D1174425

The *THING'S INCREDIBLE!*

The Secret Origins of

Weird Tales

BY JOHN LOCKE

Off-Trail Publications
Elkhorn, California

THE THING'S INCREDIBLE!
THE SECRET ORIGINS OF WEIRD TALES
By John Locke
Copyright © 2018 ▪ Off-Trail Publications
ISBN: 978-1-935031-24-6 (softcover)
ISBN: 978-1-935031-25-3 (hardcover)

All Rights Reserved. No part of this book may be reproduced or transmitted in any form by any means, electronic or mechanical, including photocopying, recording or by an information storage and retrieval system, without written permission of the publisher, except where permitted by law.

OFF-TRAIL PUBLICATIONS
Elkhorn, California

Printed in the United States of America
First printing: June 2018

The THING's Incredible!
The Secret Origins of
WEIRD TALES

CONTENTS

Acknowledgements

I would like to thank the many people who generously contributed their time, resources, and enthusiasm, all of which improved this book in countless ways.

My three weird-matter experts (WMEs), Douglas A. Anderson, Doug Ellis, and Rob Preston, shared important discoveries from their research and documents from their files, and also gave indispensable advice on the manuscript. My two colleagues, NWMEs D. Michael Thomas and Aileen Houston, provided encouragement, sanity checks, and much appreciated editorial assistance.

Numerous individuals took time to review chapters, look up buried information, scan articles from old newspapers and magazines, and otherwise sacrifice their time: Norm Davis, John Gunnison, Stephen Haffner, Matt Moring, Will Murray, Laurie Powers, Morgan Wallace, and Nicky Wheeler-Nicholson.

Christine Alexander, Registrar at Franklin and Marshall, dug out the college records of J.C. Henneberger and J.M. Lansinger. Nikki Thompson, the Assistant Registrar at Cornell College, Iowa, and Meghan Yamanishi, the Consulting Librarian for Social Sciences & Special Collections at Cornell's Cole Library, assisted on the background of the Kline family.

To recognize those individuals who gave invaluable support without always knowing they were doing so: Phil Stephenson-Payne and Bill Contento have opened up new vistas in research by building the incredible FictionMags Index. S.T. Joshi's work in writing on H.P. Lovecraft and publishing his letters allowed this story to be told in much greater detail. Neil and Leigh Mechem of Girasol Collectables deserve a Canadian-American friendship medal for their beautiful *Weird Tales* replicas, going all the way back to the first issue. Zooey Lober of the NPS Dudley Knox Library was unfailingly helpful—and successful—in prying scarce materials out of other libraries. Sandi Leavitt and the NPS Graduate Writing Center team set the best examples, believe in all the right things, and are a pleasure to be around.

Lastly, thanks were due to Joel Frieman whose 1960s correspondence with J.C. Henneberger had much to do with propelling this project. In May 2017, Joel shared valuable information not contained in the published letters. I think he would have enjoyed seeing the broader story but, sadly, he passed away at the end of 2017.

To all, my sincere gratitude. John Locke

JACOB'S DREAM

Jacob Clark Henneberger had a dream—*Weird Tales* magazine—and his dream came true for everyone but himself.

In 1923, he co-founded the magazine with J.M. Lansinger. It was their deal but it had been Henneberger's inspiration. He loved supernatural fiction, especially the work of Edgar Allan Poe, and found a dearth of it on the market. He set out to fill the void. While the first issue of *Weird Tales* was in the planning, inaugural editor Edwin Baird sketched out its aims for would-be contributors:

> For this new magazine we will want fiction of a peculiar sort. We intend featuring strange and unusual stories—the sort of stories that are commonly forbidden in most magazines—stories such as Poe's "Murders in the Rue Morgue" and the tales by Ambrose Bierce. Stories with a touch of horror, ghost stories, stories of terror and strange adventures, "creepy" stories and stories that are known as "gooseflesh" fiction are what we want.[1]

They wanted a mood, the feeling of unease that comes from pondering, at oblique angles, the mysteries of life and death. They wanted fiction that provoked a physical reaction, language that could be felt on the skin. That met their definition of artistry in the realm of the weird tale. In a way, the magazine looked backward, to ancient, primitive, but never extinct, fears. In time, the magazine would respond to the rising popularity of science fiction, peering forward into the future to explore the implications of the new age of machines that had so perturbed the new century. The magazine, like so many artifacts of the age, embodied the ferocious war between the past and the future for the souls of humankind.

But a magazine is a business even when it's a dream. From the outset, *Weird Tales* lost money. Barely over a year after it hit the newsstands, Henneberger's literary dream had turned into a financial nightmare, costing him control of the magazine. The magazine hung around, never a bestseller but always a cherished publication to its devoted fans. *Weird Tales* published the last issue of its original run in September 1954.

By then the legacy of the magazine had taken root. After author H.P. Lovecraft, the soul of *Weird Tales*, died in 1937, two of his correspondents, and fellow *Weird Tales* contributors, August Derleth and Donald Wandrei, failed to convince publishers to issue Lovecraft's fiction between hardcovers. Frustrated, in 1939 they launched their own company, Arkham House, named for Lovecraft's fictional Arkham, Massachusetts, and dedicated to publishing all of Lovecraft's writings. In time, they expanded to other *Weird Tales* authors. Henneberger took notice that his literary dream had exceeded the ephemeral lifespan of a monthly cheap-paper pulp magazine. At least for the clannish readers of weird fiction, his dream had come true.

In the 1960s, pulp historian Sam Moskowitz conducted "several interviews with Mr. Henneberger before his death as well as a number of telephone conversations."[2] In his introduction to the 1965 paperback anthology *Worlds of Weird*, Moskowitz recounted Henneberger's memories about the founding of *Weird Tales*, calling him the "forgotten creator" of the magazine.[3]

For decades, the pulp magazines had ruled the nation's newsstands as the leading forum for popular fiction in every conceivable genre. The pulps went mostly extinct in the early 1950s, but then their fiction went mass-market again. *Worlds of Weird* belonged to a growing wave of pulp reprints appearing on the paperback racks in the 1960s: Edgar Rice Burroughs novels, the great Street & Smith character Doc Savage; genres from science fiction to detective to westerns. And weird fiction, much of it from the vaunted *Weird Tales* circle—the marquee authors. Anthologies from the magazine appeared as well as individual author collections. The most popular were Lovecraft and sword-and-sorcery pioneer Robert E. Howard. Publishers were coy about the vintage of the material. The paperbacks sported entrancing new cover art, the work of talented modern illustrators. Unwitting readers could be forgiven for thinking they were reading something new.

Despite his bitter loss, Henneberger must have been pleased with the continuing legacy of his creation and the existence of a fandom which continued to grow after the magazine's demise.

One newcomer was Joel Frieman. In the '60s, he discovered *Weird Tales* through his love of Ray Bradbury's fiction.[4] Bradbury—another fan—cited *Weird Tales* as his favorite magazine. Early in his career, he placed over two-dozen stories in its pages. Fascinated by the *Weird Tales* phenomenon, Joel delved into the cobwebbed past of the magazine. In 1968, he obtained Henneberger's address in New York City and initiated a correspondence.

Henneberger eagerly shared more details of the creation of his dream. He seemed to appreciate receiving his due near the end of his life. The continuing interest in his fortunes was something unexpected, something *weird*. The dream, which had emptied his pockets and assaulted his pride, had come true for so many others—authors, editors, readers, collectors. The many authors whose careers were born in *Weird Tales* owed a part of their personal legacies to J.C. Henneberger. Hell, the field of fantasy and horror owed him a lot. *Weird Tales* planted strange, alien seeds of the imagination which continue to sprout new, bizarre, and sometimes grotesque, growths. The mortal magazine achieved the immortality of an idea.

Henneberger's letters to Joel tell a larger story than Moskowitz recounted. It was an important story, one that needed telling in greater depth. Thus, three of the letters to Joel found their way into print.[5] As did a fourth, to veteran editor Doc Lowndes.[6] The four letters, which comprise the bulk of Henneberger's known recollections of *Weird Tales*, are invaluable in piecing together the early history of the magazine, from the first issue up until the point when Henneberger lost control and its immediate aftermath, a period of about two years, after which the publication lurched forward in a somewhat stable condition. Without the letters, the creation of *Weird Tales* would be a far more elusive mystery.

But there's a vexing problem with Henneberger's recollections. Much of what he reported in the 1960s was untrue. To start, his memories, while persuasive in their specificity, were often at odds with the reliable facts. More significant, that first period of *Weird Tales*, leading up to him losing control, was fraught with painful events he preferred *not* recall. These struggles were painful to others, as well. None of them talked publicly about what really happened. Because once hands had been shaken, once differences were put in the past, they stayed in the past, never to be spoken of again. The witnesses to the forbidden knowledge, with common cause but certainly without explicit agreement, entered into a conspiracy of silence. Thus, one is struck when reading a history of the early months of *Weird Tales* by the cloudiness of the story. Who, when, why? Very little can be reliably pinned down. This is because once a false narrative is advanced, the truth must be sacrificed lest it contradict the cover story.

What follows will be a history of the origin of *Weird Tales*, and not, except for fiction which advances the historical narrative, a literary history of its content. It is a story of secrets, not just lost memories, but things which were deliberately omitted from the record, either to safeguard one's self or others, or to allow more comforting memories to prevail, or, more benignly, for professional discretion.

And, at the heart of the story, is an ominous omission from Henneberger of a personal element to the story, one of the governing secrets behind the creation of *Weird Tales*.

THE PALS

J.C. Henneberger was the son and grandson of farmers who lived in Antrim Township, Pennsylvania, near the small town of Greencastle, midway between Pittsburgh and Philadelphia. J.C.'s grandfather, John William Henneberger (1812-85), lived his entire life within two miles of where he was born.[7]

But times changed in the late nineteenth century as the nation rapidly modernized. The farm began to lose its hold over its young men as cities of excitement grew skyward into towers of stone and glass interconnected with electrical and phone wires. Selectively, male members of the extended Henneberger clan—which included J.C.'s father, Jacob Oliver Henneberger (1852-1921), and three uncles—sought higher education and professional careers. Warren (1879-1940), J.C.'s eldest sibling, earned a veterinary degree in 1906 from the University of Pennsylvania, Philadelphia. Soon after graduation, he was inspecting meat for the U.S. Department of Agriculture in Chicago, about six months after the book publication of Upton Sinclair's *The Jungle*, the fictional exposé of the brutal conditions of Chicago's meatpacking industry. J.C.'s cousin, Charlie (1886-1979), followed Warren to U. Penn, earning a medical diploma in 1910. Uncle William (1869-1928) and Charlie's brother Frank (1883-1956) attended Franklin and Marshall, a small college in nearby Lancaster. Thus, J.C., born on February 2, 1890, could hardly be considered a pioneer when he enrolled at Franklin and Marshall in the fall of 1909.

He was a thriving student, active in sports and clubs. He touched on his college years in a letter to Joel: "[Franklin and Marshall] had no press club so I organized one. I channeled its purpose to boost the college and before long I was being paid at the rate of $5 a column for my articles on sports and college activities. This income enabled me to travel to Philadelphia and New York to attend the theater."[8]

He also belonged to a fraternity, Phi Kappa Psi, another family tradition. This is where he met John Marcus Lansinger, none other than J.C.'s future *Weird Tales* partner. Superficially, they had their differences. J.C. came from a family of Democrats while the Lansingers were Republicans. J.C. was two-

and-a-half years older, though Lansinger only trailed him by a single school year. But their commonalities proved more significant: they were fraternity brothers, studying for bachelors of philosophy degrees, and members of the Sport Club.

If education was a flight from tradition for the farming Hennebergers, it was a way of life for the Lansingers. J.M.'s father, John William Lansinger (1858-1925), was practically an institution at the Pennsylvania State Normal School in Millersville, a teacher's training school just outside Lancaster. He graduated from the school in 1879, then stayed on to teach for the next quarter-century. After that, he served as business manager and treasurer. His three sons, Harold, Oram, and John Jr., not only attended the school but grew up in a house on the premises.

The 1911 Normal School yearbook offered a few tidbits about John Jr.: *nickname*: Johnny; *prized possession*: his horse; *sports*: "foot ball, basket ball, base ball"; *hobby*: dancing; *looks*: handsome; and, critical to our story, his *destiny*: "business man."[9]

Before he achieved that aim, however, his father's profession exerted its gravity. In 1912, John Jr. dropped out of Franklin and Marshall to take a job as assistant principal at the Manns Choice School in Bedford, some seventy miles west of Lancaster. It will compound a bitter irony of this chronicle that J.C., the farm boy, earned his degree while Johnny, with education in his bones, never did.[10]

After leaving college, both Henneberger and Lansinger remained active in Phi Kappa Psi, a national organization with regional chapters. Their occasional brief reports to the monthly magazine, the *Shield of Phi Kappa Psi*, contribute invaluable insights into their whereabouts and activities. Most telling was a notice in the April 1914 issue catching up with Franklin and Marshall alumni: "Lansinger . . . has left for Portland, Ore., where he will join J.C. Henneberger '13 in a very prosperous business enterprise."[11] That closing phrase brims with optimism and the language of young men, freshly issued into the dazzling new world, for whom the sky is the limit. It's our first evidence that their friendship was more than convenient. It was strong enough to unite them in a cause. And it gives them another point in common: a preference for life's unlimited possibilities over following in the footsteps of their fathers.

Their trips west—by rail, naturally—had to have been huge events for both of them, exposing them to the unimaginable vastness and grandeur of the nation's geography for the first time, while tantalizing them with the prospects of success and self-affirmation. A happy time. But this leads to the glaring omission in the Henneberger letters. The trip receives a single, mundane, indirect mention: "After graduation, I went to Portland to visit a brother."[12] We might attribute this reduction to the dulling of memory, but the key point is the absence of Lansinger. In fact, there is no reference to him, direct or oblique, in any of the letters despite his obvious role in the founding of *Weird Tales*. And so are facts buried and secrets maintained.

Warren was the brother Henneberger went to visit. By 1909, he had escaped the Chicago stockyards for Portland, still a government meat inspector. In that year, he married a Portland school teacher. In early 1913, cousin Charlie followed him to the city to practice medicine, no doubt encouraged by Warren's positive reviews. It became a virtual Pennsylvania migration when J.C. followed soon thereafter, with Lansinger in his wake.

As to that "very prosperous business enterprise," it shall have to remain a mystery. That the outcome of the enterprise proved other than expected, we can be sure of, because, while Henneberger and Lansinger remained in and about Portland for several years, they landed in employment not of their own design which led to no apparent prosperity. The evidence of their continuing friendship was their active involvement in the Portland Alumni Association of Phi Kappa Psi. In fact, we can place them together in Seattle on December 12, 1914, attending a regional gathering.[13]

Henneberger's employment record in Portland is sketchy. In late 1914, he was "general manager of the Inter State Service System."[14] The purpose of the business could not be identified; it could even have been the "business enterprise" in question. The following year he was working for the Medical Protective Society and living at the YMCA. Late in 1915, he abandoned Portland, returning east to seek employment.

Lansinger's tenure in Portland was longer and more stable. He was soon engaged as a teacher and athletics coach at Bishop Scott's Academy, in Yamhill, ten miles outside of Portland.[15] The position lasted late into 1915 when he took a job as a timekeeper with the Portland Gas & Coke Company. Meanwhile, he spent the summer of 1916 competing in amateur tennis tournaments before returning east himself.

For both of them, the great promise of Portland—and enterprise—had fallen short.

III
THE SECOND WINDS OF DESTINY

Back east, the old pals continued to follow separate paths. Henneberger set his sights on Albany, New York, but ended up in Syracuse. "I did all sorts of newspaper work," he explained.[16] He didn't actually work for a newspaper. He operated a branch office of the Stafford Subscription Agency, a company which brokered subscriptions for magazine publishers. The agency was a subsidiary of the Publishers' Promotion Company, Brooklyn, which handled advertising for newspapers and magazines.[17] Significantly, Henneberger had entered the magazine business, albeit through the back door.

Henneberger's "newspaper work" lasted until the Great War interfered.[18] Congress declared war on Germany on April 6, 1917. The first draft began two months later. A second draft began on June 5, 1918. Two days before, curiously, Henneberger enlisted in the Navy, in Buffalo. The timing suggests that he saw his number coming up and chose the Navy rather than risk being drafted into the Army. Instead of going to the Western Front as a soldier, the 28-year-old sailor went to the Naval Training Station, Great Lakes, Illinois, twenty miles north of Chicago. After 137 days, he was sent to the Naval Training School, Minneapolis, to obtain a "Chief Quartermaster Aviation" rating.[19] But history giveth and history taketh away. After serving less than a month in Minneapolis, the Armistice was signed. Two weeks later, on November 26, 1918, Henneberger was shunted back into the civilian ranks.

He relocated to Chicago, perhaps having been suitably impressed by its potential while on leave from Great Lakes, or perhaps having met his future bride, Alma K. Schneidewind, whom he married in Chicago on June 18, 1919. At about this time, his absorption into the periodical business continued. As he explained to Joel: "In 1919, I landed a job in Indianapolis with a weekly newspaper owned by the perennial candidate for President on the Prohibition ticket."[20] At this point, he had formed attachments to the two cities where *Weird Tales* would be published in its early years: Chicago and Indianapolis.

Johnny Lansinger's first destination in late 1916, after leaving Portland, was Philadelphia and the employ of O.B. Lansinger & Company, a stocks and bonds broker.[21] O.B. was Oram Byard, the second of the three football-playing

Lansinger brothers. Oram opened the firm in 1911 and soon added his father John Sr. to the payroll. John Jr. would not stay around as long as his father, though. Six months later, he was in Rochester, in the advertising business.[22] That may have introduced him to the employer which was to occupy him for the next few years: the *Orange Judd Farmer*, a Chicago magazine which began in 1888. Orange Judd (1822-92), whose company outlived him, was a proponent of scientific farming, and the leading publisher of agricultural magazines in the late-century.[23] Lansinger was a "traveling crew organizer," a manager of door-to-door magazine subscription salesmen, in other words. The position allowed him a modern, rail-borne lifestyle. For example, on his May 25, 1917, draft registration, he listed a home address back in Portland but the form was certified by the city clerk in Peoria, Illinois.[24] Later in the decade, he operated out of Cedar Rapids, Iowa.[25] Illinois and Iowa were at the heart of the territories served by the *Farmer*.

The war never interfered with Lansinger's life. His draft registration, while revealing a six-month service as an orderly in the Oregon National Guard, also claimed an exemption from military service, the reason given as "cannot see without glasses." He lost touch with the *Shield* during this period, perhaps out of embarrassment for the exemption. If one were not joining the supreme patriotic enterprise of the Great War, regardless of the justification, the safer path was to remain silent.

In about 1919, Lansinger moved to Boston for a job as New England subscription manager for the *Pictorial Review*, an attractive women's magazine which published, like most mass-market magazines of the period, a healthy selection of fiction in every issue. This job would last him until he reunited with Henneberger.

In Indianapolis, Henneberger became acquainted with the National Map Company, one of the country's leading map and atlas publishers. The company had an interesting business model. They relied heavily on student-salesmen recruited on Midwestern college campuses who worked over the summer break. The students, eager to earn their way through college, were usually male, preferably intelligent, ambitious, and aggressive.[26]

Then, as now, many colleges published magazines to serve their own student bodies. Henneberger sold the National Map Company on a broader proposition: "a national magazine for the college undergraduate."[27] It appealed to the company on at least one count: it gave them an easier way to recruit their summer salesmen. They may also have seen it as a promising investment.

For Henneberger, we can see several inducements. The launching of a magazine appealed to the entrepreneurial spirit which his early days in Portland suggest. Further, we know he enjoyed the arts—recall his trips to the New York and Philadelphia theaters. That aligns him more with the editorial rather than the business side of magazine publishing. Lastly, the inspiration for a college-themed magazine reflects the enthusiasm he had for his own college experience as represented by his continuing involvement in Phi Kappa Psi.

In his favor were the unique historical circumstances of this period which made magazine creation a potentially lucrative gambit. The expansive coast-to-coast rail system had created a far more unified and efficient economy which allowed for national markets, which in turn required national advertising. Newspapers were poor candidates because of their regional orientation; thus the need for national periodicals emerged. The reader paid for the informative or entertaining editorial content and was exposed to the advertising on the facing pages. The most popular magazines could be sold for less than their production cost with the difference made up by advertising revenue. Simultaneously, workplace automation—farm and factory—freed up time for a leisure class and rising educational levels. These and other changes added up to an unprecedented boom in publishing and reading, which accelerated rapidly through the end of the Roaring Twenties. Much of this reading occurred between magazine covers.

Thus, Henneberger's first issue of *The Collegiate World*, dated February 1920, though a quarterly, published in Indianapolis,[28] and edited by Henneberger, could have seemed like the perfect idea at the perfect time. Its content met an unfilled need and it addressed a key demographic, college students, which might appeal to certain advertisers. By 1921, the terminal flaws on both sides of the equation had been exposed. Henneberger explained the content problem: "Every college student liked [the magazine] especially if their institution was featured. Then as now, a college was known for the athletes who represented them. If I ran an article on Old Riwash, the magazine sold out there—but the others sulked."[29] The sixth and final issue, dated November 1921, showed how that problem was addressed. The cover illustration depicted a ferocious-looking football player in leather helmet with a uniform completely free of identifying insignia.

Likewise, the advertising revenue had disappointed. Outside of National Map and one other company, the magazine had little luck in selling ad space.[30] They advertised a circulation of 30,000,[31] but this sounds exaggerated. Ultimately, the poor sales of both magazines and ads led to a $30,000 debt, shared by Henneberger and his backers.[32]

As Henneberger explained, salvation came unannounced:

> One day in my office in Chicago, Illinois, pondering different suggestions by my creditors for the continuance of the publication, I was visited by the head of a self-help college located just south of Chicago. He had an article about his school that he wanted published

in THE COLLEGIATE WORLD. That I had surmised before he
broached the subject. He was very laudatory of my efforts and stated
that he liked the magazine very much. "Honestly, Mr. ——, just what
do you like about it so much?" "Well," he replied, "to tell the truth,
I like your department of college humor," a section of the magazine
I devoted to clippings of humorous college magazines and dubbed,
"The Area of Good Feeling."[33]

The conversation led to an irresistible inspiration. The next day, Henneberger
informed his creditors that he was changing the name of the magazine to
College Humor. National Map protested, no doubt fearing the diffusion
of their perfectly targeted ad campaign, but, as Henneberger boasted, "the
printer and I won out."[34] Within short order, the first issue was published,
with a Winter 1921 date, hitting newsstands near the end of the year.
Henneberger's memories of the early numbers were hazy. He recalled
that the first issue's 50,000-copy print run sold out as did a supplementary
15,000-copy run.[35] And that the first dozen issues, with a gaudy 50¢ cover
price, all sold out.[36] However, the magazine actually dropped its price to 35¢
after the first two issues which could indicate that advertising revenue had
rolled in at better than expected numbers or, more likely, that an excessive
number of the second issue had been returned. Regardless, Henneberger had
stumbled upon a winning formula. And he had learned a critically important
lesson about the ephemeral world of magazine publishing and marketing:
when the current formula is failing, when public taste is the jury, shuffling
the variables can lead to a quick and dramatic reversal of fortune. *College
Humor* went on to be a long-term success and demonstrated that college
reached a peak of hilarity in that era.

   While *The Collegiate World* struggled at the end of its run, Henneberger
added a second title to his stable, *The Magazine of Fun*, with a first issue
of August 1921. By this time, Henneberger had moved business operations
to 800 North Clark Street, Chicago.[37] Drawing from the same contributors
to *The Collegiate World*, the new monthly contained a potpourri of "verse,
jokes, skits and anecdotes and short humorous yarns [but] no fiction."[38,39]
Henneberger's New York ad representative tried to warn him off the concept:
"You simply cannot sell a national advertiser on a humorous magazine."[40] But
Henneberger was inspired by *Capt. Billy's Whiz Bang*,[41] a similar concoction
which had entered the market in 1919 and quickly rocketed into a monthly
circulation in the hundreds of thousands. *The Magazine of Fun* couldn't
nearly approach that success. In 1922, Henneberger cited a circulation of
21,344.[42]

   He was thinking ahead, though. Ads in the September and October 1921
issues of *The Writer*, and in the back of the last issue of *The Collegiate World*,

solicited detective short stories and serials for The Fiction Press, which shared the magazine's address on Clark Street.[43] It was rapidly becoming time to enter the world of the pulps.

And now the stage has been set, in 1922, for Johnny Lansinger to reenter the scene. Of course, we won't get the details of their reunion from them. Lansinger's recollections are almost completely absent from this narrative and, to reiterate, his role was mysteriously omitted from all known Henneberger letters.

The foundation of the reunion, we may presume, was the long-term friendship between the two and the unfinished business that originally united them in Portland, that "very prosperous business enterprise." All the conditions were finally in place to make the dream of partnership a reality. Both had paid their dues in the world of periodical publishing; both were ambitious, energetic young men. And they possessed complementary specialties. Henneberger preferred the editorial side and Lansinger had trained in the business end.

Henneberger might have invited Lansinger's return for practical reasons. He was in Chicago, recovered from the debt run up on *The Collegiate World*,[44] with an unqualified success on his hands with *College Humor*, and one marginal title, *The Magazine of Fun*. But he might have found himself doing too much of the work, juggling editorial and business obligations. *College Humor* was earning enough to justify an expansion of the business,[45] but to expand he would need help, someone he could trust.

Lansinger, after two-and-a-half years with the large organization of the *Pictorial Review*, may have been eager for an entrepreneurial opportunity, the chance to do better than pull a predictable salary. He acted quickly on Henneberger's good news. By March 1922, he had been named the treasurer and business manager of Henneberger's company.[46]

As a measurement of Johnny's excitement, he almost immediately returned to Portland to marry the girl he had met in his former life there. She was Lura Tamiesie, the daughter of a prominent doctor, and a pretty and popular society girl. Unlike her betrothed, she had finished college, with a Ph.D. from Stanford in bacteriology and, like him, an active Greek (Chi Omega) during and after college. As announced on June 25, the couple became engaged while he had "recently" been in the city for "an extended visit on business."[47] They married in Portland on July 12, then took a three-week honeymoon through Canada before settling in Chicago where he was "secretary-treasurer of the Independent Publishing company [*sic*]."[48] That would have put Lansinger in the office with Henneberger in early August.

Note that *The Collegiate World/College Humor* was published by The Collegiate World Publishing Company, and that *The Magazine of Fun* was published by The Magazine of Fun. Publishers commonly incorporated new magazines separately to insulate them from the business obligations of the others in the group. Accordingly, when Henneberger and Lansinger envisioned a new magazine, a new name was concocted for the joint venture: "Independent Publishers, Incorporated."[49] Soon thereafter, when the new magazine was published, the imprint had been changed to the Rural Publishing Corporation. It was an odd name for the type of material they would publish—especially *Weird Tales*. If "Rural" had been Henneberger's idea, it was probably in deference to the world of his youth. If Lansinger's idea, it may have indicated, given his experience with the *Orange Judd Farmer*, an expectation of expansion into the farm magazine field. The name may have been jointly decided for both of those reasons. In any event, they made no apparent moves into farm journalism in their short history.

IV
UTTERLY HOPELESS RUBBISH

Rural announced the new title in August 1922, *Detective Tales*, an entry into the rapidly expanding goldfield of pulp fiction magazines. The popular genres were adventure, western, detective/mystery, and romance, dominated by magazines published by big chains, like Munsey and Street & Smith, who raked in steady profits from bedrock sellers. Thus, Rural was attempting to get a toehold in the mainstream, a distinctly different strategy than Henneberger employed with *College Humor*, which sold into its own niche market. It was a fair gamble. Detective fiction was a proven perennial seller but there were only three dedicated detective pulps on the market at the time: Street & Smith's *Detective Story Magazine*, the pioneer and unassailable flagship of the genre; *The Black Mask*, a relative newcomer of uncertain prospects; and *Mystery Magazine*, a thin, shabby, cheap-paper rag which scared none of its competitors. After that, detective and mystery stories were scattered through potpourri magazines like *Argosy*, *Short Stories*, and *Blue Book*. By the 1930s, newsstands would dedicate multiple shelves to detective pulps in their many flavors, and likewise for other genres. That was to be the end state of a constant, frenzied push towards over-saturation of the market engaged in by publishers. But these were the early days of the boom, when *Detective Tales* must have looked a sure thing.

The title, *Detective Tales*, reflected another title adjustment. It had originally been conceived as *Detective Stories*.[50] Under that name, though, it would undoubtedly have drawn unwelcome attention from Street & Smith, because of its similarity to *Detective Story Magazine*. Title encroachment was considered ungentlemanly and could have led to litigation.

The first issue of *Detective Tales* was dated October 1, 1922, and appeared on newsstands September 1. Given the brief period between the end of Lansinger's honeymoon and the appearance of the actual magazine—about three weeks—Lansinger must have been late in joining the development process. While he was away on his marriage adventure, Henneberger was giving birth to the magazine.

He may not have needed Lansinger's direct assistance. It's possible that Lansinger's primary responsibility was to manage *College Humor*, freeing Henneberger to start Rural.

Henneberger did get help in Lansinger's honeymoon absence from the editor of *Detective Tales*, Edwin Baird (1886-1954), a Tennessean and the son of a postal inspector. A widower, William C. Baird (1850-1922) left the postal service soon after the turn of the century. Sometime between then and 1910, he and Edwin moved to Chicago. In a 1919 sketch, Edwin admitted that his life hadn't been very "eventful":

> I was born in Chattanooga, Tenn., and caught the writer's itch at a tender age. I was about 11, as I remember, when I constructed a lengthy poem (in which the words really rhymed) and sent it to a Nashville magazine, published by Bob Taylor. Bob wisely declined it, and my literary longing languished for a space. It broke forth again, however, with renewed violence. This time I abandoned the poetic form of expression and tried prose. Again rebuffed, I deserted literature and left it lying flat on its back.[51]

He got serious about writing in about 1907. His earliest publications were short stories which began appearing in the Munsey pulps in 1910, the start of a successful writing career. His greatest achievement as a writer was the 1913 novel *The City of Purple Dreams*, published as a book, widely serialized in newspapers, and made into a 1918 film, commanding, according to him, "the highest price which had ever been paid for motion picture rights of a novel, at that time."[52] The titular city was Chicago; the story concerned a forbidden romance between a scion of the millionaire class and the queen of a bomb-throwing anarchist gang, harkening back to Chicago's history of violent conflict between capital and labor.

Baird had married his wife Mildred by 1913. The couple initially lived in Evanston, just north of Chicago. Continuing from the 1919 sketch:

> I . . . am happily married, raise chickens and a garden, pay taxes and coal bills, and am otherwise tiresomely respectable. . . . My greatest happiness is in writing stories . . . I haven't any particular likes or dislikes—except that I'm fond of fried chicken and blue neckties, and I loathe free verse and cabbage worms. I sleep outdoors the year 'round, take a cold shower bath every morning and write three thousand words, more or less, almost every day.[53]

Baird's foray into editing was as much a career enhancement as a career change. It offered him a steady income—difficult to achieve for even successful freelance writers—while he continued to write and publish on the side.

Baird's experience writing fiction for periodicals—and his famously tireless energy—made him a promising choice to edit *Detective Tales*. In his opening editorial in the first issue, Baird made an impassioned defense of detective fiction, citing Presidents Theodore Roosevelt and Woodrow Wilson as prominent endorsers of the genre.[54] Baird's comments seem gratuitously defensive in light of the well-established position that detective fiction had earned in popular culture by 1922. The tales of Sherlock Holmes alone had practically justified the genre as susceptible to quality writing; and detective stories had been appearing for years between hardcovers, and in magazines high and low.

Baird promised readers that the magazine's priorities were in order: "No fancy covers for DETECTIVE TALES. No coated paper, or pretty pictures, or decorative names in its Table of Contents. No shallow ornamentation. But the very best detective fiction that money can buy."[55] He made the cheapness of the magazine's production values sound like a virtue. Every dime saved on the cover would go toward the purchase of better fiction. This is a lovely argument which has seldom been justified in the history of marketing. Consumers believe in their hearts that cheap packaging is a sign of a cheap product, and are usually correct. In his inaugural editor's column, Baird focused on the quality-fiction side of the argument, noting that the issue contained "the best work of some of the most noted detective story writers of England, Canada, and the United States."[56] But names, he continued, weren't paramount: "every story has been chosen, not because of the author's NAME, but solely because it was a GOOD STORY. . . . One of our chief pleasures, in editing DETECTIVE TALES, will be the discovery of new talent." This, of course, is another slippery euphemism, which ignores the fact that authors tend to become popular and famous because they produce the most entertaining fiction. Rural couldn't afford to pay top dollar for the good stuff and this was their way of disguising it.

Detective Tales was ambitiously planned for twice-monthly publication but, immediately beset with difficulties, it never achieved that goal. The first problem was that the expanding magazine market attracted an endless parade of would-be writers, like ants to a bowl of wet sugar. The August announcement for *Detective Tales* had unleashed an avalanche of submissions which the meticulous editor insisted on handling respectfully. A mere two months after the announcement, he reported:

> In dealing with authors, I always try to put myself in the writer's position and treat him as I like editors to treat me. Since becoming editor of *Detective Tales*, I have read upward of 1000 manuscripts and declined more than 900—and I have yet to return a manuscript without writing a personal note to accompany it.[57]

On the surface, it appeared to be an embarrassment of riches, even at the high rejection level, producing more than a sufficient number of acceptable stories for a bimonthly publication. But in a painfully funny article for a writers' magazine (reprinted complete in Appendix C), Baird described his experience after a year on the job (by which time *Weird Tales* was also under his control):

> We knew, of course, that all editorial offices were under constant bombardment from inept and half-baked armies of writers; but we never would have believed (to change the figure) that such an overwhelming sea of utterly hopeless rubbish was inundating these offices. The thing's incredible! Manuscripts improperly punctuated, manuscripts with misspelled words and ludicrous blunders in grammar; manuscripts with muddled plots, impossible plots, and no plots; manuscripts tattered and torn and disgracefully dirty—these pour in upon the bewildered editor, a never-ceasing deluge of words. And from this muddy torrent he must pluck material to construct his magazine![58]

So much for the joy in discovering new talent.

A bigger problem for *Detective Tales* was its precarious financial status. In that era, magazines were clearly delineated by economic class, not of the authors, editors, and readers, but of the magazines themselves. The "upper class" consisted of magazines that could afford to pay for manuscripts "on acceptance." The "lower class" paid "on publication," meaning that payment was deferred until the last reasonable moment and that no risk was taken in buying material that ultimately went unused. The contributor typically had to suffer for months before receiving the check while their masterpiece languished in a seemingly decisionless purgatory. *Detective Tales* immediately assumed its place in the demimonde, to Baird's chagrin. Two months in and he was already apologizing to the world, via an up-and-coming journal, *The Student Writer*:

> While it is true that *Detective Tales* has been somewhat slow in paying for contributions, it is equally true that I have been exerting every effort to make warm friends of all my contributors. This has been no easy task, because of the numerous difficulties (far too numerous to mention here in detail) that assailed us at the very outset. I realize, of course, that every first-class magazine should pay for acceptable material promptly on acceptance. So far, I have been unable to do this, but, to repeat, I've been doing the very best I can. Things are looking somewhat better now, and I hope, before long, to pay on acceptance and at a much better rate.[59]

In fact, despite Baird's best intentions, the lower-class status would haunt Rural's short lifespan like a looming spectre of death. The situation undermined the sense of professional integrity he felt toward his fellow writers. And it complicated his life. As the face of the company, letters from unhappy contributors went to his desk, not the publisher's. But while acknowledging Baird's difficult situation, it should be said that his willingness to air the company's dirty laundry in print was highly unusual and may have contributed to the reluctance of professional authors to offer stories to the magazine.

Baird never specified the "numerous difficulties," but they're easy to fathom: high print costs, high returns on unsold issues, low ad revenue, etc. It wouldn't necessarily have indicated a disaster in the making to its young publishers. Problems should be expected in the early months of establishing a magazine and patience is required. And the success of *College Humor* helped underwrite the incubation of *Detective Tales*.

THE BIRTH OF WEIRD

We come at last to the creation of *Weird Tales*, or, as it was aptly subtitled, "The Unique Magazine." Inexplicably, in the midst of the difficulties with *Detective Tales*, Baird announced the new magazine in the January 1923 *Student Writer*, which probably meant that the announcement had been mailed in two months earlier. That makes November 1922, then, the proximate date of the Big Bang, the birth of the *Weird Tales* universe. That was when all the trend-lines converged: the modernizing times, the opportunity-laden rise of magazine publishing, the friendship of two old frat buddies, their experiences in the magazine world, their budding partnership and Henneberger's longstanding love of Poe.

There was undoubtedly a financial motivation to creating *Weird Tales*, though fans—and disgruntled contributors—may have thought of it as a labor of love. Perhaps the partners thought that by having two Rural titles they would achieve an economy of scale. Perhaps Henneberger expected to hit pay-dirt a second time. He had scored a winner with *College Humor* by discovering an unmet need in the marketplace, one that appealed to readers and advertisers.

Similarly, while pulps specializing in specific genres were thriving— *Adventure*, the Street & Smith suite, etc.—fantastic literature lacked a natural home and presented an opportunity. Some weird stories could be found in the magazine market of the early '20s. *The Black Mask*, a detective pulp which debuted with an April 1920 first issue, included occult fiction through 1921. Bernarr Macfadden's company, flush from the runaway success of *True Story Magazine*, which debuted with a July 1919 first issue, experimented with a variety of magazine concepts. Two of these, *Brain Power* (September 1921 – May 1924) and *Midnight* (August 19, 1922 – February 3, 1923), included occult features and fiction.[60] But none of these magazines made weird fiction the central focus. Henneberger knew of the Macfadden magazines, their titles and content, as will become apparent later.

In his letters, Henneberger covered in detail his personal motivations for starting *Weird Tales*. "Much of a man's life, if he be of an inquiring mind," he wrote, "is devoted to speculation about his physical world. Science never intrigued me as much as the metaphysical."[61] Science took an unqualified second billing in this incident recalled from his childhood:

> At the age of ten [~1900] my hands were literally covered with small tumors, commonly called warts. The family doctor could do nothing about them but a neighbor advised me to see an old lady in the neighborhood who could help me be rid of them. She did. In a month or so they were gone. Whether it was by her incantations or a natural course of nature, I am not prepared to say. It was my first real adventure into the UNKNOWN.[62]

In this anecdote, Henneberger seemed to strain to explain the origins of *Weird Tales*, the initial object of Joel Frieman's inquiry.

A more tangible explanation arose out of his experience at the Staunton Military Academy, in Staunton, Virginia, where he spent a year at age sixteen, approximately 1906, for motivations unknown. A certain Captain Stevens, head of the English department, spent an entire semester on Poe using the standard collection at the time, *Tales of the Grotesque and Arabesque*, first published in 1840. Poe's gothic short stories reeked of doom and morbidity; his detective stories helped craft the genre. Henneberger considered Stevens and Poe to be such an important variable in the *Weird Tales* equation that he mentioned it in all three of his letters to Joel. In two of them, he couldn't resist noting that Stevens was a "hunchback." No doubt, for an unworldly farm boy of the time, having someone of such unencountered oddness obsess on a writer of such strangeness as Poe was a delightful nightmare come true. At any rate, the memory lasted his lifetime.

Prior to *Weird Tales*, the effect of Poe on Henneberger's imagination can be found in the very first issue of *The Magazine of Fun*, which included two Poe pastiches, both poems. Though unsigned, we assume that Henneberger composed them. The first, "Poe-Tic?," not traceable to a specific poem of Poe's, appears to be the confession of a murderer: "All the world says I'm a failure, / And I guess they all are right; / For my hands are red and gory, / And my soul as black as night." The "poetic" outcome is the damnation he faces at the hands of Satan's minions: "In a moment they will be here / With their white-hot pointed spears / And they'll drop me, unrepenting, / In the Vale of Human Fears."[63] The poem was surprisingly grim for a *Magazine of Fun*. The second pastiche, "The Raving," amusingly turns "The Raven" into the risqué pleasures of a modern ballroom:

> Then the mystic weird contortions of the dancers' upper portions
> Drove them into a frenzy such as never seen before,

Till one of the attendants cried with wrath upon his features
> "O thou wild and willful creatures, cease this, cease this I implore.
>> If you do not cease this you will be compelled to leave the floor,
>>> And be seen here nevermore."[64]

Poe gnawed at Henneberger's imagination. A little under two years later, *Weird Tales* would be the result.

Henneberger's devotion to Poe actually led to the selection of *Weird Tales* for the name of the magazine. It was inspired by this couplet from his poem "Dream-Land": "From a wild weird clime that lieth, sublime, / Out of SPACE—Out of TIME."[65] These lines aptly capture the mesmerizing, dream-like quality of the best *Weird Tales* fiction.

At Franklin and Marshall, Henneberger had been exposed to the stories of Ambrose Bierce. But Poe remained by far his favorite, perhaps of any author. "I recall everything I read by Poe, and of Bierce only one tale: *The Damned Thing*."[66] Early on, Poe and Bierce were invariably mentioned in descriptions of the kind of fiction desired for *Weird Tales*, for example the initial announcement quoted on the opening page of this narrative.

Ultimately, though, "the unique magazine" was a reflection of Henneberger's literary sensibilities, as he himself revealed: "When everything is properly weighed, I must confess that the main motive for establishing Weird Tales was to give the writer free rein to express his innermost feelings in a manner befitting great literature."[67]

The first issue of the magazine, dated March 1923, was on newsstands "on or before February 18."[68] The regular monthly editor's column was named *The Eyrie*, a nice double entendre suggesting, in its literal meaning, a nest where birds of a feather—the editor, the authors, and the readers—could congregate, layering on the further sound-alike with "eerie," the mood of the magazine. Baird—and no doubt the publishers—harbored fear that the aims of the magazine might be misconstrued. After all, the fiction would touch on morbid subjects like life after death, haunted houses, cannibalism, obsession with cemeteries, and the like, especially in its Poe-inspired early issues. Therefore, in his inaugural column, Baird laid out a defense for readers—and potentially wary distributors. The magazine, while wandering far afield of the mainstream, would not flirt with immorality:

> WEIRD TALES is not merely "another new magazine." It's a brand new type of new magazine—a sensational variation from the established rules that are supposed to govern magazine publishing.
> WEIRD TALES, in a word, is unique. In no other publication will

you find the sort of stories that WEIRD TALES offers in this issue—and will continue to offer in the issues to come. Such stories are tabooed elsewhere. We do not know why. People like to read this kind of fiction. There's no gainsaying that. Nor does the moral question of "good taste" present an obstacle. At any rate, the stories in this issue of WEIRD TALES will not offend one's moral sense, nor will the stories we've booked for subsequent issues. Some of them may horrify you: and others, perhaps, will make you gasp at their outlandish imagery: but none, we think, will leave you any the worse for having read it.[69]

Rest assured, no minds will be destroyed by *Weird Tales!* And yet, story after story, in that first issue, stoked the deepest and darkest of readers' fears: "The Grave," "The Ghoul and the Corpse," "The Gallows," "The Young Man Who Wanted to Die." If indulging in fear offered no risk, the story "Fear" offered a counterpoint in four pages, demonstrating "how fear can drive a strong man to the verge of insanity." *Weird Tales* was indeed unique, inviting readers to test themselves at the edge of emotion against the worst depravations imaginable.

In the second issue, April, a more down-to-earth anxiety asserted itself in *The Eyrie*, the life and imminent death of a magazine, the fear of financial failure:

> But, says the boss, are we also making money? A fair question! As we remarked before, WEIRD TALES is an experiment. There has never been another magazine quite like this, hence nobody knows whether or not such a magazine will pay. And, of course, if a magazine doesn't pay it promptly ceases to exist
>
> We do believe, though, that WEIRD TALES has entered upon a long and flourishing journey. We know there are multitudes of readers who like this kind of magazine and are willing to buy it. Are these readers numerous enough to support WEIRD TALES? The answer is up to you.
>
> But we'll never get anywhere unless we all work together. It's our job to publish the right sort of magazine. It's yours to buy it. If we both do these things as we should—why, then, of course, WEIRD TALES is sure to succeed. Nothing can stop it.[70]

Baird's remarks were not rhetorical. The publishers of *Weird Tales* were already worrying about its commercial viability. A particularly burdensome expense that Henneberger recalled was printing: "[The Cuneo-Henneberry Company, Chicago] printed the first six issues and the estimated cost per issue was always several thousand less than their final billing."[71] His reference was to Rural's first six issues, not exclusively those of *Weird Tales*. The March 1923 issues of *Detective* and *Weird Tales* were the company's fifth and sixth. The April 1923

Weird Tales was the first Rural magazine printed by the Cornelius Printing Company, 325 North Capitol Avenue, Indianapolis. (*Detective Tales* skipped April.) That became the Rural business address.[72] The bottom line is that *Weird Tales* essentially started life in a financial hole.

Baird's pleading to readers to pull together as a group speaks to his dedication to say whatever it took to make the magazine succeed, while also hinting at an underlying sense of desperation. It also reaffirmed the idea that the magazine and its participants belonged to a special society of like-minded savants. We can see in these early columns the shaping of the cult-like following that *Weird Tales* readers would inculcate.

A frequently misinterpreted point regarding the establishment of *Weird Tales* is that Henneberger solicited prestigious Chicago writers to contribute, but that once the magazine had been created they reneged on their promises. It's helpful to see the full quote that created this misinterpretation, from one of Henneberger's letters:

> Before the advent of Weird Tales, I had talked with such nationally known writers as Hamlin Garland, Emerson Hough[,] Ben Hecht and other writers then residing in Chicago. I discovered that all of them expressed a desire to submit for publication a story of the unconventional type but hesitated to do so for fear of rejection. Pressed for details, they acknowledged that such delving into the realms of fantasy, the bizarre and the outre could possibly be frowned upon by publishers of the conventional. I cited numerous writers like Bierce, Poe, Cabell and many others but they only shook their heads.[73]

It's clear from the passage that Henneberger discovered common interests with Garland et al., or at least polite interest, but it's not evident that he spoke to them about an actual plan for a magazine; he may simply have been engaging them in conjecture. The closing phrase makes their skepticism final. There is, finally, no indication that Henneberger received assurances. Once created, there would have been other reasons for these writers to avoid *Weird Tales*, beyond the taint of the bizarre. *Weird Tales* was an untested concept and would have been viewed as having dubious commercial merit. Professionals might have sniffed out from its young publishers that it was headed for lower-class status, even before it appeared. Payment was likely to be low. And for name authors, it would not have been simply a question of the quality of their writing, but their names would have been used to market, indeed launch, the magazine. For all these reasons, name writers would have risked placing an asterisk next to their reputations by being associated with the magazine. Publishers and readers would wonder whether their careers had hit a rough patch.

In fact, rather than stake the magazine's success on famous names, the publishers reiterated the approach taken for the sister magazine. As Baird wrote in that first announcement for *Weird Tales*:

> The author's name doesn't matter. I am not interested in names. In fact, when passing upon a manuscript I rarely even glance at the name on the first page. If the story is what I want it doesn't matter to me who wrote it. I am following this policy in selecting material for *Detective Tales* and I shall follow the same rule in editing the new magazine.[74]

The strategy was to cast the widest possible net and hope that the crème de la crème would be fortuitously high-quality material that could be bought at little cost, at least until the magazine was earning a healthy profit. *Weird Tales* was seldom a big moneymaker and consistently maintained a reputation for being uncommonly open to newcomers. Superficially, that can be presented as literary open-mindedness or a rebellion against the perceived closed-door tyranny of the publishing world. It may be either, but it's also part of a set of policies shared by the lower-class magazines: low word-rates, payment-on-publication, and a willingness to sift the haystack for the rare golden needles.

The second announcement, in the February 1923 *Student Writer*, played some very admirable politics. Baird talked up a story to be featured in the first issue of *Weird Tales*:

> "The Dead Man's Tale" is a masterpiece of gooseflesh fiction— undoubtedly one of the most hair-raising things that I've read since Edgar All[a]n Poe's "Murders in the Rue Morgue." Hardened reader of manuscripts that I am, this story made a tremendous impression upon me—and the memory of the thing clung to my mind for days.[75]

Baird amplified the compliments by leading off the inaugural issue with the story. Its author was Denver journalist Willard E. Hawkins, none other than the editor of *The Student Writer* (soon to be renamed *The Author & Journalist*).[76] It could not have hurt to compare Hawkins to Poe if one was angling for favorable coverage from *The Student Writer*.[77] In fact, *Weird Tales* would receive a lot of coverage from the magazine during its tumultuous first two years, not necessarily to its advantage.

Another Poe-esque entry in the first issue was Walter Scott Story's "The Sequel," a "new conclusion" to Poe's "The Cask of Amontillado." But Baird, having followed Henneberger's dictate for neo-Poe, may have found himself suffocating in it. He wrote in April's *Eyrie*: "Too many authors place too much stress upon atmospheric conditions when they take their trusty typewriters in hand to turn out a goose-flesh thriller. Seven in ten, when opening their stories, employ a variant of the well-worn dictum: ' 'Twas a dark and stormy night.' Why is this?" Baird, inundated with clichés, really needed fresh plots and creative atmosphere. It would take time to cultivate writers capable of providing "the unique magazine" with material that fulfilled the promise.

Another of Baird's bugaboos, for both *Detective Tales* and *Weird Tales*, was manuscripts with "too much feminine interest."[78] For *Weird Tales*, that would be the "damsel in distress" motif popular in the silent serials. Richard Epperly's cover to the first issue delivered on the promise of weirdness but, ironically, sent the wrong message in regards to plot. Illustrating Anthony M. Rud's "Ooze," the crude painting depicts a shapely lass entwined by the tentacles of some hideous swamp monster while an angry, bug-eyed male rushes to the rescue with rifle and blade. Baird must have been swamped with "Ooze"-like imitations as a result. The image of the menaced maiden would become dominant in Depression-era pulps, especially in detective and horror titles, but that had much to do with the impoverished times and the desperation of publishers in using sex and violence to jolt sales. In being that backward, the cover to the first *Weird Tales* was ahead of its time.

Predictably, by the inscrutable laws of arithmetic, adding a second magazine to Baird's responsibilities doubled his grief, which he gladly, if indiscreetly, shared with readers in the April *Eyrie*:

> And if anybody thinks that ours is the easiest task he should sit at our desk for a day or so and wade through the rivers of manuscripts that are flooding us like the waters of spring. . . . Although most of the manuscripts we receive are obviously hopeless, all must be read. Of the thousands of manuscripts sent to our office not one has been returned, or ever will be returned, unread. We cannot afford to take a chance on missing something really good.[79]

He continued to harp on the problem in the following issue with absolutely no reluctance in sharing his mockery with the readers:

> These manuscripts come from all parts of the civilized world, and they come from all sorts of people—lawyers, truck drivers, doctors, farmers' wives, university professors, carpenters, high school girls, convicts, society women, drug fiends, ministers, policemen, novelists, hotel clerks and professional tramps—and one, therefore, would naturally expect their stories to possess a corresponding diversity. But not so. With rare exceptions, all these stories, written by all these different kinds of people, are almost exactly alike!
>
> Not only do they contain the same general plots and themes—one

might understand that—but practically all are written in the same style; all have the same grammatical blunders, the same misspelled words, the same errors in punctuation, the same eccentric quirks of phraseology. After plowing through fifty or so of these stories (and we often read that many in an evening), a man acquires the dazed impression that all are written by the same person.[80]

At last, a common cause to unite the drug fiends and university professors of the world.

In sharing the inside dope on the editor's life, Baird's sense of humor shines through—indeed, blazes through with a blowtorch in each fist. Readers who appreciated H.L. Mencken's cynicism—or Bierce's—would have enjoyed Baird, as well. But that hardly describes the totality of the *Weird Tales* audience. For every literature-lover who honored the Poe-inspired artistic ambitions of the magazine, there must have been ten who simply enjoyed a spooky story of the supernatural. While ridiculing the army of would-be authors, Baird may have inadvertently alienated ordinary—and potentially loyal—readers who fantasized about submitting a story to the magazine while knowing they lacked the writing skills, people who may have thought, "he's making fun of me, too." The balancing trick for the editor was to create an exclusive club that anyone could join. Baird's condescension betrayed his inexperience as an editor. The pulps, while frequently the target of decency monitors who presumed to protect the public from offense, were actually highly sensitive to reader feelings. Operating on tight profit margins and preferring the largest possible readership, they couldn't afford to alienate their audience any more than any other commercial enterprise. This principle applied to both the fictional and editorial content. We would be hard-pressed to find comments similar to Baird's printed *in any other pulp*, which makes *Weird Tales* "the unique magazine" in a totally unexpected dimension.

Baird's editorial challenge had two axes: the phenomenal quantity of submissions, each of which he insisted on giving a professional examination, and the generally unsuitable quality. He was being crushed under a mountain of inept manuscripts: editor's hell. Notwithstanding his tirelessness, there are still limits to human performance, and Baird was already up against them with *Detective Tales*. The obvious thing would have been to hire him an assistant or two when *Weird Tales* was first published. That didn't happen, for obvious reasons. Labor costs money, a sensitive point when the enterprise has yet to prove itself. Plus, editing *Weird Tales* required a highly specialized form of labor, not necessarily easy to find.

THE APPRENTICES

Thus, Baird soldiered on alone through the creation of *Weird Tales*. But that couldn't go on forever. For Baird to live to see his thirty-seventh birthday, help had to be found. Consequently, two assistants entered the scene: Farnsworth Wright (1888-1940) and Otis Adelbert Kline (1891-1946). Wright would become famous in due course as the editor of *Weird Tales* during its golden age. Kline would achieve even greater renown as, for several years, one of the magazine's star authors.

Full-fledged members of the conspiracy of silence, the details of how either joined up were never documented. However, each gave similarly vague descriptions of their service. In a 1930 profile, *Weird Tales* regular E. Hoffmann Price wrote that, "While occupied as reporter and editor, Wright was selling stories to *Munsey's* and other magazines. When *Weird Tales* made its appearance, he sold material which appeared in its initial issues; and later, he read manuscripts for both *Weird Tales* and *Detective Tales*."[81] Kline, in a 1941 letter to Robert E. Howard's father, regarding his son's estate, provided a lengthy description of the early years of *Weird Tales* to help establish the integrity of the magazine's management. Touching lightly on himself, Kline wrote: "They began buying stories in 1922; I sold them a story of my own for the first issue, in 1922."[82] This suggests that Kline had responded immediately to the announcement in *The Student Writer*, which would have been on newsstands in early December 1922. Elsewhere in the letter, addressing the situation in early 1924, Kline noted that "both Farnsworth Wright and I had previously read manuscripts for Baird."

That's the most they were willing to offer.

The publication records of Wright and Kline in 1923 issues of *Weird Tales* are notably similar. Wright placed short stories in each of the first two issues and then disappeared until the September issue, ending the year with five appearances. Kline sold a longer story which Baird ran as a two-part serial in the first two issues, then reappeared in the June, July-August, and September issues, also ending with five appearances. (Kline also appeared with shorts in the September and October issues of *Detective Tales*, and supplied unbylined true-crime fillers to both issues.[83]) Of interest, both earned the condemnation of H.P. Lovecraft, the author most closely identified with *Weird Tales*. Never loath to slight a fellow writer, he referred to Wright in February 1924 as a "mediocre Chicago author,"[84] though later tempered his view. In 1930, he described Kline as an "amiable hack."[85]

Wright and Kline, as well, had practical matters in common, as *Weird Tales* opened for business. They both lived in Chicago and they both were already employed. We might suppose, then, two scenarios under which they became acquainted with Baird, and maybe Henneberger. In the first, one or both of the authors, noting that *Weird Tales* was a Chicago publication, stopped by the office to meet the editor and pitch their stories. This was a common approach for pulp writers in the flourishing New York publishing hub. In the second scenario, Baird noted the Chicago addresses of two of his contributors and became acquainted through the mail, or over the phone, as deals to purchase the stories were struck. In either case, Baird knew of two local authors who were smart, professional, and savvy to the magazine's focus.

We now have three data points for estimating the timing of when Wright and Kline joined the magazine as assistants: both temporarily stopped appearing in the magazine after the April issue, suggesting a shift from writing stories to reading manuscripts. The third, corroborating, point is the time at which Baird stopped complaining in *The Eyrie* about how overwhelmed he was. After his broadside in the May issue, the June column delivered this haymaker:

> The time has come to talk of cats and Chinamen, and rattlesnakes and skulls—and why it is these things abound in yarns for WEIRD TALES. Particularly cats and Chinamen. Believe it or not, every second manuscript we open (and that's placing the average rather low) is concerned with one or the other, or both, of these. . . .
> Sometimes the result is interesting. And sometimes it is awful! And again, sometimes, it is a ludicrous thing, unconsciously funny.[86]

Still irritated, he was now restricting his complaints to the *quality* of the submissions. We can dismiss the possibility that Henneberger instructed Baird to tone down his columns. As we will see in due course, Baird became even more untamed before the year was out. At any rate, it was not until the November issue that the question of quantity arose again.

This gives us a range of from April to May, when the May and June issues were largely prepared, for Baird to have received assistance. (Of course, we can't assume that Wright and Kline joined simultaneously.) Wright was probably absent for some of this time. He took a spring vacation to Seattle in this approximate period, duration unknown.[87]

What's missing from the account are a myriad of other details. Did they work in the office or take manuscripts home? How many hours did they work? How many manuscripts did they actually review? To what extent did Baird oversee their work? How much were they paid? Was it a salary, an hourly wage, or based on piecework? While we can be certain that the arrangement was unorthodox, we won't be able to answer these questions, and they won't answer them for us. But given that both men were employed otherwise, and that the budget at Rural Publishing was crimped, it seems likely that they treated the work as a fascinating little side job.

So who were Farnsworth Wright and Otis Adelbert Kline? Their very names carried an aura of old American distinction, names that matched the ancient bones of the magazine. They might have been Poe's confidants in a previous life. Their names contrasted starkly with Edwin Baird's, the plainly appointed pessimist who always wore a straw hat in the office. And where did Wright and Kline gain their aptitude for fantasy? And what strange forces brought them to Chicago—into the oblong orbit of *Weird Tales*?

FARNSWORTH WRIGHT AND THE ART OF THE NIGHTMARE

No one in the *Weird Tales* circle wrote as much about Farnsworth Wright as E. Hoffmann Price. He sold a story to Wright in 1924 and was a more or less regular contributor into the mid-'30s. When Price took a job with Union Carbide in Hammond, Indiana, forty minutes from Chicago, it was inevitable that author and editor would meet in person, which they did when Hoffmann visited the Chicago offices of *Weird Tales* in late '26. Over the years, Price socialized on many occasions with Wright and Kline, in particular, and with other members of the circle. Price's friendship with Wright and their many conversations gave him ample material when Wright's widow Marjorie urged him to collect his memories in writing. The result was a lengthy profile for the amateur magazine *The Ghost*, in which Price confessed:

> I know practically nothing of Wright's earlier years, of his family, or his background. I'm hazy as to his age, though he did once mention it. . . . In many respects, he was a total stranger; what I saw and remember is all that I can offer as a clue to what he had seen and been. And when Marjorie Wright, his widow, sent me some information about his earlier years, nearly every statement was a revelation.[88]

He reprinted key portions of Marjorie's letter in his memorial and it comprises much of what we have heretofore known about Wright's background prior to his involvement with *Weird Tales*. The following outline will fill in many of the missing details, show where he acquired the traits to successfully edit *Weird Tales*, and explore his reluctance to dredge up the dark secrets of his past.

The Farnsworth name can be traced all the way back, on his mother's side, to his great-grandfather Samuel Farnsworth, a drummer for Colonel Enoch Hale's New Hampshire Regiment in the American Revolution.[89] Farnsworth's father, George Francis Wright (1848-92), a farmer's son, was born in Elgin, Illinois, about twenty-five miles west of Chicago. George entered the U.S. Naval Academy in 1865 during the restoration of the institution which followed the divisions of the Civil War. He received his diploma from President Grant, who personally handed them to the 1869 graduates. George was immediately assigned to the USS *Lancaster*, a three-masted sloop-of-war which patrolled South American waters. He resigned his commission on April 25, 1871, after less than two years of service, to study civil engineering. Farnsworth's mother, Genevieve Farnsworth Hard (1850-1913), hailed from Aurora, just south of Elgin. Two days before Christmas 1873, George and Genevieve married in Aurora. She, possessed of a fine voice, gave up a promising career in opera to raise a family.[90]

George and younger brother Edward Thomas Wright (*b.* 1851) both worked for the civil engineering firm of Cleveland & French. They resigned to open their own civil engineering business in Chicago in 1874, but the climate soon took a toll on Edward's health.[91] The brothers and their wives relocated to the sunny climes of Southern California, along with other members of the extended family: their father Paul Raymond Wright (1819-1908), their mother, and their sister. In 1875, Edward went to work for the city of Los Angeles, while George did likewise up the coast in Santa Barbara. Both were instrumental in the planning and development of their respective cities. Paul R. Wright, a lawyer, settled in Santa Barbara where he became a judge.

The first child born to George and Genevieve was Fred Hard Wright (1875-1932), on Christmas Day in Santa Barbara. He spent ten years as an only child. The family history is difficult to trace for a number of years, as George traveled to far-flung places in the western states for assignments of lengthy duration. It's not always clear that his wife and children accompanied him. In some instances, they stayed behind in Judge Wright's home.

After three years in Santa Barbara, suffering ill health himself, and apparently the victim of dubious medical advice, George took a job in Washington Territory with the Northern Pacific Railway to escape the coast. He laid out the city of Spokane Falls, as Spokane was then called. Subsequently, as an engineer for the Union Pacific Railroad, he scouted a possible route through the Sierra Nevada mountains.

In 1879, George, Genevieve, and Fred were living in Oakland. She earned extra money by teaching "voice culture," often entertaining clients in the home. A second child, Paula Eunice, was born in Oakland in 1885. That year, they returned to Santa Barbara where George was elected city surveyor; he served three years. The last two children were born in Santa Barbara, Farnsworth, on July 29, 1988, the only child not given a middle name and, in 1890, Paul Raymond, named for his grandfather. Paul went by his middle name, for obvious reasons.

In October 1891, George moved his office to Los Angeles, again for health reasons as the move allowed him to work in the mountains. The rest of the family remained on the coast. In spite of George's itinerant and lengthy civil engineering jobs, the family appeared to be stable and thriving. That is, until disaster struck at two p.m. on August 20, 1892, the moment when George collapsed in San Bernardino, his lungs hemorrhaging, while on the job as chief engineer of the Arrowhead Valley Water Company. Genevieve received the telegram in Santa Barbara that evening.[92] Her husband was dead at the painfully young age of forty-three. Farnsworth was a mere lad of four. "About his only recollection of [his father] was that he could take a sliver out of a small boy's finger without hurting him."[93]

The family remained in Santa Barbara, no doubt welcomed by Judge Wright and his wife Emily. Genevieve taught music to get by. In 1897, when Fred enrolled at Stanford, Genevieve and the rest of the kids accompanied him to Palo Alto. While Fred put himself through school studying electrical engineering, Genevieve continued to sing, teach, and organize musical events. She was credited with starting the Stanford Girls' Glee in 1898.[94] Eventually, she expanded her repertoire of instructional topics to the new fad of "physical culture," probably in response to the popularity of Macfadden's magazine *Physical Culture*, established in 1899.

At this point, Farnsworth's interests and aptitudes begin to come into focus. On March 27, 1898, the *San Francisco Call*, on the children's page, supplies our first record of him in print:

> This is my first letter to you. I enjoy the new fairy tales very much. I would like to have "Jack and the Beanstalk" next. I am not quite 10 years old. I am a little over nine.
> I like "Jack and the Beanstalk" stories best of all. I might make up a story for the boys and girls' page. I have made up my mind to take for a subject, "How the Lily Got Her Pistil."[95]

There are several things we might take away from this youthful epistle. The most obvious, perhaps, is: "He loves fairy tales! This is the true birth of *Weird Tales!*" But, of course, most children love fairy tales. The real lesson here is Farnsworth's engagement with journalism, unusual for a nine-year-old. Not only did he write a letter to express his preferences, he was already thinking about making a creative contribution.

In late 1900, after three years at Stanford, Fred received a year's leave of absence to take a position with the Vulcan Iron Works of San Francisco.[96] He never returned to the university. Within a year, Genevieve and all four children were living in the city. By this point, a pattern had emerged. The fatherless family moved from town to town like a tightly-knit Gypsy clan, a way of life they may have adapted to during George F. Wright's frequent absences. Fred's role was critical. As Marjorie recalled, he was "more than just a big brother." He was "the most wonderful fellow Farnsworth ever

knew. He took his father's place in the family and helped with all his youthful
might to eke out the family income. He was the most unselfish and kindest of
brothers, and he had that same rare sense of humor that Farnsworth had."[97]

In San Francisco, Farnsworth's journalistic proclivities continued
unabated. As Price reported:

> Farnsworth Wright tumbled into the magazine business before
> he was out of grammar school in San Francisco, where he not only
> wrote and edited a publication called "*The Laurel*," but set the type
> and printed it on a hand press, being editor, author, printer's devil,
> compositor, and pressman.[98]

Presumably, this was an activity at the Pacific Heights School, where
Farnsworth graduated with honors in 1903.

From this time forward, the record shows his increasing involvement with
intellectual activities and the arts. He moved on to San Francisco's prestigious
Lowell High, where he made the three-member debate team. In one losing
effort, the team was defeated by visitors from the California Institution for
the Blind, who crossed the bay from Berkeley to argue over U.S. interests
in "Santo Domingo and Hayti" before a raucous audience of 300 spectators
and rooters.[99] In another losing effort, the Lowell club took the ferry to spar
with the Oakland High team over the issue of Japan's interests in the Russo-
Japanese War of 1905.[100] In the arts, he acted alongside Paula and Raymond
in "A Russian Honeymoon," the Pilgrim Sunday-School Christmas play.
Farnsworth played Father Petros, a Russian priest.[101] His nascent publishing
career is represented by a poem, "Nature," in the January 1904 issue of an
amateur magazine, *The Scribe*.

For all the reasons that San Francisco was a wonderful place to live in
the early years of the century, there was one which nullified those qualities:
the Great Earthquake and Fire of April 18, 1906. Thousands were killed and
hundreds of thousands left homeless. Families were torn apart and fortunes
destroyed.

The Wrights, living at 3006 Steiner Street, in the Cow Hollow
neighborhood, some two miles from the hard-hit downtown, were spared
the worst of the devastation. Ironically, it was the earthquake's impact on
employment that split the family. Genevieve had become prominent in the
musical life of the city, managing musical groups and teaching. At the time
of the quake, she taught voice at the Irving Institute, 2126 California Street.
The building survived without serious damage, but the unavailability of gas
and water, and the inability to heat the building, caused the school to close
early for the summer. Paula was similarly affected. A 1905 graduate of Girls'
High School, she had been accepted by Stanford, but instead took a position

as chair of domestic science at a San Jose school. Before she could start, the school closed as a result of the quake.

Six weeks after the quake, Genevieve and Paula moved to Reno, Nevada, where Genevieve opened a music studio. Fred, Farnsworth, and probably Raymond, stayed behind in San Francisco.[102] Presumably, Fred was not earning enough to support the entire family without Genevieve's contribution. Farnsworth, by remaining in San Francisco, completed high school, graduating from Lowell in 1908 just before he turned twenty.

Having grown up in California, the catastrophe of 1906 was undoubtedly not Farnsworth's first earthquake, but it was his worst—it was everybody's worst. It must have created a raft of painful memories, both for the experience of the devastation and what it did to the beautiful city and its people, what it might have done to his friends and classmates, and for what it did to his family. He apparently never wrote of his personal observations, only making one incidental—and misleading—comment: "Lived in San Francisco until 1906 when the earthquake threw him out."[103] Neither Price nor Marjorie ever mentioned the quake. However, Farnsworth did refer to it in two of the short stories he published in the San Francisco magazine, the *Overland Monthly*. In "Enemies" (February 1917), he wrote that "the Great War broke out with the suddenness of an earthquake," an astute comparison of two events, each of which are remembered as changing the world in an instant. The second story, "A Cookery Queen" (December 1919), offers a more detailed insight into his state of mind. By the time of its publication, Farnsworth was well-situated in Chicago. It's the story of a restaurant patron who becomes obsessed with a waitress (no, it's not another *Of Human Bondage*) during his futile search to find a Chicago restaurant as good as the ones he remembers from San Francisco:

> Time was when Standish MacNab was a tireless explorer among Chicago's eating houses. Memories of San Francisco drove him from one to another in search of something to remind him of the sea-girt city of the Golden West. For San Francisco is the best fed city on the continent, while Chicago, for its size, is the poorest fed. . . .
>
> He nibbled at egg "fo young" in the Mandarin Inn and King Joy Lo's in search of something as tasty as the chop suey and bird's nest hoong chop blooey of Chinatown-by-the-Golden-Gate, but Chicago's almond-eyed waiters soon saw him no more. He manipulated spaghetti in Italian restaurants over saloons, and mourned the days before the earthquake (this word has disappeared from California lexicons) when for two-bits in the Fior d'Italia on the Barbary Coast he could eat a meal that shamed anything Chicago could offer, for a dollar.

His reference to the earthquake reflects his own behavior: it's an event you scarcely hint at. More telling, the story is drenched in nostalgia—mourning—for the good life that existed before Fate stole it away. The earthquake occurred when Farnsworth was three months shy of his eighteenth birthday. Most of us can blame the loss of our youth on the passage of time. He could blame his on the earthquake, lending a false sense that it could be recaptured. The earthquake was his dividing line between youth and experience.

After high school, Farnsworth apparently rejoined the family in Reno, where he attended the University of Nevada. His 1917 draft registration indicates three years of military service as an infantry private at the university.[104] Nevada had no statewide militia during the years Farnsworth was in Reno,[105] and the nature of his service remains unclear.

By early 1910, the entire family was reunited in Reno, though Paula lived with her new husband, a young Reno lawyer. It was to be Farnsworth's last year with the Gypsy clan, as he left home for good in the fall to attend the University of Washington, in Seattle, as a twenty-two-year-old freshman. Fred helped Farnsworth with the expenses, and Farnsworth helped himself. As described in an interview: "Had to work his way through college. Spent one year surveying, one summer canvassing books, another summer as entomologist for the British Colombia Hop-Company, campaigning against the hop-fleas and the hop lice."[106] One of the few things Price recalled about Farnsworth's past was that he had worked during a school vacation "as a labor foreman in charge of a gang of Hindus."[107]

In the summer before departing Reno, Farnsworth started to demonstrate his facility for languages, becoming active in the use and advocacy of Esperanto, an invented language introduced in 1887 and designed to be a universal second language. He appeared frequently in the magazines *Amerika Esperantisto* (*American Esperanto*) and *La Simbolo* (*The Symbol*). The magazine's content was almost exclusively written in Esperanto and Farnsworth provided translations of short poems (e.g. Longfellow's "Evangeline") and excerpts from literature. His heaviest involvement with Esperanto was during his college years.

At school, he spoke publicly about the language and gave recitations. Early on, he belonged to the Department of Italian, then switched to the Department of Forestry. He was quite active in college life. He served as president of the Social Democratic Club in 1912, and was an avowed socialist. In 1913, he was president of the Debating Club and an officer of the Cosmopolitan Club. He often joined committees setting up social events, generally handling publicity.

On July 27, 1913, tragedy struck Farnsworth's life again, this time self-inflicted.[108] He was by then established as a top student in the Department of Journalism, his taste for newsprint having survived the earthquake, or perhaps been fed by it. On that Sunday, he and law student John P. Rauen, his friend and roommate, were visiting Westport, a small fishing town on the ocean. Westport sits atop the southern of two peninsulas which hold Grays Harbor in its jaws. In its geographical situation, the town resembles a miniature San Francisco. While wading in the ocean, the two friends were "caught in a deep hole made by eddying currents," right in front of the lifeguard station. Rauen was a good swimmer but drowned nevertheless. Farnsworth, who could not swim, managed to keep his head above water until help arrived. To further the strange set of ironies, the man who rescued the journalism student was a professional printer. Were it not for the tragic circumstances, Farnsworth could have dined out on the joke throughout his long career as a writer and editor. "It's not the first time a printer has saved my life. . . ."

Instead, it became another subject he never talked about directly. The experience did find its way into his fiction, however: a short story, "In the Depths," which appeared in the same issue (December 1919) of the *Overland Monthly* as "A Cookery Queen," meaning that he placed two psychologically revealing stories in the same magazine—with only three pages separating them. Freud could have filled a book analyzing "In the Depths," so laden with suggestion is it.

The story concerns a young reporter for a daily, three days on his first job, who has fallen short on his previous assignments. Pleading for one more chance, the city editor sends him in pursuit of a story which eluded a veteran reporter. His goal is to interview a diver, McLeod, who survived a "thrilling struggle with a giant octopus," but now can't be found.[109] The story begins: "Dan Carlson looked down at the oily waters of Puget Sound and wondered what strange creatures lived in its slimy depths, and whether they were not really happier, after all, than he." Having failed to find the diver in the waterfront saloons, "he stood on the wharf and speculated on the things that live under the water, and on his own drowning career." In reality, the story Carlson pursued was his own:

> The mystery of the ocean depths had always fired his imagination, but now it depressed him. He compared himself to the diver. The world was an enormous octopus, twisting its arms about his neck to drag him down.

In "the muddy depths of his despondency," Carlson spots "a roughly-dressed, ragged man, unshaven, dirty and hatless." Naturally, it is McLeod. He appears to be drunk and at risk of falling into the water. Carlson pulls him to safety, saying: "You don't want to make fish-food of yourself, and be washed out into the sound where the devilfish can twist his snaky tentacles around your neck and little fishes come and swim through the holes in your skull, where your eyes are now." They retreat to a saloon, where Carlson buys beers and hears McLeod's harrowing tale of life-and-death struggle against the devilfish—the octopus. The final twist is that the diver is too traumatized to remember how he escaped the situation, which engenders Carlson's sympathy:

> Dan felt a strange sinking of the stomach as he looked at the moaning creature before him, who was still fighting hopelessly on in his mind, with blank horror always at the end of his tale. For the diver's mind had given way under the strain of the desperate struggle under the waves and recorded no memories beyond that terrific combat, nor gave any glimmer of hope as to the outcome.

Psychologically, McLeod is trapped in the terrible moment, with no means of escape.

"In the Depths" is a story about being saved. Carlson's career is saved because he "had his story." The diver is saved, not just from the octopus, but from his trauma when, as observed in the closing sentence, Carlson's "tender hands took McLeod into their care and ministered to his overwrought nerves and anguished brain." Within the story, Carlson and McLeod save each other by giving what the other needs most. Outside of the story, knowing of the drowning tragedy in the author's life, we get a broader suggestion. A deeply depressed Farnsworth needed saving from his own painful memories. He was a haunted man, haunted by memories of the earthquake, the splitting up of the family, the drowning of Rauen, his own near-death experience, and who knows what else.

The drowning of Rauen took its irrevocable place in Farnsworth's memory and the end to 1913 gave no relief. In 1911, Fred had gone to the Philippines to work as a surveyor for the U.S. Army, all part of the aftermath of the Spanish-American War, the Philippine-American War, and the Moro Rebellion, three American wars in the Philippines in fifteen years. A year later, Genevieve abandoned Reno to join Fred in Manila. Raymond went over and enrolled in the University of the Philippines, a school established by the U.S. authorities. On December 22, 1913, Genevieve died in her abode. She was 63. Marjorie described the relationship of mother and son and his receipt of the news:

> Farnsworth was devoted to his mother. They were very close to each other. I have a lovely poem he wrote to her for a birthday present when he was a student in the University of Washington, and she was out in Manila with Fred and Raymond. Mrs. Wright died out there. The cablegram was a terrible blow to Farnsworth. He told me he was going home to the dormitory through the woods on the corner of our campus and that he felt his mother's presence so strongly that

he called out to her, "Mother!" When he got to the dorm there was the cablegram. It was Christmas vacation and the dormitory was practically deserted, and Farnsworth was awfully alone and grief stricken.

The family, so close for so long, could never be reunited.[110]

Farnsworth's solace came in his college achievements. He had served two years on the *University of Washington Daily* and for his last, 1913-14, was managing editor. In school, he was an honor student. His crowning achievement occurred on April 25, 1914, when the *Seattle Star* surrendered news operations for the day to an all-university staff. The students were "all to blame," joked the *Star*, but Farnsworth deserves a healthy measure of the credit for getting all the daily editions out.[111] He was managing editor and wrote the lead editorial, an argument on the merits of leadership. "One man with energy and capacity for leadership can accomplish more for good or ill than a thousand men who simply follow." It sounds like the way an editor might think about his mere readers. "[C]ollege training gives to the student who seeks it a broad outlook on life, it gives him vision, and it develops the latent powers of leadership within him."[112] Mere words, unless the author has proven it through action, and Farnsworth certainly had. When he collected his degree two months later, it wouldn't have taken a genius to recognize that success lay in front of him.

By tradition, the regional papers recruited fresh University of Washington journalism graduates to serve apprenticeships of about a year. Farnsworth ended up at the *Seattle Sun*, his first professional job.[113] In an unrelated note, he soon had occasion to write New York's *Harper's Weekly* to complain about Eastern attitudes toward the West: "We are considered by the effete Easterners, barbarians who dare not paint their houses for fear the mountain lions will lick the paint off and die in the front yard."[114] His loyalty to the Golden West notwithstanding, in the fall of 1915, he moved to Chicago and took a reporting job with the *Chicago Tribune*.

We don't know *why* Farnsworth left the barbarians and mountain lions behind. It may have been because of his potential and the fact that the biggest opportunities in publishing were back east; then again he may have had relatives in the Chicago area; and perhaps the dissolution and dispersion of the family weakened his need to remain in the West.

According to Marjorie, "one of the first things Farnsworth did was to pay Fred back [for helping with college], after he got his first job as a reporter in Chicago."[115] Still, he doesn't seem to have lasted very long at the *Tribune*, perhaps only a few months. Having two short-tenured jobs on his record raises the likelihood that he wasn't flourishing as a workaday news reporter. Recall that the young reporter of "In the Depths" (published in 1919) was failing badly at his first job. In some sense, Farnsworth must have drawn upon his own experience for inspiration.

In 1916, June at the latest, Farnsworth landed what may have been his dream job, as the Chicago correspondent for the New York-based weekly *Musical America*. It was a natural. Music ran in the family, from drumming Samuel to singing Genevieve. She "had a marvellous voice, and the most glorious trill of any singer he had ever heard."[116] She had taught voice since before Farnsworth was born. He grew up with music in the house, where Genevieve trained most of her clients. It seems that Farnsworth inherited his strongest instincts, appreciation of music and the arts, from his mother, while inheriting less from the practical father he barely remembered. As Marjorie emphasized, "Music was the breath of life to him."[117]

As critic for *Musical America*, he attended Chicago musical events, concerts and operas by local or visiting talents, wrote about them and issues related to the musical world, an article or two per week. His emphasis was on classical or fine music; he paid little attention to the popular arts or "show business."

While reporting for *Musical America*, he started selling fiction to the *Overland Monthly*, placing two well-crafted short stories in 1917. Both are war stories centered in Belgium. Both express a staunchly pacifistic perspective and both incorporate the idea of language creating barriers that must be overcome, ideas that flow directly from his engagement with the universal language of Esperanto. In "Enemies" (February), two soldiers, one French, one German, separated from their compatriots, face off on a Belgium battlefield. After futilely trying to kill each other, they meet over a flag of truce. Through diligent effort, they overcome their language differences, and thus their mutual hatred, by recognizing each other's humanity. They desert to Holland together, where the puzzled Dutch officer who takes them into custody mutters the question on the reader's mind: "Fools! What would happen if all the soldiers should do that?"

"The Vow" (August) takes place in the imaginary postwar period. On a train, an American—reading the *Chicago Tribune*—meets a German veteran of the war. The German recounts a story of three friends—himself, a Frenchman, and an Englishman—who vowed before the war to favor the idealism of internationalism over the insularity of nationalism. They sign their pledge using the Esperanto names of their nationalities. In spite of that, when the "thunderclap" sounds, each is drawn into fighting, either through war fever or the draft. On a Christmas Day, the anniversary of their pledge—reminiscent of the time of Genevieve's passing—Fate places the trio in the same location. The German is captured as a spy by a group of soldiers which contains the other two friends: the Frenchman, commanding, and the Englishman, acting as interpreter. The Frenchman lets the German escape and is eventually shot as a traitor. Every Christmas, the Englishman and the German meet at the ignominious grave of the Frenchman to pray for his soul. "He died a martyr to his country, which was the world."

By the time "The Vow" was published, Farnsworth had just registered in the first draft, which he did on June 5. Judging from the story, he was weighing his own feelings about participating in the grand conflict. For years, the dispatches from Europe had shocked American readers with tales of wanton carnage on the battlefields of the Western Front. At the same time, the Germans had emerged as the unqualified villains, an impression fueled by the rampant homefront propaganda which abetted American entry into the war. The pacifism which seemed like a natural part of enlightened thinking quickly began to look like a puny response to the threat of the monstrous German death machine.

The mobilization of American soldiers included stateside training followed by transport overseas. In February 1918, while 10,000 American soldiers a day were pouring into France, Farnsworth was still writing for *Musical America*. He was called up soon after, though he didn't have far to go. He was one of thirteen Chicago newsmen assigned to the Army's 161st Depot Brigade at Camp Grant, just south of Rockford, Illinois, about sixty miles west of Chicago.[118] After joining the Army, he resigned from *Musical America*. On June 1—a Saturday—Corporal and Acting Sergeant Wright returned to Chicago and visited his old office where he provided the following account of his situation, slanted for *Musical America* readers:

> The one desire of my heart now is to get to France. I expect to go "Over There"[119] by the first of August. Army life, even as it obtains at a home camp, is intensely interesting and grows more so as France draws nearer. Music plays a great part in the soldier's life and seems to be the thing most craved for.
>
> Even the men whose lives before they joined the ranks were lived without even a faint interest in music fall readily under its spell, and the spell is permanent. We are making recruits for opera and concert of the future as well as fighting men for Uncle Sam. I have been helping train Negroes from South Carolina, and the semi-barbaric folk-songs of these fellows have given me some ideas which I hope to work out musically after the subduing of the Hun is fully accomplished. The army is full of material for the man with any trace of creative ability.[120]

Promotions were cheap in the U.S. Army with the ranks rapidly expanding with green recruits but, still, the fact that Farnsworth made sergeant so rapidly is a testament to his natural leadership abilities, which we've seen repeatedly through his life: his debate team activities, his top position on the *University of Washington Daily*, his summer job as a labor foreman, his forthright advocacy of leadership, etc.

The quote reveals an interesting spectrum of his thinking and personality. Clearly, the pacifism of the *Overland* stories had been elbowed aside by the patriotic fervor "to get to France" and "subdue the Hun." Of course, he probably suspected that he would never be sent to the front; half the soldiers weren't. One passage that jumps out is his reference to the "Negroes from South Carolina" and their "semi-barbaric folk-songs." After spending the first twenty-seven of his thirty years out West, being thrown in with African Americans must have been strange for him. Chicago had a large and growing black population, owing to the Great Migration of southern blacks to the industrial north, but it's unlikely that Farnsworth had occasion to fraternize. A company of African Americans from the South must have seemed like aliens from another world, although it appears that he enjoyed getting to know them. Lastly, the quote has two instances indicating that Farnsworth was thinking about life after the war. The second, the ideas inspired by the African Americans, suggests that he fancied himself a composer. We can only wonder what those ideas might have led to.

An August 1 departure date corresponds with other information on his wartime service. It would have put him in France with about three months left in the war before the November 11 Armistice which halted combat. Still, for those sent into the fray, it was a bloody three months. That was not Farnsworth's fate, however. He served for a year as an Army interpreter, reminding us that the Armistice didn't allow everyone to return home immediately. A Reno newspaper reprinted observations from a local woman who visited France in March and April, 1919: "I have met a few Nevada boys . . . Farnsworth Wright is interpreter in the town major's office in Roeze."[121] Roeze is in the Sarthe Department (i.e. county) of France, well on the other side of Paris from the war zone. Later in the year, Farnsworth, cited as a member of the Piano Club of Chicago, reported in a musical paper on the prevalence of pianos in provincial France. The piece mentioned that he had been stationed in the Sarthe region for "a great part" of his year in France.[122]

As for his job as translator, Farnsworth's extensive experience with Esperanto and study of Italian has already demonstrated his aptitude for languages. It's unlikely that those two languages were much in demand, but as E. Hoffmann Price noted:

> Farnsworth's facility with words made a single language insufficient. His command of French had won him the Sphinx insignium of the World War One interpreter. He had a good command of German and Spanish, Latin and Italian. Whimsically, he disparaged

his linguistics by saying that having once bossed a crew of East Indian section hands, he'd learned sufficient Punjabi to give orders, and even to call for a drink of water.[123]

Upon his return, Farnsworth immediately resumed writing shorts for the *Overland Monthly*. The first to appear, "Lonesome Time" (October 1919), showed its author to be in a deeply contemplative mood. Set in France, it's a story of an American combat aviator in training who imagines how the girl he loves, the girl back home, would react to news of his death. His musings are interrupted by the arrival of enemy aircraft which draws him into his first aerial combat. He manages to shoot down his more skillful German opponent and sees him kiss a "small pasteboard object" before dying. Examination of the wreckage reveals the object to be a photo of a beautiful girl. The aviator weeps, wondering, "How many tens of thousands of girls in the warring countries must wait in vain for their soldiers?"

The empathetic story seemed to close the circle on any ideas Farnsworth may have taken into the war about "subduing the Hun." Back was the internationalism of "The Vow," in which all people are sons and daughters of the same humanity. "She knew how eager he was to go," Farnsworth wrote of the aviator's girl. But for the aviator, the fantasy of war quickly surrendered to the reality of war. For Farnsworth, going to war had been the "one desire of his heart"—the only one; there was no girl back home. Like millions of others, he may have felt suckered into thinking that participation in this particular war could not be anything less than heroic. "Lonesome Time" provided his last written words on the war, so far as we know. It became yet another subject he didn't care to talk about.

Quickly following "Lonesome Time," Farnsworth's next appearances in *Overland* were the two revealing stories already discussed, "A Cookery Queen" and "In the Depths," both in the December 1919 issue. All three postwar stories sharply reflect his experiences and feelings. They suggest an author who is out of sorts, pondering the qualities of his personal and professional life; indeed, even deeply reconsidering his views of the world. It may have been a lonely time. He may have had difficulty, like many returning veterans, reintegrating into the tame predictability of peacetime. He may have lacked a strong sense of purpose—or a cause.

We know of four more shorts he published through the end of 1920. If there are more, there are certainly not many. Price noted that "whereas [Farnsworth] could sell fiction readily enough, he couldn't produce sufficient to earn a living."[124] The stories were strictly a sideline to his journalism. It's not clear who employed him upon his return from France. He may have reconnected with *Musical America*. By November 1920, at the latest, he was a reporter for the *Chicago Herald-Examiner*. He departed the newspaper business, if the sequence is correct, to edit a magazine called *Health*, but the "untimely death of the publisher" ended that opportunity.[125] This was probably the Chicago magazine, *Health: A Notional Magazine for Home, School, Industry*, which did actually produce issues from 1921-24.

The four stories from 1920 incorporate Farnsworth's interests and views, but are less psychologically and intellectually revealing than the ones we've already examined. In "The Silent Shot" (*Overland*, February 1920), a reporter investigating a suicide decides there is more to the story. It turns out to have been an accidental shooting but the reporter drops the story out of sympathy for the shooter, reasoning that nothing would be gained and that additional lives would be ruined from the official prosecution of the case. The story offers a radical perspective on two levels. It features the selflessness of the reporter in forgoing headlines and glory while arguing for individual preemption of the cruelties of the press and legal system. "Out of the Frying Pan: An Operatic Tragedy" (*Overland*, May) is the first of two music-themed stories. A comic piece, it displays Farnsworth's inside knowledge of the music business, good and ill, and the relationship of performers to reporters. In "The Stolen Melody" (*Overland*, November), a story which incorporates a lot of technical music criticism, Farnsworth uses music as a metaphor for social class. A composer, Mascal, writes a great symphony whose central theme is a "tawdry ragtime melody." After a description of the critical debate over the symphony, the narrative concludes with "what none of them has understood": "the melody was never tawdry. It was a noble melody from the first, and Mascal simply restored it to its primal estate." The story suggests that Farnsworth may have enjoyed slumming to the popular music of vaudeville, though remaining reluctant to sign his name to such sentiments. Additionally, "The Stolen Melody" may be where the thoughts inspired by the African-American soldiers finally found a home.

The fourth story, "The Medal of Virtue," appeared in the December 1920 *Munsey's Magazine*. If *Overland*, his reliable magazine of choice, had rejected it, that would help explain why his fiction career faded out at this time. The story concerns Josephine, a young woman in Orléans, France, on the occasion of her twenty-first birthday. She unexpectedly receives in the mail the Medal of Virtue from the Society of Jeanne d'Arc for the Encouragement of Morality. Feeling entirely unworthy, she endures a rain-soaked walk in order to present the medal to a nun. But this selfless act proves her virtue, thus marking her passage into adulthood. Farnsworth was "exceedingly proud" of this story because it contained a "sacrilegious pun in French."[126]

It was in this period, roughly, that Farnsworth began to suffer from Parkinson's, a chronic disorder of the nervous system with symptoms ranging from tremors to rigidity of the limbs. Though the disease is progressive, the afflicted can live for many years. Still, if the early onset made him question his mortality, added to the thought that his father died young, it offers an additional reason why he might have abandoned his fiction career.

Seriousness of demeanor is an indication of Parkinson's, due to the effect on facial nerves. Indeed, an impression of underlying sadness comes through in photographs of Wright, which uniformly capture his dour expression. If he's smiling in any of them, you can't tell. E. Hoffmann Price echoes this sentiment in his memory of meeting Farnsworth for the first time in the *Weird Tales* office: his "face seemed expressionless, giving no hint of the wit and sparkle I'd later discover."[127]

Happily, Price contradicts the downbeat images by expounding repeatedly upon Farnsworth's love of puns, limericks, jokes of all kinds, his quick wit, and his love of a good laugh, as in this passage:

> Farnsworth's sense of humor covered the entire field, and with his knowledge of French, Spanish, German, and I think, Italian, as well as Latin, that field was wide. No matter from what you dredged a quip, you did not have to supply blueprints to get a hearty laugh from Farnsworth. There was nothing too subtle, nor anything too bawdy; in a flash, he would switch from a *jeux d'esprit*, as delicate as Hungarian Somlyoi, and to a barrackroom jest as rugged as Demerara rum. To say that the man was no prude is the ultimate in understatement.[128]

In early 1921, Farnsworth was writing for *Musical America* again, while serving as music critic for the *Herald-Examiner*. Late in the year, he jumped to the *Chicago Journal of Commerce* before returning to the *Herald-Examiner*. That is where we find him at the end of 1922, at the ripe old age of 34, when *Weird Tales* made its initial solicitation for material. The veteran newsman answered the call, placing stories in each of the first two issues, his first published fiction in over two years.

Who was Farnsworth Wright when *Weird Tales* was born? What emerges from the record of his past is a portrait of a complex man, intelligent, literate, and confident in his judgment. What fails to suggest itself is a simple equation that would explain his attraction to *Weird Tales*. There is no straight line from a singular event or interest to the realms of fantasy and horror, no obsession with Poe like Henneberger's. And, of course, Farnsworth, the king of secrets, never provided an explanation.

However, there are aspects of his past which contribute to an understanding, any or all of which may hold the answer. The simplest plausible explanation is that journalism had become an unexciting routine, he missed composing stories, and the advent of a hometown magazine trying something bold sparked his interest. It was a lark that accidentally turned into a cause.

Another explanation is his love of language and literature which may have been reignited by the appeal made in the early solicitations for *Weird Tales* for stories in the vein of those two masters of the language, Poe and Bierce. Price described Farnsworth's love of words: "Prose, to him, needed rhythm, sonorous phrases; it needed balance and imagery, for he had the heart of a poet."[129] He was "scholarly, talented, with a musical background at least as full and rich as his literary and linguistic background."[130] For Price, having met Farnsworth through his editorship of the magazine, the musical background was a discovery, Farnsworth's hidden side. For us, having worked through Farnsworth's background from the beginning, the literary side is the revelation. Music had been his dominant interest. Outside of his handful of published shorts, the record only hints at his literary impulses. But he was clearly well-read and desirous of more self-expression than journalism allows. Possessing a parallel appreciation of music and words gave him a broader perspective of each. For him, sounds had language and words had music; the art forms of music and literature overlapped. This perspective comes through in the often florid work of writers he developed, as editor, in the pages of *Weird Tales*.

Additionally, the *Weird Tales* solicitations openly appealed to nonconformists, asking for "fiction of a peculiar sort" and "the sort of stories that are commonly forbidden in most magazines."[131] Farnsworth's independent streak asserted itself repeatedly through his life. We might suppose that growing up without a father allowed him to develop in the absence of a potentially strong, or even overbearing, influence. After the war, judging by the rejection of high-art snobbery expressed in "The Stolen Melody," he appeared to be turning toward the popular arts after years as a pure classicist. *Weird Tales* offered something fresh which may have appealed to his changing tastes, a balance of the low art of the pulps and the high art of literature. He could slum if he had the promise of art to keep his sensibilities from being obliterated. It's hard to imagine him editing one of the weird menace pulps of the '30s for which sensations were the overbearing object.

Finally, there is a powerful theme to his life—his abnormal acquaintance with death—that may have connected with the inherent sense of morbidity that belongs to the horror story in general and to *Weird Tales* in particular. It starts with the early loss of his father and the painful loss of his mother, both events having serious implications for his emotional life. Added to that are the Great Earthquake, the drowning of Rauen, and the devastation of the Great War. Even if he escaped injury to life and limb in those events, they all provided a close-up experience of death and suffering. The contraction of the slowly evolving curse of Parkinson's may have made him feel that he'd run out of close calls, that Fate was catching up to him. How could he not be scarred?

Given that lead-in, we might expect his two early appearances in *Weird Tales* to bludgeon the mind with metaphors bloated like foetid corpses on a river of blood. While neither story draws upon his state of mind as blatantly and thoroughly as "In the Depths," the home-schooled psychoanalyst can still find much on which to ruminate. . . .

The first entry, "The Closing Hand" (March 1923), is a short account of two sisters left alone for the night in an old, abandoned, and perhaps haunted house. The spooky scene is suitably captured by Farnsworth: "The elder sister soon dropped into slumber, but the younger lay open-eyed, staring into the black room and shuddering at every stifled scream of the wind or distant growl of thunder." The younger sister wakes the elder to alert her to the sounds of a possible prowler downstairs. The elder leaves to explore, but what eventually returns is something quite different. . . . The story ends with a grim shock. While strong on atmospherics, the tale is weak on plot. The setup is particularly unsatisfying—and the strangest part of the story. The girls were left in the house by their mother, for reasons totally unexplained. "Mother shouldn't have left us alone in this gruesome place." The father receives an incidental mention. It's impossible to overlook the connections: the mother is Genevieve, the abandoned children are the young Wrights, and the gruesome place is the world. The story expresses the frightful insecurity and genuine dangers of being alone without a protector.

Accompanying the text was a boxed ad for Farnsworth's story for the April issue, "The Snake Fiend." Baird advertised the five-pager on the contents page as "A Tale of Diabolic Terror," and it certainly delivers on the promise. It's a genuinely creepy tale, one which Baird must have been very happy to receive. The protagonist, Jack Crimi (short for criminal?) is a venomous, vengeful snake-lover. Marjorie, the girl of his dreams, reminds Crimi of his mother. Unaware of his affections, she marries Allen, a young civil engineer. Crimi remains friends with the pair, though secretly desiring revenge. The newlyweds relocate to the sagebrush region of northern California, near the Nevada border, so that he can work on a western railroad. Clearly, the newlyweds are based on Farnsworth's parents. His father was a civil engineer who worked on railroads, only the location has been moved to the landscape which Farnsworth knew from his days in Reno. And Farnsworth eventually married a woman named Marjorie, whom he had met in college. Perhaps she reminded him of Genevieve. At any rate, the fictional Marjorie writes Crimi, telling him how infested with rattlesnakes their new land is. Crimi moves nearby, to remain sociable with them and ostensibly to study rattlers for a monograph. Like Farnsworth . . . he's a writer! The opportunity for revenge arrives when Allen and Marjorie are gone for the day. Crimi nails their cabin windows shut. After they return and go to sleep, he empties boxes of rattlers into the cabin, then barricades the only door. The account of their awakening to the reptilian menace is harrowing and horrifying. They do manage to escape, though Allen is badly wounded. A fired and disgruntled cook is blamed for the deed while—in a bit of unconvincing plotting—Crimi, the snake expert, goes unsuspected. When the couple pay a surprise visit, Crimi, mistaking them for the ghosts of his murder victims, goes insane. This story is more directly connected to the factual details of Farnsworth's life, yet the significance seems less. Crimi is the only distinctive character; Allen and Marjorie are good-natured but otherwise undeveloped. Farnsworth appeared merely to be drawing upon his past for characters and settings, as opposed to working out any inner turmoil. It's perhaps most significant that when he searched his memory for character inspiration, he kept coming back to his parents, his mother, in particular.

Both stories had an abundance of the verve that Baird sought for the new magazine. Although, as he wouldn't have known at the time, Farnsworth Wright had found a new family, the *Weird Tales* circle.

OTIS ADELBERT KLINE AND THE INVISIBLE HAND

In the pulp era, credentials for being a writer were not measured in degrees earned, conferences presented at, and workshops attended. The men, at any rate—the women just had to have hearts—preferred to establish that they'd lived life on the margins of prudence. Writing power was born of adventures in dangerous places, near-death experiences, and the number of tough, man-sized jobs undertaken. And, of course, newspaper experience was almost obligatory. That explained where the words came from. Thus, in the '30s, when Otis Adelbert Kline was called upon to share his background with his fellow writers in the American Fiction Guild, he struck the rhythms of so many writer biographies of the time:

> Knocked around country on various jobs, bonded rails behind a steel gang for Hall Signal Co., hiked poles on toll line for Bell Tel. Co., worked in factories, a shoe store, learned printing trade, became both compositor and pressman in a small shop. Later advertising manager of a newspaper. Has been traveling salesman, sales manager, manufacturing chemist.[132]

Having proven his hardboiled bona fides, he went on to describe his creative accomplishments, which were noteworthy. We don't question the above resume, but we can only corroborate the last two sentences. As to the final item—manufacturing chemist—it refers to the professional responsibilities which grew out of the family business, governed his life when he became involved with *Weird Tales*, and gave him the latitude to dabble in such diversions.

To understand where he came from, his paternal grandfather, John Adam Kline (1830-1912), makes a convenient starting point. He and his brother George L. Kline (1833-1892) were druggists by trade.

George was by far the more colorful of the pair. As a young man, he hunted and captured wild animals in the Klines' native Pennsylvania. His finest specimens ended up at the Smithsonian and other natural history museums. Hunting was a popular activity among the males in the family, including Otis.

George's hunting of animals made a natural lead-in to the hunting of men. When the Civil War erupted, he joined the Pennsylvania Bucktail Rifles, participating in numerous battles for the Union. In the Battle of Gettysburg (July 1-3, 1863), he suffered a grievous injury which sent him to the hospital. He was released from the hospital, and service, in early '64.[133]

By that time, John had relocated to the small town of Geneseo, in the heart of Illinois farm country, become the town druggist, and married the educated Julia Maria Oliver (1840-1916), a farmer's daughter from nearby Dixon. She was one of three sisters who attended the progressive Methodist school, Cornell College, in Mt. Vernon, Iowa.[134] George obviously liked the example his older brother was setting. He joined him in Geneseo, learned the druggist trade, and married Julia's little sister, Lucretia Adelaide Oliver (1842-1903), who had actually preceded Julia at Cornell. John and Julia were the first to start a family. Their son, Louis Adelbert Kline (1864-1938), Otis's father, was born in Geneseo. With the apparent death of an infant sister in 1867, Louis grew up an only child.

In the same year, 1867, with George sufficiently educated in the business, he and Lucretia moved to Sterling, about twenty miles northeast, where he set up shop, with Lucretia's little brother Oscar assisting. George's newspaper ads read: "G L Kline, Druggist and Apothecary, Sign of Red Mortar."[135] The couple started their own family. They would have three children who survived into adulthood and one who didn't.

By 1880, John, Julia, and Louis had abandoned Geneseo for a little farm outside of Rock Falls, a town separated from Sterling by the Rock River. The Sterling-Rock Falls community would be home to the extended Kline family for decades to come. John opened a pharmacy in Rock Falls while George continued to serve Sterling. Sterling was a growing town of 5,000, while Rock Falls, also growing, was yet to reach one thousand which, perhaps, explains why John supplemented his income with farming. George, the veteran of Gettysburg, seemed to be the more prominent of the pair. At their stores, they sold such estimable products as Acker's Blood Elixer, Electric Bitters, Hale's Cough Cordial, Simmon's Liver Regulator (warranted not to contain a single particle of Mercury), Rough on Rats, and—who could be without Kline's dog soap? "Save your dogs! Save your dogs! with Kline's dog soap, or keep them off the street."[136]

In 1882, Louis followed the family footsteps to Cornell College. The school was becoming an institution in the Kline-Oliver family. George and Lucretia's daughter, Lillie, preceded Louis there by several years. It was news back home when Louis bagged an eagle.[137] But back home was where Louis went when one of the stores needed help. He never graduated from Cornell. Instead, his next stop was Chicago, where he went to make his fortune. Like the Henneberger men of the same era, he abandoned the farm for the big city. He ended up, unromantically, as a stenographer for a large insurance company.

Louis came home for the 1888 Christmas holidays. Rock Falls, a hundred miles due west of Chicago, was an easy train trip. On that Christmas day, he married Ora Kate Sides (1870-1949) of Sterling, Otis's mother. The quiet wedding, at the bride's home, was witnessed by only the two sets of parents.[138] It appears to have been a quickly-arranged affair. After Christmas dinner, Louis took his bride straight back to the big city.

Their first child, Ora Sides Kline, was born in Chicago on June 27, 1890. It's a sad story. She succumbed to dysentery, at the age of nine months, while mother was six months pregnant with Otis. Louis's mother journeyed to Chicago and accompanied the bereft mother back to Sterling, bringing the child's remains for burial at the Riverside Cemetery, the final resting place for many family members. Louis, extremely ill at the time, was forced to remain in Chicago.[139] Whether his illness and the baby's death are connected is unknown. The story reminds us of the fragility of life in those days. White infant mortality had begun to decline rapidly due to advances in sanitation and medicine, but in 1890 it was still about 15%.

Otis was born in Chicago on July 1, 1891. But the Chicago experiment had ended. The family soon made a new home in Rock Falls, occasionally traveling to Chicago to visit friends or inviting them back to the small town. Otis's brother, Allen Sides Kline, was born in Rock Falls on December 19, 1893. The fourth sibling, Julia M. Kline, named after her grandmother, was also born in Rock Falls, on December 30, 1895. Louis had a severe cold at the time and the baby only lived for five weeks, the last two spent battling pneumonia. Another question. To compound the series of calamities, little brother Allen, at age three-and-a-half, fell twelve feet off a barn door and snapped his left wrist.[140] That's how close Otis came to being an only child like his father. He seems to have been the lucky one who passed through childhood unscathed. Allen bore a deformity for the rest of his life.

Meanwhile, in 1891, John Adam Kline, Otis's grandfather, had purchased the Dow & Son drugstore, in Rock Falls.[141] By 1895, it had been renamed J.A. Kline & Son, with Louis the son. Other family members pitched in with the business, like George's son, and Otis's uncle, John L. Kline. George was a partner in the store, but it was the last year of his life; he was too infirm to be of much help. When he died on February 12, 1892, days short of his fifty-ninth birthday, the cause was attributed to the long-term effects of the wound suffered at Gettysburg. Once a source of pride and a badge of honor, the injury finally finished him off. He's at Riverside Cemetery, too.

In business, Louis embraced modern practices. The *Sterling Standard* marveled when Louis telephoned Chicago wholesalers on a Friday afternoon and received his shipment on the train Saturday morning.[142] Overnight delivery! Much, much more than the goods, it was the age of miracles that had arrived. Three weeks later, he had a phone booth installed in the store.[143]

Louis was known and respected in the community. He belonged to the Knights Templar, and taught Sunday school at the Lutheran church (in deference to his wife's denomination). By 1892, he was committed to the cause of alcohol prohibition. In his later years, he wrote on the topic for religious magazines. E. Hoffmann Price recalled the one time he met the elder Mr. Kline. Otis, who indulged in a wide variety of alcoholic concoctions as an adult, had warned Price: "My father is a strict Prohibitionist, lifelong teetotaler. Let's have no reference to liquor, past, present, or future. He won't stay long."[144]

In about 1894, Louis purchased a ten-acre farm two miles west of Rock Falls. This is where Otis grew up (and where Allen fell off a barn door). Louis raised chickens on a commercial scale. He was particularly proud of his prize-winning Black Langshans. In a letter to the *Reliable Poultry Journal*, he invoked Darwin's *Origin of Species* as it applied to the cross-breeding of Langshans with Cochins.[145] On another front, he planted a hundred fruit trees under the "model orchard system."[146] All of which reminds us that druggists are scientists, as well. All signs point to his prosperity, right down to the gay new carriage he bought in 1895 to take him into town and the drugstore.[147]

Otis was an avid reader from the age of five, indulging in adventure stories in magazines like *St. Nicholas* and *The Youth's Companion*.[148] In the following insight into his childhood, Otis expands on his father's scientific temperament, an influence which explains Otis's later attraction to *Weird Tales* and his writing of fantastic fiction set on other planets:

> When I was still quite small, my father, who took considerable interest in all of the sciences, and who had quite a large, well-chosen library, used to take me out in the evenings when the sky was clear, and point out to me the planets and constellations, evoking eager questions which he answered to the best of his ability according to his astronomical knowledge of those days—the middle nineties. We frequently discussed the possibility that planets, other than our earth, might be inhabited, and I read and reread [Richard Anthony] Proctor's *Other Worlds Than Ours* first published in England in 1870, and later reprinted here. It was a great day for us when Wells' *War of the World* [*sic*] came out in 1898. I was seven years old at the time, curious about the planets, and highly imaginative. We both read this excellent novel, Dad and I, and had many talks about it. The science-fiction of Jules Verne also intrigued me mightily in those days.[149]

He went on to describe how he had found the "fossil remains of a small creature" which his father was able to identify. He ventured that his "greatest thrill of all" came when his father took him to the Dearborn Observatory at Northwestern University. "We had splendid views of Jupiter and Saturn but Mars, which we had wanted chiefly to see, was too low in the mists to be clear."

Otis's youngest daughter quoted her father as admitting that "he had so many creative talents and interests, he did not know which one to follow."[150] Our first evidence of his artistic undertakings occurs in 1901. Just short of his tenth birthday, his painted landscapes went on display in J.A. Kline & Son, "attracting considerable attention."[151] It's the first of several uncanny similarities to Farnsworth Wright. Recall that at age nine, Farnsworth expressed himself publicly by writing the *San Francisco Call* to announce himself as an avid reader and probable writer.

Throughout his schooling, Otis expressed his artistic impulses in varied ways, acting in a school play, singing in a male quartet. His mother, Ora, sang and played piano. The family hosted parties at their home with musical entertainment. Otis and Allen sang together at these events. The brothers shared an almost identical list of artistic interests: illustration, writing, acting, and music.

The mirrored childhoods of Otis and Farnsworth are again apparent: both had a musical mother and music in the house. But the difference in parentage altered their destinies. Whereas Farnsworth drew mainly on his mother's influence, in the absence of his father, Otis appeared to merge both parents into the writer he became, blending the scientific interests of his father with the artistic sensibilities of his mother. At his peak of popularity, he wrote Edgar Rice Burroughs-inspired scientific romances which appealed equally to both sexes.

While Otis had been getting a public-school education, big changes were happening at J.A. Kline & Son. John Adam was getting old; he turned 70 as the new century clicked over. He seems to have drifted away from active operation of the store, leaving the responsibility to Louis and other family members. One of their main products, traditionally sold in drugstores, was ice cream. In 1907, Louis disposed of the store and went into business with a Sterling resident, Richard Massey, to manufacture ice cream-related products: fruit extracts, syrups and, especially, vanilla extract. They also produced cleaning chemical aromas, perfume, and essential oils. The family business had essentially moved from pharmaceuticals into a related branch of chemistry. The company was best known as Massey & Massey until a 1920s merger resulted in a name change to Neilson-Massey. Amazingly, the company is still in business and their signature product is still vanilla extract.[152]

Otis finished high school in either 1909 or '10. Although the doors at Cornell would certainly have been open to him, he chose another path:

"When I graduated from high school, I decided that I would launch on a musical career, and gave up my plans for going to college," despite that "going to college had been a sort of tradition in our family."[153] In 1912, it fell to Allen to become the third-generation of the family to attend the school. He spent a fruitful four years there, contributing editing and illustration to the school magazine, and meeting his first wife, the class valedictorian.

The four to five years following high school were probably the period when Otis went on the odd-job adventures recited for the American Fiction Guild, using any kind of income as a way to support his musical ambitions. Sometime in this period, he was advertising manager for the *Sterling Standard*.[154] That period of his life leaves little other concrete evidence. One activity that we can count as a near-certainty is that he, like so many of the reading public, had been swept off his feet by the Edgar Rice Burroughs novels which appeared like clockwork after the sensation caused by the publication of *Tarzan of the Apes* in the October 1912 issue of *The All-Story* magazine.

This is the same period in which Kline became acquainted with his "invisible hand." Their lives would crisscross for many years to come, and the hand would influence Otis's step-by-step shifts into the worlds of music and literature. His name was Harold "Harry" Emmons Ward, although pulp readers, and specifically *Weird Tales* readers, would know him as simply Harold Ward. What made him invisible was that, although a constellation of fixed facts connects the two, they never publicly acknowledged their longstanding relationship. Kline, in particular, was deliberately vague about points in his past where Ward played a pivotal role. Ward, for his part, was a newsman and publicist of many years' standing, with ample opportunities to draw attention to his published work, yet rigorously avoided the temptation. Simple modesty could explain it, but Ward was also a pillar of the community, well-known and involved in a great many civic enterprises, and may have been self-conscious about his slightly disreputable pulp-writing sideline.

Like J.C. Henneberger, Ward was the son and grandson of farmers. He was born on January 5, 1879, in Coleta, Illinois, a town situated about twelve miles northwest of Sterling which is still little more than a crossroads in farm country. At age three, "he emigrated to South Dakota, where he settled on a ranch near Mitchell, which was then as wild and woolly as any budding writer could desire. Here he remained until 17 years of age, filling up on Western atmosphere."[155] This detour was related to his mother's health.[156] In 1897, he attended Sterling Business College, learning shorthand and typing, the mechanical skills required to be a newspaper reporter. He started out as a copy boy.[157] In the summer of 1897, he traveled to Springfield, the state capital, as a member of Company E of the National Guard, an organization he belonged to for decades, eventually achieving the rank of major. As a special correspondent, he reported back to the *Sterling Standard*. They must have liked his work because, in November, they made him the Rock Falls reporter while another reporter went on vacation.[158] Still a teenager, his career as a newsman had begun.

From 1897 through 1909, he worked for a number of the small-town papers in the area: both Sterling papers, the *Standard* and the *Gazette* and, in nearby Dixon, the *Sun* and the *Star*. Twice he went to Colorado to work, where he thought the change in atmosphere would better serve his poor health. As he impersonally described his experiences: "he tramped thru the mountains soliciting subscriptions for a paper in Idaho Springs. Later he tried range riding. He gave this job up in despair when he learned by bitter experience that it takes more than a pair of chaps and a broad-brimmed hat to make a cow puncher."[159] When the western sojourn didn't improve his condition, he returned home. Twice, he tried his luck with new magazines: *Rural Life* (1904), published in Sterling, and the *Middle West Advocate* (1906), published in Moline, twenty-five miles away. Neither lasted long. He changed employers frequently, moving to another paper, then back to the first with a better position, and so forth, while he climbed the ladder to editor-in-chief responsibilities. In late 1904, he went north to edit the *Freeport Democrat*. In Freeport, he met his first wife, Theresa Loos (1882-1918). They married in Dixon in 1906, after he took a managing editor job with the *Sun*. She already had a son, Van Dyke, born in 1898. In April 1907, Ward appeared to have settled down—for awhile. He rejoined the *Standard*, for perhaps the fourth time, as top editor, serving in that capacity into 1909.

Over these many years, he would have had ample opportunity to become acquainted with the Klines, but the exact manner of their meeting remains unknown. There's a small chance that Otis was advertising manager for the *Standard* while Ward was editor, but it's probably too early in the chronology for Kline. While the time and place of their meeting can't be established, the motivation is quite clear. Despite a twelve-year age difference, they possessed something powerful in common. They both started songwriting careers at approximately the same time.

Our first record of Otis's efforts as a songwriter and composer occurs with the publication of "Girlie" in 1910. This corresponds with the start of the 1910-15 dance craze at the end of the ragtime era. (Note that brother Allen is known to have written ragtime music.) Otis also wrote sentimental material like "I Wonder Why the Moonlight Always Makes Me Think of Love" (1911). Making money as a songwriter in those days usually meant getting sheet music published and having it sold in music stores, and hoping it became a hit among people who owned and played pianos. Phonograph players and records were still something of a luxury and there's no evidence that any of Otis's songs were recorded.

An even better way to make money was to establish the song in a musical stage-play. That was how Ward did it. In 1925, he reminisced about "a life time spent in [and] around the edge of the show business."[160] The first clear evidence of these activities comes during his last year with the *Standard*. He sent some of his lyrics to Arthur Gillespie, a successful Springfield composer and playwright.[161] Gillespie was famous for the 1900 hit song "Absence Makes the Heart Grow Fonder," for which he wrote the lyrics. Impressed by Ward's work, Gillespie invited him into a writing partnership. Very quickly, in 1909, they sold lyrics for two plays, sentimental stuff like "It Makes a Lot of Difference When You're With the Girl You Love." Their 1910 composition, "I've a Longing, Dear, For You, and Home Sweet Home," had words by Gillespie and music by Ward. As a lyricist, Ward confessed "to the authorship of some two hundred songs of the soft, mushy, sentimental variety—the kind wherein the singer informs his beloved that 'Under a moon is a good place to spoon some night in June,' etc."[162]

Gillespie and Ward's masterwork was the 1909 play *The Question of the Hour*. The question in question was "the drink question": what was to be done about the scourge of alcoholism? The melodrama spelled out the debate through the depredations of a village drunkard. In October, Ward resigned his newspaper position to head publicity for Chicago's Garrick Theatre, owned by the Shuberts, and to oversee the staging of *The Question of the Hour*.[163] When it received a tryout in Montgomery, Alabama, the audience "was worked up to such a frenzy that men shrieked and women sobbed," and partisans came to blows, necessitating police intervention. Accordingly, the play had to be toned down for the sake of community safety.[164] All press-agent puffery, of course, but let's pretend it's true anyway, as a touching testament to the power of drama. It's fair to say that the play had a successful touring run and contributed to the brewing debate over prohibition.

A year later, demonstrating the same restless pattern of his newspaper career, Ward became business manager for the famous touring actress, Clara Lipman.[165] Duration unknown. His last known song with Gillespie was "The Girl I Left at Home (A Sea Song)," copyrighted in September 1912. But it appears that by then he'd long since returned to life in Sterling. Gillespie died in 1916.

At about the same time as Ward's primary involvement with "the show business" seemed to have wound down, Kline was struggling to break in: "In early days of [the film] industry did short movie comedies which brought $25 a reel when they clicked. Wrote plots for revues, acts for [vaudeville] teams, etc."[166] Based on his pulp stories, his comic sensibilities don't spring to mind, but his grown daughter made a point of describing his "good sense of humor": "He enjoyed puns, limericks and funny stories. His business was words, so they naturally were more meaningful to him in all their nuances."[167]

Another likeness with Farnsworth Wright. More important, Otis referred to another writer in this period with whom he "collaborated on songs and movie scenarios, and one musical comedy."[168] That unnamed writer later became Otis's first client when he turned to the literary agent business in 1923. Their collaborations couldn't be identified but the collaborator undoubtedly was Ward. The crucial elements—the place, the time, the activities, their future association—all fit. If Ward had grown comfortable working with a collaborator, the timing of his association with Kline may have followed the dissolution of the partnership with Gillespie.

While Kline wouldn't identify the collaborative works, some of his individual achievements came to light. They may have followed his "apprenticeship" with Ward. At any rate, we can sense the influence of Ward's invisible hand, as Otis seemed to enter a higher level of professional dedication. He was employed by Clayton Summy, a Chicago music publisher, then Harold Rossiter, a Chicago composer.[169] Neither individual could be connected to Ward. Kline also alluded to having "owned and operated a music pub. co."[170] These activities appear to have occurred before Otis's songwriting peak, late 1915 through late '16. His first song in this period was "The Egyptian Dip," a "syncopated song of the Nile," which sounds like an attempt to launch a new dance. It may have been inspired by the time he played an Egyptian priest in "Egypta," a community musical in which his mother played a Hebrew maiden.[171] Other songs he published at this time include "Mary From Tipperary," "You're Sweeter To Me Than the Rose," and the catchy "Virginia Blues." Allen illustrated some of the sheet music. Otis described his musical endeavors as "fairly successful."[172] He also confessed that "it was a hard life, with much night work, plugging songs in theatres, dance halls, and cafes."[173] It was also an unpredictable life, at mercy to the whims of public taste.

Ward may have lectured his acolyte on having a backup plan because, in the end, Otis closed the door on the music world: "I decided on a business career, and went to a business college."[174] Most likely, it was Ward's alma mater, by then called Brown's Business College. Soon after finishing college, he settled down into a job and got married, in Rock Falls, to Ellen "Curley" Grove (1890-1988). The date of the wedding—to prove their romanticism—was Valentine's Day, 1914. He was 22 and she was 23, making it an unusual marriage in one respect: men rarely married older women in those days. They had three children: Elinor Marie (*b.* November 29, 1914), Allen Paul (January 28, 1916), and Ora Fay (October 20, 1918). Unlike his father's generation, and every prior generation dating back to the dawn of man, Otis and Curley had a reasonable expectation that their children would survive the perils of infancy, which they did. Such are the miracles of our modern age. For the World War draft, Otis claimed an exemption based on his wife and then two children;[175] he remained stateside whereas Allen, as yet unmarried, went to France at the tail end of the war, an Army private, and served in the Judge Advocate General's Department in Paris.

The job Otis landed after business college—by early 1917—was none other than his father's firm, Massey & Massey. The long reach of the family business had finally claimed him. Though Otis often added "manufacturing chemist" to his potpourri list of occupations, his real role at Massey was in advertising. Price called him a "master salesman."[176] In 1919, the company moved to Chicago to be near the major transportation hub. Otis, his new family, and his parents, left Rock Falls for good. Otis was not a routine employee. According to Price, he was a "partner" who could "quit his desk on little or no notice."[177] In fact, he traveled widely to represent the company and had a dozen salesmen working under him. He made a nice income from the company. Price recalled the Klines' "lavish hospitality" at their Chicago home.[178]

Despite his commitment to the new employer, Otis never gave up his desire for self-expression. "My evenings were my own. I decided to use them for the improvement of what I optimistically called my mind."[179] Planning to improve himself one subject at a time, he determined the order thusly:

> One of the old philosophers had said there were but three things in the universe, mind, force and matter. Mind controls force and force moves matter. Which was the most important of the three? I felt that mind, which was in control, was the most important, and so began a study of psychology and psychic phenomena. I read everything I could find on the subject, conducted numerous experiments, and eventually felt the urge to write. At first, I tried to write fact material and to present hypotheses based on these facts. However, this placed too much restraint on my imagination.[180]

The "fact material" was an overly-ambitious scientific treatise which was soon abandoned.

According to a *Gazette* profile instigated by Ward in 1929: "While on the road for Massey and Massey . . . [Kline] made the acquaintance of a number of magazine editors, who urged him to turn his talent to story writing."[181] It's a rather curious recollection on Otis's part. He did indeed deal with editors on behalf of the company, but they were the editors of industry journals like *The Ice Cream Review*, *The American Perfumer and Essential Oil Review*, and *The Creamery and Milk Plant Monthly*, not the kind of editors who would have spontaneously suggested a turn to creative writing, unless he had brought up the subject himself seeking affirmation.

The more plausible influence was Ward. From August 1915 through the end of 1923, Ward served as the Sterling city clerk, working out of city hall. His own self-expression bug was far from dead, though. At night, he wrote stories—and rewrote stories—polishing them to a professional sheen.[182] According to current records,[183] his first published story was "Ethics," a short in the September 1917 *Snappy Stories*. Until 1920, the bulk of his sales were to the "sophisticate" magazines like *Snappy*, *Saucy Stories*, *Breezy Stories*, and Chicago's *10 Story Book*.

In 1920, Ward leaped to take advantage when *The Black Mask* came onto the market. In time, the magazine would become legendary for developing the hardboiled detective genre and launching the careers of Dashiell Hammett and many other two-fisted typists. But for its first iteration, its content blended detective and mystery with stories of horror, ghosts, and the occult, the latter grouping being exactly the kind of thing *Weird Tales* would try to make its living on. After a year-and-a-half of issues, *The Black Mask* restricted itself to detective and mystery, with a few westerns thrown in. Henneberger should have been paying attention.

Ward was an important author for *The Black Mask*. He appeared in the first issue of April 1920 and most of the subsequent issues through the end of 1922. He contributed 47 stories in that period, mostly shorts, but on six occasions he supplied the lead novelette. He specialized in the weird stories, with entries like "The Man Who Would Not Die" (September 1920) and "The Mystery of the Haunted House" (December 1920). He was popular enough with the magazine's editor that he occasionally appeared with an additional story in an issue under the pseudonym of Ward Sterling, the deciphering of which we leave as an exercise for the reader. The November 1921 issue included *three* of his stories and yet another pseudonym had to be concocted: H.W. Starr. The February 1922 issue had a third story under H.A. Haward. On two occasions (September 1920, April 1922), *The Black Mask* ran a Harold Ward story alongside two Ward Sterling stories, which raises the question of whether the editor, Florence M. Osborne, understood that the pseudonym was supposed to conceal the lack of variety in the magazine.

Kline's writing in this period should be considered against the backdrop of Ward's success in the pulps, and with fantastic fiction. Kline kept on writing, but it took him some time before he considered himself a candidate for magazine publication. He may have lacked confidence or feared that his stories didn't fit any of the current markets. At any rate, in early 1921, he folded his psychological musings into a novelette, "The Thing of a Thousand Shapes." Still inspired by his father's interest in astronomy, he followed up with an interplanetary novel set on Venus, *Grandon of Terra* (later renamed *The Planet of Peril*).

It was not until 1922 that he got serious about actually selling these works. "The Thing of a Thousand Shapes," as he recalled, "was turned down by most of the leading magazines." *The Black Mask* wouldn't have wanted it; their weird phase was long gone by then. *Grandon of Terra* had narrower potential: Gernsback's *Science and Invention* and Munsey's *Argosy-All Story*, but the latter possibility never occurred to him. Therefore, "after writing and rewriting, polishing and re-polishing"—he still sounds like Ward's student—he sent the manuscript to Gernsback who turned it down "because of the paucity of mechanical science."[184]

Meanwhile, when Osborne departed *The Black Mask*, and new editor George W. Sutton began to reshape the magazine, Ward may have found himself unwelcome. Opportunistically, he quickly jumped on another new magazine, none other than Rural's *Detective Tales*. He planted a short story in the second issue of October 16, 1922. The announcement for *Weird Tales* was equally good news, as it restored the market for spooky stories that had dried up at *The Black Mask*. Ward appeared in the first two issues. After seeing the first issue, he sent in a fan letter (attributed to "H.W. of Sterling, Illinois") which Baird printed in the April *Eyrie*:

> My dear Mr. Baird: I have just notified my attorney to start suit against you and your new magazine for personal injury. My eyes are rather poor, and the first number was so interesting that I sat up nearly all night reading it—and as a result I've been wearing smoked glasses ever since. WEIRD TALES seems to me to fill a long felt want in magazine circles. I have always delighted in stories of the 'Dracula' type and that Sax Rohmer stuff, and I never could understand why the editors didn't wake up. You, as a pioneer in the field, are giving them something to think about. Meanwhile, if you make the next number as interesting as the first, I'll likely go blind.

Baird joshed: "Despite the danger to H.W.'s eyesight, we tried to make this number even more interesting than the first."

We can now assess Kline's situation in late 1922 when *Weird Tales* dropped the hook into the pond. He was back in Chicago, the city of his birth. He had a wife and three children, aged four to seven. He had a nice job and a comfortable living. And he had two unsold stories. *Weird Tales* was "made to order" for "The Thing of a Thousand Shapes," and Ward was telling him all about the new magazine. It made a fateful intersection of Otis's long-held love of fantastic-fiction, his desire to be an artist, and the emergence of a perfect home for his unpublished novelette.

He acted quickly, like Wright, and sold his story to Baird in 1922. "The Thing of a Thousand Shapes," Otis's print debut as a fictioneer, ran as a two-part serial. Baird must have appreciated its suspense to have broken it in two so that the first part would lure readers into buying the second issue.

Indeed, it is a well-constructed and compelling story which fairly brims with weird and spooky elements, and some very effective imagery, just the kind of submission to make Baird think the new enterprise had hope in spite of the utterly hopeless rubbish arriving in the daily mail.

"The Thing" concerns the visit of William Ansley, the narrator, to his Uncle Jim Braddock's farm near Peoria. Peoria just happens to be fifty miles south of Sterling and was likely a town Otis had occasion to visit. As the story opens, Uncle Jim has just died and his fond nephew feels obligated by loyalty to supervise the funeral and burial preparations. He remembers Uncle Jim as a "scientist and dreamer" whose hobby was psychic phenomena, and whose discoveries were recorded in a book, *The Reality of Materialization Phenomena*. As Ansley recalls, "His thirst for more facts regarding the human mind was insatiable." Clearly, Uncle Jim is Otis. When Ansley sees the body in an open casket, he declares, "Uncle Jim is *not dead!* He is only sleeping." The other attendants, two helpful neighbors, are confused because Jim has been declared deceased by a physician and shows all the signs of a corpse. The three take turns watching over the body through the night before their common terrors bring them together again. All three had experienced similar visions: a white vapor coming out of Jim's nostrils, cloudy, white shapes moving about the room and, most frightening of all, a misty, white vampire bat.

During the day, Ansley walks through the yard contemplating the dimensions of nature. "It is but a step," he reflects, "from the natural to the supernatural." But is there such a thing as the "supernatural"? he muses. He connects his reflections to the changing world: "Telegraphy, telephony, the phonograph, the moving picture—all would have been regarded with superstition by an age less advanced than ours." This type of observation is common for the period, an age of miracles so much more dramatic to its inhabitants than our own.

Finally, on one night's watch, Ansley witnesses strange creatures in the air before him, one creature morphing into another, one after one, and "Only half of the night gone!" This is the tantalizing cliffhanger which ends the first part.

The concluding part of the story, in the April issue, throws all sorts of phenomena into the mix: psychological concepts, telepathy, automatic writing, hypnosis, ventriloquism, and "psychoplasm," the white substance— and a term that Otis was rather proud of coining.[185] The human drama of the tale expands when indignant neighbors who have heard rumors of vampirism come as an armed vigilante mob to destroy Jim as they would any vampire, by putting a stake through his heart. Ansley notes that the gang is comprised of "superstitious farmers," and perhaps this describes a class of people Otis was all too happy to escape when he moved to Chicago. In the end, the gang is thwarted and Jim is awoken. He had not been dead, as Ansley had surmised, but merely the victim of a "sleeping sickness" which had been sweeping Peoria. The story, therefore, is science fiction masquerading as horror, but nonetheless weird.

Otis Adelbert Kline had joined his brother weirdsmiths, Farnsworth Wright and Harold Ward, in singing the music of wonder.

DEATH GASPS

This then was the general state of affairs as *Weird Tales* faced its own risks of infant mortality: In the futuristic, modern metropolis of Chicago, Henneberger launched his dream magazine in partnership with old pal Johnny Lansinger. If there was any hope that the new creation would lessen the struggles of their first—*Detective Tales*—that hope was soon extinguished. The struggles of the Rural Publishing Corporation simply expanded to encompass two magazines instead of one. For Henneberger and Lansinger the struggles were financial and operational; for Edwin Baird, they were editorial. The problems of filling two magazines fell to him. Despite his tireless efforts, he was overwhelmed and happy to tell the world about it in gory detail. He picked up two part-time helpers, Wright and Kline, aspiring local writers who had landed material in the first two issues of *Weird Tales*. The pair had much in common: a love of the arts, especially music and literature. Although they were drawn to the outré aims of *Weird Tales* for different reasons, they were both grounded by a robust sense of humor. They both had outside employment and could work with the magazine out of belief in the cause. Given all that, it's easy to imagine the pair circling into the orbit of Henneberger and Baird. For the publishers, the business challenges remained.

We can't examine the progress of *Weird Tales*—as a commercial product—in isolation, though. Once *Weird Tales* entered the scene, *Detective* and *Weird Tales* were Siamese twins who followed a collective destiny. Adjustments were made in tandem—in size, logo style, etc.—making both magazines readily identifiable on the newsstand as products of the same publisher. Consequently, the business history of *Weird Tales* really begins with the introduction of *Detective Tales*.

As new products for their inexperienced publishers, the two magazines would require experimentation and refinement, applying the lessons that Henneberger had learned in transforming the inconsequential *The Collegiate World*—through alterations in title, format, and content—into the successful *College Humor*. Development would have been part of the business plan. Thus it's not surprising to find a great variety of changes from the 1922 introduction of *Detective Tales* through the upheaval of 1924. Indeed, it may have been the initial struggles of *Detective Tales* which encouraged the publishers to openly champion *Weird Tales* as an experiment. Had the upheaval never occurred, we would interpret the changes as the understandable growing pains for an insurgent company like Rural. With the benefit of hindsight, knowing of the tremendous financial losses caused by the company's failures, we interpret the changes, increasingly as the magazines progressed though 1923, as being half about improving quality and half as acts of desperation aimed at salvaging the magazines' fortunes. The events of 1924 will tell a different story, as we shall eventually see.

There are numerous variables contributing to the financial fortunes of a magazine, which the publisher can balance in seeking the winning formula. The main source of income was the cover price, of which the publisher received a small percentage on issues sold, with the rest of the revenue spread through the chain of distributors and retailers. A secondary source was income from ad space sold in the magazine. Expenses included overhead, including offices and staff; prices paid for magazine content, to authors and artists; and the raw expenses of printing the magazine, which took into account the size of the magazine, the quality of the paper, the number of pages, and so forth. Within this grand equation, the publisher had tremendous leeway to play with the variables. Indeed, we see so many of these variables at play in the development of *Detective* and *Weird Tales*, the magazines make an illuminating case study on publishing strategies of the era.

The primary variable is content. *Detective* and *Weird Tales* were all-fiction magazines. That wasn't subject to change. The second variable is size. *Detective Tales* was introduced as a large-size magazine of 8.5x11 inches when every other all-fiction title on the market was produced in a standard pulp-size of 7x10 inches. Therefore, radical experimentation is evident from the outset.

It wasn't simply a question of dimensions. More important, it was a matter of status, an attempt to mingle with the upper-class on the newsstand. The large-size slicks were popular mass market magazines printed on high-quality "slick" paper, as opposed to the cheap woodpulp which gave the pulps their favored nickname. Slicks were of generally higher quality in all regards. They had wide circulations, contained better printing, and published sophisticated work from the nation's top journalists, fictionists, and illustrators. The content of the slicks entered the national conversation the way a popular television program does today. The pulps, in a distinctly lower tier, were taken less seriously. At the time, the difference between the slicks and the pulps was perceived as upper or middlebrow versus lower or working class literature. Given the prominence of popular culture today, we see that a different narrative played out. The cream of the pulps, including many stories to appear in *Weird Tales*, were fated to have a longer-term influence than the mannered or topical fiction found in the slicks.

For Rural, publishing at slick-size had a practical implication. Slicks and pulps were shelved in different sections of the newsstands, Main Street respectability on one side and the cheap-paper ghetto on the wrong side of the literary tracks. Therefore, upsizing *Detective Tales* was an attempt to get the magazine seen by a different class of customer. However, it was still printed on pulp paper, and cheaply produced in several aspects, suggesting that the commitment to slick-world, or financial wherewithal, was less than complete. *Detective Tales* may have lived in a better neighborhood on the newsstand, but it remained a pulp in slick clothing, a social climber in an ill-fitting suit.

For its first four issues, *Detective Tales* was published as a thin, 48-page magazine at 15¢, putting it in direct competition with the flimsy 10¢ *Mystery Magazine*. At a larger size and higher price, *Detective Tales* was being marketed as the superior product. After skipping the January 1923 issue, it reemerged in February at a whopping 192 pages, with a 25¢ cover price, and a bold claim on the cover to be "America's Biggest All-Fiction Magazine"—which it certainly was. Inside the magazine, an announcement claimed: "With this issue of DETECTIVE TALES we take an important forward step. In one leap, we've grown to FOUR TIMES our former size!" Even better: "For less than twice as much money you are getting twice double the amount of excellent reading."[186]

Then came March, the month in which *Weird Tales* debuted. Inexplicably, both *Detective* and *Weird Tales* appeared as standard pulps. The jumbo experiment for *Detective Tales* had ended after a single issue. The step forward had hit a wall. Baird, in his *Detective Tales* column, *A Chat With the Chief*, published a reader's letter complaining that the February issue was "too large and unhandy." Baird replied that "we" had come to the same conclusion and thus made the change to the smaller size. "Quick service!"[187] But it's just as likely that poor sales, and the excessive costs charged by the Cuneo-Henneberry printing company, rather than size, provoked the move. If the big issue had been a hit, *Detective Tales* would have lived on in that format.

The rapid changes continued. While *Detective Tales* skipped another issue, the second issue of *Weird Tales*, April, was the first produced by the Cornelius Printing Company. It was shorter in height by about three-quarters of an inch and narrower in width by about a half-inch. It may have been as unhandy in the one direction as the large magazines were in the other.

Sales of the second issue of *Weird Tales* may have been even worse than the first. Among collectors of the original magazine, it is believed to be the rarest in the entire three-decade run. This can possibly be explained by publishing industry practices. Typically, unsold copies were destroyed by the distributors and retailers, with the covers returned to the publisher as proof, meaning that relatively few copies remained in circulation. There may also have been transition issues in moving to the new printer.

With the May issues, both magazines jumped from pulp-size up to an even more unhandy 9.5x12.5 inches, the size they would remain for the foreseeable future. For *Detective Tales*, the March issue became a true anomaly as the only issue in the magazine's many-year history to be published as a true pulp. For *Weird Tales*, it may have pleased Henneberger to have elevated his pet project to the size of the classier magazines, reflecting his view that it was at heart a literary magazine. What emerges from the first eight months of Rural's life is an erratic pattern. The first five issues of *Detective Tales* were large-size; then, across the two titles, three pulp-size magazines were published in two months; and then the final move was made to the extra-large size.

One of the most important variables was the cover price of the magazine. *Detective Tales* debuted at 15¢ for 48 pages then jumped to 25¢ for 192 for the jumbo issue. The 25¢ price carried over to March for the debut of *Weird Tales* and both magazines would stay at that price through 1924. *Capt. Billy's Whiz Bang*, cheap in all ways but one, sold for 25¢; Chicago's *10 Story Book* was a thin magazine for 25¢, but offered racy glamour photography. Rural may have thought 25¢ a fair price for their far more substantial contributions to American letters. A quarter for a magazine might not sound like much today, but in 1923 it was relatively expensive, even for a slick. Despite their higher class status, the popular weeklies, like *The Saturday Evening Post* and *Collier's*, could be purchased for a nickel an issue. They were actually cheaper than the pulps because they subsidized the sale price with expensive advertising. The slicks ran full-page ads by national brands—using the best color printing of the day—allowing them to sell the magazine for below production cost. A typical slick ad was a lavish two-page spread featuring the latest automobile model. The ads in *Weird Tales* sold vocational training and cheap, mail-order handguns.

Even among the pulps, *Detective* and *Weird Tales* were expensive. The Competition Table (following pages) lists the vast majority of the fiction magazines on the market in March 1923, when *Weird Tales* debuted.

The cheapest pulp was double the price of the legendary *Saturday Evening Post*. The weekly *Argosy* was the newsstand bargain with its 10¢ price and high page-count, understandable because it had a wide circulation, featured some of the most popular authors, and ran numerous serials, which meant that readers bought the magazine routinely if not religiously.

On the upper end of the scale, which the Competition Table makes all too apparent, Rural had positioned its two pulps as premium products, with a high page-count and the 25¢ price, ranking them with the only other 25¢ pulps, *Short Stories* and the prestigious and highly popular *Adventure*. (The naughty *10 Story Book* belongs to a special class of risqué magazines.) Moreover, the List column shows that the Rural sisters were the only pulps to couple "upper class" pricing with "lower class" policies. List B indicated author word-rates of less than 1¢. Otis Adelbert Kline recalled that payments to new writers at *Weird Tales*—i.e. Rural—were only one-third to one-half cents a word.[188]

Another point to note in the table is how few monthlies there were compared to more frequently published magazines. This highlights a hidden trend in pulp publishing of the time. From late 1921 through mid-1924, eleven of the twenty-eight listed magazines increased their publishing frequency. For example, *The Black Mask* and *Sea Stories* advanced from monthly to semi-monthly (two issues a month); *Adventure* went from semi to thrice monthly. However, seven of the eleven reverted to their former frequency, usually within a year or two, the gambit having fallen short of expectations. This gives us a loose indication of how hot the publishers perceived the market to be. They sensed that there was a lot more for the taking; after all, going from once to twice a month is an attempt to double the business. For *Detective* and *Weird Tales*, it added another challenge: selling into a saturating market. That last variable may even have worked to their favor. The pulp field as a whole grew throughout the decade, but the growth occurred through the diversification of titles, not by the same titles appearing more frequently.

All the same, it was risky to price new magazines at the high end, more so if they were cheaply produced. Henneberger and Baird compounded the problem by ignoring conventional wisdom. Most pulps were marketed on the basis of the popular authors who appeared within. A magazine had a reputation, but it rested on the shoulders of quality writers whose names featured prominently and frequently on the front cover. But, as we have seen, both *Detective* and *Weird Tales* de-emphasized this obvious concept. "The author's name doesn't matter," as Baird wrote in the first issue of *Weird Tales*.[189] Indeed, for its first seven issues only a single story title with author name appeared on the cover, and a couple of those were difficult to read. Beginning with the November 1923 issue, there were *no* authors listed, for reasons to be explained later. *Detective Tales* followed the same pattern. It wasn't until the March 1924 *Weird Tales* that a name appeared again on the cover, and that name was . . . Houdini! Eventually, after the cataclysm that these missteps led to, *Weird Tales* would fall in line with standard practices: cultivating unique talents, building its reputation on their contributions, and emphasizing their names on the covers.

Competition Table

Pulps (or fiction-oriented magazines) on the market when *Weird Tales* was introduced, ranked by price and size. The "List" classification comes from the regular quarterly market report in the June 1923 *Student Writer*. List A magazines paid on acceptance at rates of 1¢/word and up. List B magazines paid on publication at rates of less than 1¢/word.

Magazine Genre	Publisher	Price	Pgs	List	Frequency
Mystery Magazine					
detective/mys	Frank Tousey	10¢	64	B	semimonthly
Lover's Lane					
romance	Clayton	10¢	64	A	semimonthly
Argosy All-Story Weekly					
general	Munsey	10¢	160	A	weekly
"I Confess"					
romance	Dell	15¢	80	B	semimonthly
Detective Story Magazine					
detective/mys	Street & Smith	15¢	144	A	weekly
Love Story Magazine					
romance	Street & Smith	15¢	144	A	weekly
Sea Stories					
adventure	Street & Smith	15¢	144	A	semimonthly
Top-Notch Magazine					
general	Street & Smith	15¢	144	A	semimonthly
Western Story Magazine					
western	Street & Smith	15¢	144	A	weekly
Brief Stories					
general	Brief Stories	20¢	96	B	monthly
Ace-High Magazine					
western/adv	Clayton	20¢	128	A	semimonthly
Live Stories					
romance/adult	Clayton	20¢	128	A	semimonthly
Action Stories					
adventure	Fiction House	20¢	128	A	monthly
The Black Mask					
detective/mys	Pro-Distributors	20¢	128	A	semimonthly

Magazine Genre	Publisher	Price	Pgs	List	Frequency
Breezy Stories					
romance/adult	C.H. Young	20¢	128	A	monthly
Droll Stories					
romance/adult	C.H. Young	20¢	128	A	monthly
Saucy Stories					
romance/adult	Inter-Continental	20¢	128	A	semimonthly
Snappy Stories					
romance/adult	Clayton	20¢	128	A	semimonthly
Telling Tales					
romance/adult	Clayton	20¢	128	A	monthly
Young's Realistic Stories Magazine					
romance/adult	C.H. Young	20¢	128	A	monthly
People's					
general	Street & Smith	20¢	192	A	semimonthly
The Popular Magazine					
general	Street & Smith	20¢	192	A	semimonthly
The Blue Book Magazine					
general	Consolidated	20¢	192	A	monthly
10 Story Book					
general/adult	10 Story Book	25¢	64	B	monthly
Short Stories					
adventure	Doubleday	25¢	176	A	semimonthly
Adventure					
adventure	Ridgway	25¢	192	A	thrice-monthly
Detective Tales					
detective/mys	Rural Publishing	25¢	192	B	monthly
Weird Tales					
fantastic	Rural Publishing	25¢	192	B	monthly

. . .

While maintaining the high cover price, *Weird Tales*, throughout its first year, showed numerous signs that cost-cutting was the underlying motivator of its "experimentation." (Data for *Detective Tales* is incomplete.) As a purely quantitative matter, the magazine declined in page count, and the number of stories and illustrations; introduced reprints; and skipped issues.

While pulps occasionally touted an increase in the number of pages, no pulp ever drew attention to a decrease. Cutting back on pages was a subtle method of giving the reader less for the money. The first two issues of *Weird Tales* numbered 192 pages. The first two large issues had 120 pages. Beginning with the fifth issue (July-August 1923), the count dropped to 96 pages, where it stayed until the massive Anniversary Issue of 1924, the terminal event of the cataclysm.

The reader, of course, was not paying for paper; they were paying for words, the unit the authors were paid by. The cost of the paper was trivial compared to the cost of the content. Fewer pages meant fewer words and usually fewer stories. The first issue of *Weird Tales* was an embarrassment of riches with 26 stories, about double what the average pulp offered. The second issue had the same page-count, but less type on the smaller pages, and 20 stories. With the drop to 96 pages, issues averaged 16 stories apiece. All the while maintaining the onerous 25¢ cover price.

Another way to save money on content was to not pay for it. There were two methods for doing this, the second to be discussed later. The *more* honorable way was to reprint stories that one already owned the rights to or were in the public domain. The honorability is relative. The reprinting of stories was an immortal scourge in the pulps which spread like a drug-resistant bacteria whenever financial stress was at its greatest, such as in the early years of the Great Depression. Reprints cheated the readers who had a reasonable expectation that a new issue of a magazine contained all new material; the sin was exacerbated if the evidence of the reprinting, like an old copyright date, was omitted or hidden in the fine print.

Rural owned no stories which could be reprinted and so they went the public-domain route. We suspect that reprints weren't an initial part of the plan because none appeared until the third issue, which introduced a feature titled *Masterpieces of Weird Fiction*. That was the reprint disclosure to the reader, thinly disguised. The inaugural classic was an abridged version of "The Haunted and the Haunters; or, The House and the Brain" (1859), by the great Edward Bulwer-Lytton of "It was a dark and stormy night" fame, Baird's ill-favored opening. The story occupied a full 8 pages, 6.7% of the 120-page total, thus providing a rough savings of 6.7% on the fiction expenditures for that issue. Baird printed a reader's lament in a subsequent

Eyrie: "You reprinted old 'Pappy' Bulwer's ridiculous ghost bunk over which our ancestors laughed, the fathers guffawing, the mothers giggling, at his frantic and most amusing attempts to be awfully terrorizing! Never was spook story so overdone."[190] The fourth issue featured another 8-pager, "The Murders in the Rue Morgue" (1841), by the spiritual godfather of the magazine, Edgar Allan Poe. This story, in particular, was of no particular value to the readers since it could have been read for free in any public library, if not in any living room with a shelf full of books. Henneberger may have been wary of reader disgruntlement because, once the magazine shrunk to 96 pages, the reprinted masterpieces were kept to 2-3 pages. The other spiritual godfather, Ambrose Bierce, appeared in the September 1923 issue with the only story of his that Henneberger favored, "The Damned Thing." It occupied most of 3 pages, or about 3% of the total content. Poe was to appear four times in subsequent issues with "The Pit and the Pendulum," "The Black Cat," and so forth.

A method of deferring financial problems was to skip—not publish—issues. *Detective Tales* began as an every-other-week publication in October 1922, quickly dropped to a monthly, then skipped the issues of January, April, July, and December 1923. *Weird Tales* skipped July and December 1923. When Baird originally announced *Detective Tales* in *The Student Writer*, he promised that it would appear "every two weeks."[191] The quick retrenchment to a monthly may have embarrassed himself and Henneberger, because thereafter they were careful to never announce the publishing schedule of *Detective* or *Weird Tales* in the writers' magazines; the only place *Weird Tales* is explicitly described as a monthly is in its title-page indicia—the fine print.[192]

Likewise, skipped issues were never acknowledged editorially; rather, the issue following a skip was awkwardly labeled with both months to give the readers an ex post facto clue that they hadn't missed anything. Consider the July-August 1923 issue of *Weird Tales*. For a typical publisher, a date in that format would indicate that the month being skipped was August, sparing the reader a fruitless search at the newsstand. The publishers of *Weird Tales* did the opposite. The skipped month was July. They never planned far enough ahead to spare the readers, or didn't understand the problem. We can be sure that July was the skipped month because of two clues in the magazine. First, the front cover lists the date as "July-August," with "August" in larger type. Second, in *The Eyrie*, Baird noted that he wrote the column on "a blazing hot afternoon in mid-July," proof that it could not have been a July issue. A third clue, the readers' experience, came through in this complaint published in the October *Eyrie*:

> With my discovery of WEIRD TALES, I felt the problem of finding interesting reading matter for the little leisure I have was solved. Getting my copy for April wasn't all beer and skittles—I secured the first copy in a town where I was stopping at the time, and when I came to look for the magazine in San Francisco, I entered several bookstores and stopped at many magazine stands before I found an enlightened druggist who supplied me with the April number. I went there for the May and June issues.
>
> To my consternation, when I called for the July number, the druggist said it hadn't come in. Since then, I have haunted that drug store—daily at first, till the clerk greeted me with a grin and a shake of the head before I had time to ask him the momentous question.[193]

Other skipped issues contain similar clues pointing to the same backwards pattern. In any event, the most important point is that *Weird Tales* was intended and implied to be a monthly, and holding to a regular schedule was critical in establishing reader habits for a new magazine, especially an untested concept.

The first impression made by any magazine on the newsstand, and the strongest element to induce a new reader to buy, is its cover: the graphic design, the artwork, the use of text. Pulp and slick covers of that era featured colorful paintings by refined illustrators. Magazines never looked more beautiful, turning newsstands into art galleries of modern illustration with a constantly changing exhibit.

In time, *Detective* and especially *Weird Tales* would contribute their masterpieces to art history as it flowered on the newsstand. But in the months before the upheaval, the covers reflected the forces already documented here: near-schizophrenic experimentation and cheap production values. The discussion will focus on *Weird Tales*, but the design changes were paralleled at every step by *Detective Tales*.

The cover design for *Weird Tales* changed frequently during its first year, a dubious strategy.[194] For a new magazine, in particular, it was important to establish a recognizable identity on the newsstand, notwithstanding that change requires time, effort, and sound judgment. Many pulps underwent cover redesigns in their history, but as a rule changes were infrequent or subtle.

The first issue of *Weird Tales* had a black logo with letters set at slightly off-kilter angles, and wavy orange lines highlighting the top and bottom of the logo; the logo had an oddly happy look, a style more appropriate for a book of nursery rhymes. *Detective Tales*, of the same month, had a matching style. As always for *Weird Tales*, "The Unique Magazine" was printed below the logo. The entire cover, like all covers up to the upheaval, was printed in two colors—black and red—an indication of the limited budget.[195] The best magazine covers used four colors. R.R. Epperly did the cover art for both March magazines. His octopus-attack cover illustration for *Weird Tales*, all shades of orange and gray, vignetted in an orange border, had a semipro look, attractive enough but not on par with the mainstream pulps.

The shrunken second issue of *Weird Tales* was given a radically different look, a redesigned—and more appropriate—white logo on a bold red background. The motif gave a preview—for one issue—of how the magazine would look from about 1925-31. R.M. Mally's artwork for "The Whispering Thing" made fine use of its limited palette in illustrating a scene of a gentleman being immobilized by the "icy breath" of some big-eyed creature in the shadows.

With the third issue, we enter the large-size period and get the third redesign in as many issues, though this revamp would last three issues. The logo was a bold red on a feathered black background, with the entire cover having a white background. It was different without necessarily being better. Below the title block, the issue data was printed between two horizontal lines in the manner of a newspaper, an illogical choice for the kind of magazine it was. The issue data included, naturally, date and price, but also the numbering (Vol. 1, No. 3) and, in parentheses, "Printed in U.S.A." The artwork, by the third new artist, was a sketchy but effective depiction of a witch performing magic over a boiling cauldron, a now-clichéd image which probably had a stronger impact in 1923. The artist was William F. Heitman, a journeyman artist for the *Indianapolis Star*,[196] who had probably supplied illustrations for Henneberger's college magazines. Heitman returned for the next issue with what may rank as the worst cover in the magazine's thirty-two-year history. His amateurish illustration of a gorilla attacking a damsel in her living room was undoubtedly delivered at the deadline when there was no time to replace it; thereafter he was banished from the covers and relegated to his specialty, interior illustrations. Mally returned for the fifth issue and would remain the house cover artist through the upheaval. But his contribution—a startled man entering a forest from a field of flowers—was unclear in its and the magazine's purpose.

Yet another redesign—the fourth, if we're keeping count—visited the sixth through eighth issues. The background switched from white to black. The redesigned logo was in white script. The "W" and "T" of "Weird Tales" were red with a three-dimensional effect that only half-worked and only if studied closely. The newspaper bar was eliminated with the data moved to the bottom of the cover. The illustration, unsigned but in Mally's style, was an all-grayscale depiction of a lion attacking a damsel, with the red lettering for Austin Hall's "The People of the Comet" barely visible. The overall tone of this and the next two covers was quite dark, dooming the magazine to indistinctness on a newsstand of vivid, four-color covers. The eighth issue, November, at least had an effective illustration of a ghost with skeletal hands menacing a man in a crypt, perhaps the closest cover yet to capture the essence of the magazine.

After skipping the December issue, *Weird Tales* returned for January 1924 with redesign #5, which lasted for five issues. This time the artwork covered the entire cover. The logo, in a classier reworked script, was superimposed on the unused portion of the image. The date and price, the only other text, were printed near the bottom in red. Mally's drawing of a ghost rider pursuing a cowboy saturated the image with sunset-reds, contributing to a very striking overall design. With the March issue, Houdini entered the scene and content-related text returned to the cover. But the heavy, dark overtones returned as well. For the final issue—before the magazine skipped five months—the deluxe 50¢ Anniversary Issue dated May-June-July 1924, the publishers actually splurged for a third cover color—yellow—for a scene of the Sphinx and the Pyramids illustrating Houdini's ghostwritten "Imprisoned with the Pharaohs."

This tour through the cover art puts a full range of experimentation on display, while also exposing the indecisiveness and missteps of the publishers. In general, they struggled to endow their choices with a clear sense of direction. The cheap production values contradicted the high cover price and the covers seldom conveyed to potential buyers the true nature of the magazine.

For a sense of what the reader may have taken away from all the changes, we have the comments of Robert Barbour Johnson. He began as a teenage pulp reader in Louisville, Kentucky, who discovered the first issue of *Weird Tales* on the newsstand, and later contributed half a dozen stories from 1935-41. Of that first issue, he recalled, "Its value . . . most certainly was not due to its appearance. It was, in fact, just about the worst-looking pulp magazine I've ever seen in my life." But he loved the content. Soon thereafter, he moved to the larger New Orleans:

> And though there were newsstands, there did not appear to be any *Weird Tales*, either! I missed two issues before I discovered what happened. The magazine had changed its format completely; I was walking past it, and not recognizing it. It was now almost as large as the *Saturday Evening Post*, though still on pulp paper. The name was in script at the top, there was a crude drawing in the center of the cover, and it was surrounded by blurbs. While the issues looked terrible, they contained some great stories . . .[197]

Despite the burden, he scraped together the monthly quarters to buy the magazine. But he was a dedicated fan. For the more casual buyer, the cheap appearance, the high price, and the disorientingly frequent changes in appearance, were negative inducements.

Covers weren't the only source of artwork in the pulps (nor the slicks). The vast majority had interior illustrations in black-and-white line art, a commonplace style in newspapers before photography matured in the early twentieth century. In 1923, and through most of the pulp era, line art was the only style that would print reliably on the coarse pulpwood paper. Interior art was, of course, another expenditure for the publisher, who paid freelancers by the piece. Therefore, the number of pieces in an issue is another index into whether the publisher was attempting to save money or enhance the magazine. The early issues of *Detective Tales* lacked illustrations, as did the first two issues of *Weird Tales*, the pulp-sizes. The May *Weird Tales*, which introduced the expansion to large-size, had nine illustrations, all by Heitman. He would supply all the interior illustrations through the upheaval; only a handful received his signature, but his style is recognizable. Nine is a reasonable amount for a pulp in that period but, scattered through the magazine's 120 pages, did not create a particularly impressive display, especially not for a premium-priced magazine. And it was nine stories earning one illustration apiece, with the remaining 12 stories in the issue receiving none. In contrast, the lavish Street & Smith pulps of the day contained up to 40 illustrations in a single issue, with numerous stories getting multiples, with line-work more refined than Heitman's. For a tempted customer thumbing through an issue at the newsstand, they were hard to resist.

For the June *Weird Tales*, the illustration count dropped from 9 to 7, but then jumped to the high-water mark of 10 for July-August. The average number of illustrations through the upheaval was 8. The low-water mark was 5, achieved twice: September 1923 and March 1924. This may indicate some particularly budget-sensitive periods. The latter issue received an additional distinction. The expenditure was for only 4 illustrations, since Heitman's page 7 depiction of a wandering man clutching his throat was the same as that used on page 25 of the January issue for a different story. Of course, that may have been a production error; it's the only incidence of a reprinted illustration in the first year. In any event, it's another sign of disarray.

Another key issue with the interiors was quality. Did the illustrations add value to the magazine? Typically, the artist was given a manuscript and expected to illustrate the critical moments from the story which most captured the genre elements attractive to the readers. In a western pulp, these might include a shoot-out, a rodeo event, a galloping horse, or a cowboy in full regalia. For a magazine featuring fantasy and the supernatural, we would hope to see the weird elements of the stories brought to life, to find out what the ghosts and monsters might really look like to an artist's imagination. This concept didn't appear to be completely understood in the early months of *Weird Tales*. Heitman's sense of the strange was very hit or miss. For example, in the May 1923 issue, of the nine illustrations, only three attempt weird visions and, even at that, they are somewhat prosaic. For A.G. Birch's "The Moon Terror," the cover story, the interior illustration depicts an unconscious woman tied to an altar, while a priest holds a long blade over her heart, ready to perform the sacrifice. Vincent Starrett, a fixture in the Chicago literary scene, supplied the short story "Penelope"; the accompanying illustration shows a man on the floor gazing at an upside-down dining-room-set on the ceiling. G.W. Crane's "An Eye for an Eye" receives a nicely-executed picture of three startled grave-diggers. The rest of the illustrations tend to be static depictions of one or two characters, in ordinary dress, perhaps talking to each other in a bland setting, with maybe a pistol in one person's hand. As the magazine progressed, the percentage of weird scenes gradually increased, as if the publishers and the artist were gaining a better appreciation for what would make the magazine appealing.

Previously, we discussed the semi-honorable method of not paying for stories, that is, by reprinting stories whose rights were in the public domain. We also discussed the two classes of magazines, the upper classes which paid on acceptance and the lower classes which paid on publication. *The Student Writer* inventoried these on Lists A and B of their quarterly market survey, as shown for pulps in the Competition Table. The pay-on-publication policy was a frustration to authors but, then, freelance writing and frustration are more or less born of the same mother. A deal is a deal. However, many contributors to the Rural publications discovered that a third option existed, even more aggravating than the second. We'll call it "pay *after* publication" and it's really more of a consequence than a policy. It was a failure of the publishers to meet their obligations because of the need to pay other creditors first. The authors were near powerless in the line of creditors, ranking behind landlords, printers, editors, secretaries, and virtually all others. The only power belonging to the author was to refrain from further business with the publisher. But in the case of *Weird Tales*, that introduced a painful dilemma: no better market existed for the unique thing that *Weird Tales* would buy. Thus, many contributors, even those knowing the score, waited painful months after seeing their masterpieces in print before receiving the payment they had bragged about to friends and family and anyone else who would listen. Lastly, there was a fourth possible policy: *never pay*. Some fly-by-night pulp publishers, though there were fewer of these than might be expected, flat-out stiffed their authors. Henneberger and company never fell into this category, except as an accident of sloppy recordkeeping. They were generally considered an honest—but tortured—operation. Many of their impatient contributors, though, wondered at times who they were dealing with.

Reminiscences from first-year contributors are scarce, but Otis Adelbert Kline described the situation in his 1941 letter to Robert E. Howard's father:

> Under the first owners and the first editor, Baird, material was bought as cheaply as they could possibly purchase it. Their top rate was 1¢ a word, payment was never made before publication, and sometimes long months or even a year after publication. They didn't pay any more than they had to, or any sooner than they had to . . .[198]

The pay-after-publication policy was not to be limited to that first year, when growing pains could be expected. In fact, it would haunt *Weird Tales* through the 1920s and '30s, presumably through the 1938 sale of the magazine to William J. Delaney, publisher of *Short Stories*. The history of *Weird Tales* during its legacy years is littered with accounts of writers becoming increasingly irate—or even despondent—as their promised checks failed to arrive. E. Hoffmann Price told the story of his first sale, "The Rajah's Gift." Accepted by the editor in March 1924, it lay dormant in the period following the upheaval, and finally appeared in the January 1925 issue, at which point Price expected to be paid. When he was not, he started mailing "pointed" letters.

> Wright answered one inquiry. Bill Sprenger answered another. By then, feeling sour, I retorted, "I have heard of penniless and starving authors, and have fancied myself one. However, the novelty of a penniless publisher is appealing, even refreshing. Only one thing could be more refreshing—to wit, since I've heard from editor, and from business manager, I should now get a message from the third member of the Trinity, Mr. Cornelius, the Treasurer."[199]

The letter created quite a stir in the *Weird Tales* offices. (William Roeder Sprenger [1902-72] was the young Chicagoan who served as business manager.)

Paul S. Powers, best known as a prolific contributor to Street & Smith's *Wild West Weekly*, got his start in *Weird Tales*. His first acceptance, in late 1924, excited him so much that he "ran around the house like a man demented."[200] In short order, several more submissions were accepted. He explained what came next, the interminably long next:

> Unfortunately, there was that strange "pay on publication" fly in the ointment. I have a little notebook before me in which I kept the records of those days, and I find that it was eight months almost to the day before I was paid the $21.75 for that first story. The checks for the others were equally belated. Of course, this is an unfair practice.[201]

So chastened, he abandoned *Weird Tales* as a market, which paid off for him in the long run. A sour memory, he referred to the magazine as a "Class C market," a sort of insider's insult, playing off the fact that List B magazines occupied the lowest tier; *Weird Tales*, from his perspective, ranked below even them. Selling to Rural was scraping the bottom of the barrel.

The situation was particularly bad during the Depression when a stalwart like Edmond Hamilton, who contributed popular space epics, was forced to abandon the magazine. The worst example of author desperation has to have been Robert E. Howard, one of the distinctive talents cultivated by the magazine. When he killed himself on June 11, 1936, *Weird Tales* owed him over a thousand dollars.[202] While the death of his mother was the immediate cause, his inability to get paid by the market which best suited him, which would have allowed him to persevere as a professional writer, is generally believed to have contributed.

Regarding the early period, lest we think that Henneberger or Baird were cavalier toward their contributors, a parallel tale of turmoil unfolded behind the scenes. Recall that two months after the launch of *Detective Tales*, Baird was already apologizing for slow payments to contributors, but remaining optimistic: "Things are looking somewhat better now, and I hope, before long, to pay on acceptance and at a much better rate."[203]

Neither dream came true. Rural's advertised policies in *The Student Writer* (and *The Author & Journalist*) remained pay-on-publication and less than a cent-a-word, though they intimated that some contributors might get a cent on acceptance. In fact, *Weird Tales* spent the rest of the 1920s languishing on List B, a decade during which the pulp field expanded to ridiculous extremes both in number of magazines and extravagance of pay to authors.

Baird, however, continued to fight the good fight. The June 1923 *Student Writer*, in their monthly *Literary Market Tips* column, passed on his remarkable report of the situation:

> *Detective Tales* and *Weird Tales*, 854 N. Clark Street, Chicago, bid fair to become "pay on acceptance" magazines. Edwin Baird, editor of both publications, has always shown a very commendable attitude in the matter of securing payment for manuscripts, but apparently has not received perfect co-operation from his business office. Mr.

Baird tells us that he hopes the magazines may begin paying for all manuscripts on acceptance within the course of a very few months, stating that he considers this the only businesslike way to conduct a fiction magazine.[204]

By "business office," Baird may have included Sprenger, the business manager, but he was certainly aiming his criticism at the chief culprit, publisher Henneberger. Comments of this nature, in which the internal problems of the publisher are spotlighted in a public forum, are virtually unrivaled in the six-decade history of the pulps. Authors and editors complained about publishers, quite naturally, but they did so in private; in the dimly-lit corners of speakeasies, we'd like to think. Editors, above all, *never* singled out their employers for blame, suggesting that Baird had the upper hand in the relationship, that because of his critical role in keeping the magazines going, Henneberger needed him more than he needed Henneberger. Without Baird, the enterprise might collapse completely.

The blurb in *The Student Writer* was paraphrased with sympathy by editor and *Weird Tales* alumnus, Willard E. Hawkins. The success of any magazine was good all-around: good for the publisher, good for advertisers, good for contributors, and good for writers' mags selling opportunity. Within a few months, though, the journal—reluctantly, no doubt—began to turn against Rural. They started adding the "slow" payment problem to the List B descriptions for *Detective* and *Weird Tales*, essentially moving the magazine from "fair opportunity" to "author beware."[205] They made the point in detail in the October 1923 issue (the first after retitling the journal):

> *Weird Tales* and *Detective Tales* . . . are far behind in their payment for manuscripts. THE AUTHOR & JOURNALIST has found Edwin Baird, the editor, anxious to deal fairly with contributors, but it is evident that the magazines are not yet firmly established financially. It is our hope that they will get on their feet, but authors should realize that in submitting manuscripts to these publications at the present time they do so at a risk of being compelled to wait indefinitely for remuneration.[206]

Two months later, Baird's pointed finger zeroed in on a name:

> *Detective Tales* and *Weird Tales* . . . are doing all in their power to straighten up with their numerous author creditors, according to Edwin Baird, editor of both magazines, who writes: "I am making every effort to clean up our indebtedness, but so far I have not been able to do so. Mr. Henneberger has told me more than once, in the talks I've had with him about this, that everything will be paid, that

the authors to whom we owe money need not fear they will lose, but I realize that this is slight consolation to a man who wants cash. In any event, I hope you will appreciate that I am doing my utmost to deal fairly with all our contributors."[207]

Baird had made a much sharper distinction between the innocent and guilty parties in the crisis. Gone was the "business office," replaced by "Mr. Henneberger." To appreciate the full weight of this escalation, note that Henneberger's name had never been in print before in association with Rural Publishing. He had previously been mentioned once in *The Student Writer*, in association with *The Magazine of Fun*, but only because he listed himself as the editor. Traditionally, the editor was the public face of a magazine; publishers stayed in the shadows, ran the business affairs, and pocketed the theoretical profits. By naming Henneberger, Baird dragged him out of the shadows and into the light, making *him* the face of the crisis. We can sense Baird's growing discomfort, as if he were afraid that the company's problems would turn into a stain on *his* honor.

In another two months, as the hole deepened, the next report surfaced in *The Author & Journalist*:

> *Detective Tales* and *Weird Tales* . . . are continuously reported as slow in their dealings with writers. In many instances, stories published months ago have not been paid for. It is our understanding that the publishers are making every effort to catch up, but until they succeed in getting on a better financial basis, authors should understand conditions.[208]

Note the phrase "continuously reported." This blurb finally makes clear what had only been implied in previous reports and explains why the reports surfaced in the first place. Unpaid authors had been bombarding the journal with complaints, forcing Hawkins to solicit Rural's side of the story, an unpleasant duty which fell to Baird.

This is a good point to revisit the relationship between a central editorial policy of the Rural magazines and the company's financial status. From the first, they had de-emphasized authors by arguing that the story was the thing and by minimizing the inclusion of author names on the covers of the magazines. This created barriers which inhibited the authors from gaining status through their contributions to the magazine, arguing for competitive word-rates, and expecting to be paid on publication, as promised. It kept Rural from having to admit that authors helped sell magazines. In essence, the company's behavior provoked a backlash: the authors appealed their grievances to a higher authority, *The Student Writer/Author & Journalist*, whose only real power was in conducting a forum which could be used for public shaming. The appearance of the June report may even have rallied more, otherwise silent, authors to add to the complaints. In the terms of the labor movement, the press facilitated a de facto unionization which organized the disparate voices of powerless workers into one. It's probably no coincidence that Rural, as the controversy reached full boil, eliminated *all* author names from the covers of *Detective* and *Weird Tales*, starting with the November 1923 issues, a design decision with a nasty bite of revenge to it. We can imagine a disgruntled, and unpaid, author writing the office to say, "Look, Mr. Henneberger, our names on your covers sell magazines!" Once the names were gone, that argument was removed.

These unprecedented events in pulp publishing—the public battles, that is; not the financial difficulties—only happened with Rural and only in this brief period of their existence, evidence that "the unique magazine" was published by a unique company.

Could matters get worse? Indeed, they could.

BIRTH PANGS

Before indulging in the maelstrom to come, we should relish the thought that out of the chaos, against all odds, the *Weird Tales* that we know and love, the *Weird Tales* that continues to extend its influence over fantastic fiction, was born. The baby screamed to excess, drove its parents and neighbors insane, but ultimately survived its tortured infancy.

Outside the pages of the magazine, the publisher, the editor, and the authors struggled to make the dollars and cents work. Inside the magazine, within the stories, the ghosts of the dead floated from page to page attempting to rectify past injustices. Mixed among their company, another group of spectres slowly sowed the seeds of the magazine's future. These were the select authors whose names and works would make the magazine's reputation through the 1920s and '30s. A surprising number of them infiltrated the magazine's pages in that perilous first year, emerging from the "inept and half-baked armies of writers" who turned Baird's office into a paper-piled purgatory. It's a tribute to his editorial acumen, his thoroughness in sorting out the mess, that the gems were discovered among the dross.

The central figure in the magazine's legacy is, by popular consensus, H.P. Lovecraft. He discovered the magazine early, bought the April 1923 issue off the newsstand, and immediately contributed. His complicated relationship with the magazine, especially during the first year, deserves special treatment and will be explored in the next chapter.

We've already encountered Farnsworth Wright, who appeared in the first two issues of *Weird Tales* and would become its most illustrious editor. We've also met Otis Adelbert Kline, who appeared in the first two issues, and four of the first five. His career in the magazine would most epitomize the reversal of the "anonymous author" policies of the first year. At the peak of his popularity, his serial, *Tam, Son of the Tiger*, was cover-featured on four straight issues (July-October, 1931). He snagged another four covers for *Buccaneers of Venus* (November 1932 - February 1933). No other *Weird Tales* author received that honor even once. For Kline, the honor reflected his popularity at the time; being an old acquaintance of Wright's couldn't have hurt.

■ ■ ■

The honor of appearing in the first two issues also fell to Hamilton Craigie, Anthony M. Rud, Julian Kilman, and Harold Ward. Though none of them would loom large in the magazine's future, their experiences are worth mentioning. Craigie was a high-producing pulp writer who actually appeared in the first four issues, again in the November 1925 issue, and never thereafter. The 1925 story had probably sold in 1923, leaving Craigie to wait over two years for his check. Rud, a Chicago writer soon to be a New York writer, was another high-producer. He had the immortal distinction of inspiring the cover to the first issue. In *The Eyrie*, Baird passed along Rud's enthusiasm for the new magazine: "Delighted to hear that you contemplate WEIRD TALES! . . . The Poe type of yarn invariably makes me shiver—and then for a week I prefer the grape-nut road, shunning the dark places after curfew. But I come back avidly for more shock!"[209] Rud offered a second story, "A Square of Canvas," for free, so eager was he to have it appear, which it did in the second issue. Baird may have taken him up on his offer, or put him at the bottom of the accounts payable list. Rud was not seen again for another decade—1934—when he made two more appearances. Kilman was a moonlighting attorney who regularly appeared in print.[210] He also made the first four issues, appeared again in the September 1923 issue and, like Poe's raven, nevermore. Craigie and Rud, in particular, trying to earn a living as professional writers, would not have expended further effort on writing for *Weird Tales* when more reliable and lucrative markets were readily available. These authors didn't contribute much to the literary legacy of the magazine, but their absence robbed them of the chance to try.

Ward, with his success in *The Black Mask*, may have fancied himself becoming a true writing pro one day, but *Weird Tales* probably convinced him that he was fated to remain a hobbyist. His short in the first issue, "The Skull," set on the "Islands," concerned hostile relations between natives and whites. The story, lacking supernatural elements, revolved around a decapitation of a murdered white man. It's a typical pulp adventure of the era, with racist overtones and language. Ward's story in the April issue, "The Bodymaster," was better attuned to the magazine's direction. Baird headlined it as "An Amazing Novelette Filled With Weird Happenings," and it certainly fulfills that promise. The tale, about the ghoulish goings-on in a sanitarium run by Doctor Darius Lessman, featured common occult concepts like hypnotism and soul transference. Ward's next appearance came in the February 1924 issue. Like Craigie, et al., he may have suspended his support for the magazine upon experiencing firsthand the non-payment problem.

Returning to the brighter stars in the heavens, the July-August 1923 issue—the fifth—marks the first appearance of Clark Ashton Smith (1893-

1961), a California poet destined to rank in the upper echelon of the *Weird Tales* circle. He was recommended to Baird by his penpal, H.P. Lovecraft.[211] It was an inauspicious debut. His two short poems—the first poetry published in the magazine—weren't listed on the contents page. They were buried in the graveyards of miscellanea that fill the leftover spaces at the end of stories, costing Baird little to acquiesce to Lovecraft's wishes. Smith's fiction wouldn't appear in the magazine until the September 1928 issue. Once he started writing fiction in earnest, he produced a phenomenal string of truly bizarre stories for *Weird Tales*. Set in a handful of fantasy worlds, like the lost continent of Hyperborea or the future world of Zothique, Smith's stories were distinguished by strange characters, unsettling plots, and a dazzling vocabulary that required readers to keep their dictionaries at the ready. In a review of Smith's third book of poetry, *Ebony and Crystal* (1922), Lovecraft attempted to match Smith's intense weirdness and language in describing the work, a description which could also apply to Smith's fiction:

> [He captured] realms of exalted and iridescent strangeness beyond space and time yet real as any reality because dreams have made them so. Mr. Smith has escaped the fetish of life and the world, and glimpsed the perverse, titanic beauty of death and the universe; taking infinity as his canvas and recording in awe the vagaries of suns and planets, gods and daemons, and blind amorphous horrors that haunt gardens of polychrome fungi more remote than Algol and Achernar. . . . [The] content is equalled only by its verbal medium; a medium involving one of the most opulent and fastidiously choice vocabularies ever commanded by a writer of English.[212]

The October 1923 issue—the seventh—was published when the payments problem chronicled in *The Author & Journalist* had been downgraded from "slow" to "far behind," the situation rising in temperature from bothersome to dire. How remarkable, then, that three major *Weird Tales* contributors made their first appearance in that October issue—and with their stories appearing three in a row. In ascending order of importance, they were Frank Owen, Seabury Quinn, and the cornerstone of the *Weird Tales* legacy, the aforementioned H.P. Lovecraft.

Owen (1893-1968), born and died a New Yorker, wrote numerous short stories set in China and the Far East despite never having been there. Once he hit *Weird Tales*, he split his output among the magazine and would-be sophisticated pulps like *Droll Stories* and *Breezy Stories*. He had a nose for the lower-paying markets. From 1930-33, he shifted into *Weird Tales's* companion magazine, *Oriental Stories*, and its successor, *The Magic Carpet Magazine*, mostly supplying poems under the scurrilous pseudonym of Hung

Long Tom. From 1936-44, Owen caught a second wind with *Weird Tales*, appearing in the magazine with thirteen scattered stories. By the time of his last *Weird Tales* appearance, November 1952, he had supplied well over 30 stories and a handful of poems.

Owen was a mere pretender next to Seabury Quinn, the most prolific—and popular—author to appear in the pages of the magazine. Quinn was a lawyer who, for many years starting in 1925, edited and wrote a column for *Casket and Sunnyside*, a mortuary trade journal. His first published fiction appeared in *Detective Story Magazine* in 1918. He had five scattered stories over two years, then a near-four-year layoff before he linked up with Rural. He debuted in the October 1923 *Weird Tales* with two pieces, a spooky story of werewolf romance, "The Phantom Farm House," and the first in a true-story series under the heading of *Weird Crimes*. The series ran for seven installments before Quinn appeared with a short story in January 1925. He then started a new nonfiction series, *Servants of Satan*, in March 1925. Meanwhile, Baird started running a Quinn series in *Detective Tales*. The lead character, Major Sturdevant, appeared in twenty-five stories before giving way to another Quinn series, Professor Forrester, who appeared thirteen times. With nineteen Sturdevants under his belt, Quinn introduced a series character to *Weird Tales*, the French detective of the supernatural, Jules de Grandin, Grandin being Quinn's middle name. From "The Horror on the Links" (October 1925) through "The Ring of Bastet" (September 1951), de Grandin, and his trusty accomplice Dr. Trowbridge, appeared in 93 tales, frequently receiving the cover illustration. Quinn's peak year of productivity was 1925, measured by number of stories: 22. All sold to Rural. For three years (late '25 through late '28), Quinn juggled the de Grandin and Sturdevant/Forrester series simultaneously. The number of stories declined, but the stories got longer. The peak of de Grandin mania may be marked by *The Devil's Bride*, a six-part serial which ran from February to July 1932. In the mid-'30s, Quinn (or the readers) tired of the character, easing him out of his *Weird Tales* contributions. Quinn's last story for the magazine appeared in the March 1952 issue. It was the end of his pulp-writing career and, indeed, an approximate date for the end of the pulps, though they limped on in diminished form.

Quinn's career is a curious reflection on the fate of *Weird Tales*, for while the grandeur of the magazine was frequently coupled with the ill practices of a struggling business, Quinn presents an inversion: he was a middling author—Lovecraft took "a dim view of his endless array of clichéd stories"[213]—and the magazine was the best thing that ever happened to him. His prolific thirty-five-year writing career was built almost exclusively on *Weird Tales* and its publisher offshoots. It began with *Detective* and *Weird Tales*. When *Detective Tales* spun off into a separate company, Quinn continued to supply both publishers. He had a handful of contributions to the *Weird Tales* companion magazines, *Oriental Stories* and *The Magic Carpet Magazine*. After *Weird Tales* was purchased by the publisher of *Short Stories*, the latter became his secondary market. In aggregate, 92% of his approximately 250 published stories went to *Weird Tales* and offshoots.

We would be remiss in neglecting to mention one last name for the list—excepting Lovecraft—an author who made his *Weird Tales* debut in the Anniversary Issue, Henry St. Clair Whitehead (1882-1932).

Born in Elizabeth, New Jersey, he had a varied schooling. "I was educated in Connecticut and New York City, at the Berkeley School in the latter."[214] He attended Columbia University as a freshman from 1900-01, then was a classmate of Franklin Delano Roosevelt at Harvard, though he never graduated.[215] An athletic youth, he played team sports, and loved to go to sea. With a reputation for prodigious strength, he was frequently called upon to tear a pack of playing cards in two with his bare hands.

Writing attracted him from an early age. His first story sale landed in *Outdoors*, December 1905. He became a newspaper reporter, then editor. He'd had his fill of newsprint by mid-1909 and entered Berkeley Divinity School, Middletown, Connecticut, graduating in 1912 with a theology degree. He was immediately ordained a deacon in the Episcopal Church. After a year's apprenticeship, he was appointed rector of Middletown's Christ Church. To some degree, it was a writing job. Clergymen, if they lead a parish, are writers by default, delivering fresh sermons on deadline every Sunday. After four years, he became children's pastor of the Church of St. Mary's the Virgin in New York City. In the ensuing years, his writing— articles and letters—could be found in religious journals like *The American Church Monthly*. "Of course I like to write," he said. "I've written with a certain ideal in mind, I think, always."[216] Occasionally, short poems of his would turn up in print.

In 1919, he became senior assistant to Dr. William Harman van Allen, rector of the Church of the Advent, Boston. Dr. van Allen was quite fond of the pulp *Adventure* and inspired Whitehead to start writing his own fiction.[217] In 1922, Whitehead left Boston to do "special work" in the Virgin Islands. Upon his return, from December 1922 through August 1923, he filled in for another pastor at the Christ Episcopal Church in Chattanooga, Tennessee. Then he returned to New England, serving as rector at the Trinity Church, Bridgeport, Connecticut. The parishioners must have been impressed with their new pastor. Soon after starting, his story "The Intarsia Box" appeared in *Adventure*, November 10, 1923, and then was one of 58 stories first-listed for the year by the prestigious O. Henry Awards.

While in the Virgin Islands, he wrote a short article, "Editorial Prejudice

Against the Occult," which appeared in the October 1922 issue of *The Writer*, a strange bit of timing since this was the very period in which *Weird Tales* was being hatched. He opened the piece complaining about those narrow-minded individuals who stood in the way of all fictioneers at one time or another, the editors:

> Said a famous editor not so very long ago in writing to one of his contributors: ". . . but my dear fellow, if you are aiming to enlist against you the suspicion—nay, the actual *enmity*—of the average editor, send him a Ghost Story, a Fairy Story, or a Dream Story. If you want to be absolutely certain of such an effect, make it a Dream Story!" . . . "the occult" in this general sense of the term is banned by most magazines. Authors who "try one on an editor" are apt to get their tales back in haste.

We can read into his comments that Whitehead himself had been writing "occult" stories and receiving only perfunctory rejections in return. If so, these stories would have found new life as his early submissions to *Weird Tales*. He continued the article with a quick survey of occult literature, by category, demonstrating that he was steeped in the genre. He closed with a point about the universality of such fiction:

> In Erse and Choctaw, in the Hieroglyphics and in the Sumerian; in Kalmuck, and Finnish, and Hebrew, there are and always have been Ghost Stories, and Fairy Stories, and Dream Stories. They have been told and are being told—and read—from the bazaars of Oodeypore to the Steppes; from the lamaseries of Tibet to the Beach of Easter Island. In China, in Afghanistan, in Ireland, and Down in Maine, people are positively clamoring for Ghost Stories and Fairy Stories and Dream Stories.
>
> Why, O why, do not the magazine editors give the people what they want?

His argument—if one chooses—operates like the setup to one of his subtle stories of the supernatural. An earnest clergyman publishes a reasoned plea for editors to accept stories of ghosts, fairies, and dreams and, by some strange magic, a few months later, against all business reason, the ideal magazine for the purpose appears on the market—*Weird Tales*—and the earnest clergyman publishes his formerly rejected stories of the supernatural in that very same magazine, his prayers answered by forces beyond understanding. The only hitch in the tale is that Whitehead was late in discovering the magazine. It came on the market while he was preoccupied in Chattanooga. When he discovered it back in Bridgeport, he immediately sent off words of support, which Baird printed in the January 1924 *Eyrie*:

> Dear Sir: You may be familiar with my work which has been published in numerous magazines here and in England since 1905. . . . It is very interesting to me to have seen WEIRD TALES for the first time today. I have long contended that such a magazine would go well, and I think I can see something of your internal problems—the necessary balance between the kind of work Arthur Machen and Montague James are turning out in this field in England and that which will not be caviare to the newsstand. . . . I congratulate you on your courage in going ahead with WEIRD TALES. It should, when well established, fill a real need, and no one has, apparently, dared to risk this type of publication.

His first story for the magazine, "Tea Leaves," appeared four issues later in the Anniversary Issue. For all we know, it accompanied the above letter and awaited Baird's discretion. "Tea Leaves" was not an obvious choice for the magazine; it seemed to be entirely out of place in a universe of snake fiends and terrifying apparitions, and must have flummoxed many a *Weird Tales* reader, which reinforces the notion that it had been intended for and rejected by another, tamer magazine. The story proceeds, for a long while, like an artful Henry James story of an American in Europe. Miss Abby Tucker, "a frugal little New England school-teacher," has saved up for a Cook's tour of the continent. On board the steamship:

> Her attention to the tea leaves [in her cup] diverted her fellow travelers greatly. By long practice she had become accustomed to mixing the tea about with her spoon so that the tea leaves would accumulate on the bottom of the cup, and then, deftly she would drink the remaining tea and set the cup down with a kind of snap and peer at the picture on the bottom. She had acquired great skill in discerning the meanings in these omens! Now for the first time in her life however, the patterns puzzled her. . . .

As she visits various cities, she buys presents for her friends, and finally a souvenir for herself, spending a little more than she had budgeted on a badly soiled necklace in the window of a back-alley London shop. Back home, a nice young man, a jeweler by trade, spots her wearing the necklace at a country party, introduces himself, and suggests getting the necklace appraised. This leads to a series of escalating good fortunes, which change her life immeasurably for the better. Unlike the typical *Weird Tales* fare, there is no grim comeuppance to end the story with an ironic jolt. Instead, the reader is left with a mystery. Was her habit of studying the tea leaves merely a small insight into her character, or did the ambiguous patterns in the leaves lead to what happened? The story is unwound so delicately, one cannot be sure, leaving a lingering feeling that the true nature of the world is outside of our grasp.

Whitehead's Christian beliefs—that is, the sense of a greater reality beyond the physical world—appear to underpin his storytelling perspective (put on display in some two dozen stories for *Weird Tales*, and a handful for the 1931-33 *Strange Tales* and other pulps). That makes Whitehead an analogue of J.R.R. Tolkien, who wove his Christian worldview into *The Lord of the Rings* without ever mentioning Christianity, or even the practice of religion. Tolkien wrote about the mythical Middle-earth, though, while the majority of Whitehead's stories were set in the contemporary world, raising the question of whether he actually believed in the supernatural dimension of his fiction. It's not an idle question. Christians inherently believe in a supernatural force and the central myth of a man tortured to death and returned to life. In his sermon of February 25, 1923, to the Episcopal Church of Chattanooga, Whitehead shed some light on the question, if the accuracy of the following news report is to be believed. Note that the Ouija board, by which one purports to channel messages from beyond, was enjoying faddish popularity in the early '20s. According to the report: "Father Henry S. Whitehead . . . warned his congregation against the use of the Ouija board, declaring that he believed that it originated in the mind of the devil himself. He also declared his belief in spirits, saying that evil geniuses lurked behind the veil with humanity as their field of operation."[218] If the Devil speaks through the Ouija board, then surely God speaks through the fiction of an Episcopalian minister.

Whitehead, the subtlety of his style notwithstanding, was ultimately a welcome addition to the *Weird Tales* circle, and validated the magazine's claims to literary relevance. Whitehead's stories found their best home in *Weird Tales* but their quality may well have served many mainstream or literary markets—were it not for those recalcitrant editors.

In March 1925, Whitehead resigned from his Bridgeport ministry over doctrinal differences, determined to do "mission work." Through the rest of the decade, he sailed numerous times to the Virgin Islands to spend his winters. Naturally gregarious, he met islanders from all walks of life and thus became acquainted with religious beliefs quite alien to his own. Or perhaps not. Subsequently, many of his stories, starting with "Jumbee" (*Weird Tales*, September 1926) were set in the West Indies and involved Voodoo practices and phenomena.

H.P. LOVECRAFT, THE ALIEN SEED

Howard Philips Lovecraft (1890-1937) could not have been a more different writer than Quinn, a singular creative talent where the latter was, like so many pulp writers, a wage-slave to a successful formula. Lovecraft, the man, could have been a character in many of his weird stories—and undoubtedly was. He led a complex and fascinating life, primarily as a man of letters, a man of antiquarian tastes who endeavored to carry the past forward.

Born in Providence, Rhode Island, he identified himself with the city and, excepting brief detours, spent his life there. Carved into his gravestone is the declaration, "I Am Providence."

He was the son of Sarah Susan Phillips (1857-1921) and Winfield Scott Lovecraft (1853-98). Like Farnsworth Wright, he grew up without a father. Lovecraft's father went into the hospital for an illness when Howard was not yet three, and died five years later, still in the hospital. Early on, there were aunts and grandparents in the picture, but he essentially grew up with his mother.[219]

As a boy, he was frail and drawn to books. As he explained:

> I grew up with a large family library in a big house, and browsed at random because I was too ill to attend school or even follow a tutor's course with any regularity. Somehow I acquired a fondness for the past as compared with the present—a fondness which had plenty of chance to reign because my semi-invalidism continued and kept me from college and business despite the most extravagant ambitions of boyhood.[220]

In fact, he only finished the eleventh grade.[221] His erudition and abilities were overwhelmingly the product of self-education.

His intellectual predilections were apparent from an early age. He read American and European classics, and was especially drawn to myths and fairy tales. He also slummed on dime novels before moving on to the early pulps.[222] He voraciously devoured the Munsey magazines. By 1914, he had read *every* issue of *The All-Story*, dating from the first issue of January

1905,[223] and every issue of *The Cavalier* which began with October 1908.[224] A man of sometimes broad tastes, he read every issue of *Railroad Man's Magazine* (1906-19),[225] a mere 159 issues of a pulp which numbered 192 pages through most of its life.

Just as prolific a writer, he wrote short stories and self-published small books of poetry. Like Kline, he had a strong interest in science, particularly astronomy. Beginning in 1903, Lovecraft published his own magazine, the *Rhode Island Journal of Astronomy*. In 1906, letters expressing his astronomical views began to appear in his local papers. A letter on "Trans-Neptunian Planets" made it into the August 25, 1906 *Scientific American*. "I have a vast affection for the celestial spheres," he wrote Baird in 1923.[226] He later joked to one of his favorite penpals, James F. Morton, "The aeons & the worlds are my sport, & I watch with calm & amused aloofness the anticks of planets & the mutations of universes."[227]

After he passed his teens, his creative efforts were disposed towards poetry. His first poem in a professional publication, "Providence in 2000 A.D.," appeared in *The Providence Evening Bulletin* of March 4, 1912. While developing creatively, he published numerous articles and editorials on science, philosophy, literary criticism, current events, etc. With all of these varied efforts running simultaneously, his writing reveals the evolution of his thinking and talents on multiple fronts.

Over the course of his life, he wrote a staggering amount of material, much of which has found its way into modern print. His output was broader than the pulps, but his numerous stories in *Weird Tales* are central to his and the magazine's reputations. Our main interest here, his entry into *Weird Tales* during its first year of publication, represents a tiny subset of his writing.

Without question, the largest category of his writing was his correspondence. He wrote letters estimated to number in the tens of thousands. On peak days, he wrote over twenty letters. He had dozens of correspondents; he would write any reasonable person who wrote him, in some cases up to three long letters a week to a single correspondent. These people included editors, of course, but mainly friends, fellow authors, collaborators, clients, and fans. Many of these letters have been preserved. The sheer amount of energy he put into correspondence, while undoubtedly a detriment to his literary output, created a virtual diary of his life, albeit with many gaps, especially when the focus is as narrow as the present narrative.

Most pulp writers—of the thousands—are challenging to profile because of the absence of documentary evidence outside of their published work. They didn't leave much of a paper trail. Lovecraft presents the opposite problem. He's daunting because of the amount of material. Perhaps the only pulp author who *can* challenge him on that account is that one-man corporation, Edgar Rice Burroughs, a Lovecraft favorite who rose to popularity in the Munsey pulps during the period of Lovecraft's addiction. Lovecraft must surely prevail in sheer complexity, however, due to the amount of detail contained in letters he wrote, letters he received, the reminiscences of the many people who wrote about him, and his many published works. Thankfully, Lovecraft scholar S.T. Joshi has tackled the Herculean task of sorting out and analyzing the vast morass. Of his many works on Lovecraft, the centerpiece is a massive and meticulously detailed two-volume biography, *I Am Providence: The Life and Times of H.P. Lovecraft*, which provided invaluable guidance for our remarks on Lovecraft.

Lovecraft's writing was at its most varied and diffuse in the years leading up to his involvement with *Weird Tales*. His amateur astronomy journals proceeded while, in parallel, he contributed weekly astronomy columns to his local papers. In 1911, his first letter to a Munsey pulp appeared in the November *Argosy*. Two years later, he engaged in a debate in the *Argosy* letters column over the merits of schmaltzy author Fred Jackson.[228] Joshi credits this experience with drawing Lovecraft out of his isolation and exposing him to differing views. It also garnered him an invitation to join the United Amateur Press Association.[229]

The amateur press movement was essentially a set of writing clubs, in which members wrote, duplicated, and distributed their material, either selectively or to a central point where the contributions were assembled into journals and redistributed to the membership.[230] The system was tailor-made for Lovecraft's promiscuous writing habits and frequent disavowals of commercial writing. With *ars gratia artis*—art for art's sake—always the top dish on the menu, it actually cost him out-of-pocket to be involved. A highly active participant, he contributed to a variety of journals and published his own, *The Conservative*, which debuted with an April 1915 date. In the world of the amateur press, he met many of his correspondents and began to find himself as a fictionist.

After his boyhood attempts, he abandoned fiction for poetry for many years. For his return, he unearthed two early efforts for publication. "The Alchemist," originally written in 1908, appeared in *The United Amateur* for November 1916. "The Beast in the Cave," a 1905 story, reemerged in the June 1918 issue of *The Vagrant*. Still, he remained committed to poetry and journalism. In the middle of 1919, he started publishing fresh stories, on an increasing pace, so that by 1922 they dominated his output. Most of these stories were decidedly weird and written while *Weird Tales* was still a gleam in Jacob Clark Henneberger's eye.

In 1922, George Julian Houtain, known to Lovecraft from amateur press circles, recruited the author to supply a series of horror stories in a new, commercially-distributed humor magazine, *Home Brew*. He enticed the wary Lovecraft with an offer of $5 per installment, advising, "You can't make them too morbid."[231] Lovecraft agreed to the deal, "for friendship's sake."[232] To his friends, Lovecraft chafed at writing to order. He complained to Frank Belknap Long, Jr., an amateur press pal, and another future *Weird Tales* contributor, about being reduced from "art to the commonplace level of mechanical and unimaginative hack-work."[233] Lovecraft contributed two series to *Home Brew*. The first, under the rubric of *Herbert West—Reanimator*, was a six-part sequence of loosely-connected stories featuring a student at Miskatonic University Medical School in fictional Arkham, Massachusetts, who experiments with bringing people back to life in increasingly baroque fashion. The episodes ran from the first issue of *Home Brew*, February 1922, through July. The restrictions of conforming to Houtain's requirements bothered Lovecraft: "I can assure you I was sick of the job before I was half done."[234] The second series, a serial called *The Lurking Fear*, illustrated by Clark Ashton Smith, ran from January through April, 1923, *Home Brew's* last issue. Lovecraft supplied the story only because Houtain allowed him to write it as a serial.

Why would a humor magazine need horror stories? To misanthropes, death is a punchline; the grimmer the fate, the more hilarious. Added to which is the iconoclasm of the amateur press which spawned *Home Brew*. The title alone is a dead giveaway, innocent enough for most times, but highly irreverent for Prohibition, conflating the ideas of do-it-yourself journalism and homemade booze, as if they were equally daring, scandalous, and fun. The covers were littered with supporting witticisms, as on the first issue: "A Thirst Quencher for Lovers of Personal Liberty," "Full of Moonshine," "A Sparkling Effervescing Stimulant of Wit and Humor." That first cover depicted the cross-section of a house, revealing a cartoon couple tending a basement brewery. An inch below, their identities are revealed, if we interpret the comical proximity correctly: "Edited by Missus and Mister George Julian Houtain." Framed by all this satirical hooliganism, the subversive idea of horror as a source of humor seems perfectly natural. Lovecraft, the misanthrope, may have secretly enjoyed the concept, yet, as a teetotaling proponent of Prohibition, had to balance that against the mortification of being in the magazine. As he would later complain to Henneberger, the magazine was a "ribald rag."[235]

The run of Lovecraft's weird stories, ending with *Home Brew*, bumps up against the creation of *Weird Tales* and marks his transition from the ranks of amateur magazines to professional markets. Note that the last two issues of *Home Brew* (March and April) overlap the first two issues of *Weird Tales*.

The first question is how the man from Providence found his way into the magazine from Chicago. There are two versions of the story, Henneberger's romanticized and inaccurate memories, recounted in letters to August Derleth, Sam Moskowitz, and Joel Frieman, and Lovecraft's contemporaneous reporting, extracted in bits and pieces from his letters. The glaring discrepancy is that Henneberger claimed to have discovered Lovecraft in *Home Brew*, while Lovecraft discovered *Weird Tales* after being alerted by his friends. Henneberger's memories, particularly the ones recounted for Joel, are so detailed as to be persuasive on that count alone, but nevertheless they're mostly incorrect. We review them here to clarify the question of Lovecraft's introduction to *Weird Tales* and to comment on what these memories say about Henneberger's association of Lovecraft with the magazine.

Henneberger explained that after the "phenomenal success" of *Capt. Billy's Whiz Bang*, "Soon there were a number of these small magazines on the stands,"[236] like *Home Brew* and Henneberger's own *Magazine of Fun*. In fact, while *Fun* was priced at a ridiculous 20¢, *Home Brew* was priced at a 25% more ridiculous 25¢, like *Whiz Bang*. But Henneberger misinterpreted the nature of *Home Brew*; except for its size, it was not an imitation of *Whiz Bang*, which published cartoons and quips suitable for teenagers, or less; *Home Brew* contained risqué articles and stories, material that the sophisticates in the amateur press movement would savor.

Henneberger's faulty memory of discovering Lovecraft in *Home Brew* was set by 1940, the date of our first evidence. When Henneberger heard about the foundation of Arkham House (1939), he was eager to obtain any publications of Lovecraft's work and initiated a correspondence with publisher August Derleth. Through scattered correspondence, he told Derleth the *Home Brew* story, and a few other brief tidbits about the founding of *Weird Tales*.[237]

By the late 1960s, when Henneberger wrote Joel, his memories were more elaborate and touched on more issues. Quoting from the later letters: Henneberger recalled that *Home Brew* "introduced me to Howard Lovecraft ... although it pained me to find such an excellent craftsman in its pages."[238] He confessed that he found in Lovecraft a writer "whose style and craft were . . . the equal of Edgar Allan Poe."[239] Further: "I discovered a story by Lovecraft in a nondescript little pocket-sized magazine. I wrote to him in care of the magazine and correspondence with him ensued."[240] In one letter, Henneberger made the only statement that links his version with Lovecraft's: "The arrangement with Lovecraft was mutual. *He knew of the magazine I was publishing* [italics added] and professed a desire to submit his work for publication at the rates I offered."[241] What might otherwise make Henneberger's account plausible is that he could have discovered *Home Brew* simply as a matter of paying attention to his competitors or by having the magazine brought to his attention and, having discovered and liked Lovecraft, he would naturally have coveted his Poe-esque fiction for *Weird Tales*.

The disproof of Henneberger's memories is the absence of evidence for his version in Lovecraft's letters. Lovecraft was forthcoming to his assorted correspondents about his progress with *Weird Tales*, yet throughout 1923 he never mentioned Henneberger. All of his contact was with Baird. Lovecraft's first mentions of Henneberger followed his receipt of a letter from the publisher in late January 1924, to which he replied on February 2.[242] The follow-on communications reveal that Lovecraft was discovering Henneberger for the first time, which wouldn't have happened if they'd been in contact since early 1923. On February 7, he wrote Long of a letter received "from Henneberger, who it turns out is . . . the actual owner of the magazine."[243] Two days later, Lovecraft wrote Morton about "The baby what owns the whole damn outfit—a bolognee called Henneberger."[244] (Lovecraft seemingly wrote in a different voice for every correspondent and was at his most jocular with Morton—or "Mortonius," as Lovecraft called him.)

If detailed memories like Henneberger's are found to be untrue, the initial impulse is to impute dishonesty. But numerous scientific studies have demonstrated that memories grow steadily more distorted with the passage of time.[245] Henneberger's faulty 1940s memories of the founding of *Weird Tales* were sixteen or more years old; by 1968, they were forty-five years old. What he did over time was to compress the entire experience of *Weird Tales*'s first year into one aggregate memory. Having lost track of the details, he associated *his* acquaintance with Lovecraft with Baird's. In fact, Henneberger referred to discovering Lovecraft in the "second year" of the magazine,[246] making his faulty memories as self-consistent as they were detailed. What's interesting is the perspective of the distortion. When Sam Moskowitz approached Henneberger in the mid-1960s, he must have set him on a path of determined recollection, which then resulted in the detailed reconstructions of events which Henneberger delivered to Joel Frieman several years later. What Henneberger "remembered" was what really mattered to him then as the end of his life neared: the legacy, the creation of *Weird Tales* and the discovery of Lovecraft, the author who best made the magazine's claim to quality. He merged the two in his mind because, to him and to a great extent the world, the two had become a single larger thing, one that he was responsible for creating.

Of course, the question remaining is how he could have formed such detailed memories of seeing *Home Brew*, discovering Lovecraft, initiating a correspondence, and so forth. When Henneberger wrote Lovecraft in late January 1924, he mentioned *Home Brew*, evident from Lovecraft's reply: "I am interested in the idea you originally formed from my stuff in HOME BREW---especially interested because I consider that stuff among my poorest." We suspect that Lovecraft's first letter to *Weird Tales* had discussed his publication record, but that these details were excised by Baird when he published the letter in the September 1923 *Eyrie*, our only record of the letter. In this theory, Henneberger then obtained one or more copies of *Home Brew* in order to flatter Lovecraft about the stories when he initiated communications. Further, after Lovecraft's move from Providence to New York City, in early March 1924, he wrote his Aunt Lillian requesting that she ship a number of his personal effects, including his files of *Home Brew* and *Weird Tales*.[247] On March 18, he wrote her implying that he'd received his *file copies* of *WT*, and presumably the *Home Brew* set, but actually needed his duplicate set of *WT* for loaning out to friends.[248] Not long after, Henneberger visited Lovecraft in Brooklyn. It's only natural that Lovecraft would have shown him the *Home Brews*. In Henneberger's blurred memory, either obtaining the magazine or seeing them in Lovecraft's apartment became his "discovery" of them, and Lovecraft. It perfectly fits his condensing of the entire *Weird Tales*/Lovecraft experience into the events of early 1924.

In Lovecraft's version of events, he got the news as soon as *Weird Tales* went on sale. The earliest evidence is in a letter he wrote Morton on March 29, 1923: "[New York writer Everett] McNeil tipped me off to that *Weird Stories* [*sic*] thing, which he says is published out in Chi, but I ain't saw it yet."[249] He promised to look for it on his next visit to a newsstand and suggested that he would submit some of his past work. His first purchase of a *Weird Tales* was the April issue, which had been on sale since March 18. (Recall that the March issue went on sale "on or before" February 18.) By the time he wrote Baird in April his list of informants had grown significantly: "Having a habit of writing weird, macabre, and fantastic stories for my own amusement, I have lately been simultaneously hounded by nearly a dozen well-meaning friends into deciding to submit a few of these Gothic horrors to your newly-founded periodical."[250] He knew the magazine was nationally distributed, as he subsequently wrote Baird, "from the fact that people in Massachusetts, New York, Ohio and California have been equally prompt in calling my attention to it and urging me to try my luck!"[251] Joshi identifies the probable candidates for each state, all Lovecraft acquaintances from the amateur press world; the Californian would have been Clark Ashton Smith.[252]

As a postscript, we should note that Lovecraft was not tipped off from the announcements for *Weird Tales* in *The Author & Journalist*, which appeared beginning in late 1922, showing how detached his amateur press friends were from the commercial magazine world. An exception was Lovecraft's friend Arthur Leeds, who wrote a column for *The Writer's Monthly*. In the May 1923 issue, he talked up the new magazine, which he referred to, variably, as *Weird Stories* or *Weird Tales*. Leeds welcomed a magazine that would "occasionally dip into the weird and the creepily grotesque, and even into the frankly terrible—the Grand Guignol type of plot." With the actual *Weird*

Tales still a work in progress, with undefined scope, Leeds saw only the upside, the literary as opposed to the pulpish possibilities. His speculation on its potential ranged from Kipling, to Irvin Cobb's notorious short story "Fish Head," to Conan Doyle, and other name authors.[253]

In an alternate history where, say, Lovecraft heard the news at the earliest opportunity and appeared in the first issue of *Weird Tales*, the magazine's destiny might have proceeded on a completely different trajectory from the one it took. Nevertheless, the discovery of *Weird Tales* several months later was a momentous event for him, because it appeared to offer the impossible dream: a commercial market with literary pretensions that matched his taste in fiction, a cross-pollination of his opposing needs for art and money. He could not have hoped for such a thing if he lived to be a hundred.

Despite the tantalizing possibilities, Lovecraft was immediately pessimistic about his chances. As he continued in the March 29 letter to Morton, regarding his intention to submit material, "a guy's gotta sling a mean line . . . to put anything over on them magazine bimboes. They're hard eggs, Archie!"[254] In the amateur press world, he could get everything he wrote printed, even if it meant publishing his own journal. But that's for material whose value is defined by the writer, not the reader. In the commercial world, he had already received impersonal rejections of two stories from magazines which were open to weird fiction—"Dagon," by *The Black Mask*; and "The Tomb," by *The Black Cat*.[255] The sting left him in doubt of his ability to rise above amateurism.

As Lovecraft progressed in his relationship with *Weird Tales*, his pessimism became more pronounced, as we shall see, coloring his value as a witness. His letters are an excellent source for dating events and identifying issues between himself and the magazine, but his outsider sensibility caused him to continually misjudge events, outcomes, and people; life within his insular society of *ars gratia artis* writers, combined with a lack of real-world working experience, leaving him at a disadvantage. At times, his contemporaneous observations could be as unreliable as Henneberger's elderly memories.

Soon after obtaining the April issue of *Weird Tales*, Lovecraft, in his zeal, actually submitted an opening salvo of five old manuscripts, instead of the normal submission of a single story. Four of the stories had already appeared in amateur journals and a fifth was unpublished (original and *Weird Tales* appearances in parentheses): "Dagon" (*The Vagrant*, November 1919; *WT*, October 1923); "The Statement of Randolph Carter" (*The Vagrant*, May 1920; *WT*, February 1925); "The Cats of Ulthar" (*The Tryout*, November 1920; *WT*, February 1926); "Facts concerning the Late Arthur Jermyn and His Family" (*The Wolverine*, March 1921; *WT*, April 1924, retitled "The White Ape"); and "The Hound" (unpublished, written in 1922[256]; *WT*, February 1924).

Technically, the first four were reprints when they appeared in *Weird Tales*, but not in the pejorative sense described previously. However, it's not clear that Baird knew of their prior publication. In his cover letter, Lovecraft told him that the stories had been "written between 1917 and 1923," but in the version of the letter published in the September *Eyrie*, no mention was made of their publication history. These may have been further details omitted by Baird. Nevertheless, the amateur journals had such a limited publication, the readers of *Weird Tales* would have had no practical opportunity to read them, nullifying the reprint question.

Given his annoyance with the heaps of rubbish, Baird must have gulped when he opened the envelope and pulled out the five manuscripts. It was an instant clue to the strangeness of this new contributor. Baird may have thought he was looking at someone's life work freshly excavated from the cupboard.

Though both were fiction writers, Lovecraft and Baird seemed to be complete opposites. Lovecraft was one of life's impractical human beings and Baird a hard-working editor of mass-produced pulp magazines, a role and phenomenon that Lovecraft held beneath him. And yet beneath the surface they may have been more alike than either realized. In particular, they shared an outspoken contempt for the masses. Baird's views came through loud and clear in his comments for the April *Eyrie*. Lovecraft would have nodded in appreciation at Baird's description of the river of hopeless manuscripts the daily mail delivered. He would have loved Baird's exhortation against the obvious: "Must the heavens weep and the thunder growl to make a weird tale! We think not." Like Lovecraft's disdain for many of his fellow writers, he was equally forthright in revealing his distaste for the reading public. In his February 2 letter to Henneberger, Lovecraft managed to compress an essay on the topic into one (literally) breathtaking sentence:

> We have millions who lack the intellectual independence, courage, and flexibility to get an artistic thrill out of a bizarre situation, and who enter sympathetically into a story only when it ignores the colour and vividness of actual human emotions and conventionally presents a simple plot based on artificial, ethically sugar-coated values and leading to a flat denouement which shall vindicate every current platitude and leave no mystery unexplained by the shallow comprehension of the most mediocre reader.[257]

Still, Baird, as his job required, had the practicality that Lovecraft lacked. The magazine was a commercial product that needed customers. Lovecraft preferred failure to compromise. E. Hoffmann Price noted that:

> Without ever putting things in such terms, [Lovecraft's] attitude implied that any mode of presentation other than his own would be catering to morons whose patronage crass, commercial editors sought to win, whatever the cost in sacrifice of "integrity."
>
> He appeared oblivious of the fact that he had no readers other than the moronic pulp readers he despised.[258]

When Baird read the remarkable cover letter that accompanied Lovecraft's five manuscripts, it confirmed the author's eccentricity. He recommended which stories be read first, to spare the editor the remainder if the first should be found insufficient. He betrayed his self-indulgent, amateur press bias: "I have no idea that these things will be found suitable, for I pay no attention to the demands of commercial writing. My object is such pleasure as I can obtain from the creation of certain bizarre pictures, situations, or atmospheric effects; and the only reader I hold in mind is myself."[259] He continued, hinting at his pessimism while demonstrating a fussiness which threatened to make the pessimism a self-fulfilling prophecy: "Should any miracle impel you to consider the publication of my tales, I have but one condition to offer; and that is that no excisions be made. If the tale can not be printed as written, down to the very last semicolon and comma, it must gracefully accept rejection. . . . But I am probably safe, for my MSS. are not likely to win your consideration." He confessed to the prior rejection of "Dagon," noting that the submission had been made "under external impulsion," as had the five enclosed manuscripts. It was oddly Lovecraftian for the author to volunteer a negative association to his work, but Baird would not have been scared off by the rejection. With *The Black Mask* a direct competitor to *Detective Tales*, he would have understood that "Dagon" had been too offbeat for *Black Mask's* discontinued occult offerings, but just right for *Weird Tales*. Finally, after saying that he liked *Weird Tales* "very much," Lovecraft criticized the contents for being "more or less commercial—or should I say conventional?" Baird could be forgiven in thinking that Lovecraft was simply obeying his friends in submitting the stories and was actually trying to convince Baird to reject them. But Baird had his eye out for the unconventional; he was begging for it. When he published the letter in the September *Eyrie*, he added: "Despite the foregoing, or because of it, we are using some of Mr. Lovecraft's unusual stories, and you will find his 'Dagon' in the next issue of WEIRD TALES."

Lovecraft completely underestimated his chances. He wrote to Morton on May 3: "what I'm betting is that the editor (like those of the tenebrous feline [*The Black Cat*] & falseface [*The Black Mask*]) doesn't bother to write a personal letter to accompany the returning manuscripts."[260] Then he criticized the magazine, admitting that he'd only enjoyed one of the stories ("Beyond the Door," J. Paul Suter). Then he belittled the editor: "I've heard of the bimbo that edits *Weird Tales*—Edwin Baird—he used to write mediocre serials for the old *All-Story*."

Baird surprised Lovecraft with a reply—and a personal note. He defended *Weird Tales* against Lovecraft's criticisms that the magazine was too conventional.[261] He also told Lovecraft that he liked the stories, as Lovecraft soon reported to Long and Morton.[262] There was only one catch. Lovecraft's five manuscripts had been typed single-spaced, presumably because in the amateur press world authors self-edited and there was no need to mark corrections between the lines—and it conserved the precious paper of starving artists. Baird was unsympathetic. Lovecraft had put him on high alert. This excerpt from a 1927 interview demonstrates Baird's view on the subject:

> [Baird] showed me a manuscript from the pile of "unknowns." It was single-spaced in blurred purple ink, with half-inch margins at the left and words running over the edge at the right, and it was held together by a needle. "If I should buy this," Mr. Baird exploded, "I wonder where the author thinks I could edit it—or maybe she thinks it doesn't need editing."
>
> "Is single-spacing your test of the amateur?" I asked.
>
> "One of them. Professionals double-space—some even triple-space."[263]

Baird certainly put his finger on it regarding Lovecraft, who didn't want anyone editing his stories, down to the character and comma. Baird, of course, reacted to Lovecraft's manuscripts like a man who spent his eternal hours trying to extract order from chaos. He requested that Lovecraft resubmit them double-spaced before the stories be considered. What he couldn't have known was that Lovecraft had a near-pathological aversion to typing, a point that comes up repeatedly in his letters. "The editor reply'd that he liked [the stories]," he wrote Long on May 13, "but could not consider their acceptance till I sent them in double-spaced typing. I am not certain whether or not I shall bother. I need the money badly enough—but ugh! how I hate typing!"[264]

This was the thread from which the legacy of *Weird Tales* hung. Lovecraft had a highly particular nature, and could easily have turned away from the opportunity. Baird, on the other hand, had a sense of professional decorum upon which he insisted. They both had dared each other to end the relationship at the start, in a way that tested the other's commitment to the cause as each of them saw it. Lovecraft risked being written off by Baird as unprofessional and unmanageable. Baird knew that Lovecraft was eccentric, yet risked calling his bluff and losing a potentially valuable source of material for the struggling magazine. Neither of them could have foreseen how intertwined the destinies of the magazine and the author would become. What kept the thread from snapping was that Baird liked the stories and said so in a personal note. That was the bare minimum that Lovecraft needed to consider retyping.

He immediately set to work on "Dagon." Like any perfectionist, he couldn't resist a little rewriting with the retyping. As he explained to Baird in his cover letter, "In copying it I have touched up one or two crude spots—it having been written in 1917."[265] We might also suppose, given Lovecraft's concern with "the very last semicolon and comma," that he took care to make the manuscript immaculate, the better to stay Baird's editorial hand. He explained his choice of story to Baird, again daring him for a rejection. "I shall venture 'Dagon' as a sort of test of my stuff in general. If you don't care for this, you won't care for anything of mine. . . . It is not that 'Dagon' is the best of my tales, but that it is perhaps the most direct and least subtle in its 'punch'; so that for popular publication it is most likely to please most."

After putting "Dagon" in the mail approximately a week or two after hearing from Baird, the waiting game began.[266] Baird's interest in his material had done nothing to alleviate Lovecraft's pessimism. "Hain't heard from the little Bairdie yet," he wrote Morton, "but betcha a plugged 1804 dollar he shies at 'Dagon' now it's put up to 'im straight without no chanct of dodging."[267] He threatened to abandon *Weird Tales* if the story was rejected. "I hates to stick around where I ain't popular."

Lovecraft didn't remain "unpopular" for long. Within a few days, Baird had written to accept the story, promise payment of an undisclosed amount on publication, and ask for more stories. The failure to obtain agreement on a price (and the rights sold) in advance of the sale fell short of professional standards on Baird's part but Lovecraft, if he understood this, did not make it an issue. At any rate, he was shocked by the sale, pleasantly so. Still, he managed to find a dark cloud in imagining how small the check would be.[268] A new waiting game began. He resolved that before retyping another story, he would wait on the size of the check.[269] Baird, at the mercy of the magazine's insufferable policies, treated Lovecraft like any run-of-the-mill contributor, again putting the sensitive author's feelings to the test. If Lovecraft was to be the Christ figure who saved *Weird Tales* from its sins, no one realized it yet. As the days dragged on, though, Lovecraft surrendered to temptation and started to retype "The Picture in the House" (*The National Amateur*, July 1919; *WT*, January 1924) which, curiously, had not been one of the original five submissions. "Picture" tells a tale of cannibalism in the Massachusetts back country which starts innocently enough before giving way to a mounting sense of dread. More daringly horrifying than any of the original five, it showed an emboldened Lovecraft testing Baird's limits, and thus his character as an open-minded editor.

When Baird accepted "Dagon," he promised that it would appear in the July issue[270] but, as we have already determined, there would be no July issue. That month was skipped and the next issue to appear was August, deceptively labeled July-August. Lovecraft joined who-knows-how-many other loyal readers who dutifully traipsed to their newsstands on June 18, or soon thereafter, and wondered why the latest *Weird Tales* wasn't available. With so much at stake, he probably made the pilgrimage repeatedly: weekly or even more often. To no surprise, the absence of *his* issue only fueled Lovecraft's already gloomy outlook. He waited until June 24, then wrote Morton: "I've no idea that leetle Bairdie'll ever take another. 'Dagon' was a luck shot, & Ed probably asked about the others to be polite. I've fixed 'The Picture in the House' for him, & am bettin' heavy it'll come back with or without thanks."[271] On July 30, Lovecraft complained to Clark Ashton Smith that the July issue was still not out, which means that July-August, which presumably should have been available on July 18, was delayed by more than the skipped month; its actual date of publication is uncertain. (From this point forward, we can no longer reliably assume that *Weird Tales* went on sale the 18th of the month prior to the cover date.) Nor had Lovecraft heard back on "The Picture in the House." He added: "I certainly hope the magazine isn't going to fail before 'Dagon' . . . & the cheque therefor . . . . can put in an appearance! . . . But it rests with the gods."[272] It was one of the few times that he interpreted the events inside Rural Publishing correctly. The skipped issue was indeed a bad sign.

On August 6, Lovecraft shared his mounting anxieties with Morton: "I don't think I'll publish nothin' more—unless that slow-motion Bairdie decides to release his mag after all, & to loosen up wit' de heavy sugar."[273] This suggests that Lovecraft had *still* not seen the July-August issue. He bitterly complained about "the vulgar necessity of financial striving," lamenting to Morton, "Oh, leetle Bairdie, why in gawd's name dontcha come acrost with de price o' 'Dagon'?"[274] In his July 30 letter to Smith, he had thrown a punch at the magazine's quality: "The flounderings of second & third raters are pathetic. *Weird Tales* has pitifully few really good things . . . Cheap weird writers sometimes have delightfully clever ideas, but *atmosphere* seems to be utterly beyond them."[275] To Morton, he added: "I ain't sure but what authorship's a bit vulgar anyway. A gentleman shouldn't write all his images down for a plebeian rabble to stare at. If he writes at all, it shou'd be in private letters to other gentleman of sensitiveness & discrimination."[276] These mirror views he expressed many times throughout his life but, in this context, he was probably thinking out loud that not appearing in the company of inferior writers—and readers—might be the superior moral path. Were it not for the badly needed moolah.

When Lovecraft finally saw the July-August issue, it was another bad tiding, for "Dagon" was not included. The time he made this horrifying discovery is the same approximate time he set to work writing another of his classics, "The Rats in the Walls," his longest story to date. He wrote Long on September 4, reporting that he had just finished it, plus "The Unnamable."[277] He submitted "Rats" to the great Munsey editor, Robert H. Davis, to be considered for the *Argosy All-Story Weekly*. Davis rejected it, finding it— in Lovecraft's characterization—"too horrible for the tender sensibilities of a delicately nurtured publick."[278] This confirmed for him "the essential insipidity and conventionality inculcated into our writing public by some of its leaders."[279] Davis's rejection of "Rats" is less surprising than Lovecraft's rejection of *Weird Tales* as his market of first refusal. The timing of this choice suggests that he had concluded his involvement with *Weird Tales* was a failed experiment, that he needed to hedge his bets by opening up a second market. In a sense, he was acting like a spurned lover, overly eager for romance on the rebound. It's true that *Argosy* was a larger, more reliable, and better paying market, but it's hard to believe that Lovecraft would have tried them with his style of story if *Weird Tales* hadn't placed him in limbo.

It remained for the September issue to resolve the mystery of "Dagon's" delay. Baird published the Lovecraft cover letter that accompanied the original five manuscripts along with the announcement that "Dagon" would be in the next—October—issue. Baird apparently never explained the delay in getting the story into the magazine; undoubtedly, the skipped month and the resulting backlog of material had tossed a grenade into his otherwise tidy plans.

Lovecraft had been fully absorbed into the *Weird Tales* "contributor's club," some of whose frustrated members were then complaining to *The Author & Journalist*. He had experienced the agonies and insults inflicted upon the author by the pay-on-publication world. For a seasoned pro, the delays would simply have been an annoyance. For a writer awaiting his first professional appearance, it must have felt like extreme cruelty. Nevertheless, he eagerly recruited his friends into the very same club. After "Dagon" had been accepted, he sent Baird samples of Clark Ashton Smith's poetry.[280] Baird wrote Smith and, despite the magazine's aversion to poetry, two of Smith's poems appeared in the July-August issue, ironically beating the long-suffering Lovecraft into the magazine's pages. Lovecraft also urged Long to contribute,[281] though his first story would not appear until the November 1924 issue. Lovecraft, Smith, and Long all became more or less regular contributors, as if *Weird Tales* was an amateur journal they all could take part in. Lovecraft's recruitment of the pair gave birth to the clannishness which would unite a number of *Weird Tales* authors over the years.

Finally, the October issue appeared on newsstands with, as promised,

"Dagon." Lovecraft wrote Long on October 7 to tell him that the issue was available.[282] If we assume that Lovecraft wrote at the first opportunity, it means that the issuance date of the magazine had slid by two or three weeks (not including the skipped month) past its normal circa-the-18th date. From the time that Lovecraft had originally submitted material in mid-April, at least five torturous months had passed. Still, Baird rewarded him with a favored position in the magazine. "Dagon" came third after the first part of the cover-illustrated serial, "The Amazing Adventure of Joe Scranton," and Seabury Quinn's well-received novelette "The Phantom Farm House."

However, what Baird gave with one hand, he took away with the other. He risked another potential wound to his relationship with Lovecraft by printing in its entirety the May cover letter that accompanied the retyped "Dagon."[283] In it, Lovecraft apologized for his former criticism of conventionality in *Weird Tales*, and clarified his point. He also poked fun at Vincent Starrett's "Penelope" from the May issue, for its "ignorance of astronomy." He told Baird that Smith had shown "Dagon" to his friend, California poet George Sterling, who made an "absurd" suggestion for improving the story. Lovecraft never imagined that Baird would commit these views to print and was mortified when he did. He worried what Starrett and especially Sterling would think. He fretted to Long, "If Starrett and Sterling don't start out after their Grandpa Theobald with stilettos and automatics, it'll be merely because they don't believe in bothering to swat small skeeters."[284] To Smith, he instructed, "For gawd's sake don't let George Sterling see [the issue]," adding that he had "the most profound respect for his work & influence in American letters."[285] He resolved to guard his words in the future: "the incident teaches me that Baird is one of those indiscreet persons to whom one must be careful what one writes!"[286]

The incident also seemed to reinforce his notion that *The Eyrie* was a place of peril. Baird wrote in the October column: "In a way, 'Dagon' is a radically different sort of story, even for WEIRD TALES, and those that will follow it are even more so. For this reason, we shall be particularly interested in hearing what our readers think of the Lovecraft tales." That second sentence put Lovecraft on edge. "I am indeed glad [Baird] likes my material so well," he wrote Smith, "& only hope his readers will not reverse his judgment with adverse comments."[287] In his perpetually gloomy outlook, Baird's approval was still not enough. What the editor gave, hostile readers could take away.

He needn't have worried. Baird happily announced in the January *Eyrie* that "H.P. Lovecraft's uncanny stories are making a decided hit, it seems." Baird printed a few of the initial responses. Poet Clement Wood called the story "sustained and excellent to the end." Another fan gushed: "H.P. Lovecraft manipulates an inimitable pen: he is extraordinary, as is 'Dagon.' "

And what of this tale which provoked so much back and forth and turmoil, all leading to such a favorable response? Indeed, it is a strange and elegant story, and a shock to the sprouting *Weird Tales* culture, for it showed how different a weird story could be and how not-different much of the magazine had thus far been. "Dagon" is the account of a marooned sailor who wakes up aground on an expanse of black slime. As he explores the bizarre environment on foot, it becomes apparent that he is on the sea floor which has risen above the water, bringing the mysteries of undersea life with it. When the sailor ascends high ground, he looks down and sees something ancient and horrifying and alive, something that upends his understanding of the world, something so outlandish that his delirious words receive "scant attention" when he later attempts to describe what he saw. It is a story filtered through the imagination of a writer who had spent years of astronomical study pondering the vastness and mystery of the universe. In a sense, the sailor is Lovecraft's view of himself, risen up from ignorance to a high point and afforded a far-reaching view that few can truly appreciate.

In addition to the praise to come, Lovecraft had much to be happy about. In the storyhead to "Dagon," Baird bylined his new author "H.P. Lovecraft, Master of Weird Fiction." And Baird satisfied the author's perfectionist impulses, as Lovecraft confirmed in a letter: "I was exceedingly pleased with the appearance of 'Dagon,' which seems virtually free from misprints."[288] Additionally, the impoverished Lovecraft could already look forward to more checks. Baird had passed Lovecraft's taste test by accepting the unsettling "The Picture in the House"; it had been an easier test for Baird to pass than Lovecraft might have guessed, because the magazine was losing money and eager to experiment in any way that altered its fortunes. It appeared in the January issue. Next in line was his retyped "The Hound" (*WT*, February 1924). Baird also queued up Lovecraft collaborations from Sonia H. Greene, the future Mrs. Lovecraft, a widow whom he had met in amateur press circles ("The Invisible Monster," *WT*, November 1923); and his Providence friend and fellow weird-fiction aficionado C.M. Eddy, Jr. ("Ashes," *WT*, March 1924; "The Ghost-Eater," *WT*, April 1924). In exchange for Lovecraft's revision work on the latter's stories, "Eddy types my own manuscripts in the approv'd double-spac'd form; this labour being particularly abhorrent to my sensibilities."[289]

The publication of "Dagon" seemed to mark a turning point in Lovecraft's regard for Baird. Lovecraft had entered the relationship with extreme distrust, from not even expecting a personal reply to thinking that if Baird didn't accept "Dagon," "he knows where he can go!"[290] He soon began referring to the editor using terms like "Leetle Bairdie." Nicknames are common to Lovecraft's epistolary style, so it's difficult to measure the balance of sarcasm and affection contained therein; it may have started as the former and slowly shifted to the latter. Despite any commonalities in temperament, the pair got off to a rocky start with Lovecraft's "caustic" cover letter and Baird's retyping request, and there were more bumps along the way: the publication delays, Baird's indiscretion, and Lovecraft's irritation with title changes, for Sonia's story and, worse, one of his own. He wrote Morton in December: "Lettle Bairdie wants to call 'Arthur Jermyn' 'The White Ape'. Blah!!!!"[291]

But these all ended up as side issues. Central to the relationship was Baird's appreciation for Lovecraft's fiction and his unwavering desire to get it into print. After "Dagon" finally appeared, and Baird's promises had been realized in black and white—and green—and more stories had been accepted, the relationship appears to have found itself—improbably—on solid ground. As Baird was accepting a succession of Lovecraft works, the author wrote Morton of Baird: "This worthy man not long ago writ me in a manner which elevates my inherent vanity to unbearable altitudes. He says, 'my work makes a peculiar appeal to readers', as attested by numerous letters from them; & he desires I shou'd address my mail to his home in Evanston hereafter, & he may be certain of early perusing it."[292] His main complaint was the slowness of payment, which was beyond Baird's control. Lovecraft wrote Long at this time: "Leetle Bairdi is become a very great friend of mine and designs to publish my efforts with much regularity."[293] By the end of January, Baird had written Lovecraft that he was one of the magazine's two "star writers" (Seabury Quinn being the other).[294]

The relationship between the pair—only fathomable because of Lovecraft's letters—makes a great case study in Baird's author-relations style, though admittedly Lovecraft was a special case. If anyone can be said to have "discovered" Lovecraft, it would be Baird. In truth, Lovecraft discovered him, but it was Baird, the professional editor, who immediately recognized the value of his work and set the stage for Lovecraft to be discovered by the wider world. This contradicts the long- and widely-held view of an out-of-touch editor who mismanaged his responsibilities and almost killed the magazine as a result. He made mistakes, but his handling of Lovecraft was not, as it happened, one of them; and the fate of the magazine was mainly in the hands of others.

Late in his life, from a distance of a dozen years, Lovecraft remembered Baird as having never rejected a story of his.[295] It was almost true. Baird never rejected a Lovecraft story for *Weird Tales*; however, in 1925 he rejected "The Shunned House" for *Real Detective Tales*, as it had been renamed.[296] But what did Lovecraft really think of Edwin Baird, the pro who had promoted him? He never—that we know of—gave a detailed description. But Long included a very complimentary memory in his 1975 Lovecraft biography: "Baird had read widely in many fields . . . and was a very able editor possessing a keen awareness of the vast gulfs which might exist, not just between a good story and a bad one, but between genuine literary excellence and the sort of mediocre offering which all editors are compelled to accept occasionally when nothing better is available."[297] Long, however, had experienced little contact with Baird. His recollection, therefore, is more likely to be based on what his friend Lovecraft had told him.

XII

A Case For and Against

Returning to Farnsworth Wright and Otis Adelbert Kline, recall that both writers appeared in the first two issues of *Weird Tales*, then pitched in to keep Baird from drowning in a churning sea of sewage. Kline's fiction was absent from the third issue—May—then appeared three more times in 1923: June, July-August, and September. Wright was absent until a run of three straight appearances starting with the September issue. We have already speculated that April and May was the likely period in which the two began to assist Baird by reviewing manuscripts. Since this overlaps the period of Lovecraft's package of five submissions, the question arises as to whether Wright or Kline had the opportunity to read the single-spaced manuscripts.

With no one willing to talk about the past, we don't know how the office operated. Would Baird have returned the manuscripts before his assistants had a chance to read them? Would he have farmed out Lovecraft's submissions to one of his new assistants for a first opinion, or divided them between the two? Would Baird have talked up Lovecraft's merits in the office, arousing curiosity for the material? Would a manuscript get reviewed by one or more people?

It's interesting to speculate on what happened, and the trace amounts of evidence doom us to a high degree of uncertainty, but there is an undeniable underlying issue. Wright and Kline, once they had joined the office, had the inside track on selling to Baird. For them to be reviewing unpublished manuscripts *and* selling stories to him created, in modern terms, a conflict of interest. In the pulps, it was not unusual for editors or staffers to sell to the magazines or publishers they worked for. There are countless examples. Still, it was a questionable practice, akin to insider trading in the stock market. In the particular case of *Weird Tales*, the incoming manuscripts, while generally useless for the magazine, were also a spectrum of story ideas from which a creative writer could draw inspiration for new or better variations. Without making accusations against either Wright or Kline, they had the opportunity, for instance, to recommend passing on a manuscript, then borrow its ideas. The question, then, is whether either of them read Lovecraft's manuscripts and drew inspiration for their own material. We have only the stories to guide us, Lovecraft's original five and the subsequent stories of Wright and Kline in the magazine. Their stories will indeed reveal thematic connections and uncanny similarities.

Recall that Wright's stories for the *Overland Monthly*, and his first two for *Weird Tales*, "The Closing Hand" and "The Snake Fiend," drew upon his past in ways that reflected, sometimes deeply, on his philosophies and feelings. In moving from a mainstream to a genre magazine, the parameters for personal expression decreased significantly, and so the two *Weird Tales* stories yield diminishing returns. Wright's subsequent stories for the magazine reveal virtually no self-reflection apart from the occasional incidental reference. For instance, in "An Adventure in the Fourth Dimension" (October 1923), the setting is Chicago and the narrator, who had been in the army in France during the war, swears in French because, "I liked to show off my knowledge of the language." If the restrictions imposed by the "weird story" constrained his imagination, Farnsworth didn't compensate by selling fiction elsewhere. It was as if he had already given as much to his fiction as he could bear. His remaining memories would stay locked inside him, off-limits for conversation with friends, off-limits even for metaphorical representation in fiction.

Wright's third short story for *Weird Tales*, "The Teak-Wood Shrine" (September 1923), has no obvious connections to its author's life. The story is told from a woman's point of view, but that element ends up having no bearing on the outcome. The plot revolves around an ornament from India, a teakwood devil with ruby eyes. Touching the eyes opens a little door, revealing a chamber. Whoever looks inside learns its terrible truth and dies as a result. The story has three elements suggestive of Lovecraft's submissions. First, a foreign artifact plays a significant role in "The White Ape," Baird's annoying retitling of "Arthur Jermyn." The Jermyns are an old family whose men were African explorers, scientists, and curio collectors. Arthur, the last of the bloodline, receives a boxed object from Africa. Upon opening the box and seeing its contents, he's so aghast that he immolates himself. Additionally, the events of "The Statement of Randolph Carter" are set in motion by an "ancient book in undecipherable characters" which came from India. Finally, "The Hound" contains Lovecraft's first mention of another book, "the forbidden 'Necronomican' of the mad Arab Abdul Alhazred." The second commonality between Wright and Lovecraft is the terrible thing which when looked upon shatters the mind leading to death. The third commonality is the technique of ending a story with a terrifying mystery left to the reader's imagination. "The Teak-Wood Shrine" never reveals the horrible truth contained within the ornamental devil; it forces the reader to ponder its dark, unfathomable depths. Similarly, in "The Statement of Randolph Carter," Harley Warren, a researcher into the unknown, takes his friend Carter to an ancient cemetery. Warren, guided by his Indian book, uncovers hidden stone steps leading underground. He descends alone while unraveling a telephone wire which allows him to communicate with Carter back on the surface. He eventually encounters something terrifying. He urges Carter to escape, warning of "hellish things." He never returns and we never discover what Carter saw.

Neither Wright's fourth or fifth stories, "An Adventure in the Fourth Dimension" and "Poisoned" (November 1923), suggest connections to Lovecraft. "Fourth Dimension" is a comical tale of visiting Jupiterians who act bizarrely and are given phantasmagoric analysis by a Professor Nutt. The story turns out to have been a dream of someone who had been reading Einstein. "Poisoned" is a yarn about an old friendship turned bad. It's only borderline weird and lacks fantastic elements.

As for Kline, after being absent from the May issue, he returned in June 1923 with "The Phantom Wolfhound." The title alone arouses suspicions about the potential influence of Lovecraft's "The Hound." The timing is tight for Kline to have read "The Hound" and been inspired to compose a similar story in time for the June issue, but it's still possible.

But are the stories similar? Both follow a plot in which violent retribution for a bad deed is visited upon the perpetrator by a ghostly hound. Both, of course, share a common ancestor: Conan Doyle's 1901 Sherlock Holmes novel *The Hound of the Baskervilles*. In keeping with the earthbound logic of the Holmes stories, the seemingly supernatural hound turns out to have a rational explanation; and the bad deed is the creation of the murderous hoax. Lovecraft and Kline flip the formula on both counts. Their hounds are genuinely supernatural, and the retribution is the result of the bad deed.

Lovecraft's "The Hound" features a pair of cultivated grave-robbers, the narrator and his friend St. John. The narrator/friend model mirrors the relationships in "The Statement of Randolph Carter" and, indeed, that of Dr. Watson and Sherlock Holmes. In "The Hound," the two Englishman travel to a crypt in Holland to steal an amulet hinted at in the *Necronomicon*. After returning to England, they are haunted by the "daemonic baying . . . of some gigantic hound." While walking home at night from the railway station St. John is "seized by some frightful carnivorous thing and torn to ribbons." The narrator arrives in time to "hear a whir of wings and see a vague black cloudy thing silhouetted against the rising moon." The thing is not a hound *dog* but rather a thing that hounds. Fearing for his own life, the narrator travels back to Holland to return the amulet to its resting place, discovers something frightful, and the story closes with him poised for suicide.

Kline's "The Phantom Wolfhound" is a sequel of sorts to "The Thing of a Thousand Shapes." That story had a major narrative defect: the most interesting character, psychic researcher Jim Braddock, is mistakenly thought dead through of most of the story and thus is dormant to the drama. Kline apparently aimed to rework the formula. The main character in "The Phantom Wolfhound" is Doctor Dorp, a friend of the absent Braddock. Dorp is a psychic investigator whom the police bring their strange cases to, Holmes without a Watson. Braddock's book, *The Reality of Materialization Phenomena*, is mirrored by Dorp's book, *Investigations of Materialization Phenomena*. Books of forbidden knowledge play a role in both Lovecraft's and Kline's stories, but Kline's usage in "Thousand Shapes" predates his possible reading of Lovecraft's manuscripts. Kline also reused the idea of psychoplasm, the white substance, for "The Phantom Wolfhound." The story concerns a Mr. Ritsky who is haunted by the ghost of a dog he has shot, which manifests itself as a grayish white apparition. He is ultimately found frightened to death with a white slime of psychoplasm on his chest. It turns out that the murdered dog was the beloved Russian wolfhound belonging to Ritsky's niece, who he was slowly poisoning for her money, a motive similar to the perpetrator of the hound of the Baskervilles.

Kline's next two stories in the magazine don't bear any obvious similarities to Lovecraft's five submissions, or Kline's previous two. "The Corpse on the Third Slab" (July-August) is the tale of Officer Ryan, a policeman assigned to keep watch in a morgue because a body had been stolen the night before. He drinks moonshine on the job—another lampoon on the impracticality of Prohibition—gets drunk, wakes up, and is confronted by one of the corpses. It even talks! For the reader, Ryan's impairment creates ambiguity about his state of mind. Is it all a drunken hallucination? Ryan falls down, hits his head, is knocked unconscious, and ultimately woken by his chief. The story closes with physical evidence that the corpse really had reanimated: a freshly painted wall has a palm-print which matches the white enamel stain on the corpse's palm.

"The Cup of Blood" (September) owes more to Poe than to Lovecraft. Two American pals touring Scotland on foot spend the night in the supposedly haunted Bludmanton Castle where, long ago, a love triangle involving Sir Malcolm Blud, his wife Lady Helen, and the young minister she secretly loved, led to tragic and mysterious consequences. Sir Malcolm, suspecting a secret affair, made Helen drink the blood, from a cup, of the dying minister. The two pals solve the mystery of their disappearance by discovering a tomb with two skeletons, where Lady Helen had been left to starve to death while trapped with the minister's corpse. One senses the influence of "The Fall of the House of Usher," with the long lineage of a family meeting its tragic end and Roderick Usher realizing of his last living relative, his twin sister: "*We have put her living in the tomb!*"

At this point, we can see an interesting symmetry between Wright's and Kline's stories as regards their resemblance to Lovecraft's five submissions. For both, it was their *first* story in the magazine after the arrival of the Lovecraft manuscripts which bore copycat elements: Wright's "The Teak-Wood Shrine" and Kline's "The Phantom Wolfhound." The immediate follow-up efforts don't suggest further connections.

Admittedly, the timing is suspicious but the case for influence is ambiguous. We're left with a spectrum of interpretations. On one extreme, Wright and Kline read Lovecraft's manuscripts and were inspired to adapt his ideas for their own work. On the other extreme, the connections with Lovecraft are arbitrary and all three writers were simply recycling the familiar tropes of the weird tale. The first interpretation may seem to be the most serious because it implies impropriety and plagiarism, but the deeds are ultimately incidental and without long-term consequence. But the second interpretation gets at the existential dilemma of *Weird Tales*: if readers become bored with the sameness of stories, then old readers depart as new ones arrive, inhibiting the magazine from growing.

Recall that Baird recounted in *The Eyrie*, almost with malicious glee, on the repetitious nature of the submissions overflowing Rural's mailbox. But what about the sameness of the final, published product in the magazine? While Baird published a great many encomiums in *The Eyrie*, he was equally forthcoming with reader dislikes, and the issue of sameness bubbled up fairly quickly. The first hint came in the June 1923 issue: "The stories you have printed so far can be grouped under three general headings: Ghost Stories, Snake Stories, Insanity Stories." In the following issue (July-August): "As for 'The Devil Tree' [*sic*; "The Devil Plant," by Lyle Wilson Holden, May issue]—why, the whole world has read Poe's 'Cask of Amontillado,' and, anyway, that tree appeared long ago in a Strand Magazine story." The erudite Lovecraft joined the chorus in his first letter (September): " 'A Square of Canvas,' by Anthony M. Rud [was] reminiscent in denouement of Balzac's 'Le Chef d'Ouvre inconnu'—as I recall it across a lapse of years, without a copy at hand." And in the October issue, Baird published a letter with a litany of complaints: " 'The Invisible Terror,' in the June number of WEIRD TALES, is much like Bierce's 'The Damned Thing,' 'The Gray Death' is very like 'The Silver Menace,' published a decade ago. 'Penelope,' in May WEIRD TALES, is very like 'Phoebe' of some years ago—the better of the two."

It's hard to imagine a similar debate occurring in the letter column of, say, a western pulp, e.g. "Chuck Martin's story, in which the cowboy gets shot after running out of bullets reminded me of a similar story in *Ace-High Magazine* some years ago . . ." The readers of westerns and many other pulp genres were none-the-wiser if their favorite genre thrills were recycled with only the character and place names changed. "The unique magazine" aimed higher, not just to be unique as a concept but to be unique within its confines. Failure to deliver on that promise threatened its long-term longevity and helps explain why Lovecraft's alien seed was so welcome to Baird.

Kline—to add a postscript—placed one more story in *Weird Tales* before the big financial meltdown of 1924. "The Malignant Entity" appeared in the May-June-July Anniversary Issue. Doctor Dorp was back—with improved circumstances. This time, he had a sidekick, a Mr. Evans, "who writes a story every now and then." Dorp had his Watson, someone to chronicle his exploits while he engaged in psychical ratiocination. In the story, Dorp has been drawn into a baffling case by Chief McGraw of the detective bureau, Dorp's equivalent to Holmes's Inspector Lestrade. An inventor, Albert Townsend, has been murdered, turned into a bleached white skeleton. In trying to prove his theory that a living organism could be created from inorganic matter, Townsend brought into life a "malignant entity," a thing that feasts on flesh to survive. A blob of a creature with a visible nucleus, after it had devoured the test animals on the premises, it turned its hunger on its inventor. This tale, too, had a connection to one of Lovecraft's stories which, by late October 1923, had been retyped and resubmitted to Baird.[298] In the dénouement to "The White Ape," Arthur Jermyn opened the box which arrived in the mail, saw a mummified white ape with a face closely resembling his own, the horrifying revelation that he had ape in his ancestry. In "The Malignant Entity," Dorp captures the creature in a jar and burns it to death. Inside the jar it forms into the face of Immune Benny, Townsend's missing roomer, implying that Benny had formed part of the entity's constitution.

Dorp and Evans weren't likely to become the new Holmes and Watson. The Doyle model didn't want for successors, and the names Dorp and Evans don't roll off the tongue the way Holmes and Watson do, nor was Kline's storytelling the caliber of Doyle's. However, Dorp and Evans could have developed into an acceptable series in *Weird Tales*. As we shall see, though, financial considerations short-circuited Kline's future with the magazine. That left the door open for Seabury Quinn to introduce Jules de Grandin and Dr. Trowbridge in 1925.

XIII

The Man Behind the Curtain

Ironically, Lovecraft blossomed as a central *Weird Tales* contributor at the same time that the magazine was entering its darkest and most desperate days to date. This period, when the magazine's troubles seemed to be deepening without hope of reversal, is when Lovecraft became involved with Henneberger. As we've previously argued, Henneberger's memory of discovering Lovecraft in *Home Brew* was faulty; their relationship was initiated when Henneberger wrote Lovecraft in late January 1924, and received a lengthy reply on February 2. Prior to this, all of Lovecraft's contacts with *Weird Tales* had been through Baird.

Absent is any evidence of when Henneberger actually became aware of Lovecraft and his potential importance to the magazine. It's always possible that Baird, in recognizing Lovecraft's value early on, had been reporting developments to Henneberger. However, the weight of the evidence is that Henneberger and Baird acted autonomously in their separate roles, and that Baird, within the purview of the magazine's purpose, was free to edit without interference. He may have insisted upon such conditions when he was hired. It's more likely that Henneberger became aware of Lovecraft when he began appearing in the magazine, with his initial letter in the September *Eyrie* and "Dagon" in the October issue.

By late January, Lovecraft couldn't be ignored, having grown into a major force among *Weird Tales* contributors, accounting for nine stories. "Dagon" had been published and well-received by readers; "The Picture in the House" appeared in the January issue. Three more of Lovecraft's stories had been purchased for subsequent issues, with a fourth imminent. One of his collaborations had been published, and two more accepted. When Henneberger wrote Lovecraft, he stressed the need for unconventional material,[299] complimenting him that "The Rats in the Walls," one of the accepted stories and certainly unconventional, was "the best tale *Weird Tales* ever received."[300] He may well have assumed that Lovecraft was a bottomless well of material useful to the magazine, much of it of similarly high quality.

Henneberger had found his model, the type of writer for whom *Weird*

Tales was created. "I had a great regard for this writer of retiring nature," he recalled of his new star.[301] Lovecraft may have seemed too good to be true. He shared Henneberger's literary imperative. In his original letter to *Weird Tales*, he confessed: "My models are invariably the older writers, especially Poe, who has been my favorite literary figure since early childhood."[302] In his February 2 reply, he added: "I would give a thousand dollars not to have read Poe's 'House of Usher' or 'Ligeia', just for the thrill of following them breathlessly with pristine suspense over what was coming!"

Lovecraft also had a well-developed belief in the nature and value of weird fiction. The February 2 reply unleashed a sweeping analysis of the topic, from which the following quote is taken. Note his connection of the fantastic elements of weird fiction to the emotions they provoke, which resonates with Henneberger's original descriptions of the intent of *Weird Tales*:

> Yet from the art standpoint—from the standpoint of the effective evocation of nameless ecstacies [*sic*] of keen-edged and titillating fear—I don't think anything can equal good weird fiction. There is only a passing horror in sordid, sanguinary gruesomeness—in bloody axe murders and sadistic morbidities. What really moves the profoundest springs of human fear and unholy fascination is something which suggests black infinite vistas of cryptic, brooding, half-inscrutable monstrosities for ever lurking behind Nature and as capable of being manifested again as in the case treated.

For Lovecraft, though, the weird tale was an art form and not an interpretation of a supernatural reality. Rather, his imagination had been unlocked by his long study of astronomy and the sense of vastness it inspired. He was fundamentally and proudly a man of scientific temperament. As he wrote one correspondent in 1926: "I am an absolute sceptic and materialist, and regard the universe as a wholly purposeless and essentially temporary incident in the ceaseless and boundless rearrangements of electrons, atoms, and molecules which constitute the blind but regular mechanical patterns of cosmic activity."[303] As he wrote another in 1931: "I have not entertained any belief in the supernatural since the age of 8."[304] Frank Belknap Long said of his friend: "His disbelief in the occult was absolute."[305]

Henneberger had found a writer seemingly custom-made for his magazine. But while Lovecraft's aesthetic imperatives were ideal, in other ways, yet to be ascertained, he would prove unfit. Notably, though the unique author made his name in Henneberger's unique pulp magazine, one hesitates to call him a "pulp writer." He's only literally that. The cream of the pulp magazines, the original and interesting material, like Lovecraft's famous stories, are sometimes used to characterize the field as a vast library of overlooked classics. There are certainly known and overlooked classics, but the reality is that most pulps had a mass-produced, assembly-line quality, every story delivering an assortment of tried-and-true genre thrills served up in a fresh combination. Seabury Quinn's writing, which Lovecraft enjoyed at first then grew to despise, was the exemplar for *Weird Tales*. In his February 2 letter, Lovecraft gave an artist's perspective of the situation:

> Added to [the conformity of popular fiction], as if by the perversity of a malign fate, is the demand of an overspeeding public for excessive quantity production. Baldly put, the American people demand more stories per year than the really artistic authors of America could possibly write. A real artist never works fast, and never turns out large quantities. He can't contract to deliver so many words in such and such a time, but must work slowly, gradually, and by mood; utilising favourable states of mind and refraining from putting down the stuff his brain turns out when it is tired or disinclined to such work. Now this, of course, won't do when there are hundreds of magazines to fill at regular intervals.

Lovecraft had learned a lesson from reading hundreds of issues of pulp magazines and thousands of stories. He didn't choose the term "quantity production" idly. An obvious phrase for the era of stopwatch-wielding efficiency experts, with the rapid growth of the pulps the idea was increasingly being applied to the craft of fiction writing. Frederick Palmer, co-founder in March 1924 of the Palmer Institute of Authorship (successor to the Palmer Photoplay Corporation), a correspondence school for writers, published a syndicated newspaper article in September 1924, "Story-telling as an Industry," an unacknowledged endorsement for his new school. In it, he laid out the parameters of the brave new world of the writer:

> Quantity production explains the metamorphosis of the writing craft, just as it explains the advance of the plate glass industry, the general use of canned goods, and the cheapness of ready-made suits of clothes. There is in America a huge demand for printed stories and for those that appear on the moving picture screen. Thousands of them are supplied every week to a public which is hungry for make-believe, for the romance and adventure which the necessities of making a living prevent them from obtaining in any other way.

Lovecraft and Palmer were both correct. The fiction industry needed fast, repetitive workers more than it needed methodical, contemplative artists. Lovecraft was far too nonconformist for the formula-friendly pulps.

"Popular authors do not and apparently cannot appreciate the fact that true art is obtainable only by rejecting normality and conventionality in toto," he complained.[306] In the end, *Weird Tales* became an amalgam of Palmer and Lovecraft, and thus an abstract metaphor for the pulps as a whole. The magazine published a great deal of genre-thrills fiction with a sprinkling of genuinely unique material, of which Lovecraft was a prime example. Quinn made a living; Lovecraft made a legacy.

Not only was Lovecraft not a pulp writer, he was only barely a professional writer. With his meticulous attention to detail, the math of the profession wouldn't work for him as a long-term proposition. The magazine could live with his fussiness, but as a painstaking craftsman, he couldn't sell them enough words to make a living. He also had the disadvantage of being a single-market author. He sold many stories and poems to *Weird Tales* during the remaining fourteen years of his life, but many others were rejected by Farnsworth Wright, a few of which went to other paying markets. Most successful pulp writers learned the hard way to diversify their markets, to insulate themselves against the ever-shifting fortunes of the field: magazines living and dying, editors coming and going and, in the case of *Weird Tales*, fluctuating word-rates and publication frequency. Lovecraft was forced to scrape out a living as a freelance ghostwriter, revisionist, collaborator, and editor. His enduring popularity following his death gives a false impression of his living years. He's the weird tale of the artist who is wildly successful—after death.

The Almanac of Cosmic Occurrences—1924

Henneberger's approach to Lovecraft was not a random bit of professional courtesy; it actually fit the larger pattern of events in 1924 that would reshape the destiny of *Weird Tales*: the hydra-headed process known as the "reorganization," actions intended to rescue the magazine from its desperate condition. Before describing these events, we must define the framework that binds them together.

What has muddled the history is that, in *Weird Tales* evidentiary documents, the single term "reorganization" has been applied to different events. For one example, after Lovecraft heard from Henneberger, he wrote Baird on February 3 that "[Henneberger] spoke of a coming reorganization . . ."[307] For an opposing example, Otis Adelbert Kline, in his 1941 history of the magazine, wrote: "[The Anniversary Issue] was a three months combined issue [May-June-July 1924], and was left on the stand for three months. Then the magazine was reorganized . . ."[308] Lovecraft's comment refers to the very beginning of the process, and Kline's to the final, sudden outcome. The statements are at odds because they are using different definitions of "reorganization." What Henneberger set in motion in January was completely different than what finally resulted.

In sum, the process can be thought of as having two parts: first, Henneberger's intention to reshape the editorial configurations of *Detective* and *Weird Tales*, and the working out of that intention step-by-step, during which components of the plan shifted significantly; and second, the actual execution of a completely different plan, which included dividing the assets of the Rural Publishing Corporation between Henneberger and his near-silent partner, J.M. Lansinger. In the beginning, "reorganization" referred to a set of large-scale editorial changes; in the end it referred to the splitting of the company; in between, lay the failures of Henneberger's intentions. The single constant, from beginning to end, was the need to install the right personnel; in particular, to assign *Detective* and *Weird Tales* to separate editors.

As one historic year ended and another began, conditions were quite unsettled in the offices of Rural. The magazine hadn't taken off like

Henneberger's dreams had prophesied. Pressures had mounted behind the scenes, then become embarrassingly public in the pages of *The Author & Journalist* when the increasingly uncomfortable editor Baird called out the owner by name. Debts continued to rise along with the pulse-rates of unpaid contributors. The magazine had just skipped another issue: December. This would become apparent to readers when the January issue finally landed on newsstands. The decision to skip undoubtedly had a large financial motive behind it, but it may also have afforded an opportunity to restore the original circa-the-18th publication date which had been lost when the July issue was skipped.

Henneberger blamed "unscrupulous dealers" for some of his problems,[309] which probably meant that he was receiving more returns on unsold copies than he thought legitimate. Times were bordering on the desperate. Something had to be done.

The first evidence that a plan was afoot is found in Lovecraft's correspondence: his February 2 reply to Henneberger's late-January missive, in which his remarks are respectfully diplomatic; a February 3 reply to Baird; and Lovecraft's immediate descriptions to friends of the *Weird Tales* situation, in which Lovecraft could be as frank and forthcoming as he wanted. Lovecraft heard about the plan from Henneberger and Baird because he figured in it.

Henneberger divulged to Lovecraft the reason for the impending reorganization: the financial plight of the company. Rural had entered business $11,000 in the black and sunk to $40,000 in the red, a loss of $51,000.[310] Most of the money was owed to the Cornelius Printing Company, of Indianapolis. There is every reason to believe—but no specific, supporting evidence—that Cornelius supplied the motivation that Henneberger applied to his reorganization plans. We strongly suspect that the printer issued an ultimatum after the first of the year: either the debt stopped growing and reversed direction, or the line of credit would be discontinued.

It would have made for dire but not quite fatal news. Henneberger knew that salvation was possible. He'd been thirty-grand in the hole with *The Collegiate World* before a quick fix—redesigning around the humor column and retitling the magazine *College Humor*—had turned the tide and made Rural possible. Henneberger hadn't forgotten those lessons. He'd been experimenting with the configuration of *Weird Tales* all along, endlessly experimenting, but had no significant improvement in fortunes to show for it. It had all been half-measures, moves made in the margins. Bolder measures were called for—big thinking and urgency—without which everything could be lost. *Weird Tales*, as it was originally configured, had been the magazine he wanted, so he had been reluctant to undertake a major overhaul. But that luxury was no longer affordable. The magazine had to attract a larger readership.

He was enough of an optimist and a salesman to practically guarantee Cornelius a turnaround. In such a conversation, he would have loudly discussed his triumphant past and urged patience. By God he could work the same magic again!

The key to rejuvenation lay in the content. "I shall watch the modified future of WEIRD TALES with keen interest," Lovecraft wrote Henneberger, "looking with especial avidity for your own work, since you so emphatically share my aversion for the insipid rubber-stamp popular magazine atmosphere."[311] In other words, the root problem, as Henneberger had conveyed to Lovecraft, was not that the magazine was too "unique" but—surprisingly—that it was too commercial. Lovecraft wrote Long, "they are desperately in need of material which is basically unconventional."[312] He advised his friend to send the magazine "lots and lots of terrible things." If anything deserved the mantle of unconventional, it was Henneberger's strategy. Counterintuitively, he sought financial salvation by making the content more radical, more Lovecraftian, proving his true belief in the cause.

Henneberger's discovery of the unconventional Lovecraft certainly contributed to his awakening sense of possibilities, the chance that unconventionality and success might serve each other. The main purpose of the late-January letter seems to have been to tell Lovecraft where he might fit into the changes. Henneberger proposed replacing the magazine's dependence on a large number of shorter pieces with "a novel and two or three short stories per issue."[313] He hoped that Lovecraft would be able to supply a 25,000-word novel, which would obviously be a boon to the author's pocketbook.[314] Lovecraft replied: "My main novel idea is that of a long phantasy to be called (subject to change) 'Azathoth', dealing with bizarre scenes somewhat in the exotic spirit of the Arabian Nights." He then averred that it would be inappropriate for *Weird Tales*, "since it will be horrible only in parts." As an alternative, he proposed a yet-to-be-written story called "The House of the Worm."

The boldest element of the plan was to incorporate in some capacity Henneberger's acquaintance, the great magician and escape artist, Harry Houdini.

A final element of the plan got lost in translation between Henneberger and Lovecraft. The author wrote Baird describing one of Henneberger's proposed changes to *Weird Tales* as "the elaboration of gruesome crime material at the expense of fiction."[315] As we will see in more detail, this was to be the main adjustment to *Detective Tales*.

These then were the initial plans, plus the change in editorship. How it would play out—how any plan plays out—is another story.

. . .

For the plan to succeed, the right editors had to be in place, canny professionals who could work hard and correctly make the myriad decisions that go into producing a magazine.

In his late-January letter, Henneberger revealed to Lovecraft a highly-sensitive matter: that he was leaning toward removing Baird from the editorship of *Weird Tales*. Baird, it seems, was taking the blame for the magazine's conventionality, despite his nurturing of Lovecraft. Lovecraft did his best to defend the editor he'd unexpectedly grown to respect:

> I feel that he must have done very well on the whole, considering the adverse conditions encountered in the quest for really weird stories. That he could get hold of as many as five perfectly satisfactory yarns is an almost remarkable phenomenon in view of the lack of truly artistic and individual expression among professional fiction-writers. When I see a magazine tending toward the commonplace, the last people I blame are the editors and publishers . . .[316]

He went on to place the blame where he thought it truly belonged, on America's "very conventional and half-educated public." Returning to the Baird matter a second time, he invoked his knowledge of publishing gained from the amateur press world:

> when I read WEIRD TALES, and note here and there a story full of hackneyed stuff---the laboratory, the club-room with well-groomed men around the fire, the beautiful queen of remote planets, the ghost that is a human villain trying to scare somebody out of a house…etc. etc.…I never think of blaming Mr. Baird; for out of a somewhat wide knowledge of non-eminent writers, gained through various club affiliations, I am perfectly well aware that he had to take the stuff because no man living could get enough of anything else to fill the required number of pages at the required intervals.[317]

The day after writing Henneberger, Lovecraft wrote Long, proclaiming, "I see how solidly I stand with both Baird and Henneberger,"[318] and then, four days later, wrote Long again, saying that Henneberger "proposes . . . installing Farnsworth Wright . . . as editor."[319] In fact, Baird continued as editor for some time longer.

Baird's position was in jeopardy and the failure of the magazine to connect with a larger audience was the foundation of Henneberger's disgruntlement. But was there more to it?

As Baird's year started, he was up to his eyebrows in work. As he concluded *The Eyrie* of February 1924, written in early January: "We are pretty busy these winter days, what with conducting two magazines and watching the progress of our new book, but we always take time to read and answer every letter we get." Some of those replies went to the teenaged Robert Barbour Johnson, as he describes:

> I was planning to become a professional writer, among other things, but though weird tales were my favorite reading, my earliest writings were along quite different lines. However, I did manage to do a couple of very short tales, submitted them. Edwin Baird, the magazine's first editor, didn't publish them (for which I'm thankful). But he was most cordial, wrote me personal letters and encouraged me to keep on trying. Had he known I was merely a precocious high school boy, he might not have been so enthusiastic![320]

The only reason we know of Baird's letters to Johnson is that Johnson eventually landed in the magazine. Who knows how many weird-inclined wannabes Baird replied to, writers who never made it into print?

"Our new book," which Baird referred to, was *Fay*, published in November 1923, his second and last novel to be published in hardcovers. (He had published additional novel-length works in the pulps.) Fay is a young woman of the Tennessee mountains who flees her roots for New York grand opera success before answering the call of her abandoned romance back home.

In an unusual move, *Weird Tales* printed two ads for *Fay*.[321] The first, a third of a page in the February issue, was ostensibly run by the novel's New York publisher, Edward J. Clode. The text of the ad implied that Baird—unbelievably—had written *Fay* while editing Rural's two fiction magazines: "As editor of WEIRD TALES, Edwin Baird has read thousands of stories of almost every sort. Some were good and some were bad, and some fell in between. Then he decided to write a story unlike any of these."[322] As if he weren't busy enough. The second ad, April, occupied a full page, filled with testimonials from nineteen newspapers, and a coupon for ordering the book from the Rural publication address.[323] The offer for the mainstream novel was unlikely to have resonated with the genre readers of *Weird Tales*; if Fay had been a lady werewolf or a goddess of unholy destruction, the outcome may have been otherwise. Though well-reviewed in the press, *Fay* failed to follow up the commercial success of Baird's first novel, *The City of Purple Dreams*.

If Henneberger had donated the ad space to Baird's publisher, or expected a better return on selling *Fay* through the full-page ad, the *Fay* experience may have been an irritant. Baird, by 1924, had made a number of moves which were likely to have made Henneberger consider the alternatives. It started with Baird's cavalier attitude toward the readers, as expressed in his acerbic comments in *The Eyrie*: funny to some and perhaps not to others. It could only have made matters worse when Baird called out Henneberger by name in the December *Author & Journalist*, as the culprit behind the slow payments to authors.

To Henneberger's aging memories, the issue was Lovecraft. In one of his 1960s letters, he claimed that Baird and Wright shared his "high regard" for Lovecraft.[324] However, in a separate recollection he revealed: "The nominal editor of Weird Tales [in the first year] was one Edward [*sic*] Baird but I made it a point to read anything that Lovecraft submitted and it was published, sometimes over the objections of Baird. This probably resulted in Wright's tenure."[325] Since Henneberger's memory failed him on numerous details, we feel free to interpret his remarks broadly.

Henneberger implied that Baird was his puppet in handling Lovecraft, a radical suggestion given that the Baird-Lovecraft relationship, as we have documented, proceeded with the normal fits and starts of any editor-author relationship, starting with the retyping issue and ending with mutual regard. There is no hint of external guidance. Henneberger's memories better fit his romanticized recollection of "discovering" Lovecraft in *Home Brew* and bringing him to the world.

If Baird did handle Lovecraft exclusively before Henneberger actually "discovered" him in his own magazine, there would still be room for friction. If Henneberger had recognized Lovecraft's importance and then found out how Baird's insistence on retyping the five manuscripts had delayed his entry into the magazine, he may very well have been annoyed. With all the back and forth, Lovecraft only appeared in *Weird Tales* once in 1923. If Baird had immediately acted on the five manuscripts by, say, taking them as-is or retyping them in-house, all five stories could have appeared in the magazine by the November issue. And, perhaps, in Henneberger's thinking, a new wave of unconventionality could have been unleashed in time to rescue the magazine.

One area on which Baird may reasonably have balked was the fiction Lovecraft collaborated on with his friends, the work of Sonia H. Greene and C.M. Eddy, Jr. These stories were published without Lovecraft's byline and rank low in the greater Lovecraft canon. It's easy to imagine Henneberger wanting to placate Lovecraft's every wish, even if it meant accepting substandard material from his literary circle, with Baird arguing that every contributor compete on the basis of merit.

While the details of the working relationship between Henneberger and Baird remain murky, there is a sense of a growing schism that Henneberger allowed to fester, perhaps because, in addition to other matters, he was intimidated by Baird's personality or professional attainments. Baird was older by only four years, but he possessed deep experience in writing and publishing and, as we have seen, was not reluctant to express and repeat strong views. Perhaps Henneberger found him exceedingly difficult to negotiate with. At the same time, Baird was doing a tremendous amount of work, both on *Detective* and *Weird Tales*; thus the question of replacing him was not so straightforward.

This brings us to the final indignity in the fracturing relationship: "The Transparent Ghost." As a story, it is trivial in the history of weird fiction, but oversized in shaping the fate of *Weird Tales*.

It all began in the November 1923 *Eyrie*. Baird opened by telling readers of his dilemma in deciding whether to publish a new submission:

> We don't know what to do with it. We don't know whether it's a masterpiece of weird literature, or a new interpretation of the Einstein Theory, or a puzzle picture, or what it is. And so we're going to submit it to our readers. We're going to print the letter that accompanied the manuscript; and we ask you to read this letter, and then (remembering that the manuscript is written in the same matchless style) tell us whether or not you want us to print the story.

This is the letter, exactly as it was published in the column:

> Mr. Edwin Baird, Editor, of the Wierd Tales.
>
> Dear Sir Your Name hase been sent to me that you are in the market for short Stories. and I am going to send you one of my manuscripts. of one of my short stories. The Name of the Storie is—The Transparent Ghost, After you have looked and read my Manuscript, of this short storie and if you think you want it for your magazine, plese let me know at once and if you think you cant youse it you will find Postage. Stamps to return it back to me and if you have a plase in you magazine for it let me know soon as posaballe I have a few more short stories one Detective storie and if you like this one I would like to send to you my manuscript of the Detective Storie
>
> Hoping to here from you soon and al so that you can youse thas Storie of the Transparent Ghost in your magazine,
>
> and also that I my Have the pleasure of writing sevril more Stories for you
>
> Resp. yours
>
> Please Adress all my letters to the adress below.
>
> Mrs, D. M. Manzer.
>
>   Amarillo. Texas,
>   Gen. Del.
>
> But as the Author to all my Stories is to be as my name is asined below
>
> Author of the
>
> Transparent Ghost, Mrs. Isa-belle Manzer.

Additionally, Mrs. Manzer inserted the pages of the manuscript into the envelope out of order, which Baird didn't figure out for awhile, leading him to comment: "Another remarkable feature of this extraordinary yarn is that you may start reading it at any point and lose none of its charm. You can read it forward, or backward, or either way from the middle—and you'll never know you're off the track. A most unusual tale!"

As Baird suggests, reading the letter tells you all you need to know about the story, from its ludicrous title to its slapdash writing. It was obviously a prank. The byline, however, was not fake. Not completely. A housewife from Amarillo, her birth name was Hattie Belle.[326]

Opinions on whether to publish the story came pouring in—according to Baird. He started printing them in the February issue. The first was a pastiche of Mrs. Manzer's style: "I sincerely hope that you will publish Mrs. Manzer's 'storie' in WEIRD 'TAILS.' I have a creepy feeling that it will be the weirdest 'tail' that has ever been written or wagged." A second thumbs-up read: "By all means (this may be regarded as a vote) let us have this masterpiece of (undoubtedly) weird fiction: 'The Transparent Ghost,' even at the risk of causing the inimitable Poe to go through the proverbial change of posture in his tomb." The parade of letters continued with Baird claiming that the majority of respondents favored printing the story. He took delight in the comic forces that had been unleashed. After the year-plus of sorting through the daily slush pile, he was finally getting revenge on his predicament. And so, with the majority having yelped in the affirmative, he kept his word and published the story, to the best of our knowledge Hattie Belle Manzer's only published work.

Publishing it at all was bad enough, but Baird magnified the offense by actually running it as a three-part serial, beginning in the February issue. It didn't take up a lot of space, accounting for two, two, and one pages, respectively, but there remained the opportunity cost of the legitimate material that was squeezed out. And, once having started it as a serial, the magazine was committed to seeing it through, regardless of a potentially bad reception. Baird's positive response from his correspondents didn't necessarily reflect the response that the readership as a whole might have taken.

As for the story itself, Baird published it without alteration. "The Transparent Ghost" is not literally unreadable, but it is morally unreadable. Like Hattie Belle's letter, it's dense with random misspellings, improper capitalizations, variable punctuation, missing spaces, etc., yet contains enough solid phraseology and plot flow to assure the sagacious reader that Hattie Belle was putting one over. The point of the exercise seemed to be to break as many writing rules as possible. The story followed the exploits of Doctor Daily, who discovered a gas which when inhaled rendered him invisible for three days . . . and so forth. . . . To further synopsize the plot would be to perpetuate the pointlessness of its publication.

Baird's actions failed the magazine on several levels. Running the story smacked of desperation, suggesting that Baird had abandoned the ostensibly serious aims of the magazine. At the end of the second installment, the teaser for the next month's conclusion read, "Get It! Read It! Then Try It on Your Banjo!" It was as if the editor had finally been degraded into a punch-drunk madman determined to burn the house down.

Further, publication of the story bent the magazine's conceptual definition of "weird" beyond recognition. Absent was the unsettling Poe sense of the weird, or, as the magazine advertised their wares, gooseflesh fiction. Baird had substituted weirdness in authorial behavior for the verisimilitude of a good story.

Further, since the story was clearly a prank, Baird made the magazine the willing victim, opening it up to ridicule, promoting rather than filtering out the "rubbish" he had been grousing about for a year. And in the remote chance that it was not a prank, Baird was doing Hattie Belle no favor by making her vulnerable to public ridicule. In the March *Eyrie*, Baird allowed a lone correspondent to make a case against publication:

> [The quality of the story], apparent in the letter, would make a farce of your magazine. Writers could never be sure whether their contributions were accepted by you for the artistic merit such contributions contained, or for the laugh or amusement that you wished to afford your readers. Those having the desire to develop into good writers of fiction are usually serious, take their work in a serious manner, and hate to be laughed at. You would find that the "Unique Magazine" was deteriorating, for lack of material, into a travesty of the type of story it started with.

Baird adamantly disagreed with the writer: "That story HAD to be printed. It fairly howled for printer's ink, and we couldn't deny its plea. We shall have more to say of this story next month." But Baird wouldn't get the opportunity to say more, for the March *Eyrie* was his last.

Finally, while the humor of "The Transparent Ghost" was juvenile, the idea of including humor at all in *Weird Tales* was a dubious proposition. In a 1927 interview, Farnsworth Wright was asked whether the magazine accepted humorous stories. "Not a chance," he answered. "A while ago we featured a humorous story which we thought everybody would appreciate, and the next month our circulation dropped fifty percent. Weird stories are what the readers clamor for, and if there is humor in them, it must not spoil the effect."[327] He didn't name the story. It could have been "The Transparent

Ghost," or even his own unfortunate "The Great Panjandrum" (November 1924), the sixth and final Wright story to appear in *Weird Tales*.

If failing the magazine was a dereliction of duty, Baird's biggest blunder was in failing his employer. Henneberger had been clear—and sincere—from the start about his literary ambitions for *Weird Tales*. He considered Poe a great writer and wanted the magazine to perpetuate his legacy. "The Transparent Ghost" slapped those ideas across both cheeks, making a parody of Poe and the very concept of good writing. How could Baird not have realized that he was needling the boss where it mattered most? . . . Or maybe that was the point.

As evidence of how troubled Henneberger was, in his late-January letter he sounded Lovecraft out on "The Transparent Ghost" while discussing Baird's tenure. Lovecraft would write Morton a few weeks later: " 'The Transparent Ghost' nearly killed Henny. He froths at the mouth if ya speak of it, since he thinks it's the cheapest kind of cheap joke."[328] In his 5,000-word reply to Henneberger, Lovecraft jumped into the imbroglio in his second paragraph, its immediacy suggesting that it had been a priority concern in Henneberger's missive:

> I assure you that I was not at all disconcerted by the presence of "The Transparent Ghost" beside my "Hound". In the first place, I don't take myself too seriously; and in the second place, I can appreciate the sort of humour involved in such touches of "comic relief"---like the gravedigger in "Hamlet" or the porter in "Macbeth".[329]

Lovecraft cautiously refused to find fault in the magazine's policies even when the owner himself had called them into question, for that would have meant siding against Baird. And signing his name to it. Lovecraft went on to say that the story might very well be appropriate for the general readership of the magazine, a group we know the erudite Lovecraft held in low regard. In evaluating the situation at large, he reasoned that since Baird had made such an issue of "unacceptable manuscripts . . . the whole subject of impossible contributions has become a live issue, so that the exploitation of some comically illiterate attempt carries a piquancy which [most readers] can feel and smile at even though others may find it somewhat tedious and inapropos." We can assuredly count Lovecraft among the "others," even while he argued that the story would "make many friends for the magazine." It's not an argument that necessarily would have impressed Henneberger, since he may have deemed Baird's public crusade against bad manuscripts an irritant.

In his third paragraph, Lovecraft responded to the threat that "The Transparent Ghost" had created for the editor's tenure: "I hope, anyway, that this matter won't be instrumental in deposing Mr. Baird from the editorship until he is himself ready to relinquish it."

Lovecraft, in all his defenses, had done his best to calm the waters from afar, to rationalize Baird as an innocent victim in the "Transparent Ghost" mess. If Lovecraft had wanted to sabotage Baird, say, as revenge for insisting that the initial five manuscripts be retyped, or just for being Baird, Henneberger presented him the golden opportunity on a gilded platter and Lovecraft refused to take it.

Nevertheless, the tide had turned against Baird. Henneberger's mind was near made up when he wrote Lovecraft, and Lovecraft never found the magic words to save Baird. Baird's reign as the first editor of *Weird Tales* was rapidly drawing to a close.

In the numerous histories of *Weird Tales*, the failures of the first year are usually attributed to Baird alone but, as we have seen, there were many misjudgments along the way, many of them Henneberger's. There was plenty of blame to go around, if blame need be assigned. We prefer to look at it as the growing pains of a pioneering venture. And one of those pains was the discovery that Baird, while a suitable fit for *Detective Tales*, was a poor fit for its weird sister. The unique magazine required a unique perspective, or, in other words, *Weird Tales* needed a weird editor.

Baird's basic problems were a lack of genuine interest in the subject matter and a failure to understand the magazine's potential readership. He may have had an intellectual appreciation for weird fiction, and the legacy of Poe, but it never registered with him emotionally. He didn't believe in that fictional milieu. Baird's gifts rendered him prosaic when he needed to be imaginatively inspired. These themes are reflected over and over in *The Eyrie*, where, exemplified by the debate over "The Transparent Ghost," Baird built a cult of admiration for his jaded sense of humor more than he cultivated an appreciation for weird fiction. *The Eyrie* revealed far more of what he didn't like than what he did. What really turned him on? "The Transparent Ghost" turned him on. He was never more excited than he was when presented with the final proof of his prejudice, that most weird fiction was rubbish and that most readers were as cynical about it as he. The story forced his basic deficiencies for the job to the surface. In the long run, he was never going to be able to take *Weird Tales* as seriously as Henneberger expected and Henneberger finally reached that conclusion. He just needed a reliable replacement.

On March 18, 1924, Lovecraft wrote his Aunt Lillian: "You will note the absence of 'The Eyrie' in this issue [of *Weird Tales*]—which no doubt marks the passing of the Baird regime."[330] March 18, presumably, was the day when the April issue landed on newsstands, the first issue without *The Eyrie*. Lovecraft drew the correct inference, but he required the April issue for confirmation. That he wrote on the day of the issue's availability demonstrates how important the issue, and perhaps every issue, was to him; this one contained "The White Ape," his poem "Nemesis," and the Eddy collaboration, "The Ghost-Eater." His speculative comment on Baird confirms that Henneberger had only hinted at what was going on behind the scenes.

The Baird regime had passed at *Weird Tales*, but he had not been fired; that is, shown the door. In fact, he remained active at Rural Publishing until the impending schism, when Rural split into two companies. It would be more accurate to say that Baird's responsibilities within Rural had been realigned. One level of editing a magazine addresses author relations and the assembling of content; a higher level addresses the management of staff and other business matters. Baird remained the content editor of *Detective Tales* while still acting as managing editor for both *Detective* and *Weird Tales*. Because he stayed on, it's unlikely that there was some dramatic blow-up between he and Henneberger. In fact, Henneberger was probably diplomatic in how he handled the shift. It's clear he'd been thinking about the problem for some time. While troubled by some of Baird's choices, he was also grateful for—and dependent on—all he'd done since the inception of the company. Henneberger could have solved the Baird problem without confronting him by simply explaining that he'd decided two magazines were burdensome for a single editor and, because *Detective Tales* appeared to be Baird's preference, that would be his sole editing responsibility in the reorganization. If Baird hadn't taken a pay cut, he may not have minded the change at all. Lovecraft assumed otherwise: "I'm kinda sorry if it cuts into his incomin' heavy metal, for I like the guy—but Fate is Fate."[331]

With the impending reorganization, Henneberger had been forced to consider alternatives for the *Weird Tales* job. He had two plausible candidates in arm's reach: Baird's assistants Otis Adelbert Kline and Wright. Kline would have been the lesser choice because of his lack of experience and preoccupation with his lucrative position at Massey & Massey. That left Wright, the strangely haunted man who never spoke of his past. If Henneberger had wanted the weirdest editor available, Wright more than qualified. But Henneberger must have considered Wright untested, or perhaps Wright had equivocated about taking the job. He, too, had other work: his music journalism. Thus, Wright was appointed interim editor while Henneberger considered splashier alternatives.

The next question is when this happened. On February 19, Lovecraft wrote Morton that he was "hearin' damn near every day from Henneberger."[332] Henneberger must have done his share of thinking aloud on the mutating reorganization, inspiring Lovecraft to gossip to Morton: "*Don't spread this in advance*, because the victim han't been tipped off yet, but (*whisper*) Leetle

Bairdie is gonna be unhooked from *W.T.* in May, Farnsworth Wright reigning in his place. He'll continue with *Detective Tales*, though."[333]

However, the other available facts point to the replacement happening sooner, perhaps right after February 19. To begin, Baird's last *Eyrie* appeared in the March issue, which arrived on newsstands February 18. In the column, he promised to say more about "The Transparent Ghost" in the April issue, an opportunity which never arrived. Therefore, he must have finished editing the March issue by himself before being informed of the change in editorship. The most reasonable time for Henneberger to make the switch would not be mid-cycle in an issue's progress but at the very beginning of the cycle, which makes mid-to-late February a fair estimate. Wright's first issue as interim editor, then, with Baird looking over his shoulder, would have been April, which awarded him the dubious honor of publishing the final installment of "The Transparent Ghost"—as if he had a choice.

There is clear evidence that Wright started making decisions for the magazine in conjunction with the preparation for the April issue and beyond. E. Hoffmann Price noted that Wright accepted his first story in March 1924.[334] Arthur J. Burks, who would feature in the magazine for several years, sold numerous stories to Wright in the approximate period of late March through the end of April. On March 30, Lovecraft wrote his aunt that "The magazine is now under its new editor, Farnsworth Wright," and that Wright had accepted Long's first story for the magazine ("The Desert Lich," November 1924). Wright recalled: "When the manuscript of 'The Desert Lich' was received in the office of WEIRD TALES, the editor read it and then uttered a loud cry of 'Eureka.' The story was accepted so quickly that it must have made Mr. Long's head swim."[335] Wright had praised Lovecraft to Long, which Long dutifully reported to Lovecraft, who told his aunt, "of course the word of a mediocre commercial editor has no literary weight."[336] Finally, Wright wrote Long on April 7 to inform him that "The Desert Lich" had been typeset and that another story was under consideration, mentioning that he was "most anxious to take over the helm at Weird Tales as doing it part time and putting out a proper magazine is proving too difficult."[337] Wright was not only editing the magazine under duress in March, he was making an auspicious debut. All three authors—Price, Burks, and Long— made memorable contributions to the magazine.

But before Wright could graduate beyond his part-time, interim status, a rival would enter the scene.

THE MAGICIAN'S GHOSTWRITERS

The most dramatic and most visible element of the reorganization was the incorporation into *Weird Tales* of Henneberger's acquaintance Harry Houdini (1874-1926). The Great Houdini in *Weird Tales!* Magic times magic! How could it lose?

Houdini had taken to magic from an early age and perfected his skills on the road. His celebrated career really took off in 1898, when he dropped the standard tricks from his vaudeville act and focused on his escape artistry. Within a few years, he was one of the most popular acts on the Orpheum circuit. He never gave up on magic, though. Like any performer, he needed to keep the act fresh, to keep his public enticed with novelty and daring. Over the years, he added new escapes, new tricks, movie roles, and public service activities, making him one of the legendary entertainment personalities of the era. A New Yorker, he was no stranger to the big-time theater town of Chicago, an obligatory stop. Thus, the connection to *Weird Tales* was made effortlessly.

Henneberger described the manner of their meeting: "Not long after I had inaugurated *WEIRD TALES*, I had a call by Houdini at my Chicago office; he expressed more than usual enthusiasm for the magazine, and the meeting resulted in a friendship lasting until his untimely death a few years later."[338] The probable time for this call was during the week of May 13, 1923, when Houdini headlined the vaudeville bill at Chicago's State-Lake Theatre.[339] The visit started more than a friendship, though. In 1924, at a time when Lovecraft or Quinn—the two star writers—might have ascended to the first-rank of *Weird Tales* personalities, instead the irresistible interloper Houdini swooped in to the head of the line.

In his February 2 reply, Lovecraft commented on this jewel in Henneberger's plans: "The acquisition of Houdini ought to be a great selling asset, for his fame and ability in his spectacular line are vast and indisputable."

However, Houdini received no mention in the February issue, put to print in mid-January, suggesting that Henneberger's plans for Houdini were either undreamed of or still up in the air. By the time of Henneberger's letter to

Lovecraft, the plans were taking shape. As Lovecraft continued:

> I did not know that [Houdini] writes, or that he possessed such a notable library as you describe. Certainly, it will afford me unmeasured delight to meet this library and its versatile owner---a thing the more probable because, although not much given to long trips, it is very likely that I shall live in New York after the coming spring. I suppose his articles naturally would have the imperfect background you mention, because he has been mainly accustomed to expressing his personality in different ways. I can tell better after seeing the one in the March issue. Perhaps Houdini furnishes an instance of the condition I mentioned before---the creator of genius who needs a re-writer to give his recorded work the form which may perfectly express its spirit.

The revelations from this passage are that Henneberger was planning on personally introducing Lovecraft to Houdini, that Houdini would write articles for *Weird Tales*, that Lovecraft assumed they would be rewritten, and that the first would appear in the March issue which, at the time of Lovecraft's letter, was in an advanced state of preparation.

The finalization of the plans undoubtedly took place during the week of February 11, 1924. On that Monday, Houdini returned to the State-Lake for a five-night stand. At the end of the week, he announced that he would be giving a lecture series on "fraud mediums," and that he was "under contract to furnish a series of articles of the same subject to 'Weird Tales.' "[340] Considering what actually happened, the probable terms of the contract were that: 1) Houdini received a fee for the use of his name and likeness, that 2) he would be cover-featured, that 3) he would contribute article ideas to be written by ghostwriters arranged by Henneberger, and that 4) he would contribute to a monthly column.

Henneberger's motivation in signing Houdini is obvious. His fame and mesmerizing hold over the public imagination appeared to dovetail nicely with the needs of *Weird Tales*. Magicians, in conjuring the illusion of supernatural forces, are nothing if not weird, and the Houdini connection promised to boost sales significantly. Henneberger must have viewed Houdini's arrival as an act of divine providence, just the thing needed to shake up the magazine's image and fortunes at a time of urgent need.

For his part, Houdini may have welcomed a new national platform to replace the collapse of his film fortunes. He had appeared in a series of films beginning in 1919; the last two, putting his own money on the line, were produced by the Houdini Picture Corporation. The very last, *Haldane of the Secret Service*, which Houdini directed and starred in, was released on September 30, 1923.[341] It would be his last film. It remained to Charlie

Chaplin to prove that a vaudeville star could emerge a film auteur. Houdini's connection to *Weird Tales*, a suitable synergy between two weird entities, would put his image on magazine covers from coast-to-coast, without requiring him to do much in exchange. It also provided a potential tie-in to promotion for his new book, *A Magician Among the Spirits*, published in May 1924; though the book was only mentioned once in *Weird Tales*, buried in the Houdini biography which accompanied the first story.

Houdini was undoubtedly oblivious to the storms that had clouded *Weird Tales's* first year of business. In fact, Henneberger may have exaggerated the circulation. In March, Houdini reported that he was "connected with the publishing business, Weird Tales, a magazine of 150,000 circulation, being one of his interests."[342] This conflicts with information released later in the year by the Cornelius Printing Company, still printer of *Weird Tales*. They cited the circulation as 100,000.[343]

The term "interests" in that last quote is . . . interesting, and may mean nothing. It could also mean that Henneberger offered Houdini an interest in *Weird Tales*. We would not have mentioned it except that Henneberger, in a 1969 letter, gave a brief but ambiguously worded history of the ownership of *Weird Tales*, in which he raises the possibility: "Another man, Harry Houdini, died in 1928 [*sic*]. He was in the process of paying off some half-million dollars lost on motion pictures he made. Had he lived, he would have been an active associate of Weird Tales."[344] However, there's no evidence of Houdini's involvement with the magazine after the mid-1924 split.

At any rate, *Weird Tales* offered Houdini potential benefits, while risking little.

If, first, the contract with Houdini was signed the week of February 11 and, second, the March issue, the first featuring the magician, appeared on newsstands on February 18, then the timing for inserting him into the issue was extremely tight. We don't know how well Henneberger planned for the contingencies of including or excluding Houdini, but there are clues that the effort was rushed. The first adventure, "The Spirit Fakers of Hermannstadt," bylined "by Houdini," led off the issue. Curiously, it was the first of a two-part serial, the conclusion appearing in the April issue. The primary reason for splitting the story would have been to force the hooked-on-Houdini reader to buy the next issue. But that was unnecessary because the April issue was to have a new Houdini adventure, which it did. Therefore, "Spirit Fakers" was probably split because the ghost couldn't finish the entire story by the deadline. The artists were probably rushed, as well. Mally's cover painting for the March issue, borrowed liberally from the quintessential image of Houdini, is taken directly from the critical moment of the first installment. Naked and chained, he's trapped with a skeleton in a dark chamber, escape imperative. Heitman's interior was a stylish scene of a séance from early in the tale.

Baird's March *Eyrie*, his last—unbeknownst to him—led off with a nice introduction to Houdini and promises of the wonders to come. At the top of the page was an announcement for the *Ask Houdini* column that would start in the April issue, in which Houdini would respond to reader inquiries. On the one hand, the column needed a delay to allow readers to submit questions; on the other, it indicates that the hastened circumstances didn't allow for any Houdini commentary to be included.

Finally, if the issue did have to be significantly redesigned at the last minute, and Baird complained, it would have provided Henneberger another, and perhaps convenient, reason to relieve Baird of the editorship. The timing supports this possibility.

The first two Houdini adventures were not really "articles," as Henneberger and Houdini had advertised. That was another illusion. They were ostensibly true experiences written in first-person narration, in a fictional style. The underlying proposition was that Houdini supply themes based on his reputation, settings based on his worldwide touring, and plot ideas, and that Henneberger would have the stories written to order. There is no guarantee that the same author ghosted both stories, but they are similar in style. Henneberger recalled that: "[Houdini] often regaled me with experiences of his that rivaled anything I had ever read in books. Several of these I published, but they were written in such a prosaic style that they evoked little comment."[345] Indeed, they achieve all of their distinction from the presence of Houdini and his exploits and none from the quality of the writing, which is to say they read like competent but generic pulp stories.

In the sidebar to "Spirit Fakers," the magazine noted that it was "a story of his adventure never before recorded,"[346] lest anyone try to challenge its authenticity against existing information. They emphasized his unparalleled reputation and attainments and reinforced the themes that would appear in both of the first two stories: his skills as an escape artist and his role as a debunker of spiritualism. Of his escape artistry, they extolled:

> Volumes could be written of the various feats performed by this Master of Escape. Most of them are well known to practically every one who has seen Houdini in his numerous appearances before the American public. No man living today could equal Houdini in assembling a crowd if it were announced that Houdini would attempt one of his miraculous escapes.

And of his debunking and beliefs:

Houdini has always been profoundly interested in spiritualistic and psychic phenomena. He has personally known most of the leading spiritualists of the last thirty years and, strange to say, they are all intensely interested in Houdini from the fact that Houdini has never failed to duplicate any feat of so-called spiritualistic phenomena. He has never been able to discover one solitary fact that would convince him of spirit communication and years ago he made solemn compacts with fourteen of his closest friends that the one first to die would communicate with the survivor, through an agreed signal. The fourteen have passed on and Houdini still awaits their messages in respectful seriousness.

The challenge to the ghostwriter was to play up the danger of conflict between Houdini and fraud spiritualists, and place Houdini's escape act into a dramatic context, as his movies had.

"Spirit Fakers" catches Houdini on one of his European tours. He is approached by "Countess D—," who is being blackmailed by fake mediums on account of her late father, "Count D—," who was known to kidnap women and girls and imprison them in "Castle D—" in Transylvania. Obviously, the details are meant to invoke Bram Stoker's *Dracula*. At the castle, Houdini confronts the frauds, but is captured, stripped, chained, and handcuffed in a dark chamber, the scene illustrated on the cover. Handcuffs were a standard feature of Houdini's act. He's stripped to imply the lack of hidden tools, similar to the setups of his theatrical escapes. He escapes from Castle D— using the bones of the skeletons in the chamber as tools. The installment ends with a cliffhanger. The second part, in the April issue, opens with his escape into a river, still handcuffed, while the bad guys try to shoot him. He has to hold his breath underwater for a considerable time, which parallels the skill he demonstrated in his marquee Chinese Water Torture Cell escape, in which he's sealed upside-down in a metal-framed glass tank. He survives, extricates himself from the handcuffs, and eventually brings the villains to justice. While his standard escapes are featured in the saga, frustratingly for the reader, none of Houdini's real secrets are divulged.

The standalone story in the April issue, "The Hoax of the Spirit Lover" involves a woman being conned by a charlatan medium who brings her deceased fiancé back to visit her in a séance, the image illustrated on Mally's cover.

Speculation has circled around the question of true authorship for these first two Houdini stories. Joshi lists Walter Gibson as a leading candidate.[347] Gibson was a magician himself, a ghostwriter for Houdini and other magicians, and, in the 1930s, penned the landmark novels of The Shadow for the pulp magazine of the same name. From his qualifications, he's made to order. Other speculation centers on Lovecraft's collaborator, C.M. Eddy, who worked with Houdini but apparently didn't meet him until later in the year, and thus the timing doesn't work. But these people were outsiders. If Henneberger was in an extreme hurry to finalize the March issue on time, then the ghost was likely to be someone in Henneberger's immediate orbit, someone who could be dealt with in person. That creates three valid candidates: Baird, Kline, and Wright. All had published fiction; all were competent wordsmiths. Kline never hinted at it later, when keeping the secret would have been purposeless, so it's convenient to rule him out. Baird is a possibility, especially if he accepted the assignment as part of a reduction of his editing responsibilities. Lovecraft's theory was Farnsworth Wright.[348] In fact, in 1945 Henneberger claimed that Wright ghosted "Spirit Fakers,"[349] but by then Henneberger had a number of specific memories of the early days of *Weird Tales* which are provably false, so we are reluctant to accept any of them without corroboration. If his memory was correct, it certainly would make a nice—and nicely benign—addition to Wright's list of secrets. The argument against Wright is that if he took over editing for the April issue, he may not have had the time for the additional burden.

There is one last candidate, a writer who has been completely overlooked, someone with significant experience in writing spooky stories, someone who had been contributing to Rural publications since late 1922, and someone who was readily available to Henneberger. The author who fits that profile is Harold Ward. After appearing in the first two issues of *Weird Tales*, he next appeared in the May-June and July-August 1923 issues of *Detective Tales*. In 1924, he was at his busiest for the company, appearing with short stories in the February and March *Weird Tales*, and stories in the March, May, and June issues of *Detective Tales*. The two Houdini stories would fit into that wave of activity. But that's just an argument. There is one specific piece of evidence that ties Ward to the second Houdini story. The solution to the mystery in "The Hoax of the Spirit Lover" is that the deceased fiancé, a Chicago man, had an identical twin brother in Wyoming who his betrothed had never seen. The twin "was slowly dying of consumption and had gone west to work on a ranch in hope that the high altitude would help him." As part of an insurance swindle, he throws his lot in with the charlatan. By smearing his face with phosphorescent paint, he passes for his ghostly brother at the séance. Harold Ward was not a charlatan nor did he have a twin brother, but for three different periods he traveled west, to South Dakota as a tot for his mother's health, and twice to Colorado for his own. It's natural that in fleshing out Houdini's story ideas he would have drawn on his own past for inspiration; likewise, it's improbable that Wright, or one of the other candidates, would have picked a plot device so particular to Ward's life.[350]

. . .

The high-profile incorporation of Houdini into *Weird Tales*, while superficially a match made in heaven, was a radical departure for the magazine, no doubt a major part of its relevance to the reorganization. It represented a shift from supernatural fiction to "true" experiences told by a real-life celebrity. Henneberger may have realized how this tampered with the magazine's stated purpose, for while Houdini stories bore his byline and were cover-featured on the issues of March, April, and the May-June-July Anniversary Issue, the magician's image on the covers did a slow disappearing act. He dominated the March cover. The April cover illustrated a séance, but Houdini was barely recognizable, if at all, in the background of the image as a man in a business suit. In the Anniversary Issue's cover image of the pyramids, Houdini was not to be seen at all.

Note that *Weird Tales* had already experimented with true-story features to a slight degree, but never as a centerpiece of the magazine's content. The first attempt was a column called *The Cauldron*, which debuted in the June 1923 issue, authored, or more accurately, curated, by Preston Langley Hickey. The column printed two or three real-life tales from readers. The inaugural editor's intro, seemingly written by Baird, rolled out the welcome mat: "Readers who have had a hand in strange adventures, or who have been victims of experiences of a startling and terrifying nature, are cordially invited to send accounts of them to THE CAULDRON. . . . Manuscripts may be as horrible and hair-raising as it is in the power of the author to make them, but they must be clean from a moral standpoint."[351] Curiously, he added: "Double-spaced, typewritten manuscripts are preferred, but those in long hand will be considered if legibly written." This had to have been written very close to the time that he returned Lovecraft's single-spaced manuscripts, which were certainly superior to longhand. Perhaps Baird had entertained second thoughts. At any rate, *The Cauldron* only ran for four issues. The last installment appeared in the same issue (October) as Quinn's first edition of *Weird Crimes*, another true-story feature.

Making Houdini the front man of a true feature was a completely different proposition, much more than a change of pace. In essence, Houdini represented the opposite of what *Weird Tales* stood for. The magazine was devoted to making the supernatural and fanciful seem real to the reader. Houdini, on the other hand, was a devout rationalist who, in 1924, was devoting increasingly more time to debunking spiritualism. Baird recognized the fundamental contradiction and attempted to bridge the difference in the March *Eyrie* which introduced the "internationally famous mystifier":

> Houdini emphatically does not believe in occult superstitions, and he probably would deny, just as vigorously, that his miraculous escapes from prison cells and handcuffs are aided by disembodied

"spirits"—as so many believe they are. And yet there is no denying that many of his amazing exploits smack of the supernatural. No wonder his name is associated with things that cannot be explained!

In the narrow view, Houdini had of his own accord fallen into Henneberger's lap and Henneberger, desperate for miracles, jumped at the chance to invigorate the magazine, and merged the magician into his grand reorganization scheme, an act of sheer opportunism. The addition of Houdini falls into line with the experimental trend of the magazine. Henneberger, convinced of the rightness of his mission, was determined to find the winning formula.

In the broader view, Houdini's presence mirrors what was happening in the magazine business at large. It shows Henneberger falling under the influence of the growing Macfadden empire of true-story magazines. Bernarr Macfadden, a he-man exercise freak, had a modest publishing success with *Physical Culture*, which launched in 1899. He struck gold twenty years later with *True Story Magazine*, a monthly collection of yarns which would eventually be categorized as "first-person confessionals," ostensibly true stories told by down-to-earth people. The first issue, July 1919, made its purpose plain throughout its cover text: "Truth is Stranger than Fiction," "$1,000.$\underline{^{00}}$ in Prizes, for <u>Your</u> Life Story," "Romance, Adventure, Business," "Stories from Life." *True Story* was so rapidly and hugely successful, it allowed Macfadden to create a publishing empire that dominated newsstands for decades. Of Macfadden's many magazines, the majority were confessionals.

As in all industry, a successful model breeds imitation. Macfadden attempted to duplicate its own popularity with magazines like *True Detective*, *True Confessions*, etc. Naturally, other companies took up the challenge. For example, Dell Publishing introduced *"I Confess"* in February 1922, a pulp featuring first-person romances. Its title was telling. While managing not to infringe on Macfadden's trademarks, "I confess" captured the essence of the approach: the revelation of deep, dark secrets coming from the sinner's own mouth.

Yes, truth can be stranger than fiction, and the truth is that there was precious little of it in the Macfadden magazines. The company had a large staff of writers who amplified reader submissions into more dramatic material, simply made it up, or published the inventions of freelancing pulp writers.

The imprint of the Macfadden approach was all over Houdini's presence in *Weird Tales*. The front cover text for the first tale read: "The Spirit Fakers of Hermannstadt, by Houdini, The Most Miraculous True Story Ever Written." The stories were written in the first-person to fool the reader into believing that Houdini was the true author, but the actual writing was farmed out to freelancers. The stories were unfailingly referred to as "articles," but were raisins of fact baked into a muffin of pure fiction. And they were consistently characterized as untold tales from Houdini's private life, and not exploits from show business, the world of make-believe theatrical performance. For example: "He has traveled to every nook and corner of the globe and in his note book are recorded some of his personal experiences in different climes that if one were not acquainted with the ability of the man, would sound like fiction of the most imaginative sort."[352]

The unuttered irony was that the man who exposed fraudulent spiritualists gladly participated in the construction of his own fake biography. That was nothing new. Houdini's persona, as it had evolved, had always been as much about the magic of publicity as the mystery of his art.

In the end, though, Houdini's inclusion in *Weird Tales* was only a flirtation with a new direction, not a fully committed change, despite what the covers implied. His stories were the only first-person "true" stories in the magazine. And once the three Houdini issues were published, and the company split up, *Weird Tales* returned to its native all-fiction, no flimflamery, state.

Because the true-trend in the magazine started and ended with Houdini, his celebrity, and a mere three stories, it may look anomalous. But recall that developments at *Weird Tales* generally paralleled those at *Detective Tales*. Their shift, at the same time, was explicit. With the May 1924 issue, the title was changed to *Real Detective Tales*—the "real" avoiding encroachment onto Macfadden's "true" territory—and its makeup altered. (Macfadden's *True Detective* began publication in 1925.) As Baird informed *The Author & Journalist*:

> Beginning with our May issue we are going to make important changes in the editorial policy of *Detective Tales*. We will feature stories and articles concerning the everyday work of the metropolitan police and the exciting adventures of real detectives. In addition, we shall continue to use detective and mystery fiction of every length up to 35,000 words but shall desire only stories possessing the ring of reality, stories so true to life that the reader will believe what he is reading. For this reason, first-person stories will be highly desirable.[353]

There would be no equivalent prospectus for the newly configured *Weird Tales* because the true-story element, the Houdini stories, would be handled in-house, not by freelancers.

The initiative of publishing a genuine weird/confessional hybrid eventually fell to Macfadden, a case of robbing the robbers to get the goods back. In 1926, they introduced *Ghost Stories*, the oddest of all their first-person confessionals. No mere flirtation with the concept, the magazine featured "true" stories of ghostly encounters, mostly written by freelancers, often with "as told to" before their bylines. The company refrained from titling the magazine *True Ghost Stories*, carefully wording their editorial material to leave the question of truth up to impressionable readers.[354] A minor servant in the Macfadden empire, *Ghost Stories* muddled along its dubious journey for over five years. Lovecraft despised the magazine. With customary derision, he told Long: "You will find it quite hopeless—even worse than *Weird Tales*. Indeed, its chief merit is to me the proof it affords that a magazine can be worse than Brother Farnie's [Farnsworth Wright]."[355] With a slight twist of fate, *Weird Tales* might have followed the doomed path of *Ghost Stories*.

XVI
A GRAND UNIFIED NEXUS OF WEIRD

When Henneberger wrote Lovecraft directly in late-January, cutting Baird out of the loop, the author's writerly characteristics had already been established, both from Baird's experience with him, and his detailed letters. Lovecraft was a meticulous craftsman, not a professional pulpsmith, as he divulged all too eagerly. He concerned himself more with commas than with deadlines. He was submitting great material, but there lingered an air of unpredictability around him. Therefore, when Henneberger conceived of the original reorganization plan, the order for the ghosting of Houdini's "articles" went to a reliable pro: most likely Harold Ward, as we have argued. The timing was too tight for an unknown quantity like Lovecraft. For the first Houdini story to be ready for the March issue, it had to be finished fast, in early February. Henneberger's concept for Lovecraft was longer-term, without a deadline; he was induced to supply a 25,000-word lead novel to fit a reconfigured magazine.

However, Lovecraft's detailed reply of February 2 spurred a change of heart by Henneberger. Presumably, this happened while Houdini was in Chicago the week of the 11th and signed the contract with Rural Publishing. As Henneberger recalled, "one day [Houdini] unfolded one astounding story of a trip to Egypt that I knew only a Lovecraft or a Clark Ashton Smith could do justice to."[356] Henneberger undoubtedly misremembered Smith as part of the calculation, since Smith was several years away from establishing himself as a fiction writer. But Lovecraft! . . . now there was a high concept straight from storyteller's heaven: the great writer of weird fiction ghostwriting the amazing Houdini's astounding tale of Egypt. The idea was too good to be true, too good not to be acted upon immediately. And so it was. The publisher apparently sent Lovecraft's letter to Houdini to establish the author's credentials for the job.[357]

Henneberger, the can-do businessman, donned his blinders in moving forward with the plan, envisioning only the wondrous results in store. He chose to ignore comments Lovecraft wrote in his reply: "Ordinarily I refuse altogether to write to order, or to give my tales any mechanical limitations to suit other people." Lovecraft explained that the *Home Brew* stories came about only because Houtain had been a friend. Henneberger was not a friend but his offer of a Houdini collaboration was so far out of the ordinary that Lovecraft's objections never materialized. In fact, he couldn't wait to tell Long of the offer, writing on February 14:

> Yes, Child, *Weird Tales* is certainly shovin' a lot of work at your aged Grandsire! Entire new job—to rewrite a strange narrative which the magician Houdini related orally to Henneberger; a narrative to be amplified and formulated, and to appear as a collaborated product—"By Houdini and H.P. Lovecraft." Henneberger demanded a telegraphed reply as to whether or not I'd accept the job, and promises INSTANT PAY on delivery! I wired him an affirmative, and am now at work familiarising myself with the geographical details of the Cairo-Gizeh locality where the alleged adventure is set— especially with the singular subterranean place betwixt the Sphinx and the second pyramid known as "Campbell's Tomb".[358]

Henneberger, with time of the essence, had offered a pay-on-acceptance deal which no other *Detective* or *Weird Tales* contributor, that we're aware of, received. But then Henneberger stunned Lovecraft by doing even better. On February 19, he exploded to Morton: "Oh gawd . . . Henny has *come acrost* wit' a cheque for ONE HUNDRED BERRIES! (No spoofin'—100— count 'em—100—Not a misprint."[359] One hundred dollars paid on faith alone. It was totally unprecedented for the impoverished company—and the impoverished author. As enthusiastic as Lovecraft was, the unsolicited payment shows that Henneberger matched him in intensity. An idea entered his head and he swooned with the possibilities, throwing money around as if Prohibition had just been repealed.

Lovecraft described the assignment in detail to Long and Morton.[360] He'd received a "specimen Houdini story" from Henneberger as a guide, probably the first part of "The Spirit Fakers of Hermannstadt." The specimen was surely inadequate in conveying Henneberger's expectations, compounded by the problem that Lovecraft had never examined a Macfadden magazine.[361] Consequently, Lovecraft took the specimen more as a challenge than a guide, an opportunity to show how a weird tale *should* be written, which was not the assignment.

Lovecraft's story was to be based on an incident involving Houdini during a sightseeing trip to Cairo. Houdini's Arab guide became involved in an altercation with another Arab. According to custom, they ascended the Great Pyramid to settle their dispute with fisticuffs. But it had all been a ruse to capture the "mighty wizard of the West" and put his legendary skills to the test. The two Arabs forced Houdini, bound and gagged, to the top of the second pyramid. Using a long rope, they lowered him through an aperture to the darkness of the crypt floor below. Hours later, Houdini staggered out of the pyramid's exit, having suffered a hideous and unspeakable experience. Lovecraft's job was to write the story and fill in the missing piece, giving it his "most macabre touches." Yet he was uncertain as to how realistic he was expected to be and how much "sheer imagination" Houdini would abide. He beseeched Henneberger to press the magician for clarification. In the meantime, he amused Morton—and himself—with the horrifying possibilities:

> I'll have them guides dress as mummies to scare the bound Houdini—yet have Hoody escape without encountering 'em. And then, when Hoodie takes the police to the scene, I'll have the guides found dead—strangled—chok'd lifeless in that ancient necropolis of the regal stiffs—*with marks of claws on their throats . . .* claws . . claws . . . principal & subordinate clawses . . . *which could not by any stretch of the imagination belong either to their own hands or to the hands of Houdini!!!* Brrr . . .[362]

The nature of the assignment gives another clue as to why Henneberger saw such exciting potential in this particular Houdini-Lovecraft collaboration. A theme which had emerged through two of Lovecraft's submissions was "the horrors that lie beneath." "Dagon" exposed the unknown life under the sea which expanded the bounds of reality to terrifying dimensions. "The Rats in the Walls," which Baird had accepted by December 4 and which would appear in the March issue, was an even stronger example. The narrator of "Rats," an American, purchases the abandoned Exham Priory in England, an estate that had been in the family, intending to restore it. After occupying the priory, his black cat becomes increasingly disturbed by the sound of rats scurrying through the walls. An ancient flight of stairs descending to a crypt is discovered. On a "hideous day of discovery," an exploration party enters the vast crypt and discovers "horror piled on horror," pits of human bones gnawed by rodents, the bones of centuries. It was only natural for Henneberger to make the connection between the horrors that Lovecraft's narrator discovered beneath Exham Priory and the ones that Lovecraft's imagination could unearth beneath the pyramid.

Lovecraft immersed himself in research. He began by giving Houdini the benefit of the doubt that a foundation of fact underpinned the tale. But that turned out to be a mirage. He wrote Long on February 25: "My Egyptian research at the library proved indubitably that Houdini's story is *all* a fake, and that there is no great sunken temples on the Gizeh pyramid-plateau."[363] His quandary was that Henneberger insisted on "literal verisimilitude." Thus, he delayed the writing while he mulled over the possibilities.

The importance of the assignment, to Lovecraft, Houdini, and Henneberger, made the work a major life event for Lovecraft. But Lovecraft found himself in a larger dilemma. He was actually juggling two major life events, with the clock relentlessly ticking. Henneberger asked for the story by Saturday, March 1.[364] And, on March 2, he was to move from Providence to New York City for a Monday marriage to Sonia H. Greene. He had too much to do. His obligations were on a collision course. Something had to give. With the deadline elapsed, on late Saturday he pulled an all-nighter,[365] like a student cramming for finals.

Lovecraft finished the story! But it would arrive late to Henneberger's hands.

On Sunday morning, in one of the most famous incidents in Lovecraft's life, disaster struck. In Providence's Union Station, the poor, sleep-deprived author stepped onto a New York-bound train, leaving the typed manuscript in the station. At the first opportunity, he purchased a lost-and-found ad, which appeared in Monday's *Providence Journal*.[366] The ad failed to produce the lost manuscript, but even before the realization of that outcome, with Henneberger's deadline slipping further behind by the minute, Lovecraft set to work doing the thing he hated most: typing. He half-finished the job on the morning of his wedding. Sonia helped on their wedding night by deciphering and dictating his handwritten manuscript while Lovecraft typed. And you can bet it was double-spaced. In Philadelphia for the honeymoon on Tuesday and Wednesday, the newlyweds completed the task.

It took a toll on Lovecraft. On March 9, by which time Henneberger had the manuscript, Lovecraft complained to his aunt of the headache "induced by the Houdini-Henneberger rush."[367] To Morton, he said: "BOY, that Houdini job! It strained me to the limit, & I didn't get it off till after we got back from Philly." Then he boasted about the story in vintage Lovecraftian style: "when I buckled down to the under-the-pyramid stuff I let myself loose & coughed up some of the most nameless, slithering, unmentionable HORROR that ever stalked cloven-hooved through the tenebrous & necrophagous abysses of elder night."[368]

It also took a toll on Henneberger's ambition to feature the story in the April issue (his "rush" and the March 1 deadline would have been meaningless if the story was targeted for May). Lovecraft's delay undoubtedly caused the story to miss the April deadline in the office. Not only was Wright rushing to put together his first issue as new interim editor, Lovecraft's story would need extra time since it would be cover-illustrated. On March 12, Lovecraft wrote Morton: "I have an idea Henny will have to stand for it, because it came in so late that there won't be a damn second to change it."[369] He was correct and Henneberger's inability to alter the text created a crisis.

Henneberger immediately conveyed his concerns to Lovecraft. On March 14, Lovecraft mailed the dispatch to Morton, which he mostly let speak for itself. The nature of Henneberger's complaint is implied in this passage of Lovecraft's: "Gawd knows what the bozo is really after, but as I says, why come to me if nameless phobic convulsions ain't wanted? It's clear the guy looks for some zippy dream stuff—dead Pharaohs doin' sinister shimmies by the light of pale torches—so what was an egg like me to do but take the cue?"[370] These comments refer, as we shall soon see, to the way Lovecraft let his fancies run wild in the final act of a story that was supposed to be a plausible incident in Houdini's life.

"Imprisoned with the Pharaohs," which led off the May-June-July Anniversary Issue, was an inspired effort by Lovecraft, worthy of his best work, and far more colorful and imaginative than the first two Houdini stories. It managed to seamlessly blend the product of his research, the requirements for "a Houdini *Weird Tales* story" as represented by Henneberger's specimen, and Lovecraft's own expression of cosmic horror. He plowed his research into the opening section which, as Joshi notes, has a travelogue quality. It's the kind of material that many pulp editors would have excised, to spare their thrill-seeking readers the didactic intrusion, and to spare themselves from paying the word-rate for library-book content. That it was left in reinforces Henneberger's artistic pretensions and, more important, his fear of altering Lovecraft's text. This opening section inspired Mally's cover illustration, a pleasant but rather bland depiction of the Great Pyramids and the Sphinx with nary a clue as to the epic wonders contained in Lovecraft's story, which dramatize events *inside* the second pyramid.

The story follows the same general model as the first two Houdini stories. Told in the first-person, it dramatizes Houdini's unique talents. The story is essentially one monumental feat of escape, owing to the framework that Houdini recited to Henneberger. Lovecraft's additions aren't as robust as in the other two Houdini stories. But he does include a nice sequence following Houdini's lowering, in bondage, to the floor of the cavern. Houdini needs to free himself but can't risk tugging on the descending line and alerting his captors to the escape attempt. Before he has time to solve this puzzle, the rope begins to fall on him, burying him in an "avalanche of hemp," and magnifying his challenge. Many words are expended describing the condition of his bondage and the suffering which he endures. Ultimately, though, as with the other two stories, none of Houdini's magical dexterity is exposed, leaving the fan underwhelmed with this aspect of the tale.

The worrisome payoff to the story is all in its Lovecraftian final act. He was clearly more inspired by the potentials for cosmic horror than in the techniques of escape. In this, the story goes ridiculously further than the other two. Bearing Lovecraft's inimitable stamp, it's a "confession" tale like no other. As Houdini struggles to find his way out of the cavern, he witnesses a ceremony and a monstrosity beyond belief, visions of an underground army of mummies and a terrifying thing of gargantuan proportions which emerged from a giant hole in the cavern floor. . . . Then, in the last sentence, in a cursory nod to Houdini's credibility, he exposed the fantastic finish as a dream, showing that Houdini was as phenomenal a dreamer as he was an escape artist. But how disappointing to the reader of fantasy. And how disappointing to Henneberger, to be stuck with a problematic text with no time for a rewrite. Nevertheless, Lovecraft had captured the great sense of underground scale that elevated "The Rats in the Walls" while topping it for imaginative splendor.

A fretful Henneberger traveled with the manuscript to Murfreesboro, Tennessee,[371] to seek the opinion of Houdini, who was completing his first-ever tour of the South. Bless his mysterious heart, he loved the story, which calmed Henneberger's frustrations with the delay and the dream sequence, and immediately reversed his outlook.

Houdini quickly sent Lovecraft a laudatory note.[372]

Better still, Henneberger elated Lovecraft with a second, and unexpected, $100 payment. "GLORIOUS REALITY! Mail just came, and in it the cheque ...... for another HUNDRED fish!"[373] Henneberger and Lovecraft had never discussed payment details for the Houdini collaboration. As Lovecraft had replied to Baird's queries: "Yes indeed, I have heard from Mr. Henneberger! Cheque? Bless me, no! Such details are so vulgar!"[374] He then confessed that because of the $40,000 "minus" that Henneberger had revealed he felt that he "ought to be a very meek and inaudible minus." In other words, Lovecraft was afraid to bring up the money question, content to discover his remuneration when the check arrived. In fact, in his 1923 letters, Lovecraft writes of waiting for payments, but never about rates or total amounts. Too vulgar. We can assume the payments were low. With the mounting debts, Henneberger could not afford the altruism of paying authors what the quality of their work deserved. He would not have approved a higher rate for any author unless forced into it, and Lovecraft would not have pressed the issue. Just the opposite, he foolishly confessed in his first letter to the magazine that "I pay no attention to the demands of commercial writing."[375] He was more interested in commas than cents. Finally, to repeat Otis Adelbert Kline's recollections, "material was bought as cheaply as they could possibly purchase it . . . They didn't pay any more than they had to."[376]

However, when Henneberger envisioned Lovecraft as an important leg of the reorganization, his attitude changed. Lovecraft became an investment in the magazine's survival, a hope realized when the author delivered quality work on the Houdini story.

In that light, the $200 total payment for "Pharaohs" merits further examination. The published story runs about 10,800 words, which probably means that Henneberger asked for something in the neighborhood of a round 10,000. Since its inception, Rural Publishing, for both *Detective* and *Weird Tales*, advertised a rate of "up to 1¢, on publication." Therefore, when Henneberger offered Lovecraft the job, he expected to pay him the top rate of 1¢/word for 10,000 words, or $100, the amount of the first check. With Houdini's unqualified approval, Henneberger doubled Lovecraft's rate with the second check to an unprecedented—for *Weird Tales*—rate of 2¢/word. Effectively, Lovecraft received a lower *rate* because of the additional 800 words which he essentially wrote for free. While those 800 words—the unnecessary travelogue material, if you will—took up space in the magazine, Henneberger, in his mind, didn't end up paying for it.

The payment had been highly satisfying to Lovecraft, and yet nothing is ever perfect to a perfectionist. First, his title, "Under the Pyramids," had been altered to "Imprisoned with the Pharaohs"—a clear improvement since it emphasizes the escape motif threading through the series. Lovecraft never complained, that we have discovered. As a commissioned work, he may have felt a reduced ownership over its particulars. Additionally, he may not have known about the alteration until the issue appeared, on approximately April 18, by which time he was ensconced in the life of a New York newlywed and less engaged with Henneberger's troubled publication.

The bigger issue to Lovecraft was Henneberger's broken promise on the story credit. In the original agreement, the byline was to be "By Houdini and H.P. Lovecraft."[377] To the relatively unknown Lovecraft, the linkage to the famous magician promised to be a tremendous boon to his name. And the byline made sense since Lovecraft had elevated himself above normal ghostwriting responsibilities, albeit without explicit authorization; he had served his own needs as a fantasist while serving Houdini's reputation as a preternaturally dramatic escape artist. But after gaining Houdini's approval, Henneberger wrote Lovecraft to renege on the joint byline. Lovecraft reacted scornfully, writing his aunt: "The Houdini story may appear without my name, for Henny is so dull that he doesn't see how a collaborated work can be written in the first person—he expected third, and indulged in several saline tears because I didn't write it thus!"[378]

It's a perfect example of Lovecraft misunderstanding the subtext. There are two more shades to the byline issue and neither occurred to Lovecraft. The charitable interpretation is that Henneberger made the promise in haste, before thinking through the need for consistency among the Houdini stories, and consistency with the broader plan of the reorganization, to recast more material in the popular first-person confessional format. Lovecraft, following the model of the specimen, dutifully wrote "Pharaohs" in the first-person.

The cold-blooded, and most plausible, interpretation is that since Lovecraft had been adamant about not "writing to order," Henneberger conned him into the job with the irresistible inducement of being mentioned in the same breath with the Great Houdini, a promise he never intended to keep.

In either case, Henneberger's claim of expecting a story in the third-person was just the excuse he came up with to justify Houdini's lone byline. Lovecraft's "saline tears" comment suggests that Henneberger had laid his argument on thick, to discourage Lovecraft from fighting him on the issue. Henneberger essentially used Lovecraft's tardiness in submitting the manuscript against him: since it had arrived late, there was no time to rewrite it in the third-person and therefore no opportunity for a joint byline. But, realistically, a third-person narrative was never in the cards.

In the growth of the confessional magazine world, it became a convention to list joint bylines in the form of, as it might have been in this case, "by Houdini, as told to H.P. Lovecraft," but Henneberger apparently never considered that possibility, and shouldn't have, since it would have implied that Houdini was not a full-fledged participant and was merely selling his name and reputation to *Weird Tales*. Adding Lovecraft's name would have suggested that the magician's assistant was necessary to the magic. The name of the legend needed to be as undiluted as the legend itself.

Nevertheless, for the astute *Weird Tales* reader, a joint byline would have made little difference. Anyone who had read the prior Lovecraft stories in *Weird Tales*—"Dagon," "The Picture in the House," "The Hound," "The Rats in the Walls," and "The White Ape"—would have borne no illusions that Houdini had written "Pharaohs" by himself. Dripping Lovecraft from every sentence, it was galaxies removed from the generic pulp style of its two ghosted predecessors.

As a final note on the byline issue, Henneberger recalled in 1969 that he "received scores of letters from readers for not giving due credit to Lovecraft." But his memory betrayed him once again when he claimed that it was Lovecraft who asked for his name to be removed from the byline. "This pleased Houdini," he said, "who received full credit for Lovecraft's work."[379] It's a further example of how integral Lovecraft's stature was to Henneberger's memories of *Weird Tales*.

Houdini did actually provide original written material to *Weird Tales*, namely his answers to reader questions in the *Ask Houdini* column. Baird teased the new feature in his last edition of *The Eyrie*:

> Houdini, Master of Escape, authority on the subject of spiritualistic and psychic phenomena and creator of the weird and mysterious, will answer through the columns of this magazine any rational question

that is deemed of general interest to our readers. No attention will be paid to questions regarding the solution of feats generally performed by Houdini but he will attempt to offer a scientific and logical explanation of any phenomena you may have witnessed or encountered in your private life.[380]

Within that passage is buried the fatal flaw to the column. Like the three ghosted stories, which depicted Houdini making seemingly impossible escapes without really explaining how, the column took discussion of his magic/escape act out of consideration. The column reflected his transition into lecturer and spiritualism debunker. But, again, this would disappoint a reader who preferred to believe in magic. The column and the three ghosted stories were at odds with the fantasy fiction of the magazine. Only Lovecraft's extravagant finish to "Pharaohs" attempted to bridge the divide.

In his foreword to the first edition of *Ask Houdini*, the magician pretended to be at home with the readers in the world of fiction:

Ingrained in me is a love of mystery and marvel. As a child, Red Riding Hood, Ali Baba, and the Arabian Nights found as much favor with me as the stories from the Bible. All were read to me by my mother. Stories of the weird and wonderful exercise a surpassing charm over my imagination. I feel there are many thousands like me and from these I will be delighted to hear. Who knows but that this department may be the means of bringing to light another Poe or another Hawthorne? Only by writing can you learn to write. By throwing off restraint, the greatest pieces of literature have been produced. This department is yours as much as mine.[381]

It's a further irony that the man whose name fronted ghostwritten and stereotypically deceptive first-person confessionals should speak of learning to write through writing and of producing great literature. In fact, the two editions of *Ask Houdini* (April and May-June-July) lacked any further discussion of weird fiction, or any other kind of fiction, except for several references to the events of "The Spirit Fakers of Hermannstadt." Reader questions typically asked about the reality of séances or dowsing, and Houdini often provided disappointingly brief answers to their occasionally essay-length questions. Of further disappointment, in some cases he advised readers to look elsewhere for answers, e.g. "The Psychical Research Society have gone thoroughly into [dowsers], and I would advise you to look up their literature on this subject."[382]

Ah, for the late, lamented Edwin Baird! He may have been wild at times, and wildly inappropriate, but he kept *The Eyrie* focused on debates over weird fiction. And he was never boring.

■ ■ ■

The April issue with the first edition of *Ask Houdini* was also the first issue of *Weird Tales* edited by Farnsworth Wright. The column contains intriguing evidence that the issue was rushed to the newsstand. In *The Eyrie* or *Ask Houdini*, from April 1923 through the Anniversary Issue (the March 1923 *Eyrie* contained no letters), the average column contained 13 reader letters, with a high of 19 and a low of 7. The April 1924 column was one of two that hit bottom at 7 letters (October 1923 being the other).

But April 1924 uniquely stands out with another low mark. The column had the most limited geographical dispersion of any of these early columns. The 7 letters originated from Illinois (Evanston, Peoria, Springfield), New York (Buffalo), Indiana (Terre Haute), Michigan (Detroit), and Kentucky (Louisville). Aggregating all the letters which list author location gives a rough idea of how widely *Weird Tales* was distributed in this early period. (Appendix A includes the complete list.) The leading letter-states were New York (26), California (19), Illinois (15), Pennsylvania (9), Michigan (6), Texas (6), Indiana (5), Minnesota (5), North Carolina (5), Florida (4), Missouri (4), Ohio (4), and Rhode Island (4). There is scant representation from the southern, plains, or desert states. For instance, there were no letters from Tennessee, which accords with Whitehead never seeing the magazine while serving in Chattanooga. As a disclaimer, the small sample sizes can be misleading; for instance, all four Rhode Island letters were from Lovecraft. But even the October 1923 issue, with 7 letters, represented both coasts. The 7 letters from April 1924, originating in relatively close proximity to Chicago, suggest that the issue was put to print early in the cycle, before letters from farther away had reached the Rural offices.

THE CALL OF CHICAGO

While the drama over the completion and approval of "Imprisoned with the Pharaohs" played out, Farnsworth Wright persevered in his new role as interim editor of *Weird Tales*, with Baird nearby to assist with sage advice or commiserate about the poor quality of submissions. Wright couldn't escape the "interim" tag, according to the shifting accounts of his status Lovecraft received from Henneberger. Wright hadn't had enough time to prove himself, but he also wasn't Henneberger's dream candidate. That honor fell to Lovecraft.

Henneberger kept his designs a deep, dark secret until after visiting Houdini in Tennessee. Once the magician had approved of Lovecraft's flamboyant ending to "Pharaohs," that troubling issue dissipated in an instant. Lovecraft had come through, he had delivered the goods, and he had pleased a god. For Henneberger, that settled the question of Lovecraft's potential editorship. The story hadn't been the most important variable in Henneberger's calculus; the bigger need was for Lovecraft and Houdini to forge a strong relationship. For all anyone knew at that point, *Weird Tales* would survive, maybe even thrive, and the Lovecraft-Houdini collaborations would continue as the center of the magazine's identity.

When Lovecraft received Henneberger's offer, he shared the bombshell news with Aunt Lillian:

> But it is from Henneberger that the startling thing came—the thing which has aroused vast excitement in this placid and newly-founded household. This honest but uncouth worthy writes that he is making a radical change in WEIRD TALES, and that he has in mind a brand new magazine to cover the field of Poe-Machen shudders. This magazine, he says, will be "right in my line", and he wants to know if I would consider moving to Chicago to edit it! My gawd, Pete, bring the stretcher![383]

By "brand new magazine," Lovecraft (no doubt echoing Henneberger's language) referred to an overhauled editorial approach as opposed to the creation of a new publication; in other words, part of the evolving reorganization. Henneberger was offering to cede creative control of *Weird Tales* to Lovecraft's judgment, indicated by his crafting of the offer to Lovecraft's tastes—"the field of Poe-Machen shudders"—and noting that the magazine would be right in Lovecraft's line. Lovecraft's admiration for Poe had been well-established in his correspondence to Baird and Henneberger. But his love for Arthur Machen (1863-1947) had been equally well-established. Lovecraft never missed a chance to praise the Welsh fantasist: "Arthur Machen is the only living man I know of who can stir truly profound and spiritual horror" (*The Eyrie*, September 1923); Machen is "my revered idol" (*The Eyrie*, January 1924); "Arthur Machen is the only living master---in the full sense of the word---I could possibly name in [the horror field]" (February 2 reply). Henneberger had read Lovecraft's missives closely and zeroed in on the factor that he thought would make his offer optimally alluring. Lovecraft began serious consideration, despite his initial repulsion to the ghastly prospect of Chicago.

By the time the offer was made, Henneberger had accumulated many reasons for favoring Lovecraft. First and foremost was the quality of his contributions, the best evidence of his argument for originality in the weird tale. His presence in *Weird Tales* gave an immediate boost to the magazine's literary integrity, so important to Henneberger. Second, Lovecraft displayed editorial vision. The letters to Baird which ended up in *The Eyrie* hinted at a deep acquaintance with the field, a view confirmed by the February 2 letter which contained a virtual manifesto on American magazines and readers, the role of weird fiction in American literature, and a lengthy analysis of the merits of stories already published in *Weird Tales*. The letter demonstrated a comprehensive knowledge of the field which far surpassed Henneberger's or Baird's. The tone of the letter suggested a blunt frankness meant to be helpful, but if it had been an interview for the editor's job, Lovecraft could hardly have delivered a more suitable set of remarks.

Further, Lovecraft had continually demonstrated a loyalty to *Weird Tales* as a cause. He couldn't resist the magazine even if he disapproved of much of its content. "I like WEIRD TALES very much, though I have seen only the April number," he wrote in his initial communication.[384] When he sent back "Dagon," retyped, he wrote: "My love of the weird makes me eager to do anything I can to put good material in the path of a magazine which so gratifyingly cultivates that favorite element. I shall await with interest the next issues, with the tales you mention, and am meanwhile trying to get the opening number through a newsdealer."[385] In the February 2 letter, he reviewed a story from the "very first issue," showing that he achieved his quest. By then, he had a full run (plus a duplicate set for loaning) and had apparently read every issue cover to cover, or close to it, not unlike him considering his heroic reading of the Munsey magazines.

After Lovecraft married Sonia, they took up house in her Brooklyn flat. He had less cause to write Frank Belknap Long since his friend lived nearby, but Long recalled from their frequent visits the commotion surrounding the editorship offer. In his 1975 Lovecraft biography, he wrote, "there were many moments when Howard remained on the verge of accepting."[386] Sonia encouraged him to take the job and expressed her willingness to move to Chicago, where her prospects in the millinery trade would match those in New York.[387]

Nevertheless, Chicago remained a barrier. Because he had never visited the city, Lovecraft, in remarks reconstructed by Long, could react with revulsion to two seemingly opposed characteristics, Chicago's reputation as a hellish slaughterhouse and its modernity:

> "*Chicago!*" I can still hear him saying. "Think of what just one month in that dreadful metropolis would do to the old gentleman! When Sandburg called it 'Hog Butcher For the World,' he thought he was paying it a compliment, which is what you'd expect of a decadent urban poet. He wouldn't have the remotest idea of how *I* would feel if I came within fifty blocks of the stockyards. The Fulton Street fish market [in the Bronx] is bad enough, and as for the buildings—you can be just as much outraged by total newness, stripped of all aesthetic meaning. Chicago is a bare, bleak, hideous city."[388]

If the reality of Chicago had been half as bad as Lovecraft's estimate, it still would have provided chilling inspiration for his horror fiction; we can only imagine.

Henneberger's offer was tempting, but the location was repellent to Lovecraft. He couldn't live with Chicago and without the "Colonial atmosphere" of the East. He pondered accepting the offer if he could edit the magazine remotely, from New York,[389] a completely unrealistic idea. Proven editors didn't get that deal; they went to the office every day where the mail, the phone calls, and the visitors came, and where the rest of the staff did their business. Lovecraft and Long discussed the possibility of persuading Henneberger to bring Long to Chicago for the job. It wouldn't have been too abhorrent for *him*. That plan never reached Henneberger's ears.[390]

Additionally, Lovecraft harbored doubts about the validity of Henneberger's offer. With his customary pessimism, he wrote Aunt Lillian, "it may be all hot air anyway."[391] The deep indebtedness of Rural Publishing had haunted Lovecraft since he'd read Henneberger's confession in late-January, since it threatened the continued existence of *Weird Tales*. The same cloud hovered over the editing offer. "The trouble is," he explained to his aunt, "that the darned thing might fail after a few issues, leaving me stranded in uncongenial Western scenes."[392] As events would unfold, his fears were well-founded.

In late March, about a week after the offer was made,[393] Henneberger, ostensibly in New York to raise capital for Rural,[394] met with Lovecraft face-to-face to press the editing offer.[395] Long implied that Lovecraft had already turned him down, but that Henneberger had "apparently not completely abandoned his efforts to persuade HPL." Lovecraft was discreet enough not to make his refusal definitive.[396] This visit, most likely, is the time when Lovecraft would have shown Henneberger the run of *Home Brews*. Lovecraft's account of the visit is missing from available letters, but Long recalled the evening that "Howard [Lovecraft] and Henneberger rang the doorbell of the Long apartment and Howard introduced him, followed by a whispered aside to me that he had taken the liberty of inviting him to be our dinner guest."[397] As brief as Long's anecdote is, it's the most detailed description of Henneberger that exists from the era:

> Henneberger was as highly energized in an extroverted, successful-businessman way as anyone I had met up to that time. He was soft-spoken and had a cultivated, widely-read side to his nature, but he kept it almost entirely under wraps and his conversation during the entire course of the evening centered around the importance of at least tripling the circulation of *Weird Tales* and proceeding from there to build a publishing empire that would dwarf MacFadden's [*sic*] in four or five years.[398]

The first noteworthy point is Henneberger's combination of business ambition and cultivation, seemingly two ingredients required for success in magazine publishing. Second, his fixation on surpassing Macfadden corroborates the centrality of the Macfadden true-story model in the Rural reorganization, and shows that the split in the company had not yet been seriously considered, if at all. Additionally, Long implied that he and Lovecraft found Henneberger's ambitions credible since he had survived a rags-to-riches cycle with *College Humor*, events he must have boasted of during the conversation.

For Long, the main benefit of the meeting was that Lovecraft convinced Henneberger to forward two Long stories to Baird. "The Desert Lich" landed in Wright's hands and became Long's first appearance in *Weird Tales*. Baird accepted the other story for *Detective Tales*, but in the turmoil resulting from the split, it never appeared.[399]

On March 30, Lovecraft informed his aunt that *Weird Tales* was "under its new editor, Farnsworth Wright."[400] In other words, after Henneberger returned to Chicago, the two big editing questions were resolved: Lovecraft's refusal became unambiguous and final, and Wright escaped his probation as interim editor. In 1968, Henneberger recalled Lovecraft's reason for turning down the job: "his spouse objected to Chicago as a domicile."[401] We might choose to dismiss this entirely, owing to Henneberger's unreliability, and because it contradicts Lovecraft's contemporaneous account. But recruiting Lovecraft as editor meant a lot to Henneberger, meaning the rejection would have been a huge disappointment, and a painful memory likely to linger with him. If Henneberger did remember accurately, it means that Lovecraft lied to him, using an argument that he wouldn't have to defend or negotiate over further since it belonged to his wife. If so, he probably used her as an excuse throughout Henneberger's New York visit. It was a small payback for the byline betrayal.

Soon thereafter, Wright made the outcome public, telling *The Author & Journalist* that *Weird Tales* "is being reorganized with myself as editor, and we hope to pay for all stories published within the next few weeks. For the present, we must continue on a payment-on-publication basis, for at least a few months longer."[402] For the present . . .

We don't know how Henneberger's faith in Lovecraft might have changed as a result of meeting him in person, but Henneberger had dodged disaster by not employing him as editor, and Lovecraft had escaped humiliation by not accepting. Objectively, the author would have made a very poor choice. While his literary qualifications were a unique asset, his *ars gratia artis*, commerce-is-vulgar sensibilities made him completely unsuited for running a professional magazine. The heaps of rubbish would have buried him. His letter-writing proclivities would have easily topped Baird's. He would have been tempted to reply to every contributor with a detailed critique of their story—to change the world, soul by misguided soul. And then there were practical considerations. Lovecraft had never held a salaried position.[403] He had no experience with any commercial enterprise, much less a magazine with a (near) intractable monthly deadline. He would have struggled to make concessions to his lofty standards with time and budget his constant enemies, descending into an ever-expanding hell of indecision. In the end, Wright, by striking a realistic balance of art and commerce, promised a better destiny for the magazine.

Lovecraft's February 2 reply to Henneberger made it evident that Henneberger wanted Lovecraft and Houdini to meet. Henneberger knew Houdini personally, and thought he knew Lovecraft from his letters and stories, and sensed the possibility of common interest. Henneberger's desire for a meeting also hinted that bigger plans for the pair were already rolling around in the back of his head.

In his reply, Lovecraft expressed enthusiasm for meeting the magician.

Houdini was game, as well. After first telling Morton about the assignment for "Pharaohs," Lovecraft reported: "Henny says that Houdini wants to get in touch with me about some books or other when he gets back from a lecture tour."[404] There may have been some meaning lost in the path from Houdini to Henneberger to Lovecraft. Lovecraft interpreted Henneberger's remarks as referring to a book proposition, whereas subsequent remarks also refer to an invitation for Lovecraft to visit Houdini's personal library. But both issues may have been present. On March 12, Lovecraft updated Morton: "Houdie has dropped me a note full of his circulars & cuttings, duly annotated, & calling attention to his home address, where he would some time like to see me. He hangs out at 278 West 113th, & is said to have the best collection of dark & weird volumes in America."[405]

Two days later, he sent Morton additional thoughts: "If I can get together with [Houdini], maybe I'll convert him to my way of thinking, & extract permission to put him through worse terrors than ever he imagined before! But time will tell."[406] These remarks came after the completion of "Pharaohs" and before Henneberger had obtained Houdini's blessing. They reveal Lovecraft's understanding that the wild ending to the story jeopardized his budding relationship with Houdini but, if he survived the danger, aided by some face-to-face persuasion, even wilder stories lay in their future collaborations. At least in Lovecraft's mind, the relationship had a chance to continue and grow. That possibility increased after Houdini approved of the story and renewed his request for Lovecraft to visit him in New York.[407]

Finally, in April, the conditions for a personal meeting arrived. Lovecraft was newly situated in Brooklyn, Houdini returned to New York from his lecture tour, and Henneberger came in from Chicago to act as rainmaker. These three luminaries celebrated their relationship by going to a play. And not just any play. It was one with particular appeal for true believers in *Weird Tales*.

First, we should note that the record of this event is burdened by two sets of misleading memories, one minor and one major. Lovecraft confirmed the April meeting in a July 1924 letter.[408] But in a 1931 reminiscence, he misidentified the month as June and the theater as the "Nieuw[New]-Amsterdam."[409] It was actually the Ritz Theatre, in Times Square. The more mangled memories occur in Long's Lovecraft biography.[410] His description of the Henneberger-Houdini-Lovecraft summit merged the April 1924 event with Houdini's early 1925 six-week stand at the Hippodrome, his first New York vaudeville bookings in three years, during which Lovecraft attended at least two of Houdini's performances.[411] Long combined the issues of 1924 with the Houdini performances of 1925, while forgetting the play.

There is no intimation in the evidence that the gathering lasted more than the one evening. Before the show, according to perhaps Long's most reliable memory, the three gentlemen discussed business, "including the splendid job Howard had done in 'revising and expanding' *Imprisoned with the Pharaohs* (not once did Houdini mention ghost-writing), what an exceptionally far-sighted businessman Henneberger was, the serious disagreements he had had with Baird, and why it was just possible that a new editor might soon be at the helm of *Weird Tales*."[412] Of course, Farnsworth Wright had already taken over by April.

Lovecraft recalled the "celebrated conjuror's" behavior before the play:

> Houdini, conversing before the rise of the curtain, aired what is said to have been a favourite parlour trick of his—apparently pulling off his own left thumb and snapping it back after it had seemed to be away from its stump for as great a distance as an inch—or perhaps two. The wholly impromptu setting, and the fact that the whole thing was in the very next seat not four feet from my eyes, made the effect highly impressive. . . . an absolutely perfect illusion . . .[413]

And a nice setup for the magical illusions of the show . . .

The play was *Outward Bound* by the young British actor-turned-playwright Sutton Vane.[414] Vane had enlisted in the British army at the outbreak of the Great War and, in 1917, was sent home from Egypt with a bad case of shell-shock while "secretly battling with the horrors of war."[415] He privately financed the production of *Outward Bound* in England; it made its American premiere at the Ritz on January 7, 1924, and was the controversial hit of the season. Presumably, Houdini had heard about it in New York and suggested the excursion as an appropriate way to make Lovecraft's acquaintance. The play closed in early May.

Outward Bound is set on a modern ocean liner crossing the seas. It lacks a captain or crew, or known destination. The ship's passengers, a motley collection of characters, are drawn from all walks of modern life. They share one thing in common, known at first only to two lovers who committed suicide together: they are all dead. They are ghosts who must discover that secret. They are making the great voyage to the afterlife—and judgment. The strength of the play was its dramatic elements. As one critic described it, the "greatest sin [of the passengers] has been the lack of courage to face life."[416] While exploring the core ethical and emotional qualities of human existence, the play lacked the supernatural pyrotechnics and horrors that might be expected in a *Weird Tales* story, which may have disappointed a certain three members of the audience on that one evening in April.

The meeting in New York was presumably intended to solidify the Houdini-Lovecraft relationship as a major part of the mutating dimensions of the reorganization. Sadly, however, "Pharaohs," in the May-June-July

Anniversary Issue, would be their only fictional collaboration. Potential additional stories fell victim to the final state of the reorganization, which degraded from a set of editorial inspirations into a deepened financial crisis. That final reorganization, which split the company, ended the magician's known association with *Weird Tales*, but not with Lovecraft. They collaborated on various projects. Lovecraft helped his friend Eddy craft a never-published book for the magician, *The Cancer of Superstition*. In October 1926, Houdini performed in Providence, by which time Lovecraft's marriage to Sonia had dissolved and he was back in his home town to stay. He and Houdini met to discuss mutual works: "raw material for a campaign against *astrology*," "an article on *witchcraft*,"[417] and "a devilish lot more."[418] But Houdini didn't last the month. He died on October 31—Halloween.

The evening of theater, and hobnobbing with Henneberger and Houdini, may have represented Lovecraft's high-water mark with *Weird Tales*. Getting there had taken a cycle of pleasure and pain. Pleasure that the magazine had come into being; pain that his manuscripts had been returned for retyping. Pleasure that "Dagon" had been accepted; pain that it took so long to get into print. Pleasure that other stories had been accepted; pain that Baird ruined a title. Pleasure that the collaboration with Houdini had come about; pain that his name had been deleted from the byline and omitted from the cover.

The play and the chance of future work had been another round of pleasure. Lovecraft was the publisher's pet, sharing the center of attention with the world-renowned conjuror. The wheel soon turned its next half-circle. *Weird Tales* stopped publishing after the Anniversary Issue, perhaps never to return. Later in 1924, it did return—from the dead, of course—with Farnsworth Wright secure as the permanent editor. Wright took his job more seriously than Baird had and resisted letting art get in the way of commerce. The magazine, crafted from Henneberger's literary ideals and Baird's freewheeling execution, had disproven its viability. Left to fill the vacuum was Wright's cautious judgment. There would be more sales by Lovecraft to *Weird Tales*, but also rejections, and no lasting peace with the magazine.

And so to Lovecraft's mail came messages of unknown terror from Chicago, a hideous place at best; a ghastly monstrosity of a city that rose ominously with cosmic arrogance above cold, dark waters; the head of the publishing octopus that thrust its disgusting, slimy tentacles from coast to coast, spreading its noxious cult of weird writing like an alien infestation. And so did "Chicago" became an accursed word, with its three syllables a corruption to the mortal soul to pronounce, and its seven poisonous letters, starting with a foreboding "C" and ending with a mocking, reprehensible vowel.

Laboring under this menacing shadow, in August 1925, Lovecraft plotted one of his masterpieces, "The Call of Cthulhu." A year later the writer who turned his nightmares into stories committed it to paper.[419] The story introduced Lovecraft's signature concept, Cthulhu, an ancient being worshipped by cultists awaiting his return. Technically, "Chicago" is pronounceable by the human voice and "Cthulhu" is not, but otherwise the two words are appallingly similar. Did one allow the other?

The yang of the masterpiece would not be complete without the yin of rejection. As Lovecraft wrote Long on October 26, 1926, "Little Farnie rejected Grandpa's *Cthulhu* story on the ground that it was too slow and obscure for his zippy morons."[420] In a universe as vast and unfathomable as Lovecraft's, there was still a place where ordinary morons held more power than old Cthulhu himself. When Lovecraft resubmitted the tale in 1927, he made a similar point, albeit with impeccable manners:

> My dear Mr. Wright:—
> In accordance with your suggestion I am re-submitting *The Call of Cthulhu*, though possibly you will still think it a trifle too bizarre for a clientele who demand their weirdness in name only, and who like to keep both feet pretty solidly on the ground of the known and the familiar.[421]

This time, it was good enough for Wright and the story appeared in the February 1928 *Weird Tales*, another episode in an increasingly aggravating relationship.

THE DEVIL NEVER FORGETS

The "reorganization" started as one thing—an editorial overhaul of the Rural magazines—and ended as another—the splitting of the company—with *Weird Tales* remaining with Rural and *Detective Tales* moving under a new corporate umbrella. The questions to be answered are: when was the decision for this dramatic switch in direction made, when did the switch happen, and why was it necessary? It's one of the murkiest areas of the narrative.

A large part of the explanation lies in the numbers, of course, numbers of dollars going out versus those coming in, and few of those numbers are available. Lovecraft's letters are a rich source of clues for explaining events up to this point. They not only document his involvement with *Weird Tales*, they timestamp events within Rural, even when Lovecraft didn't completely understand them. But, with one exception, he is of minimal help here. The gaps in the record become pronounced. Lovecraft was in New York, seemingly preoccupied with his new marriage; and after turning down Henneberger's offer of the *Weird Tales* editing job, the two had no imminent business to discuss. And it's likely that some of Lovecraft's letters from this mid-1924 period have simply been lost.

The last significant publishing event before the split, for *Weird Tales*, was the May-June-July Anniversary Issue, a jumbo collection of stories with a whopping 50¢ cover price. There was no corresponding change to *Detective Tales*, making it the biggest divergence to date between the publishing models for the two magazines, raising the question of whether the Anniversary Issue itself is evidence that a split in the company was already in the works. The size of the issue also suggests a desire to clear out the inventory of purchased fiction before moving in a new direction.

However, events argue against this. If the Anniversary Issue appeared on newsstands on or about April 18, then the approximate time for planning and preparing it would have been from mid-March through mid-April. Consider what happened in this period. Henneberger, spending freely on travel, journeyed from Chicago to Tennessee to show Lovecraft's draft of "Under the Pyramids" to Houdini. Henneberger then rewarded Lovecraft with a second $100 payment for the story and attempted to recruit him as editor of a "brand new magazine." When that failed, Henneberger installed Farnsworth Wright as permanent editor of *Weird Tales*. Finally, Henneberger traveled again, to New York, to meet with Lovecraft and Houdini. There is every suggestion in these events that the reorganization still meant editorial enhancement, and no hint that it meant a split in the company. The actual impression of events is that the editorial reorganization barreled forward to a certain point, until the bottom fell out, when all of Henneberger's big plans crashed to earth, turning the reorganization into an unforeseen split.

The Anniversary Issue itself typifies the continual experimentation with *Weird Tales* since the beginning, which expanded into the January reorganization. At a large-size 192 pages, it was the biggest issue of *Weird Tales* to date, and similar to the fat February 1923 issue of *Detective Tales*. Emblazoned in a yellow box on the front cover was "Anniversary Number." ("Number" is more commonly associated with British magazines. We've adopted "Anniversary Issue," as the issue is usually referred to.) The language suggested a special, one-time or annual, event. But, in fact, buried at the end of the first-page indicia was the text: "Issued in May, August, November and February." It's the sole piece of evidence *in the issue* that it was the first iteration of a planned quarterly.

The new format offered twice as much content—192 versus 96 pages—for twice the price—50¢ versus 25¢. Identifying it as a quarterly, with the May-June-July date and the indicia notice, may have been a crafty way of implying that it was a bargain containing triple the content for twice the price. If so, that message was botched since it was the first issue of *Weird Tales* without a front cover date. By one measurement, the issue actually represented a *shrinkage* of content since it offered two months' worth of pages spread over three months.

A genuinely deceptive message in the yellow box advertised "Fifty distinct feature novels, short stories and novelettes." In fact, there were only 37 pieces of fiction. *Weird Tales* had averaged 17.6 stories per issue up until then, but that includes the overstuffed early issues. By the July-August 1923 issue, the magazine had settled into a 16-story average. The Anniversary Issue, therefore, delivered a little better than twice the number of stories, for readers who cared more about variety than length.

For these early issues of *Weird Tales*, we can't assume that any anomaly is intentional; sometimes, they're evidence of disorganization rather than reorganization, especially under inexperienced new editor Farnsworth Wright. For example, the Anniversary Issue, the thirteenth issue of *Weird Tales*, should have been numbered Volume IV, Number 1, starting a new sequence of four-to-a-volume. Instead, it was numbered Volume IV, Number 2, on both the spine and in the indicia, which must have confused or annoyed observant readers who neatly shelved their issues with the square spines showing.

A better indicator of chaos behind the scenes at Rural is the matter of who edited the Anniversary Issue. This question has been bandied about over the years and the evidence is rife with contradictions. What follows will be our best interpretation of what actually happened. To start, three individuals—Baird and his two assistants, Wright and Kline—can all make claims on the honor. Wright never specifically addressed his involvement in the Anniversary Issue but, as we know, he had been interim editor since about late February and became permanent editor once Lovecraft turned down the job. By this time, the preparation of the Anniversary Issue was well underway, which makes Wright the leading candidate.

Kline made his case in his 1941 letter to Robert E. Howard's father. His timeline was garbled, in the manner of a spontaneously typed recollection of old events, but these were the salient comments:

> Edwin Baird was the first editor of <u>Weird Tales</u>, and continued as such until 1924. After that, I edited one issue. . . . [Henneberger] called on me for help . . . and I got out that issue and wrote the editorial, "Why <u>Weird Tales</u>" which has guided the editorial policy of the magazine ever since in the selection of material. That issue was a three months combined issue, and was left on the stand for three months.[422]

He was clearly referring to the Anniversary Issue, which contained his essay. Of note, he went on to mention Wright becoming editor *after* the Anniversary Issue and the Rural split. He omitted mention of Wright's interim status or Lovecraft's candidacy.

Finally, in the August 1924 *Author & Journalist*, Henneberger claimed that, "Up until the last issue [of *Weird Tales*], Mr. Edwin Baird handled the editorial end of both *Weird Tales* and *Detective Tales*."[423]

This puzzle has a straightforward, though not absolute, solution which logically reconciles the contradiction: all three individuals edited the issue! But to different degrees. Baird was still Rural's managing editor, in essence, for both *Detective* and *Weird Tales*. He was the *editor of record* for *Weird Tales* up until the split despite the fact that someone else did the literal job of editing the magazine. Plus, he had probably purchased a goodly amount of the stories which appeared in the Anniversary Issue. Wright was the actual editor of the issue in the early stages of its preparation, but then—the crux of the puzzle—he quit the company in anger, before the issue was finished, leaving Henneberger to quickly replace him. Kline was recruited as temporary editor, which gave him the opportunity to add his essay to the issue.

But why would Wright have quit so soon after being handed the reins of the magazine? Recall the controversy over author payments that had simmered in the pages of *The Author & Journalist* (and *The Student Writer*) since the June 1923 issue. That problem never went away and undoubtedly got worse. And, going further back, recall that after Farnsworth moved to Chicago he immediately repaid his brother Fred for assisting him with college expenses. Paying his debts, and not just to family members, was one of Farnsworth's ethical imperatives. Thus, when Wright, as the new editor of *Weird Tales*, became the new face of Rural's debt crisis, he not only may have discovered the depth of the problem for the first time, he took deep offense at his inability to treat the contributors—his fellow authors—honorably.

As the following dispatch reveals, matters quickly boiled over after Wright took over. Note that the dispatch implies that Wright quit the company after the split. We interpret the true sequence as, first, Wright quit, then after some interval the company split, and then Wright wrote the letter. These are his remarks in their entirety as published in *The Author & Journalist*:

> This is to inform you that I am no longer connected with *Weird Tales* in any capacity. As editor for the past two months I have tried without success to obtain consideration for the authors whose work has been published in the magazine, but have been unable even to collect my own salary, although I was paid some time ago for six stories and one serial that I wrote for the magazine. *Weird Tales* owes $5000 to authors for stories already published (besides about $55,000 of other debts, or about $60,000 in all). The rates for manuscripts had been cut down by Mr. Baird, former editor, and by me, acting under instructions, to as low as 1/3 of a cent a word in some cases; so when J.C. Henneberger, owner of the magazine, proposed to me that the magazine should settle with the authors for 33 cents on the dollar, I refused to be a party to any such scheme. I advise authors having claims against the magazine to send their bills directly to J.C. Henneberger, who is owner of the magazine under the corporate name of the Rural Publishing Co., and who now becomes editor as well. Just a word in defense of Edwin Baird, who is now editor of *Real Detective Tales* under entirely new ownership. Mr. Baird, as editor of *Weird Tales*, made promises of payment in entire good faith, but his promises were disregarded by Mr. Henneberger. It was Mr. Baird, however, who bore the onus of the attacks from outraged authors in the writers' magazines, and this is unjust to him.[424]

Wright's indignation comes through loud and clear. If Baird had borne "the onus of the attacks from outraged authors," Wright inherited that grief with the position of editor. He announced himself as a true man of conscience, willing to resign rather than perpetuate the injustice of mistreating the magazine's contributors. By detailing his own financial situation, he essentially sided with the contributors against the publisher. To establish his honesty, he concedes that he had been paid for all of his fiction submissions. (His sixth *Weird Tales* story appeared in the November 1924 issue. The serial is unaccounted for unless it was "The White Queen" which appeared complete in the October 1930 *Oriental Stories*, the temporary companion to *Weird Tales*.)

Of supreme interest are Wright's figures for the company's debt. When Henneberger revealed Rural's position to Lovecraft in late January, it had lost $51,000 since its inception. Wright's citation of $60,000 seems well in line, if we assume he meant to refer to Rural Publishing and not just *Weird Tales*. To approximate the change, if the $51,000 is averaged from October 1922, when *Detective Tales* first went on sale, through January 1924—sixteen months—then the company lost $3,187.50 per month. If it lost another $9,000 in the following four months, then the hemorrhaging had been reduced to $2,250 per month, which is some measure of progress. Under those figures, the Houdini gambit had worked, just not enough for Rural's biggest creditor, the printer.

However, there is a vast gulf between $51,000 and $60,000 which can't be measured arithmetically. The first figure had been told in confidence to Lovecraft, who let it slip to Long and Morton who could do no damage with it. But when Wright reported the $60,000 to *The Author & Journalist*, he was blasting the number through a megaphone to the industry of magazine professionals, an audience which included competitors—publishers and editors—as well as the army of professional writers who kept abreast of magazine markets and decided who to craft their stories for. The letter, a major attack on Henneberger's integrity, had to have deeply embarrassed the publisher. Wright had followed Baird's precedent of calling him out in public and amplified what was already a unique set of events in the history of the pulps.

Wright further poured on the humiliation by noting that Henneberger "now becomes editor" of *Weird Tales*, implying that the publisher had run out of underlings. Baird had gone with the new company and Wright had quit. Kline, employed elsewhere, didn't enter into the calculation.

Henneberger would get his counterattack, but he would have to wait a month.

The Anniversary Issue included many noteworthy features. The essay that Kline took pride in, "Why Weird Tales?," led off the issue.[425] The presence of the piece probably reflects Kline's opportunism after being handed the responsibility of finishing the issue in Wright's absence.

The essay was a scattershot manifesto on the mission of *Weird Tales*. Kline opened by complaining about editorial prejudice against weird fiction, strongly echoing Whitehead's 1922 article for *The Writer*. *Weird Tales* would counter that prejudice, as Kline asserted: "What we have done, and will continue to do, is to gather around us an ever-increasing body of readers who appreciate the weird, the bizarre, the unusual—who recognize true art in fiction." The appeal to art acknowledged both Henneberger's literary ambitions for the magazine and these remarks made by Lovecraft in the March *Eyrie*: "Popular authors do not and apparently cannot appreciate the fact that true art is obtainable only by rejecting normality and conventionality in toto, and approaching a theme purged utterly of any usual or preconceived point of view."[426]

In discussing the scope of the magazine's content, Kline described the war between the past and future without directly acknowledging it. The past was represented by supernatural fiction in literature, of which Kline made a brief survey, including a spirited defense of Henneberger's and Lovecraft's favorite author, Edgar Allan Poe. The future was served by Kline's preferences for a science-altered world. "Men in the progressive ages to come will wonder how it was possible that writers of the crude and uncivilized age known as the Twentieth Century could have had foreknowledge of the things that will have, by that time, come to pass." He outlined two categories to reflect the division: the "occult story" and the "highly imaginative story." The occult story could be told from the point of view of believers or nonbelievers, a qualification which allowed for the true-story, spiritualism-debunking of the pre-Lovecraft Houdini tales. The highly imaginative story—of "advancement in the sciences and the arts"—would be told by writer-prophets of the terrors to come.

Of these latter stories, the writer would be "at once the scientist, the philosopher and the poet." That would make an apt description of Lovecraft, yet Kline never mentions him in the essay, and neither of Kline's story categories clearly accounts for Lovecraft's fiction. Lovecraft was the best at characterizing the artistic potential of the weird tale, as he did in his February 2 letter, which Kline probably never read: "What really moves the profoundest springs of human fear and unholy fascination is something which suggests black infinite vistas of cryptic, brooding, half-inscrutable monstrosities for ever lurking behind Nature and as capable of being manifested again . . ."[427] That idiosyncratic quote, only a taste of Lovecraft's definition, makes Kline's analysis look pedestrian. Looking back from the vantage point of Kline's incomprehensible future, we can see Lovecraft as the true spirit of the magazine, but to Kline that outcome was not apparent.

The essay would have given any reader the impression that *Weird Tales* was a model of health and sound purpose. The rest of the issue added affirmation, with its thirty-seven "distinct" pieces of fiction—plus the sixth number of Seabury Quinn's *Weird Crimes* column, and the second (and last) installment of *Ask Houdini*.

The lead, cover-illustrated story was Lovecraft's daring "Imprisoned with the Pharaohs." Hidden behind Houdini's byline, Lovecraft appeared elsewhere under his own name with "Hypnos," a short story which had appeared a year earlier in the May 1923 issue of *The National Amateur*. Closer to a prose poem than the Lovecraft stories which had already appeared in *Weird Tales*, "Hypnos," whose characters enter the "caverns of dream," was narrative-heavy, vague, and lacked dialogue. It was another Lovecraft story wherein a character witnesses some great horror but the reader doesn't. The technique works well in other Lovecraft stories, but is rather dissatisfying here, particularly in contrast to "Pharaohs" which proved that when Lovecraft wanted to finish off with something terrifying, it was well worth the wait.

The issue also included Kline's "The Malignant Entity," Whitehead's introduction to the magazine, "Tea Leaves," and Frank Owen's "The Man Who Lived Next Door to Himself."

One story which sparked controversy was C.M. Eddy's "The Loved Dead," "the latter half of which *I* [Lovecraft] re-wrote!"[428] The two were working on it in late October, at which time Lovecraft described it to Morton as "a pleasing & morbid study in hysterical necrophily."[429] Baird was uncertain as to whether to purchase it, as indicated by Lovecraft's February 3 remarks to him: "I'll bet [Henneberger would] snap up that Eddy yarn, *The Loved Dead*, which is presenting such a doubtful case!"[430]

If by "hysterical," Lovecraft meant funny, there's nothing overtly humorous about Eddy's tale of a necrophiliac serial killer. It opens in a cemetery gravesite at midnight, with the language of morbidity laid on thick: "Around me on every side, sepulchral sentinels guarding unkempt graves, the tilting decrepit headstones lie half-hidden in masses of nauseous, rotting vegetation." The narrator proceeds to tell of the long path that led him to that place. He attended his first funeral, his grandfather's, at age sixteen.[431] Far from disturbing him, he enjoyed the sensual trappings, "swayed by some strange discordant sense of elation." When his mother died, "so genuine was my grief that I was honestly surprised to find its poignancy mocked and contradicted by that almost forgotten feeling of supreme and diabolical ecstasy." He became an undertaker's apprentice, addicted to dead bodies. "Every fresh corpse brought into the establishment meant a fulfilled promise of ungodly gladness, of irreverent gratification; a return of that rapturous tumult of the arteries which transformed my grisly task into one of beloved devotion . . ." Eventually, he starts murdering people at night to satisfy his need for bodies. When the world war comes, he is one of the first to arrive and one of the last to depart. The horrors of the war—the "sickening slime of rain-rotten trenches"—made for "four years of transcendent satisfaction." But the grisly war sequence, only a paragraph, is insufficient to let us see the story as a metaphor for humanity's death-addiction, which the war seemed to embody. Upon his return to the states, the narrator is reemployed at a mortuary. He commits more murders, but makes mistakes, and is forced to run, hounds in pursuit. Finally, cornered in the cemetery where we first met him, he takes a razor to his wrist. In an elegant ending, the narration dwindles into the nothingness of ellipses as the life drains from his body.

The evidence is ambiguous as to whether Baird or Wright purchased this well-executed but problematic story, or whether Henneberger contributed his approval. But in a desperate financial situation calling for drastic "reorganization," the extreme, disturbing nature of the story may have appealed. Or, perhaps, because the story was sponsored by Lovecraft during Henneberger's recruitment of him for bigger things, the need to appease the author outweighed the risks of publication. Regardless, the appearance of the story in the Anniversary Issue stirred up trouble. Later in the year, Lovecraft recounted for his aunt, "About poor Eddy's tale—it certainly did achieve fame of a sort! His name must have rung in tones of fiery denunciation all through the corridors & beneath the classic rotunda (if it has a rotunda) of the Indiana State Capitol!"[432] Late in 1925, Wright rejected his short story "In the Vault" because, according to Lovecraft, "its extreme gruesomeness would not pass the Indiana censorship,"[433] and because the Indiana senate had taken action against "The Loved Dead."[434] Years later, Lovecraft associated the problem with the Indiana Parent Teacher's Association.[435] These comments have fueled speculation that the Anniversary Issue was banned in Indiana. This thesis, unsupported by news reportage, which it certainly would have garnered, has a simpler explanation. The editorial offices for *Weird Tales* at this time were at 854 North Clark Street, Chicago; their business address was 325 North Capitol Avenue, Indianapolis, the address of a brick building constructed and owned by the Cornelius Printing Company, a well-known, family-owned Indianapolis company of solid standing, who happened to be the printer of *Detective* and *Weird Tales*, and the largest creditor of Rural Publishing. Their building sat a mere block-and-a-half from the capitol. We suspect that Lovecraft's initial comment—"His name must have rung . . ."—was based on information he misunderstood and which he turned into a delectable joke. What fun to imagine that Eddy's devilish little story threw a puritanical state government into a tizzy! In fact, what probably happened was that the PTA, a member, or even a state senator, visited the Cornelius office to complain about "The Loved Dead," and the unwholesome influence it might have on the youth of America, etc., etc., and that the company, which had financial leverage, asked Henneberger to exercise more caution in the future. Then when "In the Vault" was rejected, Lovecraft converted his initial faulty supposition into a fact.

The incident traumatized Wright, as if he needed another nightmare. It kept him looking over his shoulder for the frowning face of the censor, a problem which vexed Lovecraft on occasion. Beyond the rejection of "In the Vault," the problem persisted into the following decade. Writing Clark Ashton Smith in 1935, Lovecraft referred to Wright and his protégé Robert Bloch, who became a *Weird Tales* regular:

> I trust [your future titles] may somehow get past Little Farny's timid glance. A recent experience of little Bobby Bloch does not form an encouraging omen—for Pharnabozus turned down a yarn of his (about a chap who found that his bedfellow in an hotel was a badly decomposed cadaver) on the ground of excessive horror, bringing up the now-classic case of 1924 . . . Poor Farny—he's like a dog which has received a nerve-breaking scare, & cringes every time anything reminds him of it![436]

Once the Anniversary Issue was on the street, the final stage of the reorganization, a division of the assets into two companies, happened quickly. It occurred sometime between the two putative dates of April 18, when the Anniversary Issue was published, and May 18, when newly-titled *Real Detective Tales and Mystery Stories* appeared under its new corporate label of Real Detective Tales, Inc., with Baird as editor. One of Baird's first acts was to write contributors with the good news:

> As a writer, you may be interested to hear that DETECTIVE TALES has undergone a complete reorganization. We have changed the policy of the magazine, and we have also changed its name, and the size and general make-up. REAL DETECTIVE TALES, bigger and better than ever, is now being published by a new corporation, which enables me to pay promptly and at a good rate for acceptable material.[437]

Finally, he and his authors were free of the financial nightmare that Rural had become, ensnared no longer.

The Anniversary Issue and the May *Real Detective Tales*, its first and only issue under that exact title, constituted the last gasp of the Rural Publishing Corporation. But there was more to be divided than Rural's two magazines. Henneberger's *College Humor* was thriving. The February 1924 issue ran a banner across the bottom of the cover that read "Over a Quarter Million Circulation This Issue." It may have been a generous rounding upwards but, if so, subsequent events would not disqualify the estimate. While *College Humor* was thrown into the mix, *The Magazine of Fun* appeared to be inactive and out of the picture. There must have been anguish in the negotiations but the outcome was simple. Johnny Lansinger purchased *Real Detective Tales* and *College Humor* from Henneberger, allowing Henneberger to retain his true love, *Weird Tales*. Still, it must have pained him to surrender *College Humor*, the living proof of his magazine-making genius.

The real power in the negotiations was the Cornelius Printing Company, to which Rural owed $43,000 of its $60,000 debt.[438] Later, Henneberger would refer to them as "a mercenary and unimaginative creditor."[439] Where he saw a magazine inspired by Poe, Cornelius saw only the balance sheet. As Henneberger recalled the details in 1968:

> Nominally, the control of Weird Tales was always in my name, even unto its demise. In order to continue publication, however, I signed a written agreement with the printer (who also furnished the paper) that he would maintain a temporary control to the management until such indebtedness to him was paid. Naturally, he was in a position to see that this did not eventuate, despite the fact that the magazine had a following of hard-core readers who kept the sales at 50% of the print order.[440]

In Kline's recollection, Henneberger remained owner, Cornelius held the stock of the new company pending the payment of the debt, and William R. Sprenger, who had been with Henneberger since before the formation of Rural, was business manager.[441]

The Cornelius Printing Company, now the effective owner of *Weird Tales*, had a long and storied history in Indianapolis. The company was founded and owned by George M. Cornelius (1866-1946). In 1924, his English wife, Alice Mildred Cornelius (1870-1957), was vice president, and their son, George Hooper Cornelius (1897-1973), served as secretary. Over the decades, many other family members worked for the firm. The sire, George M. Cornelius, was born with ink in his veins. For his first business venture, at age ten, he printed calling cards for his schoolmates. He delivered newspapers on horseback. As an adult, he progressed through a series of jobs with big-city newspapers, doing everything from typesetting to proofreading. In 1900, he established the Cornelius Printing Company in Indianapolis, where he had first lived at age four. In late 1909, a new headquarters was constructed at 325 North Capitol Avenue; the company began operations there in March 1910, specializing in "publication and book work."[442]

When *Weird Tales* fell into their laps, it was an odd turn of events. Henneberger's passion project, the legendary "Unique Magazine," became the property of an entity, however tolerant and well-intentioned, for whom it was just a printed product; an entity which barely registers in the richly-documented history of the magazine. It must have stung Henneberger for the outcome to have gone that way.

Why had it happened? Why did the two old pals break off their relationship? It was like a divorce with the children split between the parents. Henneberger, at least, held on to his favorite. Neither he nor Lansinger ever spoke of their breakup, not in print anyway. Indeed, we have no evidence of further contact between the two. Johnny had been silent all along. Subsequently, he rarely spoke to the press. That's not unusual. Businessman don't normally write about their work and, in publishing, public interest is almost exclusively on the editorial side. Johnny's absence from the record is only unusual within the orbit of *Weird Tales*, wherein fan interest has guaranteed that as many voices as possible have been added to the record. The more telling silence is Henneberger's. Recall that in all his reminiscences, Lansinger's name was conspicuously absent. Henneberger's silence about his partner, added to Lansinger's, doomed some of the history to die.

Perhaps the answers reside in their essential dissimilarity: the man who had always wanted to be in business versus the publisher who believed in the demonstrably noncommercial propositions of artistic writing, weird fiction, and the legacy of Poe. Johnny had probably held up his end of the bargain. The responsibility for the losses all lay on the editorial side of the shop: the choice of *Weird Tales* as the sure-fire subject for a magazine, the poor design-decisions made along the way, and the failure to discover the winning formula, assuming one existed. We will not get their views on any of this, but the sense of defeat is palpable in the silence.

Ultimately, the editorial reorganization had failed to rescue *Weird Tales*. The Houdini gambit, the Lovecraft factor, and the true-story slant—all had failed. In promising a dramatic turnaround, Henneberger had put his head on the chopping block for temporary safekeeping and, after the last hurrah of the Anniversary Issue, that very same head was quietly lopped off, and Houdini disappeared like magic as suddenly as he had arrived.

Once the split had been consummated, Rural Publishing was reduced to one owner, one magazine, and no editor. Farnsworth Wright had stormed off in anger, his note in the July *Author & Journalist* the equivalent of slamming the door on the way out, leaving the reputation of *Weird Tales* in tatters buffeted by the backdraft. It was a mess in need of a cleanup. After the insults from Wright, and the earlier ones from Baird, Henneberger finally unleashed his response. His rebuttal to Wright appeared in the August *Author & Journalist*. The journal didn't publish everything Henneberger had to say. They alluded to his denial of "other assertions" by Wright, comments presumably too accusatory or ill-mannered for the polite pages of *A&J*. These, then, are the extracts the magazine did publish, in their entirety:

I read your magazine with a lot of interest and have been especially pleased with some of the things you feature. If you will take the trouble to ascertain the true situation regarding *Weird Tales*, I am sure you will give your readers a different story. Up until the last issue, Mr. Edwin Baird handled the editorial end of both *Weird Tales* and *Detective Tales*. At that time I disposed of *Detective Tales* and the present owners retained Mr. Baird as editor. Mr. Baird is not responsible for any of the debts contracted by either magazine. I might mention at this time that *Detective Tales* is paying promptly for its material and is in good financial condition. I disposed of this publication that I might have more time to devote to *Weird Tales*. Mr. Wright makes the statement that our indebtedness is so much, but although he is in possession of our financial statement, mentions nothing of our assets. We owe authors nothing like the sum he mentions. It would possibly aggregate that if we were to include manuscripts on hand and for which payment is promised only on publication or as soon afterwards as possible. Since the inception of the magazine we have paid to authors a sum exceeding $7000, and at the present time owe less than $4000. We are not buying a thing at present, although I am sure we are receiving daily more manuscripts than the average magazine of similar type. I specifically deny that I ever offered to settle with any writer at a sum less than contracted for. It is true that we have not been able to meet our obligations on time, and Mr. Baird was instructed at all times to acquaint writers with the true situation in regard to our financial situation. The magazine is making steady progress and the future of it is assured. Despite the handicaps we have experienced we are gradually growing. If you take the time to go over a list of authors whose names appear in the back issues of the publication and write them for their experience with us, I am sure you will find that our attitude has always been straightforward and honest. True, we have had some unpleasant experiences with writers. I think we have had almost ten cases of plagiarism.[443]

We note, to begin, an air of general obfuscation in the comments, an attempt to minimize Rural's problems. He portrays Wright as an uninformed exaggerator, making him the rug under which the problems can be swept. Wright had devalued Henneberger's competence by suggesting that he had inherited the editor's job in the wake of his employees' defections. Henneberger took his revenge here by claiming that Baird had been editor up to the end; this was the argument that Baird had edited the Anniversary Issue, undoubtedly false. In making the claim for Baird as editor, Henneberger implied that Wright had exercised delusions of grandeur in making the claim for himself. He was the underling who foolishly thought that he was the one in charge.

By noting that "Mr. Baird is not responsible for any of the debts," Henneberger muted Wright's implication that Baird had been victimized by the injustice of facing outraged authors, as well as minimizing the scale of the author-payment issue for the sake of would-be contributors. We take Henneberger at his word that authors were made aware of the magazine's precarious condition. The magazine was generally, as Kline has pointed out, impoverished but upfront with contributors.

By claiming that the split was accomplished so that Henneberger could devote more time to *Weird Tales* is clearly misleading. It implies that the effect of the split was the cause of the split, when the overwhelming evidence is that the debt to Cornelius was the driving force. Finally, his references to "unpleasant experiences with writers" and plagiarism, while inherently true to the Rural situation and the industry, respectively, are an attempt to shift the focus from the company's shortcomings to other issues.

Henneberger's optimism that the future of *Weird Tales* was assured is borne out by history, of course. His positive comments suggest that there was enough financial wherewithal in the company's assets, especially *College Humor*, that the survival of *Weird Tales* was never in as much peril as Henneberger's ownership stake.

The editor of *The Author & Journalist*, Willard E. Hawkins, had published all the dispatches through 1923 and '24 related to the troubles at Rural. He consistently acted as an honest referee, advancing the concerns of complainants against the company, while giving the company the benefit of the doubt in all of his accompanying remarks, and taking care not to take sides in the company's disputes with authors. He didn't let the fact that he had appeared in *Weird Tales*, and that Baird had flatteringly compared him to Poe, bias him against either side of the dispute. Thus, his comments following Henneberger's dispatch were guardedly reassuring, noting that "Payment for manuscripts by the concern is slow and uncertain, but if it should succeed in getting upon its feet financially, a good outlet for fiction will have been established." At the time, it was the best that could be hoped for. Hawkins had probably learned a lesson from the long sequence of dispatches: to never again let his magazine be used as a forum for a publisher's internal squabbles to play out in public.

Farnsworth Wright didn't take Henneberger's counterattack lying down. In fact, he escalated the matter beyond words—into deeds. The only account of his actions is found in similar letters Lovecraft wrote C.M. Eddy, Jr. on July 21, 1924, and Clark Ashton Smith three days later. Lovecraft implied that the information came from Frank Belknap Long: "I haven't been able to keep track of Henneberger, Baird, & Wright at all—although of course my young friend Long generally gives me the latest. Long is in Maine for the summer now, but writes his old grandpa frequently."[444] If Long was the source, the information probably passed from Wright to Long first since the two were acquainted from Long's sales to the magazine. It probably did not pass directly from Wright to Lovecraft since Lovecraft doesn't appear to have corresponded with him by this time on any matter; Henneberger took over communications with him from Baird.

And what was this incendiary news? Lovecraft reported that *Weird Tales* was "hanging in the balance betwixt extremes as widely antipodal as total extinction & reproduction by fission!"[445] The extinction extreme included the complete "evaporation" of the magazine owing to its deep debt. In between the extremes were the possibilities that either Henneberger would refinance the magazine with his own resources or that the printer would try to publish the magazine. At the other end of the scale was the bombshell, the reproduction extreme. Lovecraft revealed that Wright was seeking financial aid to launch a higher-quality competitor to *Weird Tales* to be called *The Weird Story Magazine*. "Thus," as Lovecraft concluded, "we may have *no* weird magazine, & we may have two where one grew before."

It was a ferocious attack by Wright, aimed at Henneberger's heart—his beloved *Weird Tales*—and his pocketbook. If nothing else, it showed that Wright once believed, and still believed, in the cause of a magazine devoted to weird fiction. As an act of revenge, it threatened to take everything that still remained of Henneberger's professional life: his love and his livelihood.

And that's how Farnsworth Wright, the man of languages, became the man of deeds, the permanent editor of *Weird Tales*, and the arbiter of weird in the pulps.

What!?

We reach, at this point, a glaring gap in the story: the record of precisely what happened next. This narrative is, after all, a story of secrets. These turbulent events were never even hinted at by the principals. They are not to be found in Henneberger's reminiscences. The events were too humiliating, too painful. They were memories of failure—of insurrection from the editor within and the printer without—which interfered with the beautiful memories of having given birth to the intertwined legacies of *Weird Tales* and Lovecraft. Kline must have known what happened. He never mentioned it in print. Wright had ample opportunity to reveal the story of how he became editor—how he *really* became editor—in the occasional autobiographical details he supplied to the writers' mags. He could have told the story to E. Hoffmann Price, who knew him as well as anyone in the *Weird Tales* circle. He didn't, because, of course, Henneberger remained owner—or "owner"— for the entire time that Wright was editor.

So what must have happened? Henneberger and Wright fought and then they reconciled, because it made sense to do so. Like the reporter and the diver of "In the Depths," each could save the other. Wright needed a weird fiction magazine to edit—he didn't really want to run a business—and Henneberger needed a qualified editor. So they mended the rift, shook hands and, like gentlemen of the old school, never spoke of their differences again.

In a 1933 interview, Wright claimed that he became editor in late 1924.[446] A lie, but not an evil one. "My impression," Henneberger wrote in his final months of life, "has always been that Mr. Wright's editorship of *WEIRD TALES* started with the November 1924 issue."[447]

It was a secret by mutual consent.

ARTHUR J. BURKS AND THE TRIPLE EVOLUTION

The first season of *Weird Tales* was a haunted house's garden of withered and drooping ideas, and yet amid the desolation a few sprouts could be seen emerging, notably the alien growths of Lovecraft and the reliably nourishing produce of Seabury Quinn. There is another perspective, of things that might have been, of seeds that might have borne fruit had they been nurtured properly. Of those, the experience of Arthur J. Burks illustrates why *Weird Tales* was fated to fall short of normal standards of success.

Burks made his first professional sales to the magazine in 1924. By the end of the decade, he was a high-producing pulp writer earning up to two thousand dollars a month on fiction sales.[448] A magazine profile crowned him the "Speed-King of Fiction" for his ability to spit one saleable story after another from his typewriter.[449] The nickname stuck. In the 1930s his productivity across a variety of genres, and his leadership of the American Fiction Guild, made him one of the best-known—and most popular—fictioneers in New York City.

The curious fact is that the start of his professional career formed a nexus between three forces in transition: the triple evolution. The first was Burks himself. He had struggled to establish himself as a professional writer for four years and finally, in March 1924, the means finally presented themselves. The second force was the Palmer Photoplay Corporation, a correspondence school established in 1918 by Frederick Palmer and three partners, to train freelance writers for Hollywood's movie mills. That idea slowly panned out. In March 1924, after years of consideration, the company changed its name to the Palmer Institute of Authorship and its mission to training writers for the rapidly burgeoning magazine industry. That idea endured. Burks bought the Palmer course and, when his career blossomed, became their star student. The third force was *Weird Tales*. In March 1924, as we have witnessed, Rural Publishing was in the throes of an tumultuous reorganization. The timing of the three transitions was synchronous but not necessarily harmonious. Burks would find himself in the middle of opposing forces, caught between writing dreams and reality.

Objectively, his contributions were not critical to the development of

Weird Tales. Rather, he's remembered for being one of the first quality writers ushered in during the early Wright years. His stories for the magazine have occasionally been anthologized and his permanent residence in the *Weird Tales* corpus came courtesy of the 1966 Arkham House collection, *Black Medicine*, which gathered his early work.

Burks is of most interest to this narrative for two tangential reasons. First, he submitted his first work to the magazine in the midst of its turmoil, joining Frank Belknap Long and E. Hoffmann Price, who shared the same unlucky timing. Unlike Burks, who abandoned the magazine, they became an enduring presence. The second reason is practical: years later, Burks wrote about his experiences, providing a professional pulp writer's insights into the effect of the *Weird Tales* business practices.

Burks grew up in the farm country of central Washington state, the first child of a teen bride. Soon after his birth, his parents, Lura and Richard Burks, homesteaded in Moses Coulee, a narrow, bluff-rimmed valley branching off of the Columbia River. Richard was known within the extended family as "the world's laziest man." He fancied himself a man of letters, a writer in waiting, and left the brutal job of working the snake-infested farm to his wife. Thus, Arthur inherited from his parents two qualities which would define him: from his father, a love of stories and writing, and, from his mother, a relentless work ethic. These two great traits, which in combination were the key to become a high-producing pulp writer, were, amazingly, forged into his character by the time he turned the ripe old age of four.

Richard Burks was as violent as he was lazy. One of Arthur's early *Weird Tales* submissions, "The Ghosts of Steamboat Coulee," was set in Moses Coulee and its branching tributary whose mouth was marked by a large rock resembling a steamboat. Wright thought enough of the story to use it for the cover illustration of the May 1926 issue. One of Burks's best, it hauntingly shuffles and reshuffles his earliest and most painful memories into a series of recurring nightmares.

Richard Burks abandoned the family soon after Arthur turned four, and Lura abandoned Moses Coulee for a "rock patch" near the town of Waterville, home base to her extended family. Arthur and little brother Charlie pitched in as they could and attended school. Big brother Arthur grew up fast. By age twelve, he was essentially self-sufficient, earning an adult living as a farmhand—while still minding his studies. When his high school English teacher joked that he would someday write the Great American Novel, he believed it. His ego had been given shape.

Had it not been for World War I, we may never have heard of Arthur J. Burks. He would have become a prosperous farmer in central Washington with dozens in his employ. Instead, he took the train to Seattle and enlisted in the Marine Corps, becoming another young man of the time who left the farm, never to return. He never served overseas, a small source of embarrassment later in life when he churned out a lot of WWI aviation fiction for readers who assumed their authors were inspired by actual experience. But he never shirked danger. He was simply too squared away to be wasted in battle, so they made him a trainer and assigned him to shepherd recruits through Quantico, Virginia.

After earning his corporal stripes, he took a teen bride, a farm girl, and began to raise a family. He was following in his father's footsteps, with none of the bad character. Having a family always weighed heavily in his financial decisions. He would never, like Lovecraft, have the option of leading the life of an impoverished artist.

When the war ended, he left the Corps and joined the Department of Commerce in D.C. to help with the 1920 national census. He took "a five dollar writing course"[450] and submitted a piece to Macfadden's *True Story*. It was rejected. Naturally, he moved immediately onto that Great American Novel. He spent thirty days in 1920 producing *The Splendid Half-Caste*, a 60,000-word, smoothly-written, and ridiculously-plotted, western of forbidden love set in central Washington. It was "published" by the Burton Publishing Company of Kansas City, Missouri, a vanity press. They took his $500 and did nothing. He hounded them off and on for five years before they finally printed the book. It was one of the great mistakes of his life, but the writing practice did him good. As a pulp writer, he contributed to numerous genres: stories of the weird, weird menace, science fiction, adventure, action, military, aviation, war, detective, g-men, gangster, sports, and boxing. The two genres he steadfastly avoided were western and romance, owing to the scar inflicted by *The Splendid Half-Caste*.

In April 1921, the Corps offered him a commission as a 2nd lieutenant. He leaped at the chance. After officer training, in August he was stationed in the Dominican Republic (D.R.) where he spent the next two-and-a-half years.[451] The U.S. military occupation of the D.R. belonged to the so-called Banana Wars, a series of incursions and skirmishes intended to preempt potentially hostile European powers from their own occupations in the region, which would gain them proximity to the newly-completed Panama Canal. Burks's frequently harrowing duties in the D.R. can be divided into three phases: administering a military prison in Barahona; mapping remote mountainous regions on foot; and acting undercover to disrupt gun smuggling. The famous energy of his pulp career exhibited itself in every stage of his life. While engaged in these dangerous activities, he continued to raise a family—a third child was born in the D.R.—*and* work on his writing career, selling numerous short stories to religious youth magazines with $5 his biggest check.[452] He sailed back to the States on the USS *Chaumont*, a troop transport. Passing through the Panama Canal, he saw with his own eyes what he'd been defending. On March 20, 1924, the *Chaumont* slid into the San Diego harbor.

Burks returned from his years in the D.R. debilitated by bouts of malaria, dengue, and dysentery. He'd seen death and flirted with death. The lingering effects of the diseases plagued him for years. When he arrived in San Diego, he was an exhausted wreck. Thus, the Corps granted him leave through the end of April to recuperate. We can guess what he actually did with that gift of time.

The Palmer Photoplay Corporation was founded in Los Angeles in July 1918. The idea for the correspondence school belonged to Roy L. Manker, a newspaperman turned Hollywood scenario writer. He saw a need to teach freelancers how to write for the red-hot movie market. The studios were cranking out two-reelers and features almost faster than they had time to write them. Manker lined up two financiers, but they insisted he recruit a more knowledgeable hand to develop the course materials, someone who knew the film business inside and out, and could write. Manker knew just who to ask. He looked up an old colleague, Frederick Palmer (not to be confused with the war correspondent and novelist whose name he shared). Palmer, born in 1881, was a vaudeville magician whose career started at the turn of the century. By 1914, he and wife Anna—the magician's assistant—tired of the constant travel and settled in Los Angeles. Palmer entered the film business, progressing from actor to press-agent to scenario writer. In the volatile, high-speed world of early Hollywood, ambitious men and women rose from rags to riches and returned to rags, practically in the blink of an eye. Fortunes were made and lost and made again, subject to the whims of the business and the unpredictable tastes of the public. Palmer had exchanged the grind of vaudeville for the insanity of Hollywood. Finally ready for something stable, he accepted Manker's offer. Palmer was the last founder to join the new venture but became the name and face of the school.

Manker's idea, however, was based on a bad bet, that the studios would open their doors to freelance contributors. What they actually did was build in-house writing departments. The work was too specialized for outsiders. It took some years for the Palmer gang to come around to this realization. Though the company was a legitimate operation, in the early 1920s the odor of scandal attached itself to Palmer and its less scrupulous competitors. Shop girls and factory workers were being bilked out of their hard-earned pay with false promises of Hollywood dreamstuff. Or so the critics complained. When the Palmer brain-trust finally woke up, they realized that the real dreamstuff was in the opportunities afforded by the booming magazine market. Pulp magazines, in particular, were proliferating at a pace that would accelerate until the end of the decade, turning the 1920s into the single best time in history to make money selling words. As the better bet came into focus, the Palmer school steadily shifted its emphasis toward magazine writing. The official turn came in March 1924 when they changed their name to the grandiose Palmer Institute of Authorship. Later in the year, Frederick Palmer published his views on "quantity production," the industrial idea at the heart of the pulp-fiction business, an idea tailor-made for an indefatigable fiction fanatic like Arthur J. Burks.

While still in the D.R., in late 1923, as Burks explained: "I saw some Palmer literature and enrolled for the photoplay course, not because I intended writing photoplays, but because I thought it would help me write other things."[453] The course cost $136—over two weeks of his pay—but he was desperate to break out of the rut of low-paying juvenile magazines.

Palmer's industrial perspective gradually sank in: "It was tough sledding at first, just as it is for everybody. I found, however, that after I'd thoroughly mastered the *technique of writing*, I could apply the rules subconsciously, and from then on, began to pick up speed."[454] Speed would become critical, especially during the Great Depression when the extravagant word-rates of the late 1920s, two cents and more, gave way to a pitiless penny-a-word market. One had to write twice as fast, or more, to maintain the same income. One could afford no more artistic inspiration than the assembly-line nature of the work would allow.

Once Burks returned from the D.R., he was invited to the Palmer Building in Los Angeles which housed the institute.[455] The visit was an eye-opener:

> Those chaps at Palmer Institute started in on me, told me what to do, what not to do, commented on the sloppy work I had done on the photoplay course, told me what I ought to write, ought not to write, and in general made out a patient-chart which sent my fever up to 112, and the coolness in my feet down to absolute zero, and sent me home talking to myself, absolutely sure that I hated all correspondence schools, all literary critics, all institutes of authorship—with especial reference to the Palmer Institute, which was the only one I knew. They were a bunch of crooks, I figured, hungry for those installments I had paid, or trying to scare me into buying some other course.[456]

But they never sold him another thing; never tried. Instead, he confessed, "they made me so danged mad that I resolved to show them I could write."

The "oughts" and "ought nots" are of great interest since one of the Palmer services was to steer students to appropriate markets and Burks immediately turned to *Weird Tales*. The fly on the wall has long since passed away, but we can make a reasonable approximation of what transpired in the conversation.

Though Burks supplied no further detail, we know his background and interests; and we know the institute's points-of-view because later in 1924 they published them in five volumes of faux leather binding titled *Modern Authorship*, each volume written by a different member of the brain-trust—the course materials for the institute's new curriculum, the first with the emphasis squarely on fiction.

Burks would have told them about his experiences in the D.R., of all the people he met—the soldiers and, especially, the natives—of all the notes he carefully kept, planning to turn them into stories in due course. He would have told them about the Haitians—above all, the Haitians—of their strange behavior, weird beliefs, and the disturbing practices of their voodoo religion which could be turned into excellent tales of the supernatural. The D.R. experience had taken a toll on Burks's health, but not his imagination. His experiences had given him unique story material.

If he had expected enthusiastic agreement from his new friends at Palmer, he would have been sorely disappointed—and disappointment permeates his description of the visit. From their perspective, he had given them a prescription for commercial failure, nothing but "ought nots," all of which could be found in the first volume of *Modern Authorship*, Frederick Palmer's *Author's Fiction Manual*. The title of Chapter V laid it on the line: "Subjects to Avoid." Before moving on to the bad news, Palmer opened with a concession to the good:

> The magazine writer is not confronted with the difficulties which handicap the dramatist in his choice of material. Censorship is perhaps the most serious problem which faces the screen writer of to-day. No Board of Censors, local or national, can pass upon the work of the novelist and the magazine writer. He is limited only by his own standards of good taste and ethical standards which are recognized by the publication to which he submits his work. "Let your conscience be your guide" might be the slogan for the fiction writer as he decides nice questions concerning border-line topics in his stories or articles.[457]

Palmer wasn't entirely correct. The New York Society for the Suppression of Vice could make things plenty hot for magazines published in the State of New York, as publishers of everything from Joyce's *Ulysses* to the risqué girlie pulps would find out.[458] But for *Weird Tales*, published in Indianapolis and Chicago, the range of topics and treatments was potentially unlimited—dependent on Henneberger's and Wright's—and Cornelius's—tolerance.

But the big issue for Palmer wasn't propriety; it was salability, of the magazine to the reader, and thus of the writer to the magazine. Two of

Palmer's taboo subjects were two of the *Weird Tales* specialties, "the morbid story" and supernatural stories. In regards to the former, Palmer explained:

> The morbid story has little chance with the editor. . . . When the analysis of your character's desires or inhibitions dwells upon the morbid or the insane, your story cannot be said to be amusing, inspiring or imaginatively stimulating. It is only the morbidly, curious person who cares for such stories; and these persons are, fortunately for the social fabric, in the minority. A story in a recent magazine which features the morbid and the erratic placed all the action beside the casket of a dead person who had been hated by the leading character in the story. The reaction which took place when death released this character from bondage motivated the story. The reader was conscious throughout the story of the casket and the corpse of the man who had in life been hateful and unforgiving. The morbid glee which possessed the leading character in the story and the unseemly hilarity to which he yielded formed the basis for an unusual but an entirely unsavory story. If the novice is interested in such material as this, he must realize that his market will be limited to a few magazines which have a relatively small circulation.[459]

Because there are no supernatural or overtly horrifying elements in Palmer's example, he probably wasn't alluding to a *Weird Tales* story, but the obsession with the circumstances and rituals of death and burial could have described many a story in the magazine. Eddy's necrophilia tale, "The Loved Dead," contained no supernatural element, either, and achieves the pinnacle of morbidity. In regards to the supernatural, Palmer continued:

> Most editors dislike stories featuring the supernatural, although the ghost story has a limited market if it is very well handled. The recent interest in spiritualism and in all forms of the occult creates a demand for such stories if they can be made convincing or really interesting. The difficulty is that it is almost impossible to make such stories plausible without destroying the eerie effect which is necessary if the element of the supernatural motivates the action.[460]

To further add to the "ought nots," in a later chapter, "The Basic Emotions," Palmer invoked Poe stories to define three different emotions: "terror," "horror," and "wonder." He cautioned that " 'terror' with its accompaniment of 'dread' and 'horror' and 'despair' does not strike a responsive chord in the heart of the average editor."[461] And of "horror," that "Tales of this emotional tone have a certain fascination, but they are not in general demand."[462] And, last, that "However excellent are Poe's examples of the 'wonder' tale, they are not the sort fiction editors are seeking today."[463]

The negatives piling up, the Palmer gang would have presented a comprehensive case to Burks that although his story ideas were ideally suited to *Weird Tales*, and no other publication on the market, his attraction to the weird was a losing proposition. First, the magazine would have corralled him into an unpopular niche, not conducive to building a professional writing career, with any notoriety he achieved from appearing in the magazine of dubious benefit elsewhere. Second, given the well-publicized author-payment crisis, which the Palmer staff would have known about from *The Author & Journalist*, if not from other students, *Weird Tales* was not a viable commercial entity. Placing a story in its pages, with payment low and late, was only marginally better than being rejected from a legitimate market. In short, Palmer's staff held the winning argument. They would have counseled Burks to be wary of the failing magazine or, better still, to craft different kinds of stories from his experiences.

Would Burks have listened? Did he listen? Of course not. Not at first anyway. He would have to learn his lesson the hard way. He was not the kind of person who wilted in the face of discouragement. It's what made him such a stellar marine. In closing, Palmer would have made the case for caution, but they never would have told him his writing dreams, no matter how vaporous, couldn't come true.

Weird Tales it would be.

Years later, Burks reflected on his first contacts with the magazine. "I sold my first adult yarn—to *Weird Tales*, for $15.00. I had arrived!"[464] Like many others, no doubt, he was fooled by the high cover price: "I felt it was the beginning of a great career. *Weird Tales* sold for more money than *The Saturday Evening Post*."[465] The sale was a watershed moment for Burks:

> as long as I live I shall never forget the thrill of it, nor the letter which came to me . . ., nor the name which was signed to that letter. Put it in capitals, that name, Mr. Editor, for it was the biggest, most important letter I ever received in all my days: FARNSWORTH WRIGHT, editor then, and now, of *Weird Tales*. *Weird Tales*, and its editor, were having a hard time then, and Farnsworth Wright was very plainly a much overworked man. That was evident in all his letters, yet he still had time, knowing as he did that I was a newcomer, and that he was buying my first yarn, still found time to write me about my story, to ask for more, to offer friendly criticism, and to suggest revisions for stories which for one reason or another did not click.[466]

Wright could not have known it then, but by asking for more stories he had kicked off the Reign of the Speed-King. Burks had been unleashed: "I sat down and wrote ten stories in ten days, sold eight of them, payable on publication—and then *Weird Tales* had something happen to her, and suspended publication!"[467] He couldn't blame Wright for the magazine's misfortunes. Only later would it dawn on him what it actually meant to "sell" a story to *Weird Tales*.

Burks's stories began to appear in the magazine, as soon as it resumed publication. The first two—"Thus Spake the Prophetess" (November 1924) and "Voodoo" (December 1924)—appeared under the penname of Estil Critchie, inspired by "Esther Critchfield, a girl he once knew."[468] He'd been using the penname on his youth magazine publications. Farnsworth Wright convinced him to use his real name thereafter.[469]

As much as possible, Burks tried to base his fiction on places he'd been and things he'd seen. For example, he was a big fan of boxing. In the Marines, he never fought himself but refereed many bouts. Thus, his pulp output is littered with civilian and military fight stories. Burks was renowned in 1930s Manhattan pulp circles for being able to turn any random object into a story, a challenge which frequently came up at cocktail parties.[470] This talent was established early on. Once, a dentist complained to Burks that he wanted to write but that all he knew was teeth. " 'Well, write about teeth,' advised Burks. The dentist was skeptical, so Arthur J. picked up a plaster cast of a patient's jawbone, and made a wager that he could turn out a story with that as his 'inspiration.' "[471] The result, "Something Toothsome," appeared in the March 1926 *Weird Tales*.

His early *Weird Tales* stories were set in either of the two nations which comprise the island of Hispaniola: Haiti, on the smaller western side, and the Dominican Republic. Some, like "Thus Spake the Prophetess," were based on his research into ghastly episodes from history. Others, like "Voodoo," derived from personal experience, were full of authentic detail. Wright would have welcomed a story on as weird and exotic a topic as voodoo, a stark departure from the routine fare dreamed up by homebound American writers sitting at rolltop desks. (Henry S. Whitehead's voodoo stories would not appear until 1926.)

"Voodoo" is about the grim experience of Rodney Davis, an American officer stationed in Haiti—presumably with the Marines. Burks would not have specified the service branch for the same reason that he used a penname: as an active duty officer himself, he was uncertain of how much he'd seen on the job he was allowed to divulge, or whether he was allowed to write on the side for money. After making an official inquiry, he discovered that there was no conflict between serving and writing, other than protecting classified information.

In "Voodoo," Davis is rocked when he finds his military buddy dead in the jungle, the torture victim of a voodoo ceremony. Hellbent on revenge, he mastered the Haitian *patois* over six months, then went hunting for Cerimarie

Sam, the high voodoo priest. He locates the cult and, in disguise, sneaks into one of their nighttime ceremonies. Burks's description of a woman dancing around the fire is perversely chilling:

> Her bodily postures now expressed the lowest meanings of sensuality. The brain behind that black skull must have crawled with devilish vermin. Her movements were the acme of obscenity. The lust of the beast is clean because it is natural. The natural emotion of man is clean because it is sacred. But the lust expressed in the dance of the *Maman Loi* was the lust of a man or woman for a beast—horrible, revolting, inexpressible in words. As she worked herself into a frenzy a sort of froth came to her lips; her eyes rolled until one could see the dead white of them. She seemed to be possessed of serpents that crawled within her bosom, causing her to writhe with their writhing.

But that is just the warm-up, so to speak, for the sacrifice of the "goat without horns." A nude teenage girl, "stupefied with some sort of drug," is brought forth. The high priest opens her veins and the throng falls on her for "trophies that had once been part of a fellow being."

> The ceremony proceeded to its inevitable conclusion as if there were no depth to the filth into which the devotees might plunge themselves. Men and women, one with the other, forced themselves far, far down below the level of the beasts—in the name of the most terrible religion.

After uncovering Cerimarie Sam, Davis murders him while Sam's "devotees were too far gone in their beastliness to notice what took place." The story concludes with Davis informing his commanding officer of the "strange" death of Cerimarie Sam. "I also learned the identity of Cerimarie Sam, and it is my duty to inform you that the district of San Pierre has lost a distinguished senator!"

The story expresses the racial animus that might be expected from a Washington farm boy thrust into a thoroughly alien culture in the early 1920s, and the tale must have horrified the readers of *Weird Tales*, whose reflexive hands would not have been able to stop turning the pages. But, with Burks, the questions must always be asked: Was he Davis? How much of the story was real?

Readers of Burks's *Weird Tales* stories have always assumed that he served in Haiti *and* the D.R. But that would never have happened. He was forbidden to cross the border. Haiti's colonizers were the French; in 1804, the African slaves who worked the sugar plantations revolted and founded a new nation. The D.R. was colonized by Spain. Haiti and the D.R. differ ethnically, culturally, and in language, with French and Creole spoken in Haiti, and predominantly Spanish in the D.R. While the Marine Corps occupied both nations, they were such disparate challenges that U.S. forces weren't mingled. Accordingly, Burks served all but one week of his two-and-a-half years in the D.R. That one week was his last on Hispaniola. A military chauffer drove the Burks family from the capital city of Santo Domingo, D.R., to Port au Prince, Haiti, where Burks languished on duty while awaiting embarkation on the *Chaumont* for the journey to San Diego.

Burks did, however, come into contact with many Haitians. His first assignment was to the Barahona detachment, where he soon succeeded, at age twenty-three, to the command of thirty marines. "I became several things," he recounted, "commanding officer of the detachment, warden of the prison, provost judge of the province and intelligence officer."[472] It's not unusual that he would be handed such responsibilities at his age; with the Corps stretched thin, young and inexperienced officers were the face of the American occupation. The Barahona prison of his charge filled up with desperate Haitians who had snuck into the country looking for work. As Burks described, "These men were forced, under Marine bayonets, to work on the roads."[473]

He was fascinated by these Haitians, the strangeness of their behavior and culture. "I hadn't been in Barahona over a month, spending much time among the natives, before I decided that my business in life would be to transfer them to the printed page. . . . I think the Haitian prison furnished me with most of my material at first."[474] Burks conversed with the prisoners and took notes on the things he heard; the prison registry became "a mighty roster of Haitian names" useful for fiction. The prisoners became the inspiration for the early stories he sold to juvenile magazines. But that meant he could only use uplifting material, suitable for his youthful readers. In one, "Belema Guigua was a little black boy who saw visions of future greatness, dreamed of becoming a wise man and perhaps leading his people out of bondage." But "the real Belema Guigua was a Haitian prisoner, a voodoo practitioner, and all of sixty years of age. It was rumored that he practised cannibalism, but this was never definitely proven."[475]

Burks saw and heard other terrible things:

> Once I saw a Haitian in a pesthouse with all his bones broken except his right arm. He had been beaten half to death by the inhabitants of Pinon because they had found him with his mouth over an incision he had made in the neck of a young girl he had just killed. They left him tied over an anthill, where he stayed for three days until we found him—raving mad. During his last days he carefully took his rice and beans and plastered himself with them.

> In the Tower of Homage, Santo Domingo City, we had two prisoners, old Haitians, who were in for cannibalism. We had to keep them separated because they always quarreled over who had eaten the most human flesh. One had eaten his own daughter; the other somebody else's daughter.[476]

His dependence on the juvenile magazines had frustrated Burks. He had much more dramatic, horrifying material that lay dormant in his notebooks, waiting for an appropriate market . . .

When the opportunity finally arrived, in March and April of 1924, when *Weird Tales* presented itself as the ideal destination for his ideas, "Voodoo" came together. From his roster of names, prisoners Cerimarie Leontes and Guillame San merged to form "Cerimarie Sam." For the drama of voodoo, Burks did indeed have an experience to fall back on. He didn't specify where or when he witnessed this event, whether he had illegally crossed the border with no one the wiser or whether it was during his last week in Haiti:

> Personally, I've seen a voodoo ceremony, secretly. I frankly don't believe that any other writers have—except those fake ceremonies staged for tourists. I'd have lost my head if I'd been caught. I've never seen the ceremony of the sacrifice of the Goat Without Horns. The Marines have discouraged human sacrifices and cannibalism.[477]

He combined this experience with the grislier aspects of voodoo that he'd heard about in the prisons. Finally, all it took was filling in the blanks and adding a simple plot to round off his material.

To outward appearances, Burks had made a terrific start with *Weird Tales*. He had quality material to offer, appropriate to the magazine's mission, and new (interim) editor Farnsworth Wright liked it a lot. A look at Burks's publishing record with the magazine shows his continual presence after the resumption of publication. He appeared in the November and December issues of 1924. In 1925, Wright used his stories in nine of the twelve issues. It would be reasonable to conclude that he had settled in as a regular contributor, and that a healthy relationship existed between author and magazine. In 1926, continuing the trend, he appeared in the March, May, and June issues. But then he disappeared until December. Something had changed.

Recall that Burks wrote ten stories in ten days and sold eight to Wright. At another time, Burks confessed to a tendency to get carried away with his enthusiasm. After he made his first sale to a juvenile magazine, he quickly turned out twenty-eight more; he eventually sold twenty of them but it took two years. "Later," he continued, "I hit the adult magazines and, forgetting the lesson of the immortal twenty-eight juveniles, did about twenty-nine shorts in one month."[478] This is clearly a reference to *Weird Tales* and not incompatible with the "ten in ten" reference. Like many things Burks wrote about himself, the accounts sound exaggerated, and he may have overestimated the number, but Burks was generally on the level. He omitted details but what he said was usually the truth. And it is the Speed-King we're talking about. Therefore, we can't rule out that Burks's history with the magazine was simply a matter of Wright working down the pile of manuscripts he'd bought from Burks at the very start.

When the magazine halted publication, it had to have crossed Burks's mind that his submissions, only payable on publication, may have been in vain. If *Weird Tales* went under for good, the manuscripts were probably unsalable elsewhere. And any additional submissions to Wright, if "bought," would simply take their place on top of the pile. Once the stories started appearing in November, the payment checks dribbled in slowly. There was absolutely no urgency for Burks to submit more material since publication and the payment thereof would be so long in coming. In the meantime, the experience having made him increasingly conscious of the need to diversify, Burks's career branched off in other directions. Eventually, Wright's pile of Burks manuscripts ran out. Except for a few stragglers in 1927 and '28, and an additional submission or two that didn't belong elsewhere, Burks's career with *Weird Tales* had ended.

Sometimes the things not said speak volumes. When given the opportunity, Burks voiced fond memories of Wright, but always slanted his remarks toward getting his start from him, and never in regard to having a continuing relationship. This nostalgic 1929 reminiscence is typical: "So far as I know now, *Weird Tales* is safe and sound, and Farnsworth Wright, the editor who is making her that way, is a good friend of mine, because he bought my first adult yarn, and because his letters went far to cheer me when I was in the dumps."[479] There's not a whiff in those comments to suggest that Burks would appear in the magazine again. He did, though barely. He contributed two new stories in the 1930s (January 1933, May 1936), a decade in which he sold almost 500 stories to other pulps.[480] After a lengthy hiatus, during which he rejoined the Marine Corps for WWII and struggled with his wife's cancer, he rediscovered the magazine in 1949, selling them nine more stories in their final six years.

Burks had no relationship to Baird, while Baird was still nominally connected to *Weird Tales*; Wright had already taken over as editor. Burks also had no relationship with Kline, meeting him a single time in the '30s.[481] However, after *Weird Tales* suspended publication after the Anniversary Issue, the first recipient of Burks's diversification endeavors was Baird and

Real Detective Tales. It's probably not a random happenstance. Wright, most likely, recommended Baird to Burks, and Burks to Baird. *Real Detective Tales* continued publication while *Weird Tales* hibernated, only missing the October issue in 1924. *Real Detective* continued its pay-on-publication policy which didn't relax until late 1925, tossing Burks out of the frying pan and into another frying pan, with the exception that Baird didn't have a pile of Burks manuscripts to work down.

The Burks-Baird connection didn't click instantly. "Baird doesn't write much," said Burks, "but his 'This came close, try me again,' on a rejection slip, signed with his initials, caused me to keep at it, until I finally sold him a long series of detective novelettes."[482] His first story in *Real Detective* was "Master of Silence," serialized in the January and February, 1925, issues. Baird paid him $110, ten dollars higher than Wright had offered for any of Burks's *Weird Tales* stories. Baird essentially outbid Wright, stealing Burks's loyalty, another reason for him to abandon *Weird Tales*. "Master of Silence" began a series of mysteries featuring deaf detective Ewart D'Strange. Most were set in Washington, D.C., giving the author another opportunity to cash in on a setting known to him personally.

Burks sold Baird fourteen stories for *Real Detective*, the majority at prices comparable to the first, effectively preempting him from ever returning to *Weird Tales*. They appeared into early 1927, the time when Burks went overseas with the China Composite Expeditionary Force. When he returned, he had a new exotic setting and new experiences to incorporate into his fiction. He became a star author for the Fiction House action pulps and started selling practically everything he could write at good prices, payable on acceptance. The Chicago boys receded into memory.

Burks was the popular pulp writer who got away, or one of the ones. He loved to write but he wouldn't write for love. He couldn't afford to. His ultimate goal, which he achieved in October 1927, was to resign his commission and become a full-time, professional writer.

The original goal for *Weird Tales*, and Henneberger, was to achieve artistic and commercial success. The compromised goal, in the Wright era, was to strike a balance. They seemed to have succeeded, more or less. The magazine contained a mixture of challenging artistic work with crowd-pleasing potboilers. As a commercial entity, it survived but didn't thrive.

In time, the Speed-King would disprove the necessity for any artistry in the pulps. He became Palmer's archetypal machine-age, "quantity production" author. Burks was a fine writer when he needed to be, but he's best known for his Depression-era pulp stories which he wrote as fast as humanly possible, without revision, for the diminished one-cent-a-word paychecks. An alert student of his craft, Burks realized that all editors wanted, and all that most readers demanded, were comfortably predictable genre thrills loosely held within a semblance of form. Any extra effort spent in perfecting the form was a waste of time—and money.

AFTER THE EARTHQUAKE

With the May-June-July 1924 Anniversary Issue of the new quarterly *Weird Tales* displayed on newsstands for three months, the financial crises of Rural Publishing stabilized for the time being, and the acrimonious public spat between publisher Henneberger and editor Wright resulting in a truce, normality of a sort had been achieved. Except that there was no issue in August, or September, or October. Readers were confused. As Wright explained in the December 1924 *Eyrie*: "Because of the change in ownership and consequent reorganization of the magazine, the August-September-October number was not issued."[483] *Weird Tales* finally returned with the November issue, the magazine having been "restored to monthly basis."[484] But if peace had truly returned to the kingdom of weird, why the delay?

The magazine could have used a cooling off period, if a year of negative publicity in *The Author & Journalist* had frightened away professional contributors. But the real reason resided in the preoccupation of the Cornelius Printing Company, now the majority stockholder of *Weird Tales*. Obtaining control of the magazine was only the second biggest thing that happened to them in 1924. The first was winning the account to print *The American Legion Weekly*. The American Legion was co-founded in 1915 by the famous editor of *Adventure*, Arthur Sullivant Hoffman, to address military preparedness issues in light of the devastating war in Europe. After the war, the Legion became a veterans organization headquartered in Indianapolis. The *Weekly*, established with a first issue of July 4, 1919, was printed in New York. In 1924, headquarters called it home.

Change could happen fast in those days. In May—with the Anniversary Issue only a few weeks on the stands—Cornelius purchased eleven lots of an industrial strip at 2500 East Washington Street, Indianapolis, for a new, much larger printing plant for the *Weekly*, to be furnished with brand-new equipment.[485] In August construction began on a modern "steel, brick and glass" structure,[486] while the Cornelius facility at 325 North Capitol was offered for lease. While still available, the *Weird Tales* editorial offices moved from Chicago to the old building. Farnsworth Wright relocated to Indianapolis, while Henneberger stayed put. By the end of October, the new facility was nearing completion.[487] Printing of the *Weekly* began with the December 19 issue.

The effect of the *Weekly* on *Weird Tales* is told in a single simple variable: circulation. The *Weekly* was published with 700,000-800,000 copies per week, or about three million magazines a month. *Weird Tales*, according to Cornelius, had a monthly circulation of a measly 100,000, and thus was outnumbered thirty-to-one.[488] Admittedly, the *Weekly* had a cheaper issue price (the subscription rate was $1.50 a year), like *The Saturday Evening Post*, but was similarly subsidized by higher-class advertising. The grand equation rendered *Weird Tales* an afterthought for Cornelius, and moving it to Indianapolis in the midst of a major Cornelius expansion explains the delay in resuming publication.

Meanwhile, Henneberger schemed of ways to make money, to win back *Weird Tales*, to stay relevant. Still residing in Chicago, he produced a set of twelve booklets reprinting stories from early issues of *Detective Tales*, up through March 1923. Rural had been buying all rights in that period from unwitting neophyte authors,[489] and thus could resell the stories with no further consideration. The set was offered in a splashy full-page ad on the first issue of the revived *Weird Tales*, November 1924, available on newsstands October 1, the new standard for publication date. The ad offered "12 Great Detective Story Books" for a dollar.[490] The coupon listed the 325 North Capitol address. The November issue also ran an ad for the Anniversary Issue, and a full-page ad for *Real Detective Tales and Mystery Stories*, trumpeting Baird's editorship, and showing that relations with Lansinger and Baird were still cordial.[491]

"Make sure of getting your set before they are gone," the ad for the set cautioned. The warning proved prophetic, albeit in the twisted manner of W.W. Jacobs's "The Monkey's Paw." Three weeks after the November issue had been out, this classified ad appeared in the *Chicago Tribune* of October 23:

> PUBLIC SALE—STOCK OF BOOKLETS OF J. C. Henneberger. Notice is hereby given that 20,000 sets of booklets entitled "DETECTIVE TALES," held as collateral by the undersigned upon a certain note and indebtedness of J. C. Henneberger, will be sold at public auction to the highest bidder for cash on Monday, Oct. 27, 1924, at 3 o'clock in the afternoon, at the office of the undersigned, 140 W. Ohio st., Chicago, Ill., unless the maker of said note shall before that day and hour make payment of the note and interest. General Printing Co., by P. E. Schumacher, Treasurer.

If Henneberger had expected the income from early sales to cover the print costs, it was a risky bet. In the December *Weird Tales*, there were no ads for the set, suggesting that he had no booklets to sell and may have been unable to fulfill responses to the November solicitation. He must have come up with the money somehow because full-page ads for the books resumed with the January 1925 issue.

Henneberger had another trick up his sleeve, though, one that involved Lovecraft. With *Weird Tales* on hiatus, its future uncertain, and needing to pull his weight in the marriage, the author sought freelance editing or writing jobs in New York without much luck.[492] On September 7, he received a surprise call from Henneberger, in the city on business. As Lovecraft recalled, "Going over to his hotel, I had quite a talk with him; during which he told me of the new lease of life achieved by Weird Tales, and of the fine job he had in store for me."[493] The job was to edit a humor magazine,[494] as wildly inappropriate as that seems for a writer of Lovecraft's peculiar gifts.

Joshi speculates fairly that the offer was for *The Magazine of Fun*.[495] It was not a new magazine, of course, but simply a revival of Henneberger's early companion to *College Humor*. Henneberger may have been inspired by Lansinger's first big move as sole owner of his own company. To complement the large-sized *College Humor*, he launched a like-minded pulp called *Co-Ed* (commonly known as *Co-Ed Campus Comedy*, owing to the subtitle on the cover). Intended to surpass *College Humor* in "speed and spice,"[496] *Co-Ed* was edited by *College Humor's* editor, Harold Norling Swanson (1899-1991). Swanson had been a noted writer while attending Grinnell College, Iowa, writing poems, columns, editing the humor magazine *The Malteaser*, and winning a literary prize as a senior. He graduated in 1923 and was hired as editor of *College Humor* by September of that year.[497] *Co-Ed* ran for five issues from September 1924 through January 1925 then, like most failing pulps, flopped without fanfare.

But before that eventuality had unwound itself, Henneberger may have thought he needed to climb back onto the humor bandwagon.

A few days after the initial meeting, Lovecraft again went to meet Henneberger, who "promised great things" and invited him to Belmont Park for the pony races, which Lovecraft was grateful to have wriggled out of.[498] On September 17, Henneberger asked him "to turn out some samples of [his] adapting of jokes for his proposed magazine," which kept the author busy for the rest of the day. The next morning Henneberger " 'hired' [him] on the spot."[499] Lovecraft's placement of "hired" between quotes reveals his skepticism for the proposition. Nevertheless, he wrote his aunt that:

> Am ceasing answering advts for a while, to give Henneberger a chance to prove his business sincerity.
> He has—or says he has—hired me for his new magazine at a

salary beginning at $40.00 per wk & later going up (HE SAYS) to $100.00. I'll have to give him my undivided time, of course, but I'll lose nothing thereby, since the moment he stops paying I can stop working. First payment—a week from tomorrow. His plans sound more businesslike than ever before.[500]

But the plan came to nothing. Given the close correspondence in timing of the two schemes—the reprinting of *Detective Tales* stories and this new recruitment of Lovecraft—suggests financial interference from the former to the latter.

At any rate, though Henneberger had lost Lovecraft's confidence, the publisher continued trying to work him into his plans. In September 1925, when Lovecraft heard that Henneberger was in New York, he wrote Clark Ashton Smith that "[Henneberger] is always full of chimerical plans & false alarms, but this time I shall pay no attention to his magniloquent maunderings!"[501] On May 1, 1926, he wrote Frank Belknap Long: "Just had a letter from that crook *Henneberger*, who wants me to write up a 'stupendous' new plot idea of his! I've told him that payment of past debts is an essential preliminary to further business talk!"[502] Lovecraft was still owed money for material published *before* the split, two years earlier. Aside from the "new plot," Henneberger immediately tried to entice him with another offer, which sounded suspiciously similar to the failed *Detective Tales* reprint scheme which relied upon free advertising in *Weird Tales*. As Lovecraft outlined it for Long:

> the irresponsible Henneberger is now belabouring me with requests for authority to submit some of my tales to book publishers. I have let him have some to keep him quiet; tho' warning him that I can assume no financial responsibility, and that I extend no power for him to bind me to any agreement. . . . Henneberger thinks he can 'land' the tales not on their own merits, but through guaranteeing 500 purchasers for the book (*W.T.* readers—the great 'literary' publick!) and offering free advertising in the magazine. Well—he can't say that I didn't warn him—but I have so little faith or interest that I declined to re-type such unpublished tales as needed it; sending Henny the batch as it stood, and letting him copy the stuff (a process he claims to *enjoy!*) as best he can.[503]

Though an admirable idea, this too never came to fruition, and represents the end of Henneberger's courtship of Lovecraft. Ironically, given his great contemporary popularity, Lovecraft's fiction was never collected in book-form during his lifetime.

. . .

When readers rediscovered *Weird Tales* on the newsstands in October 1924, they found a completely reconfigured format. It was not another experiment, though; it was the end of experiments. The magazine would go forward as a reliably consistent product. It would get the occasional style upgrade, but no more than the typical pulp magazine.

The new format restored the magazine to pulp-size for the first time since the April 1923 issue. The new iteration was noticeably under the standard 7x10 inches owing to Cornelius's production. The cover price remained at 25¢. A newfound commitment to quality was apparent in the attractive, full-color covers by new artist Andrew Brosnatch. Inside, the number of illustrations were increased, though the line-art that previously illustrated scenes from the stories was replaced by decorative storyheads which mimicked the style of the classy *Adventure*.

As reported in *The Author & Journalist*, *Weird Tales* was "recently purchased by a new corporation," the Popular Fiction Publishing Company of 325 North Capitol Avenue.[504] It's a telling point that the Rural Publishing Corporation title—whatever its meaning—had been abandoned, illustrating the complete, legal schism between Henneberger and Lansinger, and the "reorganization" of the ownership. The Statement of Ownership in the December issue listed all five individuals who owned more than 1% of the company's stock: business manager William R. Sprenger, Farnsworth Wright, J.C. Henneberger, George M. Cornelius, and his son George H. Cornelius.[505]

Ostensibly, business practices had been refreshed, as well. In *The Author & Journalist*, hoping to forestall the strife of the past, Wright reassured would-be contributors that sanity had returned:

> The new corporation has agreed to pay off the former owners' debts to authors as rapidly as is compatible with meeting current obligations, and hopes to do this within six or seven months. It will be necessary to remain for a while on a basis of pay-on-publication at low rates, but we hope to go on a basis of pay-on-acceptance as soon as old accounts are cleared up.[506]

As proof of their sincerity, Wright followed up with this unattributed dispatch, appended with a list of names and stories, and a hope that the unpaid authors would respond:

> In going through the authors' file of the Rural Publishing Corporation, which came into our possession when we took over *Weird Tales* recently, we find that this file does not have the addresses of a number of contributors whose material the former owners had

published. We are desirous of knowing the addresses of these authors, so that when we are in a position to liquidate these unpaid accounts, we will know where to send the check.[507]

A deceptive bit of wording, Wright made it sound like the old ownership had been completely replaced by the new ownership. By implication, the old ownership didn't pay authors, kept lousy records, and were probably scofflaws who skipped town in the middle of the night, pockets stuffed with someone else's cash. By further implication, the new ownership was honest and upright and always paid their bills which, in Wright's case, turned out to be the truth.

We see in his misleading remarks an explanation for the jettisoning of the Rural corporate title. They were scrubbing the company of any links with the past, which may even explain the move to Indianapolis. The observant *Author & Journalist* reader could have seen through this misdirection since Wright's name had already been associated with the old regime and the new; for the unobservant, the absence of his name from the dispatch consummated the ruse.

The next month, and three months after the original promises, Wright confessed that the payoff of past debts had still not yet begun, and that until those obligations were fulfilled, the magazine would remain on pay-on-publication status for new authors with a low, half-cent rate.[508] His remarks betrayed that the magazine's new format had not spurred a dramatic turnaround in sales. Long, slow nurturing would be required. In February 1925, Sprenger sent a letter to unpaid contributors explaining the situation:

> We are writing you to keep you posted on the progress of *Weird Tales* under the new ownership and management. Even though we are progressing very well and are paying our current obligations, yet it is a little too early for us to show a real profit and pay off the old authors' accounts, incurred by the former owners. It is almost beyond the imagination of one not directly connected with the publishing business to understand thoroughly just how difficult it is and how much time it requires to launch a publication successfully—especially after the rundown condition that *Weird Tales* was in. By inspecting a current issue you will convince yourself that we are putting out a real magazine, and with it success is sure to come. You will be doing your part by having patience with this new organization, and we will keep you informed from time to time of our progress.[509]

Meanwhile, *Weird Tales* did not reside for long in the old Cornelius plant. By late 1924, they had moved several blocks away to the Baldwin Building on Monument Circle, upstairs from the showroom of the Baldwin Piano

Company, which must have pleased the musically inclined Wright. At the Baldwin address, *Weird Tales* earned a listing in a New York publication, *Hartmann's Who's Who in Occult, Psychic and Spiritual Realms*,[510] an indication of the public's continuing confusion over the nature of the magazine. In early 1926, the *Weird Tales* offices moved east several more blocks to the Holliday Building, a five-story, standard brick office building. By the end of the summer, they were back in Chicago which, at least, restored Wright's ability to supplement his income as a music critic for the *Chicago Daily Journal*.

After being rehired as editor and during the transition to the new ownership, Wright did not purchase any new material for *Weird Tales*. That changed when, in anticipation of the revival, he submitted a new description of needs to *The Author & Journalist*, which appeared in the October 1924 issue:

> *Weird Tales* especially wants pseudo-scientific stories; tales of science, invention and surgery; tales of the bizarre and unusual; occult and mystic tales and tales of the supernatural, preferably with a rational explanation; good humorous and romantic tales with a weird slant; tales of thrills and mystery; unusual tales of crime and a few tales of horror, but nothing sickening or disgusting.[511]

The blurb, imposing his personal vision, illustrated his desire to broaden the magazine's palette, but was not entirely accurate as to what the magazine would become. His desire for "rational explanations" seems like an unnecessary holdover from the Houdini issues. The humor and romance slants would not be requested again. His aversion to the "sickening or disgusting" was clearly a sustained reaction to the backlash over "The Loved Dead." The inventory style of the blurb seemed to reflect the contents of the November issue. For example, the odd reference to surgery probably came from "The Brain in the Jar."

Newly purchased material would have to compete for space in the magazine with the stacks of already purchased stories, like Burks's. Two new contributors whose stories were purchased in late September illustrate the dilemma. Amelia Reynolds Long (1904-78) made the first story sale of her life to Wright, "There Are More Things in Heaven and Earth," with the promise that it would be in the November issue.[512] However, she was not in the issue nor did any story with that title ever appear in the magazine. Her first of six stories in *Weird Tales* appeared in March 1928. If it was a retitling of "Heaven and Earth," her wait—and payment—exceeded three years. Another author, Hurley Von Ruck, had better fortune. She made her first ever sale to Wright at virtually the same time as Long.[513] "The Terrific Experiment," a story of hypnotism, appeared a year later, in September 1925. Only a year but the wait must have been unbearable.

Inside the revived magazine, the number of stories, which peaked unnaturally for the Anniversary Issue, returned to the 20+ count from the original three issues of the magazine. The November issue featured a few familiar names. H.P. Lovecraft had a poem, "To a Dreamer." Kline had a supernatural western, "The Phantom Rider," seemingly inspired by the January 1924 cover painting. Seabury Quinn returned with the final installment of his *Weird Crimes* series. Henry S. Whitehead made his second consecutive appearance with a short story, "The Door." The issue introduced two authors familiar to this narrative, though not to the readers: Frank Belknap Long with "The Desert Lich"; and Estil Critchie (Arthur J. Burks) with "Thus Spake the Prophetess," a historical tale of Haiti. Another newcomer, Greye La Spina, had made her name in Street & Smith's legendary—and doomed—pulp *The Thrill Book*, which hung on for sixteen semi-monthly issues in 1919. Her reemergence in *Weird Tales* revitalized her writing career. She appeared frequently through 1925 and '26, then sporadically through 1951.

The Eyrie returned for November, no doubt a relief after the flaccid *Ask Houdini* columns. But Wright's *Eyrie* varied from past practice as much as anything in the magazine. Gone was Baird's wildman antics aimed at the wiseacres in the readership, replaced by the normal straight-talking exchange between editor and reader that would be expected in any other pulp. For his first *Eyrie*, Wright began with a direct appeal for reader advice. He highlighted two stories—"The Hermit of Ghost Mountain" (March 1924), C. Franklin Miller's story about a hermit who extended his life through a diet of human blood, and "The Loved Dead"—as having drawn strong negative reactions against their gruesomeness. Wright quoted at length from a criticism of "The Loved Dead":

> Why will you give us such sickening stories? I read Eddy's yarn late at night. It nauseated me, but I could not stop reading, for the story was fascinatingly told. My eyes must have bulged in horror as I read, for when I finished I was covered from head to foot with clammy sweat, but wild horses could not have dragged me away from Weird Tales before I had read through to the end. But please, please—why *will* you feed us such disgusting themes? . . . for the sake of all that is sweet and wholesome, spare us any more stories such as "The Loved Dead."[514]

"Shall we purge the magazine of all strong horror?" Wright asked. "If we find a nauseating story as well handled as these two stories, shall we print it anyway?" He promised to tally the results and report the verdict in a future column. Additionally, he solicited opinions on all the fiction in the magazine. He renewed the request in the December *Eyrie*. Taking a page from Baird's book of wizardry, he added, "Prank criticism is welcomed, because WEIRD TALES is a magazine for its readers."[515] He seemed to be recalling the spurt of energy that "The Transparent Ghost" brought to the magazine, as if he never realized how damaging it had been to the relationship of Baird and Henneberger. All in all, Wright's early management of the magazine suggests someone trying to forge a unique identity while only having past decisions as a reference.

To no surprise, the reader verdicts on "strong horror," summarized in the January *Eyrie*, showed a heavy bias in favor of Wright's preordained conclusion:

> Some of our readers want the magazine to drip with gore ("the scarier they are, the better I like them," writes Bessie Douglas, of Portland, Maine); but these are in a small minority. . . . Well, readers, we are going to keep the magazine weird, but NOT disgusting. The votes for the necrophilic tales were so few that we are satisfied you want us to keep the magazine clean. Stories of the Poe type— scary stories—spooky stories—mystic and occult fiction—thrilling mysteries—bizarre crime stories—all these will find place in WEIRD TALES, but those of you who want tales of blood-drinking and cannibalism will have to make your opinion register a great deal more strongly than you have yet done before we let down the bars to this type of stories.[516]

Good old Burks, fan as well as contributor, came down on the side of the ghouls: "May I . . . vote 'yes' for horror stories." He'd seen worse things in the Dominican Republic than he would ever read about in a pulp magazine. To drive the verdict home, Wright reiterated the debate in the following issue. "I would draw the line at the grave," proffered one reader. "Even in fiction the dead have a right to rest in peace." Wright, with caution's hand resting squarely on his shoulder, concluded: "those who want cannibalistic and blood-drinking stories . . . are as few as those who want no horror stories at all."[517] He was learning the editor's art, using the pretense of a poll to let the readers think that they had democratically chosen what in reality was the inviolable dictate of the man in charge.

The December issue promoted Frank Belknap Long, honoring his short story, "Death-Waters," with the cover illustration and lead-story status. Wright published Estil Critchie's "Voodoo" and vanquished the author's secret identity for all time in *The Eyrie*. Eddy reappeared with a caveman story, "With Weapons of Stone," which prompted a long digression from Wright in *The Eyrie* on the caveman genre. "Why has not someone written of a fight between a Cro-Magnon caveman and a Neandertal man?" he lamented. As Patrice Louinet has noted, Wright's remarks served as a virtual blueprint for Robert E. Howard's first submission to *Weird Tales*, "Spear and Fang."[518] Howard immediately sent in a story to Wright's ruminative specifications; by the end of November, Wright had accepted it, marking Howard's first professional sale. "Spear and Fang" appeared in the July 1925 issue. If we are to believe Howard's autobiographical novel, *Post Oaks and Sand Roughs* (1928), Wright offered him $15 for the story, payable on publication,[519] the identical terms Arthur J. Burks received for his first submissions.

In the process, Wright learned that he had two distinct avenues for attracting new contributors. The first was *The Author & Journalist* (and other writers' mags), whose readers were aspiring or professional authors. The second was a direct appeal to his readership through *The Eyrie*. Of note, Wright's fresh description of needs, in the October 1924 *A&J*, was his last such submission to a writers' magazine in the decade, with one trivial exception in 1927. The only announcements he sent to the writers' magazines were changes of address or increases in word-rate—and there were more of the former than the latter. *The Eyrie* became his one and only forum to attract new talent, from the only pool that mattered to him, the fans and readers of *Weird Tales*.

Wright was completing his transition from author. But he did have one last piece of original fiction appear in the November 1924 issue, under a pseudonym. As he described the situation in 1935:

> I have written nothing new since I became editor of *Weird Tales* in 1924, but I wrote stories for *Weird Tales* previous to that, when it was edited by Edwin Baird. When I became editor one of my stories was already in type for the next issue (a story called "The Great Panjandrum"). I thought it looked rather phony for an author [*sic*] to use one of his own stories in his magazine, even though the story had been accepted by a previous editor; so I used the name Francis Hard as the author of that story.[520]

It's clear he wanted to avoid the conflict of interest issue we highlighted previously in regards to Wright and Kline.

He concocted "Francis Hard" from his father's middle and his mother's maiden names. Thereafter, the Francis Hard name was only to be found in *Weird Tales* bylining a handful of original poems, and translations of a short story by his favorite author Frenchman Alphonse Daudet and a poem by the German Friedrich Schiller. In the early '30s, "Francis Hard" landed a story in each of the Popular Fiction Publishing Company pulps, *Oriental Stories* and its successor *The Magic Carpet Magazine*. They were two of four which passed Otis Adelbert Kline's quality test. "Two other stories, which Kline considered rotten, I quickly canned—may they rest in peace."[521]

'Tis a shame he didn't run "The Great Panjandrum" past Kline and preempt it from being published. Told in a tone of benevolent condescension, it's the ostensibly humorous story of George and Martha Washington—but not *that* George and Martha Washington. This pair is a married African-American couple living near the smelly South Side stockyards of Chicago. Martha harps on George mercilessly, questioning his manhood for not going to France. The story's theme and not-for-the-squeamish Negro slang were perhaps the last vestiges of Wright's army training camp experience. By and by, George overhears of a plot to establish an African republic in Chicago, with talk of race war. The leader of the movement is a high priest of voodoo (the popular new theme in *Weird Tales*) known as the Great Panjandrum. When George reports the plot to police, they ridicule "the nigger" in disbelief, so George takes matters into his own hands. He infiltrates the temple of voodoo and sees the bloody sacrifice of a goat. After confronting the Great Panjandrum, a scuffle ensues, and all fall through a trap-door. The police arrive in the nick of time, having heard of the plot from another source. With the plot broken up, George becomes the hero Martha always expected him to be. The story is more valuable as a relic of the times than as a piece of literature, and tends to affirm Wright's move into editing. Mercifully, the story received no reader reaction in *The Eyrie*, one way or another.

At this point, we can declare the transition complete. Wright had become in finality an editor, and *Weird Tales* had turned into a "normal" magazine. It remained unique, but in the better way, in the authors it cultivated and the fiction they produced. Still, the unique chaos of its first two years remains a spectacle to behold, ranking as the worst two-year stretch in the history of any pulp magazine.

XXI

WONDERS AND WONDERERS

Going back to the start, one is struck by the closeness in age of most of the individuals who created or contributed to *Weird Tales* early on. Most were born in the last fifteen years of the nineteenth century: Edwin Baird (1886); Farnsworth Wright (1888); Seabury Quinn (1889); J.C. Henneberger, H.P. Lovecraft (1890); Otis Adelbert Kline (1891); J.M. Lansinger (1892); Clark Ashton Smith, Frank Owen (1893); C.M. Eddy, Jr. (1896); E. Hoffmann Price, Arthur J. Burks (1898); and a slight outlier, Frank Belknap Long (1901). (Appendix B provides a more complete list.) In one respect, this tight grouping is unremarkable. They were all in their mid-twenties or thirties, old enough to have escaped childhood intact and young enough to embrace daring career choices. But there is something else in those birth-years. Those particular years welcomed its members into a special generation who came of age during an unparalleled period of technological advancement: when transportation went from horses to automobiles; when the age-old miracle of flight was proven possible; when homes were networked with electricity and telephones; when electric light replaced gas and candlelight; when phonographs brought the world's greatest musicians into the living room, and film turned the reaches of the imagination into visions of reality. Over a brief passage of years, centuries of slow, gradual progress exploded into a world of possibilities. It's easy to see this sentiment fueling the creation of *Weird Tales* and soon thereafter the science-fiction pulps. A universe of unlimited possibilities needs art forms to express the wonder. There had been fantastic literature before, but in the 1920s it coalesced into popular genres.

Following in the wake of the *Weird Tales* founding class was First Fandom, as it came to be known, the fans who most embraced fantastic literature, devouring and debating its merits passionately, forming clubs, publishing fanzines, and sometimes turning into professional creators themselves. The well-known members of this group also were born in a tightly grouped set of birth-years. Leading the curve were the Arkham House founders Donald Wandrei (1908) and August Derleth (1909). Following them, to select a number of prominent names, were Donald A. Wollheim, Bob Tucker (1914); Mort Weisinger, Julius Schwartz (1915); Robert A.W. Lowndes, Forrest

J. Ackerman (1916); Frederik Pohl (1919); and Isaac Asimov and Sam Moskowitz (1920). (Also listed in Appendix B.)

If we take these two groups to be representative samples of specific culturally defined generations—admittedly problematic—then two conclusions spring to mind. First, that the *Weird Tales* founding class had the right age and acculturation to create popular genres of the fantastic. And, second, that the future members of First Fandom were too young or too few to support *Weird Tales* in 1923-24. Most were at an age when, if they had even recognized their love affair with the fantastic, they lacked the pocket change to support it, especially a magazine at the top of the price scale.

As the decade progressed, the idea of genre specialization in the pulps expanded, sometimes to ridiculous extremes. In the realms of the fantastic, key events were the science-fiction pulps, starting with Gernsback's *Amazing Stories* in April 1926, followed by other Gernsback titles, and then *Astounding Stories of Super-Science* in January 1930. By the early '30s, the dimensions of fandom had taken shape. There was a critical mass of material being published. And the majority of First Fandom had reached their teenage years and were capable of acting on their passions. The two forces, magazines and fans, were ready to unite.

If *Weird Tales* had debuted a few years or a decade later, it might have bypassed some of its early travails. By that time, the First Fandom evangelists would have been older—with fuller pockets. The magazine's quality variances, which mattered to a general readership, didn't carry as much weight with fandom. Fandom supports its raw materials as a cause. Fans are addicts. They consume bad stories as much as good ones because bad stories offer equal, often even better, opportunity for debate. Excessive liking leads to sycophancy; criticizing makes one feel like a self-respecting participant. They are equally valid rites of passage into the community.

Weird Tales, in its beginnings, paid a price for being ahead of the wave.

XXII

A History of Silence

Those first two years of *Weird Tales* were a torturous infancy, which produced for its participants frustration, shame, humiliation, and anger. Reputations were attacked and damaged by men who had worked together. And yet the magazine survived its difficult birth. Men who had fought publicly—Henneberger and Wright—settled their differences and even stayed with the magazine. Others went their separate ways. But whether they stayed or moved on, the participants shared a common desire: to forget the dark days, to allow their memories to evaporate, to pretend the thing had never happened, to let history melt into a secret past. In this penultimate chapter, we'll examine how *Weird Tales* changed the lives of the participants and how they attempted to bury their secrets.

Edwin Baird had the fortune, to put it charitably, to be the first editor of an obscure magazine that became influential. It set his career on a different path, turning him from his first love, writing, into an editor who wrote on the side. He never stopped contributing to magazines, though his freelancing waned when he was at his busiest as an editor. His fiction could be found sporadically in the pulps, often the cheapest ones like *The Underworld* or *Cabaret Stories*, and sometimes the better ones, like *Detective Fiction Weekly*. He wrote nonfiction pieces for an immeasurable number of publications, ranging from *Popular Photography* to true-crime mags. In that great age of print, a writer could always make his or her voice heard—and pick up a little extra money.

During the 1920s, the success of Lansinger, *College Humor*, and *Real Detective Tales* translated into success for Baird. He and wife Mildred moved from Evanston into the city. MacKinley Kantor was a pulp writer (and future Pulitzer Prize winner) from whom Baird had purchased many detective stories in 1928-29. In a 1929 profile for *The Author & Journalist*, Kantor described the good life Edwin lived as a celebrity in the Chicago literary renaissance:

His luxurious apartment on the lake front, with its unsurpassed view of Lake Shore Drive, is the Mecca of fiction writers, editors, newspaper men. It is here that Baird does much of his voluminous reading, and here that many manuscripts are weighed for acceptance, or sent back "into the woods" for permanent exile. . . . Suppose one drops in on the editor of *RDT* at eleven o'clock some Saturday evening. He may find [Charles] Layng of the *Daily News* and Babcock of the *Tribune* engaged in an amiable game of chess; Vincent Starrett and Harry Stephen Keeler in one corner, discussing British agents; Jack Woodford, Snowshoe Al Bromley and Merlin Taylor in another, discussing prohibition (in no uncertain terms); "Bunker" Bean of *Hygiea* coaxing college songs from the grand piano. . . . And moving from chess to British agents with equal assurance, pausing to nudge the discussers of prohibition, and dropping over to join in the chorus with Bean, is Ed, the editor and host. He plays with as much energy as he works, and that is saying something.[522]

In a 1963 letter, Kantor was more candid in his recollections. He described Mildred as a "rich woman from the East." If so, it enhanced the lavish lifestyle. "When the Bairds traveled anywhere it was in a big Lincoln limousine, with a Negro chauffeur etc." One thing the couple shared was a personality. "Both Bairds were agreeable to their friends and associates, supercilious and scornful in their regards of the world at large," Kantor explained. "I was appalled at some of [Edwin's] utterances. He used to stand at the huge front window of their apartment, and look down at a seething mass of humanity who spread along Oak Street beach on warm Sundays. He would say, 'Look at them! Aren't they just a bunch of lice? On a real hot day, when the wind is right, you can smell them up here, too!' "[523]

Kantor couldn't resist repeating one tale from the good old days of his youth. Chicago writer Harry Stephen Keeler held a drinking party—at the height of Prohibition—for a large cross-section of the literati. Soon, many of the guests were reeling drunk. In one memorable incident:

> Baird began embracing some young chick whom he found in a vulnerable position in a corner of the living-room. The hefty little Mrs. Baird fought her way through the crowd, grabbed her husband, and whirled him toward the door. She pushed him all the way across the room, striking at his back with the flat of her pudgy hands.
>
> "Edwin!" she cried. "Edwin! We're going home. Do you hear me? We're going home!"[524]

In the immediate aftermath of the Rural Publishing debacle, and in the sobriety of the working day, Baird set himself to making Lansinger's *Real Detective Tales and Mystery Stories* a success, satisfying his writing needs through the monthly column, *A Chat With the Chief*, and the occasional editorial. He continued the practices he had learned on the low-budget Rural titles. He beat the bushes for cheaply bought unknowns; he read all the manuscript submissions himself. And he never stopped bitching about their poor quality. As he led off a 1929 article:

> It would be so much easier to tell how *not* to write one!
>
> In order to do this, one would only need to take at random almost any of the thousands of unsolicited manuscripts that come to the office of *Real Detective Tales*—or the office of any other magazine—and exhibit it as an eloquent example of what not to write. The general run of these manuscripts is incredibly bad. Less than two per cent of them are worth an editor's consideration. Less than one-half of one per cent are worth accepting.[525]

At least his days of publishing an execrable manuscript for a lark—"The Transparent Ghost"—were over. Lesson learned.

Baird's post-Rural career reminds us that legacy is a two-sided coin. Legacy is what the world thinks of the individual. It's also how the individual values their own participation. In 1927, Baird and Wright were profiled in an article for *The Author & Journalist*.[526] The author, Willis Knapp Jones, had sold stories to both editors: four to Wright in 1925 and '26 for *Weird Tales*, and one to Baird in 1927 for *Real Detective Tales*, all after the split. And so, on a visit to Chicago, Jones looked them both up for an omnibus profile. He started by describing Wright and the magazine's standards. At the end of the section, he wrote: "I left this genial editor who seems so eager to help writers, and I went to call on Edwin Baird." Then he profiled Baird and his magazine. A tale of two halves. The odd thing about the article is that it contains no mention that Baird used to edit *Weird Tales*, that he and Wright worked in the same office, and that Wright succeeded him. The article contains not the slightest clue that the two editors were even acquainted. If Jones didn't know it himself, neither Baird nor Wright filled him in. It had only been three years since the Rural split, but that's how fast history can bury its dead. Baird and Wright, with no conscious coordination, were all too happy to let the first period of *Weird Tales* go unmentioned. For them to even acknowledge their acquaintance was to open the door to unwanted questions.

Never eager to talk about himself, in general, as the 1920s progressed Baird did open up about his long-lost days on the newspaper crime beat. A 1926 *Writer's Digest* interview described his experience:

> Editor Baird was for ten years police court reporter for one of the great Chicago dailies, and that he has in consequence a wide and exact first-hand knowledge of criminals and their ways, and that you cannot

tell him any "fairy stories" in this line. His training has particularly
fitted him for just the position that he occupies today.[527]

Kantor, in the 1929 piece, managed to pry out some of the more lurid
details:

> The trail which brought him to the editorial chair of *RDT* began
> down in Tennessee some forty years ago, and led through the local
> rooms of small-town and big-town dailies, through courts and
> morgues and gambling dens, all of which he saw with the wide-awake
> eyes of a police reporter. Baird has seen men shot down and watched
> gang hang-outs being raided; he has hurtled along crowded streets in
> detective squad cars; he has been the confidant of condemned men
> who waited for the rope in shadowy cells. . . . I would like to see an
> over-ambitious writer slip any fake crook stuff over on him! . . . Baird
> *knows.*[528]

When Baird wrote about himself, as in a 1930 *A&J* piece, he erred on the
side of modesty: "During my newspaper days in Chicago, I had occasion to
meet a great many detectives of sorts and observe them at their daily work,
and it came to me, to quote a distinguished Chicago gangster, now deceased,
that most of them 'couldn't track an elephant through a snowdrift.' "[529]

All that earthy, violent excitement made a marked contrast to the life he'd
described in 1919 as being uneventful. Therefore, note the particular aspects
of these three quotes. They were all provided to writers' magazines whose
readership were potential contributors to fiction markets. Note, as well, in
the first two quotes, the warning against trying to fool Baird with inauthentic
storytelling. Baird's reportorial past was, in fact, his way of turning the
tables on his contributors with an inauthentic story of his own, a fabulous lie
designed to scare off anyone who wasn't willing to do the research necessary
for a convincing crime story. Such is the editor's art.

After seven years of editing detective fiction magazines, Baird had an
itch to write a book on detective-story technique. Instead, he produced *How
to Write a Detective Story*, a series for *The Author & Journalist*. It ran in
thirteen monthly installments from December 1929 through December 1930.
In the November 1929 issue, *A&J* editor Willard E. Hawkins introduced the
series with the MacKinley Kantor piece, the first broad profile of Baird's
life to appear in print.[530] Kantor included many biographical details from
throughout Baird's life. It also included the false account of Baird's police
reporter days while completely omitting any hint of his experiences as editor
of *Weird Tales*. In fact, none of the thirteen installments of *How to Write a
Detective Story* mentioned *Weird Tales* or his experiences.

The omission, generally excusable, was blatantly glaring in Part XII: "The Horror Story."[531] It's hard to imagine him writing this piece had he not been editor of *Weird Tales* and grappled with issues of appropriateness for the magazine, and yet the closest he came to mentioning the magazine was to imply its membership in "the two or three wood pulps that specialize in weird fiction."

Superficially, the topic of horror stories seems ill-placed in a discussion of detective-fiction technique, but Baird opened with a bold declaration of their commonality:

> Since the horror story is closely related to the detective story—a blood brother in crime, as you might say—it seems proper and fitting to dwell upon it in this glorious series of articles.
>
> Other near relatives of the horror story are the weird story, the ghost story, the grotesque story, the mystic story, and the pseudo-scientific story; and these, in turn, are kin to the subject of these sketches—the detective story.
> . . .
> While the detective story is essentially a story of plot, soundly and logically constructed, the horror story is largely a story of atmosphere, and you may make it as fantastic as you please.

It's the opening to a weak argument, for Baird never makes the case that detective and horror fiction are related, which he could have since murder and mystery are typically central to both. Rather, the article resembles that last paragraph, in which the two forms are shown to be opposites. It reads like he was fishing for new topics for the series and running out of pier. However, the idea of the article was prescient. The introduction of weird elements into pulp detective fiction was steadily growing and within a few years would constitute a major subgenre.[532]

Elsewhere in the article Baird wrote: "Of the two, it might seem that the horror story is the easier to write, since the writer may give a free rein to his imagination, without troubling to explain his phenomena; but the fact is it requires a higher degree of skill, for its success depends largely on style and subtle handling." He could have been speaking as a proud former editor of *Weird Tales*, thus the concealment of that fact is all the more telling. The emphasis on atmosphere and subtlety is also the perspective that connected him to H.P. Lovecraft. The article throws out examples of weird fiction masters, like Lovecraft favorites Poe and Arthur Machen, but omits reference to the modern master, Lovecraft himself, who Baird brought to public attention.

Finally, Baird supplied a list of horror story taboos: "gruesome themes; revolting descriptions; repulsive thoughts . . . The horror story, of course, may deal with gruesome matters—and often does—but there's no need to offend good taste." Memories of "The Loved Dead" refused to die.

The 1920s became the boom years for the pulps, especially in the closing years of the decade, the time when many people made money hand-over-fist putting genre fiction on the newsstands for entertainment-hungry Americans. *Weird Tales*, in its frequent struggles, was a sad anomaly. After the stock market crashed in October 1929, the easy money days for pulps, and a lot of other magazines, and a lot of other things, ended. The money fled the pulps in a dozen different directions: cover prices dropped, magazines thinned, contributors received less per word, etc. Almost everyone struggled during the Great Depression.

Lansinger's magazines, *College Humor* and *Real Detective Tales*, were not exempt. During 1930, while Baird dispensed advice on writing detective stories, his detective story magazine suffered as well. Adjustments were made to the makeup and, as we've seen in abundance with *Weird Tales*, change often indicates distress, a need to shake up the formula. In the middle of the year, Baird deemphasized fiction in favor of "up-to-the-minute true stories dealing with crime and police work."[533] It was the same experiment that had been tried during the 1924 editorial reorganization. With the May 1931 issue, the title was abbreviated to *Real Detective*, bravely putting it in direct competition with Macfadden's true-crime leader *True Detective Mysteries*; with the July issue, fiction was dropped altogether. The results speak for themselves. With the December issue, fiction crept back into the magazine. The magazine limped through the dog days of '32.

After Kantor had established himself with *Real Detective Tales* in the late '20s, Baird raised his word-rate to 2¢. "I remained at that figure until April, 1932," Kantor recalled. "Then, desperate for money, hounded by creditors, I came into his office with a story which he accepted immediately. Baird said, 'One cent a word. Take it or leave it.' Guess he realized he had me over a barrel. I took the check, walked out, and never saw Edwin Baird again."[534] Kantor mistook Baird's bluntness for betrayal, not realizing that the Depression had both parties over a barrel. The glory days for writers in the '20s, the days of 2¢ and more, had ended. For most freelancers, the 1930s would be a 1¢/word struggle for survival. For those who remembered the easy money days, it was a harsh and sometimes prolonged awakening.

In early 1933, Lansinger lost the company as a result of using company stock as collateral, then falling too far into debt.[535] The last Lansinger/Baird issue of *Real Detective* was dated February 1933. The new owners moved *College Humor* and *Real Detective* to New York. But the dynamic duo of Lansinger and Baird weren't finished. They scraped enough money together to launch a new magazine, *Real America*, initially published—by the Lans Publishing

Company—from Baird's home address at 1120 Lake Shore Drive, Chicago.[536] Subtitled "The Magazine of Outspoken Truth," they promised that it would "blaze a new trail in magazine publishing." No fiction would be used. The magazine would tell "the REAL TRUTH about present conditions in America . . . It will expose corruption and graft wherever found. It will be fearless in revealing conditions that should be brought to public notice. It will always be outspoken." For a nation undergoing the darkest days of the Depression, *Real America* sought to have its index finger on the pulse of the times. For Baird, a muckraking magazine made the perfect home for his acerbic temperament.

The new magazine was beset with the age-old problems of editing. Baird complained to *The Author & Journalist* about the great number of unsuitable manuscripts that were arriving in the mail.[537] "No mild, long-winded discussions," he chided, "or quotes from other publications." By the end of 1934, Lansinger threw in the towel and Baird took over as publisher, again publishing it out of his home.[538] With the August 1935 issue, *Real America* included fiction in its contents,[539] a desperate decision. Baird's tastes were strangely broad for the kind of magazine he was publishing, indeed for any magazine:

> Stories need not conform to any special type, nor need they deal with any particular theme or subject. They may be of any sort—sex, love, adventure, mystery, detective, crime, weird, supernatural, occult, Western, scientific, pseudo-scientific, or anything else. They may be tragic or comic, serious or humorous, realistic or romantic. There are no restrictions, no taboos.[540]

He was—at least theoretically—willing to turn *Real America* into another *Weird Tales*—if that's what it took to survive. Several months later, he sold off his interest. The newly owned *Real America* failed quickly but returned under even newer ownership with Baird as a contributing editor and author of the column *Baird's Bazaar*.[541] And that was the last hurrah for *Real America*, never to be heard from again.

In early 1937, with his editing responsibilities having ended after fifteen hectic years, Baird settled into the more comfortable life of a freelance writer. One of his first jobs was a piece for *The Author & Journalist* titled "A Day With Midwest Editors," in which he visited as many Chicago magazine publishers as he could in a single day.[542] He made it to at least a dozen. The biographical blurb at the head of the article noted that he had edited *Real Detective*, *Real America*, and *Weird Tales*. It's the one and only time since he left *Weird Tales*—that we could find—in which he acknowledged his service to the magazine, or even mentioned it. In the article, after describing the operations at the co-published *Esquire* and *Coronet*, he moved onto his old haunts. "But let's leave these swank offices," he wrote, "and stroll on down the boulevard to 840 N. Michigan, and call at the two-office headquarters of that two-man magazine, *Weird Tales*." The address had changed, but not much else in all those years. Baird's description of the offices was accurate, but something less than charitable—at least he didn't call them pathetic. He neglected to mention that he'd once shared similarly cramped quarters with the two men: "tall, grave-looking Wright and short, merry-eyed Sprenger." Baird covered their fiction needs briefly, as well as their policies. "The rate isn't high—a cent a word—and the payment is none too swift." *Weird Tales* had bumped its freelance rates up to that level while most other pulps in the Depression had dropped theirs to the same. The magazine had become ordinary by default. One phrase bears repeating: "the payment is none too swift." The reader of the article could have had no idea of the haunting memories that lurked behind those words—for Baird, Wright, and Sprenger—unless they remembered the vivid drama that played out in *The Author & Journalist* in 1923 and '24.

Apparently, Baird's visit led to an invitation from Wright to contribute to the magazine at long last. Baird had published a lot of fiction in the twenty-seven years since his 1910 debut, but none of it had appeared in *Weird Tales*. Thus, his only story for the magazine, "Anton's Last Dream," appeared in the May 1937 issue. An uninspired effort, it's about a chemist who invents an invisibility formula, then employs it for concealment in a plot to murder his wife and her lover. Wright published the story but omitted mention of it or Baird in *The Eyrie*. And so the secrets were judiciously maintained.

Baird's career ended as it had begun, as a freelance magazine writer. He was as likely to be found in the detective pulps as the true-crime magazines. He also, surprisingly, turned up in the love pulps: *Love Story Magazine*, *Smart Love Stories*, *Sweetheart Stories*, *Thrilling Love*. A freelancer had to diversify. His known publications are scattered across the 1940s.

He died without fanfare, a forgotten man, on September 27, 1954, at the age of 69. It was over four months before Vincent Starrett, who had sold him "Penelope" for the third issue of *Weird Tales* and became a fellow member of the Chicago literary renaissance, warmly marked his passing in his *Chicago Tribune* column. "He was the friend and encourager, sometimes the last resort, of nearly all the young men of the '20s whose talent lay in the field of mystery and melodrama. . . . He began and ended his career as a writer of mysteries."[543] Starrett mentioned Baird's editorship of *Weird Tales*; he may not have known it was a secret.

Because of his short, failed tenure with *Weird Tales*, a magazine whose success came after his departure, Baird left the impression of an unimaginative man out of his depth. But even if he wasn't the right man at the right time, his intelligence, sense of humor, and verve shone through in everything he did, mistakes as well as achievements. His legacy as the first editor of *Weird Tales* endures in spite of his every effort to eradicate it.

Mr. Weird Tales. That's how insiders referred to Farnsworth Wright, so closely associated did he become with the magazine.

He had his many secrets, as we have documented, and he protected them well, even from the insiders. In the 1927 interview, recounting Wright's origins with *Weird Tales*, Willis Knapp Jones explained that Wright and Sprenger "took over a moribund magazine with a large indebtedness which they could legally have avoided paying; but because they look on writers as their friends, they made every debt good."[544] In the continual burial of the past, Wright was again implied to have played no role with that moribund magazine; and Henneberger, the source of so much aggravation to Wright in 1924, went unmentioned. Additionally, we know of no instances in which Wright mentions the founder of *Weird Tales*. Whereas for Baird, the secret had been his very involvement with the magazine, for Wright, who would never escape *Weird Tales*, it was his association with Henneberger.

Still, the magazine treated Wright well. E. Hoffmann Price first came face-to-face with him in late 1926, just after the editorial offices had moved back to Chicago from Indianapolis. "When I met Wright, he not only had his editorial salary, but also, $80 a week as music critic for a major Chicago daily newspaper."[545] "In those days, Farnsworth lived in an hotel."[546] "In 1927 he moved to an apartment far better than I could afford. He bought an Auburn car at a time when working stiffs either drove a Model 'T' or relied on public transportation, as did I."[547]

At that 1926 meeting, Price had stopped by the new quarters at 450 East Ohio Street:

> Wright's office was not the necromancer's cavern I had so often pictured. The room was brightly lighted, overlooking the lake, large enough, though seemingly much too small for the man. He was tall, very tall, and somewhat stooped; a large-framed, long-legged man, conspicuously and prematurely bald. My first impression was that his face gave no suggestion of his wit and sparkle. Neither did his voice, which was on the subdued rather than on the hearty side, but his eyes had a twinkle, keen and blue, and friendly. . . . [Wright] wanted Bill Sprenger, *Weird Tales*'business manager, to greet [me]. Bill was short, alert, intensely on his toes; pleasant, yet all business and a go-getter. He never read *Weird Tales*. Writers were pests who always howled for money. We all had a laugh on that. He and Wright were slowly but surely pulling *Weird Tales* through a financial reorganization, devoting most of the current profits to paying off the obligations of the original management.[548]

In 1929, Wright married Marjorie J. Zinkie (1893-1974). She began life in Aurora, Illinois, about forty miles west of Chicago, but they had met at the University of Washington, both graduating with the 1914 class from the College of Liberal Arts. As she wrote Price:

> Farnsworth and I always wished we had fallen in love when we were in college, instead of fifteen years later, but we didn't know each other very well then. He was well known and very active on the campus, and I always knew who Farnsworth Wright was, but I was a campus nobody, and only had a nodding acquaintance with him. He went with a friend of mine, a *little* girl who could walk under his arm—so I *heard* lots about him![549]

In the intervening years, she worked as a librarian in diverse locations: the Seattle Public Library, the New York Public Library, and the Idaho Technical Institute.[550] It's unknown how she and Farnsworth reconnected, but he was active in alumni organizations. Their only child, born in Chicago, was Robert Farnsworth Wright (1930-93).

Wright's Parkinson's became visibly worse throughout his years as editor of *Weird Tales*, as documented by the writers who recalled the situation in their memoirs. Price wrote:

> Even in 1926, the palsy which made him handle a pen with such difficulty had contributed to a certain general slowness of motion, which was so pronounced as to be a hesitance rather than natural deliberation. This suggestion of lack of muscular coordination was revealed also in his facial expression and in his speech.[551]

Referring to 1927, Price mentioned "the ruinous sums he was spending in his fight against ill health." Skipping ahead six years:

> I was shocked, the last time I saw him, in the fall of 1933, after a two-year absence from Chicago. It took me some minutes to recover; and then, suddenly, the man's spirit took command, and I became unaware of the increasing palsy, the perceptible drag of one foot. He even convinced me he was recovering. Damn it, he always did! He wanted no sympathy.[552]

In 1936, *Weird Tales* contributor—and cover star—Jack Williamson stopped in Chicago on a drive east. "Farnsworth Wright received me warmly and took me home for dinner. To his wife's dismay, I'm afraid; his paralysis was getting visibly worse, and she was trying to protect him."[553] In 1939, according to Robert Spencer Carr, a teenage contributor to *Weird Tales* of the late '20s, Wright "could no longer walk without assistance."[554]

Yet, he continued to produce a monthly magazine. He even, for a time, edited a magazine on the side. A failed experiment ultimately, *Oriental Stories* was issued nine times from 1930-32, and its successor *The Magic Carpet Magazine* came out five times in 1933-34. According to Henneberger, the idea for *Oriental* came from Cornelius Printing, looking to fill unused capacity.[555] Wright had a different version. After *Magic Carpet* had been put to rest, he blamed ex-President Hoover for inspiring the launch. Hoover was widely reported at the beginning of the Depression to have claimed that "prosperity is just around the corner."[556]

In 1938, *Weird Tales* was sold to the company that published *Short Stories*; that is, the Cornelius stock that Henneberger never bought back was sold. Wright and the magazine moved to New York. Sprenger remained in Chicago, marrying Ruth Y. Smith in 1940. After WWII, he joined the headquarters of the Montgomery Ward department store chain, working for twenty years before retiring in 1965. He died in St. Petersburg, Florida, on January 1, 1972.

In 1940, publication of *Weird Tales* was reduced to odd-numbered months, which it remained to the end in 1954. After editing the March 1940 issue, Wright was let go because of his disabilities. The editor of *Short Stories*, Dorothy McIlwraith, took over the responsibilities for both magazines. The news over Wright's fate passed like a wave of outrage through the *Weird Tales* circle of contributors, and fandom. For example, Otto Binder, who with his co-author, brother Earl, had sold several stories to Wright, wrote super-fan Jack Darrow on March 10, 1940:

> Wright was cold-bloodedly fired from Weird Tales, because of circulation drop. It's being carried on by McIlwraith. Wright is hit pretty hard, and our gang has pledged to boycott the mag. If Wright succeeds in getting another publisher interested in backing a new weird mag, we'll submit only to him. It's all we can do for one of the best and most liked editors in our field. With Wellman, Kuttner, Hamilton, Quinn, Williamson, and others not submitting to Weird, I'm thinking McIlwraith will have to print blank pages.[557]

Binder was located in Manhattan and clearly in touch with Wright. The intimations that Wright might start a rival weird-fiction magazine are intriguing, because they parallel the events of 1924, when Wright's equivalent threat appeared to have won him back the editor's job at *Weird Tales*. If it had worked once, it might work again. But that was 1924 and this was 1940. Wright was much older, seriously infirm, and the new company didn't need a second editor for a bimonthly publication whose sales had long since proven steady but mediocre. He wasn't going back to *Weird Tales* and he didn't have the strength to go forward with something new. Binder's charge of cold-bloodedness was probably unfair. The new owners had kept Wright aboard until, seemingly, they did him the favor he wouldn't grant himself.

None of Wright's schemes would have mattered. He died on June 12, 1940, while the first McIlwraith-edited issue lingered on newsstands. According to Price, Wright's Parkinson's "indirectly caused his death."[558] He couldn't put into print what actually happened. Encomiums for Wright are easy to find in the many memoirs of writers who knew him. Even Henneberger, the man who had caused Wright so much grief, and received so much in return, remembered him fondly: "Farnsworth Wright was the ideal editor. He combined a rare wit with a thorough knowledge of literature and understanding of writers, especially those in whom he sensed a promise."[559] If Henneberger harbored any reservations at that late date in his own life, he kept them to himself.

Otis Adelbert Kline, Baird's other manuscript reader from the early days, never—that we could find—publicly mentioned that he had worked for Baird or *Weird Tales*. Had he been willing, his best opportunity was in "Writing the Fantastic Story," a 2,200-word autobiographical piece in *The Writer* (January 1931) which essentially traced his life in fantastic literature. In it, he mentioned conferring with Baird on his interplanetary novel *Grandon of Terra*. Baird rejected it as being too long for *Weird Tales* and suggested Kline shop it to *Argosy-All Story*. The connection to Baird was a clue if anyone had known how to interpret it. The most Kline said about those early days was contained in his 1941 letter to Robert E. Howard's father. But even in those private words, Kline pulled his punches. He mentioned reading manuscripts, editing an issue, and writing "Why Weird Tales?," but never hinted at the strife that lay behind those activities. Finally, E. Hoffmann Price profiled Kline in a chapter of *Book of the Dead*. Price met him in 1926 at the same time as he met Wright. Though the profile discusses Kline's past, it fails to mention his earlier relationship with *Weird Tales*, other than as a contributor, as if the subject never came up. The only hint that it may have come up is his recollection that Wright regaled him with stories "of the many crises which had threatened to finish *Weird Tales*."[560] Whatever was said was off the record.

When the turbulent events of 1924 took place, Kline was still working for the family business, Massey & Massey. However, he still wanted to pursue a writing career. On June 22, 1924, he began work on *The Bride of Osiris*, a story he finished on January 2, 1925.[561] Implicitly, he took the manuscript to Wright first:

> When Sprenger and Wright took over, the magazine was so deeply in debt they wouldn't pay more than 1/2¢ a word to anybody. They told me they could get all the stuff they needed at that price or cheaper, and if I wanted to write for 1/2¢ all right; that was all they would pay me. So I quit writing for them.[562]

But when Kline shopped it elsewhere, all he got back were rejections. Though he never expressed it, we can sense his indignation, for the story languished, unsold, for well over two years. He preferred not selling it at all over selling it on the cheap. In the meantime, his stories showed up frequently in Baird's *Real Detective Tales*.

Two careers were not enough for Kline so, also on the side, he began operating as a literary agent. As he recalled in the '40s:

> In 1923, I helped another writer, an old timer who had quit for eight years and with whom I had previously collaborated on songs and movie scenarios, and one musical comedy, to come back. He quickly told others of the help I had given him, and they told others, so presently, I had an agency, international in its scope. Soon I was selling the work of other writers as well as my own in foreign countries as well as the US.[563]

Two disclaimers: First, this passage makes it sound like the business came together fairly quickly. In fact, it took a decade to develop. Second, the "old timer" who inspired the business had to have been Kline's old mentor Harold Ward. The reference to him quitting for eight years refers to his time as Sterling city clerk, but overlooks his extensive early '20s work for *The Black Mask*. Further corroboration that the client was Ward is the appearance of his *Black Mask* article, "The Concrete Facts About Thomas Hancock" (October 1922), in the March 2, 1923 issue of the British pulp *The Detective Magazine*. The following year Ward and Kline co-authored a short story, "The Yellow Killer," that appeared in the August 29, 1924 *Detective Magazine*. Baird's fiction started appearing in British pulps, including *The Detective Magazine*, at the same time, suggesting either that Kline had been tipped off by Baird as to the possibilities, or that Baird became a client of Kline's.

As Arthur J. Burks recalled, Kline "worked the mine of foreign sales which other agents neglected because of their smallness."[564] The British fiction magazines, in particular, were an active market, though they never rivaled their American counterparts and often relied on American authors to fill out their pages. The writers' magazines periodically listed English publishers and magazines, and provided guidance. For example, H. Bedford-Jones's article, "Selling 'Em in England" (*Writer's Digest*, March 1924), explained how and what to sell and what to expect in payment.

In due course, the *Weird Tales* crew achieved a sort of normalcy. As Kline recalled:

> By careful selection of stories during the next few years, and by keeping all expenses down to a minimum while living on starvation wages themselves, Sprenger and Wright managed to pull the magazine out of its financial hole, and it started on a new era of prosperity, along about 1926. When they began to pull out of the hole, they told me they would pay me 1¢ a word once more, so I began to write for them again.[565]

The first thing he sold them was the dormant *The Bride of Osiris*. Wright ran it as a three-part serial in the August, September, and October 1927 issues. For August, the story earned an alluringly exotic Hugh Rankin cover illustration. At this point in the narrative, it should come as no surprise that, despite being featured, neither Kline nor the story received any mention from Wright in *The Eyrie*.

In 1929, both Klines, Otis and his father, sold out their interests in the renamed Neilson-Massey. Louis A. Kline was in his sixties and ready to retire. For Otis, leaving the company corresponded with the start of his most active period as a writer. Like Burks, he had to quit his day job to achieve the kind of success he most desired.

Kline's first task was to do something about *Grandon of Terra*, which had been gathering dust since 1921. The book publisher, A.C. McClurg, who had published numerous Edgar Rice Burroughs novels, agreed to issue *Grandon* provided Kline could first obtain serial publication in a magazine. When *Argosy* bought the rights, the deal was complete. Retitled *The Planet of Peril*, the novel ran as a six-part serial in the weekly from July 20 through August 24, 1929. On October 5, ads for the McClurg hardbound started appearing in newspapers.

There could be no greater tribute to the story's power than what happened during this time in Livingston, Montana. One Rollin Davisson was awaiting hanging for the murder of the police chief and another officer. He passed his time by reading *The Planet of Peril* in *Argosy*, but he was missing two installments. In sympathy, the local paper ran a story on his plight. Readers supplied "scores of copies of the two missing numbers to the newspaper and to the sheriff's office."[566] Sadly, though, Davisson would not live long enough to read Kline's sequel.

On September 7, the *Sterling Daily Gazette* ran a "local boy makes good" story on Kline's success with *The Planet of Peril*. The information had been supplied by Harold Ward after he went to Chicago to call—allegedly—on "a number of editors and publishers." The real purpose was undoubtedly to call on his agent, Kline. Kline had placed a number of his stories in British pulps during the late '20s. The article, which Ward probably supplied the copy for, took the objective reportorial tone expected of news articles, as if the reporter had no relationship to his subject. It sketched in Kline's background: "Originally a musician of ability, he entered upon his writing career as a song writer, turning out a number of songs of extraordinary merit." It gushed with praise for *The Planet of Peril*, courtesy of the "editors and publishers": "promises to be one of the six best sellers of the year," "without doubt one of the greatest pieces of imaginative fiction ever produced," "considered the equal of the work of Edgar Rice Burroughs and Mr. Kline is touted by the best writers and editors as the logical successor of that author."[567]

This was the start of comparisons between Kline and Burroughs, though Ward shouldn't get much credit for the novelty of the observation. Kline had been inspired by Burroughs's interplanetary stories and the obvious comparison was spontaneously made in numerous newspaper reviews of the McClurg book. In time, the similarity of the Kline and Burroughs novels, and the sequence of them employing each other's planets as fictional milieus led to talk of a rivalry which has been largely debunked.

Through 1933, with all the time he needed, Kline poured out novels set on Venus, Mars, and the Moon, as well as earthly jungles, drawing comparisons to Burroughs's Tarzan novels. Kline was a serial star in *Argosy*, and what they wouldn't buy at their higher rates ended up in *Weird Tales* as lavish, cover-featured attractions. Kline even got little brother Allen—the one who fell off the barn door—into the act. They co-authored a novel, *The Secret Kingdom*, which was serialized in *Amazing Stories* in the last three issues of 1929.

To outward appearances, Kline had figured out how to make his dreams come true. E. Hoffmann Price bluntly told the other side of the story: "Otis couldn't make the grade as a full-time fictioneer. He sold all that he wrote. He was however unable to produce the volume which his life-style required."[568] This was when his literary agent's work entered the foreground while his writing moved to the background. In early 1933, he took on the productive Robert E. Howard as a client. The October 1934 *Author & Journalist* featured the first ad for Kline's services, listing his home address of 4333 Castello Avenue, Chicago. It featured a lengthy endorsement from Edwin Baird that concluded with, "he is absolutely fair and square—as honest a man as I've ever known." A March 1935 Kline ad in *Writer's Digest* consisted of a laudatory letter from Harold Ward. It thanked Kline for placing so many of his materials in foreign markets. He also praised Kline's criticism service: "Even an old dog like myself sometimes runs amuck, and I respect, admire, and take my hat off to any man who has the intestinal fortitude to slap me back on my haunches when I'm wrong."[569]

The number of writers that Kline represented will never be known. His professional discretion prevented him from discussing his clients, which helps explain why his relationship to Harold Ward remained hidden for so long.

In late 1936, Kline moved his agency to New York while moving his residence with wife Curley to Short Beach, Connecticut. He promoted his Unified Sales Plan for literary properties using endorsements from a who's-who of names from the early days of *Weird Tales*, the writers he remained closest to: Edwin Baird, E. Hoffmann Price, Farnsworth Wright, Harold Ward, and Frank Belknap Long, Jr.

Kline continued to write, occasionally collaborating with Price. Their novel, *Satans on Saturn*, appeared in *Argosy* in five parts in November 1940. Kline's last piece of fiction published in his lifetime was, appropriately enough, a novelette in the July 1943 *Weird Tales* co-authored with Long. Its title, "Return of the Undead," could have referred to the magazine after its 1924 resurrection.

He passed away at his Short Beach home on October 24, 1946. Otto Binder, who had worked for the New York branch of Kline's agency, reported what Curley Kline had told him over the phone: "[Otis] had gone to his N.Y. office, seemingly fit, but came home early, not feeling well. He fell dead from a heart attack shortly after."[570]

At the same time as the Rural Publishing meltdown in 1924, events in Harold Ward's life derailed his writing ambitions. Back during the world war, he had organized a group, the Sterling Lady Zouaves, as a fundraiser to buy overcoats for the local infantry recruits. The ladies—sixteen high school girls—dressed in the striking black and red of the French colonial Zouaves and performed a fifteen-minute routine under Ward's direction. The group was such a success they stayed around as a sort of local club.[571] That was how Harold got to know a girl named Gladys (1903-96), twenty-four years his junior. On April 30, 1924, Ward resigned his position as Sterling city clerk, after President Calvin Coolidge nominated him to be Sterling postmaster and the U.S. Senate consented. Soon thereafter, Gladys became the second Mrs. Harold Ward. With an important new job and a new wife, and *Weird Tales* suspended, the writing slipped away.

The Wards had three children together: Dorothy, 1926; Milton, 1927; and Gladys Jr., 1930. If being postmaster, husband, and father wasn't enough, Ward also busied himself with other civic responsibilities, like serving as president of the Association of Commerce. Meanwhile, Kline did his best to earn Ward a little extra money from the British reprints of his American publications. Ward didn't start publishing new material again until 1929, when the market for pulp writers was peaking. He reappeared in *Weird*

Tales in 1932 starting a nice run of eleven appearances that lasted through 1937, making him a familiar name in the Golden Age without adding much to the *Weird Tales* literary legacy. Wright honored him by using his short story, "Clutching Hands of Death," a "story of weird surgery," to illustrate the cover of the March 1935 issue. Ward is perhaps best-remembered for writing the lead novels for *Doctor Death*, under the elegant nom de plume of "Zorro," one of the very few character pulps which employed a villain as lead character. Something of a last hurrah, it only lasted three issues: February, March, and April 1935. After that, Ward stories appeared in scattered pulps throughout the remainder of the decade.

In 1934, he took an editing and writing position with the *Sterling Daily Gazette*, a job he held for the rest of his life. First and last a newspaperman, he died at his desk in the *Gazette* offices on March 1, 1950.[572]

"Wright is a most bewilderingly capricious cuss!"[573] So wrote the elder H.P. Lovecraft to his young correspondent Robert Bloch in November 1933, nine years after the historic Rural split, nine years after the transition from Edwin Baird to Farnsworth Wright as editor of *Weird Tales*—the benefactor or executioner of a fantasy writers' dreams—and nine years after the passage from a mercurial to an even-tempered personality.

Though his anxieties made it difficult for him to realize it in the early days, Lovecraft had been spoiled by Baird. Baird purchased everything Lovecraft submitted; published his friends, as well. Baird not only fulfilled Lovecraft's dreams, he fulfilled Henneberger's desire for a magazine that carried on a tradition established by Poe. Then he turned around and ridiculed his boss's intentions by contemptuously publishing "The Transparent Ghost." Baird had his capricious streak, too, but the victim was Henneberger. When Henneberger took over Lovecraft relations from Baird, Lovecraft became the celebrity author who could do no wrong.

When Farnsworth Wright became editor, the manufactured anxieties of the Baird regime were replaced by genuine anxieties. Wright had his own suite of fears, no doubt amplified by the turbulent events of 1923-24. He had strong memories of the poor choices that had led to failure. Henneberger, through the marginalization of his ownership, had been neutralized as an influence over the content of *Weird Tales*. He wouldn't even move to Indianapolis. The power of his shadow—and Poe's—diminished. When the magazine relaunched in late '24, it was Wright's show. And the things that gave him nightmares in the dark of night were stories which were too wordy, too slow, too arty, too atmospheric, or too gruesome—all of the attributes which in their balance form Poe's appeal—and Lovecraft's. If there was any question as to whether a story tilted too much toward the experimental and too far away from the commercial, Wright followed duty in erring on the side of survival, an approach which seriously disadvantaged Lovecraft.

Inevitably, Lovecraft was introduced to the sting of rejection. It's a pain that every commercial writer endures, but Lovecraft, a perpetual stranger to commercial publishing, found it difficult to adjust.

Wright consistently published Lovecraft material in the magazine throughout the first year of the new regime—some from the previously purchased backlog and some from new purchases. He pressed Lovecraft for more material, and paid him at the magazine's highest rate.[574] But in September 1925 Wright rejected "The Shunned House" for "beginning too gradually."[575] It was the first clue to Lovecraft that the frictionless days had passed. Following soon after came the rejection of "In the Vault" on the nebulous grounds of Indiana censorship. Then, in early 1926, Wright rejected "Cool Air," the last of Lovecraft's New York stories, for unknown reasons though, as Joshi speculates, its "grisly conclusion" made it problematic.[576] It eventually appeared in the short-lived *Tales of Magic and Mystery* for March 1928. "The Call of Cthulhu," as previously discussed, was initially rejected by Wright before being accepted on a second submission. In 1931, a particular blow to Lovecraft was Wright's rejection of his 40,000-word novel, *At the Mountains of Madness*. According to Lovecraft, the editor found it *"too long, not easily divisible into parts, not convincing—& so on."* In despair, he added: "It is very possible that I am growing stale . . . but if so it merely signifies the end of my fictional attempts."[577] Over four years later, the novel was serialized in *Astounding Stories*.

There were good days in the universe of Wright's capriciousness. Lovecraft spent the first half of 1931 writing "The Whisperer in Darkness." It garnered $350 from the editor, the largest payment Lovecraft would ever receive for a story,[578] and appeared in the August 1931 *Weird Tales*. But Lovecraft couldn't take the good with the bad. The paradigm had become rejection. After writing "The Dreams in the Witch House" in February 1932, he mailed the manuscript around to his friends for review. Three were favorable, but August Derleth deemed it a "poor story."[579] Lovecraft's confidence was shattered. He never sent it to Wright. Approximately a year later, Derleth, on his own initiative, forwarded it to the editor. It appeared in the July 1933 issue.[580]

After that, the author who so much represented the aspirations for the magazine was a diminished presence in its pages. His classics were occasionally reprinted. He collaborated with E. Hoffmann Price on "Through the Gates of the Silver Key" (July 1934). His revisions for clients appeared sporadically. A Lovecraft letter turned up in *The Eyrie* now and then. Only two new Lovecraft stories were published in *Weird Tales* in the last four years of his life and they both came near the end: "The Haunter of the Dark" (December 1936) and "The Thing on the Doorstep" (January 1937).

"Haunter" was a fictional retort to a Bloch story, "The Shambler From the Stars" (September 1935), which had teasingly used Lovecraft as a character; "Thing" had been written in 1933.

Lovecraft began to feel quite poorly in January 1937. The end of February found him in constant pain. His last month was miserable. He died on March 15, 1937. The causes were cancer of the small intestine and kidney disease.[581]

But in many respects that was the beginning of Lovecraft's story. Once he was dead, the era of capriciousness went with him, to be replaced with literary immortality. The encomiums poured into Wright's mailbox; a number were printed in the magazine. Wright may have been surprised by the groundswell of grief for Lovecraft's passing. He responded in kind. By the end of 1937, Lovecraft was a constant presence in the magazine, mimicking his golden days of 1924. His writers' struggles had been rendered irrelevant once again. Most of the material was reprints, of course, but some previously unpublished material appeared, mostly poetry. A lot of the reprinted items had appeared in amateur press publications but never in *Weird Tales*. Wright had much to choose from.

Some of Wright's choices were laden with irony. "The Shunned House," Lovecraft's first rejection from Wright, appeared in the October 1937, one of the initial pieces of the revival. "Imprisoned with the Pharaohs," reprinted for the first time in the June 1939 issue, listed Houdini as author on the magazine's table of contents, but on the storyhead Wright added: "Though the events were narrated by Houdini, and the printer's proofs were all OK'd by him, the actual writing was done by the late great master of weird fiction, H.P. Lovecraft." It was mostly true, probably reflecting what Wright actually knew about the original circumstances. "Cool Air," rejected in 1926, appeared in the September 1939 issue. Down to the end, Wright's last issue (March 1940) reprinted a poem, "The Dweller," from Lovecraft's hometown paper, *The Providence Journal*. Only by being so parsimonious about publishing Lovecraft during his lifetime could Wright have unveiled so much about the author after he died.

Wright's successor, Dorothy McIlwraith, didn't show the same zeal to immortalize Lovecraft, but nevertheless continued to include him in the magazine. Lovecraft's novel *The Case of Charles Dexter Ward* received its first publication in the May and July 1941 issues. The six episodes of *Herbert West—Reanimator* (*Home Brew*, 1922), which Lovecraft would have preferred to remain buried, were sprinkled through *Weird Tales* across 1942 and '43.

Meanwhile, the establishment of Arkham House in 1939, with the goal of publishing all of Lovecraft's writings, took his legacy in a more sustained direction. The seed that was planted in 1923-24 grew into widespread publication of his works, an influence on other writers, an influence on horror and fantasy in the pulps and elsewhere, an influence on horror and scifi films, all of which have woven him—and *Weird Tales*—into the texture of popular culture.

Lovecraft can be omitted from one of the broader themes of this narrative: the conspiracy of silence. He is our tale's Deep Throat, the chief leaker. The trail he left in his correspondence was instrumental in peeling away the veil of secrecy maintained by the *Weird Tales* creators. And, by conspiracy, we don't mean a blood oath made in a secret meeting behind closed doors, but rather a shared understanding that some matters were best forgotten. To review the pattern of secrecy in one place, here are how the main players handled their memories.

Chief among the secret-keepers was J.C. Henneberger himself, the man whose reputation took the hardest hit. He had shared a little of the *Weird Tales* origin story with publisher August Derleth after the foundation of Arkham House; August Derleth, the man who had succeeded where Henneberger had failed, in collecting Lovecraft between hardcovers. Henneberger further opened up about his experience with *Weird Tales* in his 1960s conversations with Sam Moskowitz. A few years later, he provided Joel Frieman a more elaborate account. All accounts were highly sanitized and ravaged by memory faults. Of his difficulties, he admitted to losing "a great deal of money." He blamed the printer for his problems. That's about all for the difficulties. Lansinger's name never entered into it. In 1965, Arkham House published the first volume of Lovecraft's *Selected Letters*. It included letters that Lovecraft had written immediately after Henneberger wrote him in January 1924, indiscreetly describing the magazine's deep problems. When Henneberger heard that the book was forthcoming, he wrote Derleth about obtaining a copy.[582] That Henneberger's memory wasn't refreshed by the material in the book suggests that he either never read it or ignored its contents. As he wrote Joel: "There is no use going into details of the quirks of fortune that beset me with this magazine."[583]

His silent partner, Johnny Lansinger, became prominent as the owner of the high-flying *College Humor*, but rarely gave interviews and never mentioned *Weird Tales*. By 1932, he was apparently claiming that he co-founded *College Humor* with a fraternity brother, which is untrue but papered over the origins of his fortune.[584]

Edwin Baird, as we have seen, never mentioned his experience with the magazine. He was happy to pretend that those two years had never happened.

Farnsworth Wright talked about his background with the magazine several times, both with the writers' magazines and the fan press. He consistently claimed to have started editing *Weird Tales* with the November 1924 issue, a convenient lie that spared him from ever being asked undesirable questions about what happened during the contentious split.

Otis Adelbert Kline failed to mention his history with the magazine in his best opportunity, his autobiographical 1931 article. What little he was willing to say appeared in his 1941 letter which wasn't published until 1970, and that letter maintained the fiction of Wright only editing the magazine after the split. When he became an agent, he retreated into the cocoon of professional discretion.

Their tight lips kept the secrets intact for nearly a century.

XXIII

THE ARC OF THE COSMOS

The arc of the *Weird Tales* story is broad. It encompasses the authors, the stories, the poetry, the artwork, the history of the magazine, the wide influences on writing, film, art, and even music, and the very idea of weird fiction. But the arc of the first two years—from formation to split—is, according to this narrative, the story of its two founders, the story of two magazine makers, the story of two friends who wanted badly to be in business together. Their respective fortunes, following their division of Rural Publishing into two companies, one belonging to each of them, contains the final secret of the origin.

While the split left J.C. Henneberger with a valueless ownership of *Weird Tales*, Johnny Lansinger profited immensely from his ownership of *Real Detective Tales* and especially *College Humor*. In June 1924, immediately following the split, Lansinger paid $55,000 for a Chicago apartment building to serve as a new home for his executive staffs.[585] While the company instead moved in 1925 to an improved location at 1050 North La Salle Street, the deal introduced him to real estate broker Fred Brons.

Meanwhile, big changes were made within his Collegiate World Publishing Company. In 1924, he started the new pulp, *Co-Ed Campus Comedy*, which quickly disappeared. It was the first failed experiment in magazines that he could call his own. No matter. The failure seemingly had no major impact on the company. Lansinger quickly compensated by upgrading *College Humor*, with the February 1925 issue, from a quarterly to a monthly, while also improving the magazine in quality and content. In this form it achieved its fame as a supreme "It" item for the Roaring Twenties. Throughout the decade, it featured fiction from some of the best and best-known authors in the country, including F. Scott Fitzgerald, Ben Hecht, Robert Benchley, Arnold Bennett, and an up-and-coming Cornell Woolrich. One journalist called it "the world's most necessary adjunct to a complete college education."[586] Another referred to it as "that sprightly magazine that lies right under the ukelele [*sic*] in nine out of 10 college dormitory rooms."[587]

Katharine Brush sold her first story, "Pity Pat," to *College Humor* in May

1924 and was soon put under contract, ultimately publishing forty short stories and two serials, plus additional stories for *Co-Ed* under pseudonyms.[588] Her stories usually had clever, Prohibition-flaunting titles like "Survival of the Lit-est" and "Delirium Trimmings." In December 1924, she visited the *College Humor* office, which, in her description, "had a distinctly fraternity-house party air about it."[589] Expecting men who looked like Supreme Court justices, she was shocked at how young they all were. "The Grand Old Man was Mr. Lansinger, the publisher, who must have been thirty-eight or thirty-nine if he was a day." Actually, he had just turned thirty-two. Of wonderboy editor Swanson, she recalled: "He was perhaps twenty-three years old, easily six feet three inches tall, and he parted his hair in the middle, yes, and yes-he-had-a-raccoon-coat, and he even drove an underslung roadster in which he lay, as in a bathtub." Swanson had just turned twenty-five. Brush thought he was one of her fictional characters. Of the visit, she concluded, "I daresay the office boy was working his way through kindergarten."

In May 1925, Lansinger and Brons were in business together as the Lansbro Hotel Corporation. As equal partners they bought a lot with an existing building on the southwest corner of Maple and Dearborn, Chicago, and had the building demolished late in the year, replacing it with a ten-story "fireproof" building with 162 apartments and six ground-level commercial spaces. They called it The Lansing. In September 1926, Lansinger bought out Brons's half-interest for $230,000.[590] The building still exists. Located at 1036 North Dearborn, it's now the Dearborn Apartments.

In 1927, in conjunction with First National Pictures, *College Humor* conducted a nationwide talent search for handsome and talented college men to appear as supporting players in the Richard Barthelmess feature, "The Drop Kick," written by Katharine Brush. This gave Lansinger a great opportunity to travel around the country—especially Hollywood.

He and wife Lura started escaping the miserable Chicago winters by spending the season in Palm Beach and environs. They cruised to Havana. A frequent guest was golfing buddy H.N. Swanson, or "Swanie" as his friends called him. They made a congenial twosome—Johnny and Swanie—in the Third Annual Artists' and Writers' Association golf tournament of January 1930, where they mingled with the likes of Grantland Rice, Rube Goldberg, Arthur Somers Roche, Octavus Roy Cohen, and James Montgomery Flagg.

January 1930 belongs to a special time, those innocent, ignorant days after the great Stock Market Crash and before the realization of the Great Depression had set in. They were giddy heights for Lansinger and probably the pinnacle of his high-flying years. But the tide had turned. The publisher's first problem was The Lansing. It became embroiled in legal turmoil when its faulty foundation allowed it to settle and lean against its neighboring building.[591] By July 1930, it was in default. The second problem was his other prize, *College Humor*. Eventually, its circulation, the source of his royal lifestyle, began to decline. After 1929, to the depths of the Depression in 1932, the magazine plummeted from its peak circulation of 300,000 to 150,000.[592]

In the middle of 1932, Swanie flew the coop for a tantalizing job as a writer-producer at RKO Pictures. In 1934, he opened his own Hollywood literary agency and became one of the most prominent agents in the business, representing many of the top-name writers in Hollywood. The ad copy for his 1989 memoirs rhapsodized over his exciting life with an orgy of name-dropping: "He partied with F. Scott and Zelda Fitzgerald. Kept Raymond Chandler on the wagon. Told Elmore Leonard to stop writing westerns and 'put a girl in the story.' Along the way, he gave Ginger Rogers her first break. Cut up with Bogie at the Mocambo. Worked side by side with David O. Selznick, Irving Thalberg, and Jack Warner. He's H.N. Swanson, the grandest of the grand Hollywood agents."[593]

If Swanie's departure from *College Humor* was an omen, so was the closing of the magazine's New York offices on October 1, 1932. Soon after, Lansinger lost his publishing company and tried to start anew with Baird and *Real America*. Lansinger's involvement lasted less than two years.

Swanie must have been whispering in his ear, telling him that the palm trees were greener on the other side of the country, because he followed in his former editor's footsteps, opening the J.M. Lansinger Agency in Hollywood. It was a chance to recapture the magic stolen from him by the Depression. Aided by a valuable associate, former *College Humor* editor Dorothy Ann Blank, Lansinger's specialty was in helping eastern writers in Hollywood. The outfit got off to a promising start. An early client was Alvah Bessie, fresh off his well-reviewed first novel, *Dwell in the Wilderness* (1935), the saga of a Midwestern family. He would not achieve screenwriting success until the '40s, however. (He's best known as a member of the blacklisted Hollywood Ten.) An actual success for Lansinger was the sale to MGM of the story that turned into the Clark Gable-Joan Crawford romance *Love on the Run* (1936).

Whatever Lansinger achieved, it wasn't enough. In mid-1936, he tried, unsuccessfully, to launch *Screen Digest*, a film gab mag modeled after *Reader's Digest*. Apparently, no issues were produced. At about the same time, he lost another colleague to an irresistible opportunity. Dorothy joined the Walt Disney company as a writer for the landmark animated feature *Snow White and the Seven Dwarfs*.

In 1937, Lansinger was back in Chicago, his glamour days gone for good. The downdraft from the Depression seemed to have finally sucked him back to earth. In the summer, he ran help wanted ads to recruit undergraduates to sell magazine subscriptions door-to-door. It was the same damn job he'd held with the *Orange Judd Farmer* when he was young, hungry, and craving success. Riches to rags. His ads asked for young men with guts and determination—like the young man who had journeyed to the fabled West for a "very prosperous business enterprise."

He also worked in life insurance—to bring it back to the mundane. He'd always wanted to be a businessman. At least he was flexible in his terms.

His fate changed again, this time by the deaths of his in-laws, Dr. James P. Tamiesie in 1935 and Ruth Ann in 1938. Lura Lansinger and her brother inherited their spacious home at 21 Southeast Floral Place, Portland, across the street from scenic Laurelhurst Park. In 1939, the Lansinger family—Lura, daughter Joan (*b.* 1928), and son John (*b.* 1932)—relocated from Chicago to occupy the fifteen-room house. Lansinger took a job as an underwriter for the State Mutual Life Assurance Company. In an interview with the Portland *Oregonian*, he took sole credit for founding *College Humor*,[594] an enviable and colorful credential. Like Henneberger, his lifelong claim to fame would be the creation of a legendary magazine, though Henneberger unambiguously deserves the credit for creating both *College Humor* and *Weird Tales*; however, the credit for nurturing them to their legendary status goes, respectively, to Lansinger and Farnsworth Wright.

In the dismemberment of Henneberger, Swanie's 1989 memoirs claimed another limb—and a couple of Lansinger's fingers. According to Swanie, he began his career as a magazine writer. And then: "I also founded a magazine called *College Humor*—a national institution in its day—which I ran for eight years."[595] His original idea, coming out of college—as his account continued—was for a compendium of items taken from college-humor magazines to be called *The College Widow*. His uncle John Norling of Chicago, a former newspaperman, had put him in touch with Lansinger, a "really nice guy"—with money. After a lengthy discussion, Lansinger agreed to put up the money on one condition: the magazine would be called *College Humor*. The office was cramped: "John Lansinger and I faced each other across a big desk. . . . We were there every day, including Sundays and holidays."[596] How did the man with the financing end up sweating across from him in a cramped office? Swanie never explains. Lansinger quickly drops out of the narrative. Henneberger is never mentioned.

One is loath to accept anything at face value from Swanie's book, which is riddled with errors, the invention of *College Humor* being one of the most blatant. However, if we discount his errors of memory and pride, a glimmer of truthful possibility shines from beneath the pile of inaccuracies. *College Humor* (102 West Chestnut Street) and the Rural pulps (854 North Clark) were published at different addresses which were actually different entrances to the same building, one around the corner from the other. If Lansinger toiled with Swanie in one cramped suite while Henneberger and

Baird ran Rural from another, it would help explain the division of spoils during the 1924 split.

That diversion aside, Lansinger's 1939 life insurance job didn't last. In December, he took over *The Oregon Merchants Magazine*, a Portland food trade industry publication that dated to 1901. Over the next decade, he consolidated his magazine holdings, buying journals like *Western Frozen Foods*. He was back in the only real game he knew: magazine publishing. He also became heavily involved with independent grocery business advocacy organizations like the Oregon Food Merchants' Association. Prosperity had returned, if not the excitement. He belonged to a country club, golfed regularly.

In the 1950s, the John Marcus Lansinger entry became de rigueur in books like *Who's Who on the Pacific Coast*. His entry never changed. Among the other factual details of his life, it listed some of the successful magazines he'd been associated with: *Pictorial Review*, *College Humor*, and *Real Detective*. It omitted the two he most likely considered his biggest failures, the ones he preferred the world forget: *Weird Tales* and *Real America*.

In 1955, the Lansingers downsized to a duplex in Sandy Crest Terrace, selling their landmark house to a Catholic charity, the Sisters of Social Service.[597]

Johnny Lansinger died in Portland on June 30, 1963, leaving behind Lura, their two children, four grandchildren, and a disembodied name attached to the founding of *Weird Tales*.

Finally, we return to Jacob Clark Henneberger, the man who gave birth to the weirdest of all babies. His connection to the magazine appears to have been tenuous after his failures in late-1924 to raise enough money to regain control. There would be no more reorganizations. Lovecraft ceased mentioning him in his correspondence after 1926, after Henneberger's efforts to publish a Lovecraft collection had fallen through. The editorial direction of the magazine was completely ceded to Farnsworth Wright. There are two versions of how Wright's early-'30s pulps, *Oriental Stories* and *The Magic Carpet Magazine*, came about, but neither version includes Henneberger's influence.

Henneberger held out one last hope of reclaiming the magazine. Robert Maurice Eastman (*b.* 1869), president since 1908 of Chicago's massive W.F. Hall Printing Company, promised to bail him out. When this ill-fated pledge was made or what conditions needed to be met are unknown. According to Henneberger, "The advent of the Depression found this gentleman in a deplorable position. He was carrying a dozen or so publications on credit in order to keep a large staff of printers employed but the load was more than he could carry."[598] On November 22, 1932, Eastman died at home[599] "and with his demise went my hopes of regaining the helm of Weird Tales."[600] And with that sad event, the idea of *Weird Tales* seemingly died in his mind, lingering as a ghost. In 1969 he wrote Joel Frieman: "I never let the ownership of the magazine get out of my hands. It was simply turned over to Delaney of Short Stories on a percentage basis."[601] The purchase by Delaney happened in 1938. The magazine lasted until 1954.

"I never made any money with Weird Tales" he told Sam Moskowitz.[602] It's a claim that will not be challenged here.

How he lived all those years is another story. In 1928, he moved, permanently as it turned out, to New York City.[603] As he explained his motivation, "I found myself so hopelessly entangled with printers and paper houses that I chucked the whole thing over."[604] He abandoned Chicago, and the Indianapolis connection, and anything to do with the Cornelius Printing Company. He probably remained involved in the magazine business in some capacity. Our only hint of his employment—and it's thin evidence—is the 1940 letter he wrote August Derleth; it was typed on Magazine Builders letterhead.[605] Magazine Builders Inc. was a publisher who operated in the late '20s out of New York and Chicago. They produced the popular movie magazine *Screenland*, and a couple of other titles. But by 1940, *Screenland* was published by another party and Magazine Builders appears to have been defunct. Henneberger may have worked for the company early on—or maybe he just obtained some of their stationary, because their name was an essential description of what he tried to do with his life. The letterhead was only a tantalizing clue. He never told Derleth what business he was in; it was probably nothing to brag about.

When Joel tracked Henneberger down in the late '60s, he worked in the historic Algonquin Hotel. Located near Times Square, its bar is a traditional watering hole for New York's literary and theatrical sets. Accordingly, he ran the theater-ticket concession in the lobby. Recalling how he fled Franklin and Marshall college when he could to attend the theater in New York and Philadelphia, his life had come full-circle, a first love reasserted. It was a good gig but an anonymous recompense for someone who had accidentally ignited a literary movement.

Joel concluded that Henneberger's life was "a sad story."[606]

What we don't find from Henneberger nor Lansinger, after the split of Rural Publishing, is either of them publicly mentioning the other. They instead conducted a lifelong war of silence. Their brief partnership, born of friendship, had started with great promise. But their confidence and optimism, the source of their entrepreneurial spirit, had crashed on the rocks, dashing their expectations into shards. Worse than the failure itself, the outcome produced a deep embarrassment for both, for different reasons.

Lansinger, the college dropout, benefited greatly from the friendship, building a life on Henneberger's enterprise. Henneberger led him west to find his fortune, which took longer than expected, but still happened. Lansinger found his wife, as well. With the launch of the company that became Rural, he married the doctor's beautiful daughter, started a family. From Henneberger, he got his career as a publisher. He inherited his trusty editorial sidekicks, Edwin Baird and H.N. Swanson. He made enough to invest in expensive real estate, raking it in while *Weird Tales* toiled in virtual poverty. He lived the Roaring Twenties highlife, wintered in paradise, flirted with Hollywood dreamland. He retired in comfort, living out his closing years with the admirable imprimatur of having created *College Humor*, a credit he appropriated from Henneberger. It may have been less from pride than it was to conceal the original sin.

Henneberger's failures, on the other hand, awarded him with the worthless ownership of a magazine. Worse than worthless, *Weird Tales* was a constant reminder that the magazine-making magic he once put unbreakable faith in had been more illusion than gift.

There's no evidence that Henneberger and Lansinger remained in touch after the split of their company. It's the silences that tell the story. As Henneberger wrote Moskowitz: "the few headaches [*Weird Tales*] caused were compensated by the association with men like William Sprenger (business manager), Farnsworth Wright, Frank Belknap Long, Seabury Quinn (who ran an undertakers magazine) and many prominent men like Harry Houdini who swore by the publication."[607] Lansinger didn't make the list.[608] His rewards would have to come from elsewhere.

Therein lies the most painful secret in the origin of *Weird Tales*, the dark heart of the silence shared by its two founders. The magazine destroyed a friendship that had begun with such high hopes. The best friendship of youth—the one that was supposed to last forever.

When Joel initiated his correspondence with Henneberger, virtually all of the witnesses to the first two years were dead: Lansinger (1963), Baird (1954), Wright (1940), Kline (1946), Houdini (1926), and Lovecraft (1937). E. Hoffmann Price called his collection of reminiscences the *Book of the Dead*, because one by one all of his friends in the *Weird Tales* circle and the pulps had passed. When a person is alive they contain all of their qualities, good and ill; once dead, memory rewrites the biography, taking only what it wants and forgetting the rest. So too with a magazine; so too with the *Weird Tales* of 1923-24. Once a secret because of its shameful dimensions, at the end of Henneberger's life it could be celebrated for its successful dimensions alone, in what it spawned. And so, Henneberger's communications with Joel, and fandom, represent a reversal, a final acceptance of credit for starting something good even if the start itself was better left forgotten.

In closing his first letter to Joel, Henneberger seemed to discover his own epitaph in the experiences of Edgar Allan Poe, the inspiration for *Weird Tales*. Alluding to Poe's *The Stylus*, Henneberger wrote: "In his time, Edgar Allan Poe contributed to the success of several magazines, but he always wanted his own. When he started one of his own, unfortunately, he did not succeed."[609]

Abbreviations: Edwin Baird (EB); Arthur J. Burks (AJB); Jacob Clark Henneberger (JCH); Otis Adelbert Kline (OAK); Frank Belknap Long (FBL); Howard Phillips Lovecraft (HPL), *Selected Letters* (*SL*); E. Hoffmann Price (EHP); Clark Ashton Smith (CAS). See **Bibliography** for full references to major sources.

Chapter I: Jacob's Dream

1 *Literary Market Tips*, in *The Student Writer*, January 1923.

2 Sam Moskowitz, *Weird Tales*, Winter 1973. This revival, published by Leo Margulies and edited by Moskowitz, lasted four issues from Summer 1973 to Summer 1974.

3 Moskowitz, *Worlds of Weird*, 9-13.

4 Joel Frieman, phone conversation with the author, May 7, 2017.

5 JCH, July 1968, October 20, 1968, and April 14, 1969. The original October 20, 1968 letter, and not the revision in *WT50: A Tribute to Weird Tales*, was used for this history.

6 JCH, May 1969.

Chapter II: The Pals

7 George Overcash Seilhamer, *Biographical Annals of Franklin County, Pennsylvania, Containing Genealogical Records of Representative Families, Including Many of the Early Settlers, and Biographical Sketches of Prominent Citizens* (Chicago: Genealogical Pub. Co., 1905), 441.

8 JCH, April 14, 1969.

9 The 1911 *Touchstone*.

10 Both outcomes were confirmed through email by Christine Alexander, the Franklin and Marshall registrar, May 23, 2017.

11 *The Shield of Phi Kappa Psi*, April 1914.

12 JCH, April 14, 1969.

13 *The Shield of Phi Kappa Psi*, February 1915.

14 *The Shield of Phi Kappa Psi*, December 1914.

15 *The Shield of Phi Kappa Psi*, December 1914.

Chapter III: The Second Winds of Destiny

16 JCH, April 14, 1969.

17 Henneberger's role is mentioned in *The Shield of Phi Kappa Psi*, April 1916. The companies are described in "Topics of the Trade," *The American Stationer*, March 27, 1915; and "Ball and Walsh Form a New Company," *The Fourth Estate*, July 15, 1916.

18 JCH, April 14, 1969.

19 Jacob Clark Henneberger, Naval Service Record, November 26, 1918.

20 JCH, April 14, 1969.

21 *The Shield of Phi Kappa Psi*, October 1916. The item only mentions him "entering the bonding business" in Philadelphia, but it's reasonable to assume that this was his brother's firm.

22 *The Shield of Phi Kappa Psi*, April 1917.

23 The company's other big title, the leading magazine of its class, was the *American Agriculturalist*.

24 The form lists his employer as "Orange-Judd Co."

25 *Polk's Iowa State Gazetteer*, 1918-1919.

26 "Draft Compels Map Company to Advertise for Salesmen," *Printers' Ink*, June 6, 1918.

27 JCH, April 14, 1969.

28 An update to the *Shield of Phi Kappa Psi*, October 1920, lists the business address as the State Life Building, Indianapolis.

29 JCH, April 14, 1969.

30 JCH, July 1968.

31 Ad for Collegiate Special Advertising Agency, Inc., *Advertising & Selling Magazine*, January 1922.

32 JCH, April 14, 1969.

33 JCH, July 1968.

34 JCH, July 1968.

35 JCH, July 1968.

36 JCH, April 14, 1969.

37 A garage on 2122 North Clark Street, two miles up the road, was the site of St. Valentine's Day Massacre on February 14, 1929.

38 *Literary Market Tips*, in *The Student Writer*, February 1922.

39 *The Literary Market*, in *The Editor*, April 22, 1922. The second issue of *The Magazine of Fun* started a series, "See America Thirst," with apparent jabs at Prohibition coming from around the country.

40 JCH, July 1968.

41 JCH, July 1968 and April 14, 1969.

42 *N.W. Ayer & Son's Directory* (1922), 207.

43 Ad for the Fiction Press, *The Collegiate World*, November 1921, 31.

44 JCH, July 1968.

45 JCH, July 1968.

46 "J.M. Lansinger Joins Collegiate World Company," *Printers' Ink*, March 9, 1922.

47 *Society*, in *The Oregonian* (Portland), June 25, 1922.

48 *Society News*, in *The Oregonian*, July 13, 1922.

49 *Literary Market Tips*, in *The Student Writer*, September 1922.

Chapter IV: Utterly Hopeless Rubbish

50 *Literary Market Tips*, in *The Student Writer*, September 1922.

51 EB, letter to the *Chicago Ledger*, November 15, 1919.

52 MacKinley Kantor, "Editors You Want To Know: Edwin Baird," *The Author & Journalist*, November 1929.

53 EB, letter to the *Chicago Ledger*, November 15, 1919.

54 The Editor, "Speaking of Detective Stories," *Detective Tales*, October 1, 1922.

55 The Editor, "Speaking of Detective Stories," *Detective Tales*, October 1, 1922.

56 The Editor, *A Chat With the Chief* (column), in *Detective Tales*, October 1, 1922.

57 *Literary Market Tips*, in *The Student Writer*, November 1922.

58 EB, "What Editors Want," *The Story World and Photodramatist*, October 1923.

59 *Literary Market Tips*, in *The Student Writer*, November 1922.

Chapter V: The Birth of Weird

60 Locke, "The History of *Ghost Stories*" in *Ghost Stories: The Magazine and Its Makers* v1, 6-8.

61 JCH, October 20, 1968.

62 JCH, October 20, 1968.

63 Anonymous, "Poe-Tic?," *The Magazine of Fun*, August 1921, 26.

64 Anonymous, "The Raving," *The Magazine of Fun*, August 1921, 33-34.

65 JCH, July 1968.

66 JCH, May 1969. "The Damned Thing" was reprinted in the September 1923 *Weird Tales*.

67 JCH, October 20, 1968.

68 News dealers typically introduced new issues on a specific day of the week, which probably explains the uncertainty of the date. *Weird Tales* would have appeared on that day of the week nearest the 18th of the month. Since February 18, 1923, was a Sunday, then Friday, February 16, is a good estimate of the actual appearance of the issue.

69 The Editor, *The Eyrie*, in *Weird Tales*, March 1923.

70 The Editor, *The Eyrie*, in *Weird Tales*, April 1923.

71 JCH, letter to Leo Margulies, June 30, 1964, partially quoted in book dealer's catalog.

72   The March 1923 *Weird Tales* listed Cuneo-Henneberry as printer under the back-cover coupon; the May issue listed Cornelius under the back-cover coupon. The April issue omitted any specific reference to printer, but added the Cornelius address to the issue's indicia.

73   JCH, October 20, 1968.

74   *Literary Market Tips*, in *The Student Writer*, January 1923.

75   *Literary Market Tips*, in *The Student Writer*, February 1923.

76   The September 1923 issue was the last as *The Student Writer*.

77   According to Hawkins, his story was actually inspired by the 1920 film version of *Dr. Jekyll and Mr. Hyde*. "On 'Dead Man's Tale,'" *Fantasy Magazine*, April 1935, 131.

78   *Literary Market Tips*, in *The Student Writer*, May 1923.

79   The Editor, *The Eyrie*, in *Weird Tales*, April 1923.

80   The Editor, *The Eyrie*, in *Weird Tales*, May 1923.

Chapter VI: The Apprentices

81   EHP, "Editors You Want to Know: Farnsworth Wright," *The Author & Journalist*, October 1930.

82   OAK, letter to Dr. I.M. Howard, April 1, 1941.

83   OAK, "Curious Crimes: A Collection of Factual Fillers," *OAK Leaves* 12, Autumn 1979. The items were identified from Kline's publishing record.

84   HPL, letter to FBL, February 7, 1924, *SL I*, 304.

85   Joshi, *I Am Providence* v2, 745.

86   The Editor, *The Eyrie*, in *Weird Tales*, June 1923.

87   *The Washington Newspaper*, June 1923. Published by the School of Journalism, University of Washington, Seattle.

Chapter VII: Farnsworth Wright and the Art of the Nightmare

88   EHP, "Farnsworth Wright" in *The Weird Tales Story*, 12; reprinted from "The Book of the Dead: Farnsworth Wright" in *The Ghost*, July 1944. An abridged version was used as Chapter I of Price's *Book of the Dead*. The abridged version eliminates 30% of the text but also adds information not included in the original version.

89   Farnsworth Wright, Application for Membership, The Colorado Society of the Sons of the American Revolution, January 9, 1910; *Official Bulletin of the National Society of the Sons of the American Revolution*, October 1913.

90   Marjorie J. Wright, quoted in EHP, "Farnsworth Wright" in *The Weird Tales Story*, 12.

91   Details on Edward Thomas Wright were taken from *Press Reference Library (Western Edition): Notables of the West* (International News Service, 1915), 191. Details on George Francis Wright's professional career comes from two

main sources: 1) American Society of Civil Engineers, "Memoir of Deceased Member: George F. Wright," *Proceedings*, October 1892; 2) "George F. Wright" in *The United States Naval Academy Graduates Association* (Baltimore: Deutsch Lithographing & Printing Co., 1893). There is a suspicious pattern through all three sources of both brothers relocating for their health: Edward leaving Chicago (1875); George abandoning Santa Barbara (~1878); and George seeking work in the San Bernardino Mountains (1891). However, George is the one who leaves a record of ill health throughout his adult life and died at a relatively young age. This at least raises the possibility of confused details in the accounts, that it may have been George who needed to leave Chicago, and/or that George's first abandonment of Santa Barbara was confused with his later move to Los Angeles.

92   "Santa Barbara County," *Los Angeles Times*, August 21, 1892.

93   Marjorie J. Wright, quoted in EHP, "Farnsworth Wright" in *The Weird Tales Story*, 12.

94   "Stanford Girls' Glee," *The Daily Palo Alto*, November 18, 1898.

95   Farnsworth Wright, quoted in "Jack o' the Beanstalk," *San Francisco Call*, March 27, 1898.

96   *The Daily Palo Alto*, October 17, 1900.

97   Marjorie J. Wright, quoted in EHP, "Farnsworth Wright" in *The Weird Tales Story*, 13.

98   EHP, "Editors You Want to Know: Farnsworth Wright."

99   "Though Blind They Succeed," *San Francisco Chronicle*, March 19, 1905.

100 "Local Boys Win Debate," *Oakland Tribune*, November 20, 1905.

101 "Merrymaking by the Pilgrim Sunday-School," *San Francisco Chronicle*, December 21, 1904.

102 "Organizer of the Stanford Glee Club," *Reno Gazette-Journal*, June 4, 1906. This account of Genevieve and Paula moving their residence to Reno makes no mention of the three brothers.

103 Julius Schwartz, "Titans of Science Fiction: Farnsworth Wright," *Science Fiction Digest*, March 1933.

104 Registration Card, Farnsworth Wright, June 5, 1917.

105 Michael J. Brodhead, "The State Militia in Nevada: A History," *State Defense Force Journal*, Fall 2005.

106 Schwartz, "Titans of Science Fiction: Farnsworth Wright."

107 EHP, "Farnsworth Wright" in *The Weird Tales Story*, 12-13. After the Chinese Exclusion Act of 1882, laborers were imported from other Asian countries, especially India and Japan.

108 "Fatal Bathing at Westport," *Aberdeen Herald* (Washington), July 29, 1913.

109 Farnsworth wrote for the New York weekly *Musical America* starting in 1916. The masthead listed two names for the Chicago office: Margie A. McLeod, manager, and Farnsworth Wright, correspondent. The choice of "McLeod"

as the octopus-entangled victim of "In the Depths" is unlikely to be a coincidence.

110 "Mrs. Wright Dies at Home in Manila," *Reno Gazette Journal*, December 26, 1913; "Returns to Reno from Philippines," *Nevada State Journal*, August 27, 1914; Marjorie J. Wright, quoted in EHP, "Farnsworth Wright" in *The Weird Tales Story*, 13.

111 "Army of Journalists Rout Editorial Staff," *Seattle Star*, April 25, 1914.

112 Farnsworth Wright, "What Seattle Needs Most," *Seattle Star*, April 25, 1914.

113 "Students Drop Theory for Actual Experience," *Port Angeles Olympic Leader*, July 3, 1914.

114 "Cheer Up, Western Athletics!," *Harper's Weekly*, July 18, 1914.

115 Marjorie J. Wright, quoted in EHP, "Farnsworth Wright" in *The Weird Tales Story*, 13.

116 Marjorie J. Wright, quoted in EHP, "Farnsworth Wright" in *The Weird Tales Story*, 12.

117 Marjorie J. Wright, quoted in EHP, "Farnsworth Wright" in *The Weird Tales Story*, 12.

118 *Musical America*, July 13, 1918.

119 George M. Cohan's "Over There" was the signature patriotic song of the era.

120 "Chicago Notes," *Musical America*, June 15, 1918.

121 "Reno Girl Tells of Happy Life in France," *Reno Gazette Journal*, April 30, 1919.

122 "Chicago, Ill.," *The Music Trades*, September 6, 1919.

123 EHP, "Farnsworth Wright" in *Book of the Dead*, 18.

124 EHP, "Farnsworth Wright" in *The Weird Tales Story*, 8.

125 EHP, "Editors You Want to Know: Farnsworth Wright."

126 EHP, "Farnsworth Wright" in *Book of the Dead*, 14. Price describes the pun in detail in *The Weird Tales Story*, 8-9.

127 EHP, "Farnsworth Wright" in *Book of the Dead*, 10.

128 EHP, "Farnsworth Wright" in *The Weird Tales Story*, 9.

129 EHP, "Farnsworth Wright" in *The Weird Tales Story*, 9.

130 EHP, "Farnsworth Wright" in *The Weird Tales Story*, 12.

131 *Literary Market Tips*, in *The Student Writer*, January 1923.

Chapter VIII: Otis Adelbert Kline and the Invisible Hand

132 OAK, autobiographical sketch, *American Fiction Guild Bulletin*, January 2, 1936.

133 George L. Kline obituary, *Sterling* (Illinois) *Gazette*, February 19, 1892.

134 The eldest sister, Margaret E. Oliver (1838-1885), was apparently the only one of the three to earn a degree.

135 G.L. Kline ad, *Sterling Standard*, March 13, 1872. The first instance found of this ad.

136 Print ad, *Sterling Gazette*, July 23, 1881.

137 *Sterling Gazette*, March 24, 1883.

138 *Sterling Gazette*, December 26, 1888.

139 *Sterling Standard*, April 2, 1891.

140 *Sterling Standard*, August 12, 1897.

141 *Sterling Standard*, July 16, 1891.

142 *Sterling Standard*, December 24, 1896.

143 "A Telephone Cabinet," *Sterling Standard*, January 14, 1897.

144 EHP, "Otis Adelbert Kline" in *Book of the Dead*, 40.

145 Louis A. Kline, "About Langshan Color," letter, November 17, 1899, in *Reliable Poultry Journal*, December 1899.

146 *Sterling Gazette*, April 6, 1895.

147 *Sterling Gazette*, April 11, 1895.

148 "Chat About Authors," *The Tampa Tribune*, November 17, 1929.

149 OAK, "Reflections," *OAK Leaves* 11, 1975, 3-4. The editor of *OAK Leaves*, David Anthony Kraft, discovered this previously unpublished piece in Kline's files. In it, Kline refers to WWII, which dates it precisely enough.

150 Ora Rozar, "Notes," *OAK Leaves* 6, 1971-72.

151 *Sterling Gazette*, June 7, 1901.

152 The company's website, www.nielsenmassey.com, names "Otis Kline and Richard Massey" as the company's founders, apparently confusing Otis with his father. Otis turned sixteen in 1907.

153 OAK, "Writing the Fantastic Story," *The Writer*, January 1931.

154 "Fiction Writer Guest of Mother Here," *Sterling Daily Gazette*, January 6, 1930.

155 Harold Ward, "The Team of Ward and Pearce Will Now Perform Strike Up the Band!," *Chicago Ledger*, November 22, 1919. Ward described his life (in the second person) in one-half of the article, Pearce in the other.

156 Al Tonik, "An Interview with Gladys Ward" in *The Complete Exploits of Doctor Death*, 348.

157 Ward, "The Team of Ward and Pearce Will Now Perform Strike Up the Band!"

158 *Sterling Standard*, November 25, 1897.

159 Ward, "The Team of Ward and Pearce Will Now Perform Strike Up the Band!"

160 Ward, letter, *Sterling Daily Gazette*, August 13, 1925.

161 "Gillespie in City," *The Daily Times* (Davenport, Iowa), October 13, 1909.

162 Ward, "The Team of Ward and Pearce Will Now Perform Strike Up the Band!"

163 "Harold E. Ward Becomes Publicity Head at Garrick," *Dixon Evening Telegraph*, October 14, 1909.

164 "Theatrical: Woodstock Opera House," *Woodstock Sentinel* (Iowa), September 7, 1911.

165 "Ward's New Position," *Dixon Evening Telegraph*, October 28, 1910.

166 OAK, autobiographical sketch, *American Fiction Guild Bulletin*, January 2, 1936.

167 Ora Rozar, "Notes," *OAK Leaves* 11, 1975.

168 OAK, "Reflections," *OAK Leaves* 11, 1975, 4.

169 "New Song Hit," *Sterling Standard*, July 27, 1916.

170 OAK, autobiographical sketch, *American Fiction Guild Bulletin*, January 2, 1936.

171 " 'Egypta' Cast Is Announced," *Sterling Standard*, February 9, 1906.

172 OAK, autobiographical sketch, *American Fiction Guild Bulletin*, January 2, 1936.

173 OAK, "Writing the Fantastic Story."

174 OAK, "Writing the Fantastic Story."

175 Registration Card, Otis A. Kline, June 17, 1917.

176 EHP, "Otis Adelbert Kline" in *Book of the Dead*, 40.

177 EHP, "Otis Adelbert Kline" in *Book of the Dead*, 27.

178 EHP, "Otis Adelbert Kline" in *Book of the Dead*, 28-29.

179 OAK, "Writing the Fantastic Story."

180 OAK, "Reflections," *OAK Leaves* 11, 1975, 4.

181 "Otis Kline's Novel Among Best Sellers," *Sterling Daily Gazette*, September 7, 1929.

182 Tonik, "An Interview with Gladys Ward," 349.

183 The online FictionMags Index, and associated indexes, are indispensable for fleshing out the careers of magazine writers of the era.

184 OAK, "Writing the Fantastic Story."

185 OAK, "Reflections," *OAK Leaves* 11, 1975, 4.

Chapter IX: Death Gasps

186 "A Bigger and Better Magazine," *Detective Tales*, February 1923, 4.

187 EB, "A Chat With the Chief," *Detective Tales*, March 1923.

188 OAK, April 1, 1941.

189 The de-emphasis of author names was unusual but not without precedent in the pulps. *Sea Stories*, for instance, featured gorgeous sea-themed covers unmarred by any type below the title area. It could be argued that *Sea Stories* was its own form of "unique magazine," relying more heavily on the reader's interest in a specialized genre than in its authors. However, *Sea Stories*, which debuted in 1922, eventually caved in to the demands of the market and began featuring author names in 1927.

190 H.M., letter in *The Eyrie*, in *Weird Tales*, July-August 1923.

191 *Literary Market Tips*, in *The Student Writer*, September 1922.

192 In contrast, when Harold Hersey published his Good Story pulp magazines in the early 1930s, many titles were published ten times per year, and clearly announced as such.

193 Lee Torpie, letter in *The Eyrie*, in *Weird Tales*, October 1923.

194 Every *Weird Tales* cover can be viewed on Galactic Central, www.philsp.com/mags/weirdtales.html.

195 A variant of the cover swapped the orange and black plates in the vignetted portion of the cover, which had to be either an experiment or an error, most likely the latter. That both variations escaped into the market can be interpreted as a cost-saving move. Had the printed error produced an incorrect date or price, Rural would have been forced to destroy the defective copies. For a mainstream producer of a printed article, any major printing error would be destroyed rather than bring the producer's quality standards into question.

196 Terence E. Hanley, "Tellers of Weird Tales: Artists & Writers in The Unique Magazine: William F. Heitman (1878-1945)," *Tellers of Weird Tales* blog, April 18, 2012. tellersofweirdtales.blogspot.com/2012/04/william-f-heitman-ca-1879-1945.html

197 Robert Barbour Johnson, "Recollections of Weird Tales" in *The Weird Tales Story*, 56-57.

198 OAK, April 1, 1941.

199 EHP, "Farnsworth Wright" in *The Weird Tales Story*, 7.

200 Paul S. Powers, *Pulp Writer*, 125.

201 Powers, *Pulp Writer*, 126.

202 Mark Finn, *Blood & Thunder*, 315.

203 *Literary Market Tips*, in *The Student Writer*, November 1922.

204 *Literary Market Tips*, in *The Student Writer*, June 1923.

205 "The Student Writer's Handy Market List for Literary Workers: List B," *The Student Writer*, September 1923.

206 *Literary Market Tips*, in *The Author & Journalist*, October 1923.

207 *Literary Market Tips*, in *The Author & Journalist*, December 1923.

208 *Literary Market Tips*, in *The Author & Journalist*, February 1924.

Chapter X: Birth Pangs

209 Anthony M. Rud, letter in *The Eyrie*, in *Weird Tales*, March 1923.

210 Douglas A. Anderson, "Julian Kilman," *Lesser-Known Writers* blog, March 30, 2012. desturmobed.blogspot.com/2012/03/julian-kilman.html

211 HPL, letter to FBL, March 30, 1926, *SL I*, 233.

212 HPL, "Ebony And Crystal by Clark Ashton Smith" in *Collected Essays: Volume 2: Literary Criticism*, 73-74.

213 Joshi, *I Am Providence* v2, 814.

214 Henry S. Whitehead, letter to *The Camp-Fire* (column), in *Adventure*, November 10, 1923.

215 A. Langley Searles, "Fantasy and Outré Themes in the Short Fiction of Edward Lucas White and Henry S. Whitehead" in *American Supernatural Fiction*, 64.

216 Whitehead, November 10, 1923.

217 Whitehead, November 10, 1923.

218 Associated Press, "Chattonooga Rector Speaks Against Ouija," *The Tennessean* (Nashville), February 27, 1923.

Chapter XI: H.P. Lovecraft, the Alien Seed

219 Joshi, *I Am Providence* v1, pp. 10, 11, 17, 21, 28.

220 HPL, letter to JCH, February 2, 1924, Harry Ransom Center, The University of Texas at Austin.

221 Joshi, *I Am Providence* v1, 98, 102.

222 Joshi, *I Am Providence* v1, 54.

223 Joshi, *I Am Providence* v1, 140. Also see Joshi, "Lovecraft and the Munsey Magazines" in *Lovecraft and a World in Transition*, 62.

224 Joshi, *I Am Providence* v1, 365.

225 Joshi, *I Am Providence* v1, 140.

226 HPL, letter in *The Eyrie*, in *Weird Tales*, October 1923. Contains the date-range of the columns and the quote.

227 HPL, letter to Morton, March 14, 1924, *Letters to James F. Morton*, 76.

228 Joshi, *I Am Providence* v1, 143-155.

229 Joshi, *I Am Providence* v1, 155.

230 Joshi, *I Am Providence* v1, 156-159. Joshi provides a succinct history of the movement and a description of its operation.

231 HPL, letter to Anne Tillery Renshaw, October 3, 1921, *SL I*, 154.

232 HPL, letter to JCH, February 2, 1924.

233 HPL, letter to FBL, October 8, 1921, *SL I*, 158.

234 HPL, letter to JCH, February 2, 1924.

235 HPL, letter to JCH, February 2, 1924.

236 JCH, July 1968.

237 JCH, letters to August Derleth, November 1, 1940, December 27, 1944, January 27, 1945, December 5, 1945, unpublished. Additionally, JCH recounted similar memories in a letter to the editor of *Esquire*, December 17, 1945, unpublished, responding to John Wilstach's article in the January issue, "The Ten-cent Ivory Tower," in which he disparaged Lovecraft's cultish readers. JCH sent a copy of his letter to Derleth.

238 JCH, July 1968.

239 JCH, *Weird Tales*, Winter 1973.

240 JCH, October 20, 1968.

241 JCH, October 20, 1968.

242 HPL, letter to JCH, February 2, 1924.

243 HPL, letter to FBL, February 7, 1924, *SL I*, 304.

244 HPL, letter to Morton, February 9, 1924, *Letters to James F. Morton*, 66.

245 See, for example: Elizabeth F. Loftus, *Eyewitness Testimony*. In this pioneering criminology text, Loftus shows the ease with which memories can be changed and how radically they can change over time.

246 JCH, October 20, 1968.

247 HPL, letter to L.D. Clark, March 9, 1924, *Letters From New York*, 43.

248 HPL, letter to L.D. Clark, March 18, 1924, *Letters From New York*, 46.

249 HPL, letter to Morton, March 29, 1923, *Letters to James F. Morton*, 33.

250 HPL, letter in *The Eyrie*, in *Weird Tales*, September 1923. This letter, which accompanied Lovecraft's initial submission of stories, was printed without date in the September issue. The letter's date had to have been between March 29, before Lovecraft had seen the magazine, and May 3, the first known report, in a letter to Morton, that the submission had gone out.

251 HPL, letter in *The Eyrie*, in *Weird Tales*, October 1923.

252 Joshi, *I Am Providence* v1, 453.

253 Arthur Leeds, *Thinks and Things* (column), *The Writer's Monthly*, May 1923.

254 HPL, letter to Morton, March 29, 1923, *Letters to James F. Morton*, 33.

255 Joshi, *I Am Providence* v1, 452.

256 HPL, letter to Clark Ashton Smith (CAS), October 17, 1930, *SL III*, 192.

257 HPL, letter to JCH, February 2, 1924.

258 EHP, "Howard Phillips Lovecraft" in *Book of the Dead*, 47.

259 HPL, letter in *The Eyrie*, in *Weird Tales*, September 1923.

260 HPL, letter to Morton, May 3, 1923, *Letters to James F. Morton*, 40.

261 HPL, letter in *The Eyrie*, in *Weird Tales*, October 1923. Baird's reply to Lovecraft's initial submission is unavailable. Lovecraft's subsequent reply, printed in *The Eyrie*, implies that Baird had defended the magazine.

262 HPL, letter to FBL, May 13, 1923, *SL I*, 227; HPL, letter to Morton, May 17, 1923, *Letters to James F. Morton*, 43.

263 Willis Knapp Jones, "Listening in on the Editors," *The Author & Journalist*, August 1927.

264 HPL, letter to FBL, May 13, 1923, *SL I*, 227.

265 HPL, letter in *The Eyrie*, in *Weird Tales*, October 1923.

266 By May 13, 1923, Lovecraft had received Baird's retyping request. By May 17, he was still thinking it over. By May 26, he was waiting for Baird's reply.

267 HPL, letter to Morton, May 26, 1923, *Letters to James F. Morton*, 44.

268 HPL, letter to Morton, May 29, 1923, *Letters to James F. Morton*, 46-47.

269 HPL, letter to FBL, June 3, 1923, *SL I*, 233.

270   HPL, letter to Morton, May 29, 1923, *Letters to James F. Morton*, 46-47.

271   HPL, letter to Morton, June 24, 1923, *Letters to James F. Morton*, 49.

272   HPL, letter to CAS, July 30, 1923, *Dawnward Spire, Lonely Hill*, 55-56. Note that Lovecraft favored British conventions in punctuation and spelling, e.g. "cheque."

273   HPL, letter to Morton, August 6, 1923, *Letters to James F. Morton*, 54.

274   HPL, letter to Morton, August 6, 1923, *Letters to James F. Morton*, 55.

275   HPL, letter to CAS, July 30, 1923, *Dawnward Spire, Lonely Hill*, 56.

276   HPL, letter to Morton, August 6, 1923, *Letters to James F. Morton*, 54.

277   HPL, letter to FBL, September 4, 1923, *SL I*, 250.

278   HPL, letter to FBL, November 8, 1923, *SL I*, 259.

279   HPL, letter to JCH, February 2, 1924.

280   HPL, letter to FBL, June 3, 1923, *SL I*, 233.

281   HPL, letter to FBL, June 3, 1923, *SL I*, 233.

282   HPL, letter to FBL, October 7, 1923, *SL I*, 253.

283   HPL, letter in *The Eyrie*, in *Weird Tales*, October 1923.

284   HPL, letter to FBL, October 7, 1923, *SL I*, 253. "Lewis Theobald Jr." was one of Lovecraft's amateur press pseudonyms.

285   HPL, letter to CAS, October 17, 1923, in *Dawnward Spire, Lonely Hill*, 58-59.

286   HPL, letter to CAS, October 17, 1923, in *Dawnward Spire, Lonely Hill*, 59.

287   HPL, letter to CAS, October 17, 1923, in *Dawnward Spire, Lonely Hill*, 58.

288   HPL, letter in *The Eyrie*, in *Weird Tales*, January 1924.

289   HPL, letter to Morton, October 28, 1923, *Letters to James F. Morton*, 57.

290   HPL, letter to Morton, May 17, 1923, *Letters to James F. Morton*, 43.

291   HPL, letter to Morton, December 5, 1923, *Letters to James F. Morton*, 60-61.

292   HPL, letter to Morton, October 28, 1923, *Letters to James F. Morton*, 57.

293   HPL, letter to FBL, November 8, 1923, *SL I*, 259.

294   HPL, letter to Morton, January 25, 1924, *Letters to James F. Morton*, 65; and letter to CAS, January 25, 1924, in *Dawnward Spire, Lonely Hill*, 65.

295   HPL, letter to Morton, February 23, 1936, *Letters to James F. Morton*, 372.

296   HPL, letter to L.D. Clark, July 27, 1925, *Letters From New York*, 155.

297   FBL, *Howard Phillips Lovecraft: Dreamer on the Nightside*, 124.

Chapter XII: A Case For and Against

298   HPL, letter to Morton, October 28, 1923, *Letters to James F. Morton*, 57.

Chapter XIII: The Man Behind the Curtain

299   HPL, letter to FBL, February 3, 1924, *SL I*, 292.

300 HPL, letter to EB, February 3, 1924, *SL I*, 295. JCH remembered "The Rats in the Walls" as an extremely significant story for *Weird Tales*. In his 1940s correspondence, he brings the story up repeatedly. For example, he recalled it, falsely, as "the first story I bought from [Lovecraft]"; JCH, letter to August Derleth, November 1, 1940, unpublished.

301 JCH, May 1969.

302 HPL, letter in *The Eyrie*, in *Weird Tales*, September 1923.

303 HPL, letter to Walter J. Coates, March 30, 1926, *SL II*, 41.

304 HPL, letter to J. Vernon Shea, July 19, 1931, *SL III*, 382.

305 FBL, *Howard Phillips Lovecraft: Dreamer on the Nightside*, 209.

306 HPL, letter in *The Eyrie*, in *Weird Tales*, March 1924.

Chapter XIV: The Almanac of Cosmic Occurrences—1924

307 HPL, letter to EB, February 3, 1924, *SL I*, 295.

308 OAK, April 1, 1941.

309 HPL, letter to JCH, February 2, 1924. Lovecraft's reply to Henneberger echoes Henneberger's language in many respects. In this instance, Lovecraft referred to "dealers in the unscrupulous state of mind you describe."

310 HPL, letter to EB, February 3, 1924, *SL I*, 295.

311 HPL, letter to JCH, February 2, 1924.

312 HPL, letter to FBL, February 3, 1924, *SL I*, 292.

313 HPL, letter to EB, February 3, 1924, *SL I*, 295.

314 HPL, letter to JCH, February 2, 1924.

315 HPL, letter to EB, February 3, 1924, *SL I*, 295.

316 HPL, letter to JCH, February 2, 1924.

317 The remark about "the beautiful queen of remote planets" is most likely a criticism of Edgar Rice Burroughs's Mars series, which centered around Earthman John Carter and his Martian bride Dejah Thoris.

318 HPL, letter to FBL, February 3, 1924, *SL I*, 292-293.

319 HPL, letter to FBL, February 7, 1924, *SL I*, 304.

320 Robert Barbour Johnson, "Recollections of Weird Tales" in *The Weird Tales Story*, 56-57.

321 *Detective Tales* published ads for *Fay*, as well.

322 Ad for *Fay*, *Weird Tales*, February 1924, 94.

323 Ad for *Fay*, *Weird Tales*, April 1924, 93.

324 JCH, May 1969.

325 JCH October 20, 1968.

326 Terence E. Hanley, "Tellers of Weird Tales: Artists & Writers in The Unique Magazine: Isa-Belle Manzer (1872 or 1873-1944)," *Tellers of Weird Tales* blog, April 18, 2012. tellersofweirdtales.blogspot.com/2012/04/isa-belle-manzer-1872-or-1873-1944.html

327 Willis Knapp Jones, "Listening in on the Editors," *The Author & Journalist*, August 1927.

328 HPL, letter to Morton, February 19, 1924, *Letters to James F. Morton*, 68.

329 HPL, letter to JCH, February 2, 1924.

330 HPL, letter to L.D. Clark, March 18, 1924, *Letters From New York*, 46.

331 HPL, letter to Morton, February 19, 1924, *Letters to James F. Morton*, 68.

332 HPL, letter to Morton, February 19, 1924, *Letters to James F. Morton*, 67.

333 HPL, letter to Morton, February 19, 1924, *Letters to James F. Morton*, 68.

334 EHP, "Farnsworth Wright" in *Book of the Dead*, 10.

335 The Editor, *The Eyrie*, in *Weird Tales*, November 1924.

336 HPL, letter to L.D. Clark, March 30, 1924, *Letters From New York*, 52.

337 Farnsworth Wright, letter to FBL, April 7, 1924. A detailed description of the letter, from which the quote was taken, is in a book dealer's online listing offering the letter for sale.

Chapter XV: The Magician's Ghostwriters

338 JCH, May 1969.

339 Houdini also played Chicago's Palace theater for a limited engagement in October 1923.

340 "Houdini Leaving Stage," *Minneapolis Star*, February 23, 1924.

341 Internet Movie Database (IMDB.com).

342 "Houdini Removes Thumb," *Greenville News* (South Carolina), March 7, 1924.

343 "Printing Company Prepares to Move," *Indianapolis Star*, October 20, 1924.

344 JCH, April 14, 1969.

345 JCH, May 1969.

346 Untitled sidebar, *Weird Tales*, March 1924, 4.

347 Joshi, *I Am Providence* v1, 498.

348 Joshi, *I Am Providence* v1, 498.

349 JCH, letter to August Derleth, January 27, 1945, unpublished.

350 To muddy the waters, Farnsworth Wright's father and/or uncle may have relocated from the Midwest to the California for their health, but this was before Farnsworth's time and the circumstances don't match the Houdini story as closely as Ward's.

351 *The Cauldron* (column), *Weird Tales*, June 1923.

352 Untitled sidebar, *Weird Tales*, March 1924, 4.

353 *Literary Market Tips*, in *The Author & Journalist*, April 1924.

354 Locke, "The History of *Ghost Stories*" in *Ghost Stories: The Magazine and Its Makers* v1, 13.

355 HPL, letter to FBL, October 26, 1926, *SL II*, 79.

Chapter XVI: A Grand Unified Nexus of Weird

356 JCH, May 1969.

357 James Machin, "Fellows Find: H.P. Lovecraft Letter Sheds Light on Pivotal Moment in His Career," January 27, 2015, Harry Ransom Center, The University of Texas at Austin. https://blog.hrc.utexas.edu/2015/01/27/fellows-find-h-p-lovecraft-letter/

   The February 2 letter, so critical to this narrative, was unearthed by British PhD student James Machin at the Ransom Center. Machin speculates, quite plausibly, that the letter came from the center's Messmore Kendall collection of theatrical materials which included items owned by Houdini, and that Henneberger gave the letter to the magician when the Houdini-Lovecraft collaboration was being contemplated.

358 HPL, letter to FBL, February 14, 1924, *SL I*, 311.

359 HPL, letter to Morton, February 19, 1924, *Letters to James F. Morton*, 67.

360 HPL, letter to FBL, February 14, 1924, *SL I*, 311-312; HPL, letter to Morton, February 19, 1924, *Letters to James F. Morton*, 67.

361 HPL, letter to August Derleth, September 2, 1926, *Essential Solitude*, 34. Lovecraft wrote: "I know the Macfadden junk is altogether impossible—in fact, I've never so much as opened one of these publications with the exception of [*Ghost Stories*]!" *Ghost Stories* debuted with a July 1926 issue.

362 HPL, letter to Morton, February 19, 1924, *Letters to James F. Morton*, 67.

363 HPL, letter to FBL, February 25, 1924, *SL I*, 317.

364 HPL, letter to FBL, February 25, 1924, *SL I*, 317.

365 HPL, letter to FBL, March 21, 1924, *SL I*, 330.

366 Joshi, *I Am Providence* v1, 498. Note that Joshi attributes the loss to Lovecraft being in a rush; we prefer the sleep-deprivation theory, but the two ideas are not mutually exclusive.

367 HPL, letter to L.D. Clark, March 9, 1924, *Letters From New York*, 38.

368 HPL, letter to Morton, March 12, 1924, *Letters to James F. Morton*, 71.

369 HPL, letter to Morton, March 12, 1924, *Letters to James F. Morton*, 71.

370 HPL, letter to Morton, March 14, 1924, *Letters to James F. Morton*, 75-76.

371 HPL, letter to L.D. Clark, March 19, 1924, *Letters From New York*, 46.

372 HPL, letter to L.D. Clark, March 19, 1924, *Letters From New York*, 46.

373 HPL, letter to FBL, March 21, 1924, *SL I*, 333.

374 HPL, letter to EB, February 3, 1924, *SL I*, 295.

375 HPL, letter in *The Eyrie*, in *Weird Tales*, September 1923.

376 OAK, April 1, 1941.

377 HPL, letter to FBL, February 14, 1924, *SL I*, 311.

378 HPL, letter to L.D. Clark, March 19, 1924, *Letters From New York*, 47.

379 JCH, May 1969.

380 The Editor, *The Eyrie*, in *Weird Tales*, March 1924.

381 Harry Houdini, *Ask Houdini*, in *Weird Tales*, April 1924.

382 Harry Houdini, *Ask Houdini*, in *Weird Tales*, April 1924.

Chapter XVII: The Call of Chicago

383 HPL, letter to L.D. Clark, March 19, 1924, *Letters From New York*, 46.

384 HPL, letter in *The Eyrie*, in *Weird Tales*, September 1923.

385 HPL, letter in *The Eyrie*, in *Weird Tales*, October 1923.

386 FBL, *Howard Phillips Lovecraft: Dreamer on the Nightside*, 118.

387 HPL, letter to L.D. Clark, March 19, 1924, *Letters From New York*, 46.

388 FBL, *Howard Phillips Lovecraft: Dreamer on the Nightside*, 119.

389 HPL, letter to L.D. Clark, March 19, 1924, *Letters From New York*, 46.

390 FBL, *Howard Phillips Lovecraft: Dreamer on the Nightside*, 119-122.

391 HPL, letter to L.D. Clark, March 19, 1924, *Letters From New York*, 46.

392 HPL, letter to L.D. Clark, March 19, 1924, *Letters From New York*, 46.

393 FBL, *Howard Phillips Lovecraft: Dreamer on the Nightside*, 120.

394 FBL, *Howard Phillips Lovecraft: Dreamer on the Nightside*, 121.

395 HPL, letter to L.D. Clark, March 19, 1924, *Letters From New York*, 46.

396 FBL, *Howard Phillips Lovecraft: Dreamer on the Nightside*, 121.

397 FBL, *Howard Phillips Lovecraft: Dreamer on the Nightside*, 120.

398 FBL, *Howard Phillips Lovecraft: Dreamer on the Nightside*, 121.

399 FBL, *Howard Phillips Lovecraft: Dreamer on the Nightside*, 122.

400 HPL, letter to L.D. Clark, March 30, 1924, *Letters From New York*, 52.

401 JCH, October 20, 1968.

402 *Literary Market Tips*, in *The Author & Journalist*, June 1924.

403 Joshi, *I Am Providence* v1, 505.

404 HPL, letter to Morton, February 19, 1924, *Letters to James F. Morton*, 67.

405 HPL, letter to Morton, March 12, 1924, *Letters to James F. Morton*, 71.

406 HPL, letter to Morton, March 14, 1924, *Letters to James F. Morton*, 76.

407 HPL, letter to L.D. Clark, March 19, 1924, *Letters From New York*, 46.

408 HPL, letter to CAS, July 24, 1924, *Dawnward Spire, Lonely Hill*, 70.

409 HPL, letter to Wilfred Blanch Talman, March 24, 1931, *SL III*, 355.

410 FBL, *Howard Phillips Lovecraft: Dreamer on the Nightside*, 114-118.

411 HPL, letter to L.D. Clark, January 22, 1925, *Letters From New York*, 105; HPL, letter to Annie E.P. Gamwell, February 10, 1925, *Letters From New York*, 111.

412 FBL, *Howard Phillips Lovecraft: Dreamer on the Nightside*, 116-117.

413 HPL, letter to Wilfred Blanch Talman, March 24, 1931, *SL III*, 355.

414 *Outward Bound* was filmed twice by Warner Brothers: *Outward Bound* (1930) and *Between Two Worlds* (1944).

415 Sewell Collins, "Who Is Sutton Vane?," *New York Times*, January 13, 1924. Collins was a representative of the play's London producer and personally acquainted with Vane.

416 Burns Mantle, "Life Beyond Is Theme of 'Outward Bound'," *Pittsburgh Post Gazette* (PA), January 13, 1924.

417 HPL, letter to Wilfred Blanch Talman, October 11, 1926, *SL II*, 76.

418 HPL, letter to FBL, October 26, 1926, *SL II*, 79.

419 Joshi, *I Am Providence* v2, 636.

420 HPL, letter to FBL, October 26, 1926, *SL II*, 79.

421 HPL, letter to Farnsworth Wright, July 5, 1927, *SL II*, 149.

Chapter XVIII: The Devil Never Forgets

422 OAK, April 1, 1941.

423 *Literary Market Tips*, in *The Author & Journalist*, August 1924.

424 *Literary Market Tips*, in *The Author & Journalist*, July 1924.

425 OAK (unattributed), "Why Weird Tales?," *Weird Tales*, May-June-July 1924, 1-2.

426 HPL, letter in *The Eyrie*, in *Weird Tales*, March 1924.

427 HPL, letter to JCH, February 2, 1924.

428 HPL, letter to CAS, March 26, 1935, *Dawnward Spire, Lonely Hill*, 594.

429 HPL, letter to Morton, October 28, 1923, *Letters to James F. Morton*, 57.

430 HPL, letter to EB, February 3, 1924, *SL I*, 295.

431 Curiously, Henneberger was sixteen when he was introduced to Poe at his military academy.

432 HPL, letter to L.D. Clark, December 22-23, 1924, quoted in Joshi, *I Am Providence* v1, 501, footnote 30.

433 HPL, letter to L.D. Clark, December 2, 1925, *Letters From New York*, 251.

434 HPL, letter to L.D. Clark, December 13, 1925, *Letters From New York*, 252.

435 HPL, letter to CAS, March 26, 1935, *Dawnward Spire, Lonely Hill*, 594.

436 HPL, letter to CAS, March 26, 1935, *Dawnward Spire, Lonely Hill*, 594.

437 EB, letter to contributors on *Real Detective Tales & Mystery Stories* letterhead, May 28, 1924, unpublished.

438 HPL, letter to CAS, July 24, 1924, *Dawnward Spire, Lonely Hill*, 69.

439 JCH, letter to August Derleth, November 1, 1940, unpublished.

440 JCH, October 20, 1968.

441 OAK, April 1, 1941.

442 Most details taken from "The Cornelius Printing Company," *Indianapolis Star*, June 23, 1912; "George Cornelius Dies; Founded Printing Firm," *Indianapolis Star*, August 29, 1946.

443 *Literary Market Tips*, in *The Author & Journalist*, August 1924.

444   HPL, letter to C.M. Eddy, Jr., July 24, 1924, unpublished.

445   HPL, letter to CAS, July 24, 1924, in *Dawnward Spire, Lonely Hill*, 69.

446   Julius Schwartz, "Titans of Science Fiction: Farnsworth Wright."

447   JCH, May 1969.

Chapter XIX: Arthur J. Burks and the Triple Evolution

448   Unless otherwise noted, background material on Burks is based on unpublished research by this author.

449   Robert A. McLean, "Arthur J. Burks: Speed-King of Fiction," *Writers' Markets and Methods*, August 1928.

450   Mort Weisinger and Julius Schwartz, "Titans of Science Fiction: Arthur J. Burks," *Science Fiction Digest*, May 1933.

451   Burks chronicled his Dominican Republic experiences in *Land of Checkerboard Families* (1932).

452   AJB, "Pitfalls," *Writers' Markets and Methods*, April 1929.

453   AJB, "Literature as an Investment," *Writers' Markets and Methods*, February 1929.

454   McLean, "Arthur J. Burks: Speed-King of Fiction."

455   The Palmer family who owned the building were unrelated to Frederick Palmer or the institute, but you would never have known it from the institute's advertising and materials.

456   AJB, "Literature as an Investment," *Writers' Markets and Methods*, February 1929.

457   Frederick Palmer, *Modern Authorship: Author's Fiction Manual*, 69.

458   Douglas Ellis, *Uncovered: The Hidden Art of the Girlie Pulps* (Silver Spring, Maryland: Adventure House, 2003).

459   Palmer, *Author's Fiction Manual*, 73-74.

460   Palmer, *Author's Fiction Manual*, 80.

461   Palmer, *Author's Fiction Manual*, 139.

462   Palmer, *Author's Fiction Manual*, 140.

463   Palmer, *Author's Fiction Manual*, 140-141.

464   AJB, "Literature as an Investment," *Writers' Markets and Methods*, February 1929. In the following month's issue, March, Burks identified the story as "Too Many Legs," but no Burks short story bearing this title appeared in *Weird Tales*, or any other pulp. Additionally, the title doesn't have any apparent match with the Burks stories that did appear in *Weird Tales*. If Burks's memory is accurate, then Wright may never have published it—or paid for it. In "What Palmer Students Are Doing," *Writers' Markets and Methods*, February 1926, Burks listed the prices he'd been paid for numerous stories in *Weird Tales*. Two of them received $15: "Voodoo" (December 1924), and "Strange Tales from Santo Domingo: 1. A Broken Lamp-Chimney" (February 1925). The others he listed, and the prices paid, were: "Luisma's Return"

(January 1925), $25; "Strange Tales from Santo Domingo: 2. Desert of the Dead" (March 1925), $20; "Strange Tales from Santo Domingo: 3. Daylight Shadows" (April 1925), $20; "Strange Tales from Santo Domingo: 4. The Sorrowful Sisterhood" (May 1925), $25; "Strange Tales from Santo Domingo: 5. The Phantom Chibo" (June 1925), $25; "Black Medicine" (August 1925), $100; "Vale of the Corbies" (November 1925), $24; "When the Graves Were Opened" (December 1925), $40; "Something Toothsome" (March 1926), $20; "The Ghosts of Steamboat Coulee" (May 1926), $70; "Asphodel" (June 1926), $25; "Orbit of Souls" (December 1926), $60; "Strange Tales from Santo Domingo: 6. Faces" (April 1927), $25; "Three Coffins" (May 1928), $70; "Invisible Threads" (September, October 1928), $100.

465 AJB, "Otis Adelbert Kline: A Memoir," *OAK Leaves* 13, 1981.

466 AJB, "Are Editors Human?," *Writers' Markets and Methods*, March 1929.

467 AJB, "Literature as an Investment," *Writers' Markets and Methods*, February 1929.

468 Weisinger and Schwartz, "Titans of Science Fiction: Arthur J. Burks."

469 Mort Weisinger, "Why They Use Pennames," *The Author & Journalist*, November 1934.

470 See, for example Frederick C. Painton, "Wuxtry! Art Burks' Plot Clicks," *Writer's Digest*, April 1936.

471 McLean, "Arthur J. Burks: Speed-King of Fiction."

472 AJB, *Land of Checkerboard Families*, 17.

473 AJB, letter in *The Globe-Trotter* (column), *Thrilling Adventures*, October 1934.

474 AJB, *Land of Checkerboard Families*, 17.

475 AJB, *Land of Checkerboard Families*, 19.

476 AJB, *Thrilling Adventures*, October 1934.

477 AJB, *Thrilling Adventures*, October 1934.

478 AJB, "Pitfalls," *Writers' Markets and Methods*, April 1929.

479 AJB, "Literature as an Investment," *Writers' Markets and Methods*, February 1929.

480 Additionally, Wright reprinted two of Burks's early stories: "Bells of Oceana" (April 1934), and "When the Graves Were Opened" (September 1937).

481 AJB, "Otis Adelbert Kline: A Memoir," *OAK Leaves* 13, 1981.

482 AJB, "Are Editors Human?," *Writers' Markets and Methods*, March 1929.

Chapter XX: After the Earthquake

483 The Editor, *The Eyrie*, in *Weird Tales*, December 1924.

484 *Literary Market Tips*, in *The Author & Journalist*, October 1924.

485 "Buys Site for New Printing Building," *Indianapolis Star*, May 21, 1924.

486 *Indianapolis Star* August 10, 1924.

487   "Printing Company Prepares to Move," *Indianapolis Star*, October 20, 1924.

488   "Printing Company Occupies Washington Street Plant," *Indianapolis Star*, December 8, 1924. Cornelius also printed the bimonthly *United Mine Workers Journal*, at 300,000 copies per issue.

489   OAK, April 1, 1941.

490   The twelve titles listed in the ad were: "Buff," by Edwin Hunt Hoover (*Detective Tales*, October 1, 1922); "The Sign of the Toad," Clifford Burns (October 16, 1922); "The Glass Eye," George Doubleday (October 16, 1922); "The Web," Eric Howard (November 1, 1922); "Nighthawks," Edwin MacLaren (two-part serial: November 1, 1922; November 16/December 15, 1922); "Crimson Poppies," Matthew Benson (November 16/December 15, 1922); "Disappearing Bullets," George J. Brenn (two-part serial: November 16/December 15, 1922; February 1923); "The Green-eyed Monster," George Bronson Howard (February 1923); "The Valley of Missing Men," Charles Franklin (February 1923); "The Mystery at Eagle Lodge," Irvin Mattick (February 1923); "The Dangerous Hours," George B. Jenkins (February 1923); "Derring Do," Hamilton Craigie (March 1923).

491   Full-page ad for *Real Detective Tales and Mystery Stories*, in *Weird Tales*, November 1924, 192.

492   Joshi, *I Am Providence* v1, 509-510.

493   HPL, letter to L.D. Clark, September 29-30, 1924, *Letters From New York*, 70.

494   HPL, letter to L.D. Clark, September 29-30, 1924, *Letters From New York*, 75.

495   Joshi, *I Am Providence* v1, 511.

496   *Literary Market Tips*, in *The Author & Journalist*, September 1924.

497   "Swanson Makes Good on 'College Humor,'" *The (Grinnell College) Scarlet and Black*, September 19, 1923.

498   HPL, letter to L.D. Clark, September 29-30, 1924, *Letters From New York*, 73.

499   HPL, letter to L.D. Clark, September 29-30, 1924, *Letters From New York*, 75.

500   HPL, letter to L.D. Clark, September 18, 1924, *Letters From New York*, 62.

501   HPL, letter to CAS, September 20, 1925, *Dawnward Spire, Lonely Hill*, 81.

502   HPL, letter to FBL, May 1, 1926, *Letters From New York*, 315.

503   HPL, letter to FBL, May 20, 1926, *SL II*, 53.

504   *Literary Market Tips*, in *The Author & Journalist*, October 1924.

505   Statement of Ownership, *Weird Tales*, December 1924, 190.

506   *Literary Market Tips*, in *The Author & Journalist*, October 1924.

507   "Checks Due These Writers," in *The Barrel* (column), in *The Author & Journalist*, December 1924. The unpaid authors and their stories: Vida Taylor Adams, "Whoso Diggeth a Pit" (May-June-July 1924); John Harris Burland,

"The Strange Case of Jacob Arum" (July-August 1923); Paul Crumpler, "The Photographic Phantom" (April 1923); Orville R. Emerson, "The Grave" (March 1923); E. Thayles Emmons, "Two Hours of Death" (May 1923); Leonard Fohn, "The Visit of the Skulls" (March 1924); M.L. Humphreys, "The Floor Above" (May 1923); Harry A. Kniffin, "The Hand of Fatma" (January 1924); Charles Layng, "The Cataleptic" (January 1924); William Merrit, "The Finale" (May 1923); Will W. Nelson, "Voodooism" (July-August 1923); C.P. Oliver, "Black Magic" (September 1923); I.W.D. Peters, "The Gallows" (March 1923).

508 *Literary Market Tips*, in *The Author & Journalist*, January 1925.

509 *Literary Market Tips*, in *The Author & Journalist*, March 1925.

510 William C. Hartmann, *Hartmann's Who's Who in Occult, Psychic and Spiritual Realms* (Jamaica, New York: The Occult Press, 1925), 49.

511 *Literary Market Tips*, in *The Author & Journalist*, October 1924.

512 "Amelia Long's Story," *Harrisburg Telegraph*, September 20, 1924.

513 "Mrs. Silvio Von Ruck," *Asheville Citizen-Times* (North Carolina), September 22, 1924.

514 The Editor, *The Eyrie*, in *Weird Tales*, November 1924.

515 The Editor, *The Eyrie*, in *Weird Tales*, December 1924.

516 The Editor, *The Eyrie*, in *Weird Tales*, January 1925.

517 The Editor, *The Eyrie*, in *Weird Tales*, February 1925.

518 Patrice Louinet, " 'The Wright Hook' (or, the origin of 'Spear and Fang')," *REH: Two-Gun Raconteur*, October 25, 2016. http://www.rehtwogunraconteur. com/the-wright-hook-or-the-origin-of-spear-and-fang/

519 Louinet, " 'The Wright Hook'."

520 Farnsworth Wright, quoted in Mort Weisinger, "Pseudonym Sidelights," *The Author & Journalist*, August 1935.

521 Farnsworth Wright, in "Pseudonym Sidelights."

Chapter XXI: Wonders and Wonderers

No notes.

Chapter XXII: A History of Silence

522 Kantor, "Editors You Want To Know: Edwin Baird."

523 MacKinlay Kantor, letter to Peter Ruber, May 4, 1963, unpublished.

524 Kantor, May 4, 1963.

525 EB, "How to Write a Detective Story: I. Mastermind and His Problems," *The Author & Journalist*, December 1929.

526 Willis Knapp Jones, "Listening in on the Editors," *The Author & Journalist*, August 1927.

527 James Knapp Reeve, "About Some 'Specialized' Publications and Their Needs," *Writer's Digest*, May 1926.

528 Kantor, "Editors You Want To Know: Edwin Baird."

529 EB, "How to Write a Detective Story: IX. Rules and Methods," *The Author &
Journalist*, August 1930. For the record, the witty gangster was Chicago's Big
Tim Murphy, gunned down on June 26, 1928. Murphy was quoted in "So This
Is a War on Gangs, Says Big Tim," *Chicago Tribune*, December 21, 1927. It
was an old gag when Big Tim used it in 1927, and simultaneously too recent
for Baird's apocryphal newspaper days.

530 Kantor, "Editors You Want To Know: Edwin Baird."

531 EB, "How to Write a Detective Story: XII. The Horror Story," *The Author &
Journalist*, November 1930.

532 For a detailed analysis, see John Locke, "Weirdness and the Detective
Pulp," in Maxwell Hawkins, *Cult of the Corpses* (Castroville, CA: Off-Trail
Publications, 2008), 5-20.

533 *Literary Market Tips*, in *The Author & Journalist*, July, November 1930;
March 1931.

534 Kantor, May 4, 1963.

535 Bill Brannon, "Bill Brannon Remembers," *Keeler News: Bulletin of the Harry
Stephen Keeler Society*, August 2014, 7.

536 *Literary Market Tips*, in *The Author & Journalist*, February 1933.

537 *Literary Market Tips*, in *The Author & Journalist*, December 1933.

538 *Literary Market Tips*, in *The Author & Journalist*, January 1935.

539 *Literary Market Tips*, in *The Author & Journalist*, July 1935.

540 *Literary Market Tips*, in *The Author & Journalist*, September 1935.

541 *Literary Market Tips*, in *The Author & Journalist*, February 1937.

542 EB, "A Day With Midwest Editors," *The Author & Journalist*, May 1937.

543 Vincent Starrett, *Books Alive* (column), *Chicago Tribune*, February 13, 1955.

544 Willis Knapp Jones, "Listening in on the Editors," *The Author & Journalist*,
August 1927.

545 EHP, "Farnsworth Wright" in *Book of the Dead*, 14.

546 EHP, "Farnsworth Wright" in *Book of the Dead*, 11.

547 EHP, "Farnsworth Wright" in *Book of the Dead*, 14.

548 EHP, "Farnsworth Wright" in *The Weird Tales Story*, 7.

549 Marjorie J. Wright, quoted in EHP, "Farnsworth Wright" in *The Weird Tales
Story*, 13.

550 Mary Jeannette Zinkie (Marjorie's mother), letter to "Folks," October 10,
1925.

551 EHP, "Farnsworth Wright" in *The Weird Tales Story*, 7.

552 EHP, "Farnsworth Wright" in *The Weird Tales Story*, 13.

553 Jack Williamson, *Wonder's Child*, 109.

554 Robert Spencer Carr, quoted in EHP, "Farnsworth Wright" in *Book of the
Dead*, 25.

555 JCH, October 20, 1968.

556 *The Pony Express* (column), in *Writer's Review*, November 1934.

557 Otto O. Binder, letter to Jack Darrow, March 10, 1940, unpublished.

558 EHP, "Farnsworth Wright" in *The Weird Tales Story*, 7.

559 Moskowitz, *Weird Tales*, Winter 1973.

560 EHP, "Otis Adelbert Kline" in *Book of the Dead*, 32.

561 David Anthony Kraft, "The Bride of Osiris and Other Weird Tales," *OAK Leaves* 12, Autumn 1979.

562 OAK, April 1, 1941.

563 OAK, "Reflections," *OAK Leaves* 11, 1975, 4.

564 AJB, quoted in "Oakline Correspondence," *OAK Leaves* 12, Autumn 1979.

565 OAK, April 1, 1941.

566 "Condemned Prisoner Will Finish Serial Before He Is Hanged," *Great Falls Tribune* (Montana), October 10, 1929.

567 "Otis Kline's Novel Among Best Sellers," *Sterling Daily Gazette*, September 7, 1929.

568 EHP, "Otis Adelbert Kline" in *Book of the Dead*, 32.

569 Harold Ward, "A Letter That Speaks for Itself," undated letter to OAK, quoted in OAK ad, *Writer's Digest*, March 1935.

570 Otto O. Binder, letter to Jack Darrow, October 27, 1946, unpublished.

571 Tonik, "An Interview with Gladys Ward," 349.

572 "Harold Ward," *Chicago Tribune*, March 2, 1950.

573 HPL, letter to Robert Bloch, November [n.d.], 1933, *Letters to Robert Bloch and Others*, 89.

574 HPL, letter to L.D. Clark, August 6, 1925, *Letters From New York*, 162.

575 HPL, letter to L.D. Clark, September 23-24, 1925, *Letters From New York*, 197.

576 Joshi, *I Am Providence* v2, 617.

577 HPL, letter to J. Vernon Shea, August 7, 1931, *SL III*, 395.

578 Joshi, *I Am Providence* v2, 759, 765.

579 HPL, letter to EHP, October 20, 1932, *SL IV*, 91.

580 Joshi, *I Am Providence* v2, 824.

581 Joshi, *I Am Providence* v2, 1003-1007.

582 JCH, letter to August Derleth, February 3, 1965, unpublished.

583 JCH, April 14, 1969.

584 M.W. Childs, "She Gave Up 'Serious Thinking' and Became an Editor," *St. Louis Post-Dispatch*, September 4, 1932. In this article, the new editor of *College Humor*, Mary Reilly, describes the history of the magazine, an account that most likely came from Lansinger.

Chapter XXIII: The Arc of the Cosmos

585 "Publisher Buys Flats," *Chicago Tribune*, June 8, 1924.

586 Stuart Knox, "Connecticut Yankee in Cinema's Court," *Hartford Courant*, November 20, 1927.

587 "Publisher of College Humor in Miami to Rest Funnybone," *The Miami News*, March 2, 1928.

588 Katharine Brush, *This Is On Me*, 103.

589 Katharine Brush, *This Is On Me*, 136.

590 "May Build Apartments at Dearborn and Maple St.," *Chicago Tribune*, May 10, 1925; "Work to Start Tomorrow on Lansing Hotel," *Chicago Tribune*, December 27, 1925; Lansbro Building Corporation ad, *Chicago Tribune*, January 5, 1926; "Brons Sells Half Interest in Lansing Hotel," *Chicago Tribune*, September 12, 1926.

591 "Asks Injunction Against Lansbro Hotel," *Chicago Tribune*, December 27, 1929.

592 M.W. Childs, "She Gave Up 'Serious Thinking' and Became an Editor," *St. Louis Post-Dispatch*, September 4, 1932.

593 "Hollywood Glitter from a Shining Legend," ad for *Sprinkled with Ruby Dust* by H.N. Swanson, *Los Angeles Times*, October 15, 1989.

594 "Lansinger Joins State Mutual Life," *The Oregonian*, May 3, 1939.

595 Swanson, H.N., *Sprinkled with Ruby Dust*, 11.

596 Swanson, H.N., *Sprinkled with Ruby Dust*, 19-20.

597 Jessie Scott, *The Grapevine* (column), *The Oregonian*, May 22, 1955.

598 JCH, October 20, 1968.

599 "R.M. Eastman Funeral To Be Held Tomorrow," *Chicago Tribune*, November 24, 1932.

600 JCH, April 14, 1969.

601 JCH, April 14, 1969.

602 Moskowitz, *Weird Tales*, Winter 1973.

603 JCH's known residential addresses in NYC: 51 Hamilton Place (Manhattan, 1940), 7 Van Corlear Place (The Bronx, 1942, 1944-45), and 170 South Oxford Street (Brooklyn, 1965, 1968).

604 JCH, letter to August Derleth, November 1, 1940, unpublished.

605 JCH, letter to August Derleth, November 1, 1940, unpublished.

606 Joel Frieman, phone conversation with the author, May 7, 2017.

607 Moskowitz, *Weird Tales*, Winter 1973.

608 Nor did Baird, Kline, or Lovecraft.

609 JCH, July 1968.

APPENDIX A
ORIGINS OF LETTERS TO *WEIRD TALES* BY STATE

The following table lists the rank and count of the states of origin, when noted, of every letter to the *Weird Tales* columns *The Eyrie* (nine issues from April 1923 to March 1924) and *Ask Houdini* (two issues from April to May-June-July 1924), from the inception of the magazine through the split of Rural Publishing into two companies.

Since distribution figures for the magazine aren't available, the below figures give a rough—and thoroughly unscientific—estimate of where the magazine was most available and most popular.

All three Canadian letters came from cities close to the northeast U.S. border: St. Catharines, Ontario; Montreal, Québec; and Québec City, Québec. The Mexico letter (May 1923), postmarked Vera Cruz, was sent by an American merchant marine officer from New Orleans. Chief among the statistical anomalies, all four Rhode Island letters came from H.P. Lovecraft.

State	Count	State	Count	State	Count
New York	26	Nebraska	3	West Virginia	1
California	19	Wisconsin	3	Arizona	0
Illinois	15	Connecticut	2	Arkansas	0
Pennsylvania	9	Delaware	2	Idaho	0
origin not listed	7	Kentucky	2	Louisiana	0
Michigan	6	Oregon	2	Mississippi	0
Texas	6	Washington	2	Nevada	0
Indiana	5	Alabama	1	New Hampshire	0
Minnesota	5	Georgia	1	North Dakota	0
North Carolina	5	Iowa	1	Oklahoma	0
Florida	4	Kansas	1	South Carolina	0
Missouri	4	Maine	1	South Dakota	0
Ohio	4	Maryland	1	Tennessee	0
Rhode Island	4	*Mexico*	1	Utah	0
Canada	3	Montana	1	Vermont	0
Colorado	3	New Jersey	1	Virginia	0
Massachusetts	3	New Mexico	1	Wyoming	0
				Entries	**51**
				Sum	**155**

APPENDIX B
VITAL STATISTICS FOR NOTABLE *WEIRD TALES* CONTRIBUTORS

Chapter XXI, "Wonders and Wonderers," discussed the commonality in birth-years for two groups: the central *Weird Tales* creators and contributors from the early years; and First Fandom, the fantastic-fiction fans who organized into networks, generally in the 1930s. The below lists rank the names in birth order. A number of the *Weird Tales* contributors made their appearances after the first two years and are thus not mentioned in the narrative. There is some overlap in the candidates for both lists, notably Donald Wandrei and August Derleth, both of whom contributed to *Weird Tales* and fandom.

Weird Tales Contributors

Name	Birth	Death
Nictzin Dyalhis	06/04/1873	05/08/1942
Harry Houdini	03/24/1874	10/31/1926
Harold Ward	01/05/1879	03/01/1950
Hamilton Craigie	07/22/1880	08/09/1956
David H. Keller	12/23/1880	07/13/1966
Greye La Spina	07/10/1880	09/17/1969
Henry S. Whitehead	03/05/1882	11/23/1932
John Martin Leahy	05/16/1886	03/26/1967
Edwin Baird	06/28/1886	09/27/1954
Vincent Starrett	10/26/1886	01/05/1974
Farnsworth Wright	07/29/1888	06/12/1940
Seabury Quinn	01/01/1889	12/24/1969
J.C. Henneberger	02/02/1890	11/??/1969
H.P. Lovecraft	08/20/1890	03/15/1937
Eli Colter	09/30/1890	05/30/1984
Otis Adelbert Kline	07/01/1891	10/24/1946
J.M. Lansinger	09/10/1892	06/30/1963
Anthony M. Rud	01/11/1893	11/30/1942
Clark Ashton Smith	01/13/1893	08/14/1961
Frank Owen	04/20/1893	10/13/1968
Everil Worrell	11/03/1893	07/27/1969
H. Thompson Rich	11/23/1893	08/??/1974
Willis Knapp Jones	11/26/1895	03/??/1982
C.M. Eddy, Jr.	01/18/1896	11/21/1967
E. Hoffmann Price	07/03/1898	06/18/1988
Arthur J. Burks	09/13/1898	05/13/1974

Weird Tales Contributors

Name	Birth	Death
Frank Belknap Long, Jr.	04/27/1901	01/03/1994
William R. Sprenger	05/15/1902	01/01/1972
Manly Wade Wellman	05/21/1903	04/05/1986
H. Warner Munn	11/05/1903	01/10/1981
Edmond Hamilton	10/21/1904	02/01/1977
Paul S. Powers	01/31/1905	03/01/1971
Robert E. Howard	01/22/1906	06/11/1936
Robert Spencer Carr	03/26/1909	04/28/1994

First Fandom

Name	Birth	Death
Donald Wandrei	04/20/1908	10/15/1987
August Derleth	02/24/1909	07/04/1971
Clifford Kornoelje ("Jack Darrow")	05/14/1912	05/12/2001
Donald A. Wollheim	10/01/1914	11/02/1990
Bob Tucker	11/23/1914	10/06/2006
Mort Weisinger	04/25/1915	05/07/1978
Julius Schwartz	06/19/1915	02/08/2004
Robert A. W. Lowndes	09/04/1916	07/14/1998
Forrest J. Ackerman	11/24/1916	12/04/2008
Frederik Pohl	11/26/1919	09/02/2013
Isaac Asimov	01/02/1920	04/06/1992
Sam Moskowitz	06/30/1920	04/15/1997

The Story World and Photodramatist, October 1923

What Editors Want
Why Manuscripts Go Home
By Edwin Baird
Editor of Detective Tales and Weird Tales

If nobody objects, we shall employ the w. k. editorial "we" in submitting these remarks on home-coming manuscripts. The word implies a collective viewpoint and thus neatly sidesteps the accusation that what follows here is merely one individual's opinion.

That matter disposed, we should like to remark, before we go further, that we've been on both sides of the rejection slip, and every author who gets a manuscript back from *Detective Tales* or *Weird Tales* may acquire some solace from the thought that the editor shares, vicariously of course, his sharp disappointment.

When we were offering our masterpieces in the market place, and receiving many of them back as fast as we sent them, we bitterly believed, as most young authors probably believe, that an editor was inhuman and as bloodless as a fish. And we sometimes thought that the average editor, when selecting material for his magazine, blindfolded himself and grabbed at random in a barrel of manuscripts. Only thus could we explain his criminal neglect of our classic stories and his amazing attention to others. And we made a stout vow, when we undertook the job of editing two fiction magazines, that we'd do better than that.

Well, we've been at the editor's desk for upward of a year, and our ideas have changed. Today we are persuaded, somehow, that the editor is more deserving of sympathy than the author. And we marvel now, not at the vast number of poor stories published, but at the ability of any editor to find any other sort.

We knew, of course, that all editorial offices were under constant bombardment from inept and half-baked armies of writers; but we never would have believed (to change the figure) that such an overwhelming sea of utterly hopeless rubbish was inundating these offices. The thing's incredible! Manuscripts improperly punctuated, manuscripts with misspelled words and ludicrous blunders in grammar; manuscripts with muddled plots, impossible plots, and no plots; manuscripts tattered and torn and disgracefully dirty—these pour in upon the bewildered editor, a never-ceasing deluge of words. And from this muddy torrent he must pluck material to construct his magazine!

For *Detective Tales* and *Weird Tales* we receive an average of three hundred unsolicited manuscripts a week and we choose from this number, for publication, less than a dozen—and are often hard put to it to find even that many worthy of acceptance. The rest go home.

If we were suddenly asked to name the one great outstanding fault of these rejected authors, we should hastily reply, "Intellectual laziness." And later, if the same question were put to us again, we should make the same answer, deliberately. For surely the hopelessly-written manuscripts, which we send flying back home, denote mental sloth. It is inconceivable that any person, not afflicted with cerebral hookworm, could perpetrate such atrocities on the English language.

Nor are these crimes committed exclusively by the amateur or inexperienced writer. The professional writing man is quite often just as guilty. We have in mind an author—whose name, if not a household word, is at least known to every reader of mystery and detective fiction—from whom we bought a story for *Weird Tales*. The story had a weird plot, but the plot was not half so weird as the orthography.

In the course of his story this man had occasion to mention a number of seaports, and in every instance the name of the city was incorrectly spelled. That was bad enough, but downright unpardonable was the author's juggling of letters when he came to the names of his characters. These he spelled in a disconcerting variety of ways.

His hero's name, for instance, was spelled with an "i" on page one, with an "e" on page three, again with the "i" on page five, and thereafter he flopped crazily back and forth, apparently uncertain which letter he preferred. And yet this man's stories appear regularly in some of our most pretentious magazines!

Things like this cause an editor to wax pessimistic concerning the outlook for American literature.

We might, if we cared, multiply the aforementioned instance an indefinite number of times and go on to mention innumerable manuscripts that we have accepted and couldn't send to the printer until they were thoroughly overhauled. Despite their shortcomings, these manuscripts were accepted because of their unusual plots. And unusual plots are what we want. The magazine editor—particularly the all-fiction magazine editor—is looking, first of all, for plots. The matter of workmanship, or skill in striking words together, is of secondary importance.

A hasty perusal of any manuscript tells the busy editor whether or not it contains a good story. He rarely, if ever, has time to read every word when first passing upon it. Thus it sometimes happens that in our hurried search for acceptable plots we overlook the crudities of composition. But when the time comes to edit the copy for publication we must, of course, carefully read the thing in its entirety, and it is then we discover whether or not the writer is too indolent to prepare his story properly. Too often his manuscript fairly shouts at us:

"This story was written by a sluggard!"

But enough about the stories that contrive to get by. We are chiefly concerned, at the moment, with those that don't.

The most conspicuous characteristic of unacceptable manuscripts is the pronounced lack of originality. It's really amazing. These manuscripts are written by persons in almost every walk of life, and they come from almost every part of the world, and yet, after reading fifty of them, one gets the dazed impression that all were written by the same person. It is not merely that the plots are alike—one might understand that—but all have the same errors in spelling, the same grammatical blunders, the same grotesqueries of phraseology. This is a thing we've never been able to explain.

Also, after plowing through a field of these voluntary offerings (and it's mighty hard plowing, usually), one becomes afflicted with a peculiar form of mental paralysis. They drug your mind, you might say, and after eight hours or so of steady reading you find it difficult, somehow, to distinguish a good story from a bad one. They all look alike.

Occasionally we encounter a manuscript that is faultlessly written, perfectly typed, and correctly paragraphed and punctuated—and invariably such a manuscript is nothing but a waste of words. There's no thought in it, no plot, no story. It is like a wax dummy in a modiste's window—beautifully appareled and pleasing to look upon, but utterly devoid of life.

Then, going to the other extreme, we have the manuscript of the person who is almost, if not quite, illiterate. These are most pathetic of all. Written by unlettered men and women, who lack even an elementary knowledge of how to place their thoughts on paper, they yet bespeak a yearning for expression, some strange inner urge, that impels them to authorship.

A moment's glance at these tragic offerings is, of course, sufficient. We've all heard that reading a manuscript is like eating an egg—you needn't consume the whole thing to learn that it's rotten—and so, perceiving at once that a manuscript is a hopeless mess of words, it usually goes back home by return of mail.

Recently, though, this procedure slipped a cog somewhere, with the result that one of those impossibilities failed to return to its owner. Whereon we received the following interesting letter:

"Edwin Baird. Editor, of Weird Tales.

Dear Sir I am writing you in regards too my manuscript I sent you severil weeks a go it was a Ghost story and as I not heard from you any thing about my manuscript i have come to the conclusion that you have made up your mind accept my manuscript for publication. in your Weird Tales magazine.

or you would of returned it before now as I sent to you the Postage to send it Back to me if you did not care too accept it But if you dont care for my manuscript please return it to me soon as possible as I have Sevril more Magazine's wanting such articles for publication and i like to sell my Manuscripts as soon as possable

"I am sending to you more Postage Stamps to here from you soon or for you to return my Ghost story if you can not youse it.

"Resp address to

"Mrs.————————"

"———————— Texas Gen Del.

"The Name Given as the Author of my manuscript i sent to you is Mrs—

————————

"Please let me hear from you soon as possable

"Edwin Baird.

"Editor. of the Weird Tales"

On the chance that it may interest prospective contributors, and because we believe that similar systems obtain elsewhere, we shall mention here our method of judging and accepting, or declining, the manuscripts offered for our inspection. Since we employ no readers, every manuscript receives our personal attention and for this reason we find it necessary to expedite matters by grading each manuscript as we read it, employing symbols and a hard lead pencil.

Thus, for instance, a penciled "R" means "return," "70 D. T." denotes it is a seventy percent *Detective Tales* story and therefore acceptable, and "80 W. T." indicates that it is an unusually good yarn for *Weird Tales* and must go in an early issue. We have never yet found a manuscript (and we've read many thousands) that we could mark "100," and we are beginning to think we never shall find one.

We observe no rules when examining manuscripts. We have only one test that we apply to all alike, and the test is merely this: Does the thing interest us? If it does, we keep it; if it doesn't, we send it back. For we believe that others will be interested or bored by the same stories that interest or bore us.

In the case of *Detective Tales*, of course, we must of necessity draw certain restrictions. Here the material must be of the detective or mystery type. But for *Weird Tales* we accept any sort of story, so long as it is sufficiently unusual.

The bizarre, the fantastic, the grotesque, the story of stark terror and the uncanny story, the story of eerie adventure, the supernatural or ghost story, the story that other magazines decline because it conflicts with policy—these are joyously admitted to *Weird Tales*. Manuscripts intended for *Weird Tales* are read with an open mind, untroubled by prejudices, free from restriction, wholly unfettered.

And names don't matter. They never have mattered with us. Every editor is familiar with the unsuccessful author's common complaint:

"They won't buy my stuff because my name's not known."

This unhappy protest has been answered so many times by so many different editors that it seems unnecessary for us to dwell upon it; but we should like to say that we scarcely ever even look at an author's name until we've finished his manuscript. Then, if the story appeals to us, we look back at the first page to learn who wrote it. If it doesn't appeal, we slip it into the return envelope, and we never notice the name at all—unless, as sometimes happens, the rejected story offers a promise of something better to follow.

We have accepted scores of stories by writers whose names had never appeared in print, and we've turned down dozens by others whose names are known to all who read. We can say, from experience, that practically every editor welcomes the new writer and always tries to give him a square deal.

And right here—speaking of new writers and square deals—we want to mention something that causes editors no end of trouble and makes them proceed cautiously in dealing with people unknown to them. We're talking now about plagiarism. We hold this to be not only the most despicable form of theft, but a heinous crime perpetrated by thieves against whom the editor has no defense.

All editors have been victimized by these literary yeggs, and we feel we've had more than our share. For an unknown reason, all of them seem to pick on us. They've stung us a dozen times or more. The most flagrant case was that of a notorious plagiarist who sold us a story that he had clipped bodily from an old copy of *The American Magazine*. He typed the story and sent it to us as his own.

Before we discovered the theft we had bought ten more stories from him, including a short serial. And then, when we confronted him with his guilt, he calmly advised us to chuck the rest of his stories in the waste-basket! This man, as we subsequently learned, had hoodwinked a number of New York editors, to whom he submitted stolen stories signed with various names.

A more recent instance involved a man who appropriated a story written by an editor and published in an early issue of *The Black Cat*. When we informed the gentleman that he was offering us a yarn that a friend of ours had written he promptly replied:

"Well, the only thing I can see to do is to send the check to the man who first wrote the story."

Things like this convince us that plagiarists, as well as writers, are a very unbusinesslike people. Anyway, it's a losing game. Even though a crook of this stripe is not prosecuted for selling stolen property, his theft is sure to be discovered, and editors are now exchanging "black lists" of such thieves.

Moreover—to get back to what we were saying—the plagiarist makes it hard for the new writer to break into print. We have almost reached the point where we are suspicious of any story of unusual merit submitted by an "unknown," and now, before accepting such stories, we endeavor to learn something about their authors.

Plagiarism, however, is by no means an adequate explanation of Why Manuscripts Go Home. Broadly speaking, we'd say they go home because that's where they belong.

Overland Monthly, December 1919

In the Depths
By Farnsworth Wright

Dan Carlson looked down at the oily waters of Puget Sound and wondered what strange creatures lived in its slimy depths, and whether they were not really happier, after all, than he. A whirlwind racked his brain, for he faced involuntary separation from his job, and, being young, he was not used to it. For three days he had been a reporter on one of the city dailies—his first job, and he had failed on three assignments, so the city editor told him that he lacked aptitude and could not be used as a reporter. The boy pleaded for one more chance.

"I'll give you another chance," the city editor finally promised him, "if you go down to the waterfront and find a deep-sea diver named Angus McLeod and get his story of his fight with a devilfish three weeks ago. Look up the story in the files. Myers should have been able to interview him, for he has been marine reporter for years and ought to know everybody on the waterfront. But Myers hasn't been able to find him, and I can't tell you where you can locate him except that he ought to be somewhere on the waterfront. McLeod's story would have been a corker three weeks ago, but we can still use it."

Myers, the marine reporter, had learned only by chance of the diver's thrilling struggle with a giant octopus, and his rescue after he had lost consciousness, for McLeod was little known on the waterfront. The newspaper account of the battle under the waves was for the most part drawn by Myers from his imagination, for he had been unable to find and interview the dour Scot who was the hero of it.

Dan set out at once in search of McLeod, and he found that the old Scotch diver had moved from his lodgings several days before he was sent out on the job which so nearly cost him his life. Nobody seemed to know where he was living.

"He's about your height and pretty well tanned," the man in the salvage company's office described him to Dan. "He's got a grayish-reddish beard and he don't wear a mustache. He's an oldish fellow, a little bit deaf from being under the water so much, and he's got red hair and blue eyes."

On this meagre information Dan made the rounds of the waterfront saloons, but failed to find the man he was seeking. He did not want to go back to his city editor and report failure, so he stood on the wharf and speculated on the things that live under the water, and on his own drowning career.

The mystery of the ocean depths had always fired his imagination, but now it depressed him. He compared himself to the diver. The world was an enormous octopus, twisting its arms about his neck to drag him down. The breaking of the diver's air-tube was the fell stroke of chance, which had caused him to fail on his assignments and now prevented him from finding McLeod. Dan's star of hope, which had lit up his sky for an instant when he had been given this last chance to make good was sinking fast behind vast clouds of gloom. Hardly a ray now lighted the muddy depths of his despondency.

Looking up from his gloomy musings he noticed a roughly-dressed, ragged man, unshaven, dirty and hatless, leaning against a pile. His torn shirt was open at the throat. A queer moaning gurgle came from his half-opened mouth. He reeled as if he were drunk.

Dan feared the old fellow would fall into the bay, so he seized him quickly from behind, by the arms, just below the shoulders. The man shrank from his grasp with a moaning cry, and would have fallen from the dock had Dan not pulled him quickly back from the edge.

The stranger twisted around to face the youth, and he struck Dan's hands away as he did so. He gazed for an instant full into Dan's eyes with the fright of a hunted animal showing on his face. Then his gaze roved, and a puzzled, intent expression came over his face, as if he were vainly trying to recall something to his memory. He ran his fingers through his long, coarse hair and stared into Dan's eyes again. Dan noticed that the man's eyes were blue.

"You almost fell into the water," laughed Dan, reassuringly. "I guess you're sick, but at first I thought you were drunk when I saw you hanging to that post and reeling."

"Drunk," asked the stranger. The intent, puzzled expression came over his face again and he rubbed his fingertips over his stubby, reddish-gray beard.

"Drunk?" he repeated, and his bewildered look became pitiful in its intensity and suffering.

"Oh, no! I mean I thought so at first—the way you staggered! Of course you're not drunk. But you did nearly fall into the water," Dan went on, hastening to change the subject. "You don't want to make fish-food of yourself, and be washed out into the sound where the devilfish can twist his snaky tentacles around your neck and little fishes come and swim through the holes in your skull, where your eyes are now."

"Fishes?" the man asked. "Oh, ay, there are millions of 'em, lad, millions of 'em! I've seen whole armies of 'em come and look at me while I worked, and one big fish came and looked in the little window to see what made the bubbles come up. But he swam away quick when I tried to grab him."

Dan was still deep in his gloom and took in the import of the old man's strange words only vaguely as in a dream. He looked up wonderingly.

"There are strange things down there in the depths," he said slowly.

"In the depths," moaned the old man. "Oh, ay, in the depths!" His eyes opened big and he stared at Dan as at some dreadful specter.

A flash of comprehension came to the youth as he pondered the stranger's peculiar utterance about the fish armies and the big fish that looked into the little window; and Dan suddenly noticed that the stranger's close-cut beard was reddish and that he did not possess a mustache. But his hair was not red—it was snow-white!

Dan's heart jumped and the star of hope suddenly flooded his firmament with light again. The clouds of gloom were dissipated as if by the fresh wind which was springing up from the sound. Dan's thoughts were no longer vague and wandering.

"Is your name Angus McLeod?" he asked his odd acquaintance.

"Ay," answered the diver, his eyes intently searching Dan's face.

"Carlson's my name—Dan Carlson," Dan introduced himself, his eyes sparkling. "Come over and have a glass of beer with me."

McLeod did not answer, neither did he clasp Dan's outstretched hand.

"Come on," urged Dan, and he took the diver by the arm.

McLeod struck the boy's hand away as if in terror, but he followed him to the saloon. They were soon seated at a table and the bartender brought some beer.

"Now," demanded Dan eagerly, "tell me all about it."

"All about what?" asked McLeod.

"Why, about your fight with the devilfish up near Anacortes, of course."

"Oh, ay, the devilfish!"

The diver's eyes wandered; he looked terrified, and he passed his hands several times through his hair, then rubbed his stubby beard with his fingertips.

"Set 'em up again," called Dan to the bartender, for McLeod had drained his glass at a gulp.

"You were exploring an old wreck, weren't you?" he went on. "How long had the wreck been there?"

"Ay, a wreck it was. Several years old. It wasn't so awful deep, but I stayed too long."

McLeod ran his fingers through his hair again and horror was written in scarehead letters on his face.

"Come, come; you're all right now." Dan tried to calm him. "Drink your beer. Now go on. How deep was it?"

"Not too deep, for the sunlight was shimmering and shivering over the bones o' the ship, according as the waves was rippling and curling on top o' the water. It wasn't too deep, and there was a lot o' little fishes kept looking, and then they'd scamper away all of a sudden when they was frighted, like a lot o' minnows. But down in the ship it was dark and there was strange creatures there."

The diver shuddered and beads of sweat stood out on his furrowed forehead.

"Drink some more beer," Dan urged.

The former intense bewilderment again furrowed McLeod's face as if something he was seeking kept hiding Just beyond reach of his memory. He drank the beer and wiped the foam from his lips and chin on his sleeve.

"How did the octopus get hold of you? Tell me all about your fight with it. Nobody knows anything about it except what you told them through your diver's telephone while you were slicing the beast's arms off," Dan explained.

"Got hold on me? Oh, ay, it got hold on me all right," answered McLeod. "It must have got me from behind, because I didn't see it till it was around my neck. Long arms, like snakes, and it gets hold on me with two of 'em at once. First thing I knows about it, it draws me to one side, and I try to get away, but my feet are weighted and I can't move fast enough. But I'm just as cool as a clam. 'Never lose your head now or you'll never see Seattle again,' I says to myself. But it's hard to saw through those slippery, tough arms with my knife, though they look so soft and easy when the thing's captured and lying on shore, dead. But I've lost my knife," he moaned. "I tell you it's gone, and I can't pick it up."

The intent, bewildered look had again given place to horror.

"Come, come," Dan soothed him, "what ails you? Here, let me pour you some more beer. You say you had a knife?"

"I tell you I dropped it," exclaimed the diver with growing excitement. "Pick it up! Quick, I tell you!"

Pressing one knee against the table as if he were still struggling in the tight grip of the eight-armed monster, the diver gave a sudden push, upsetting the beer onto Dan, and sending his own chair backward onto the floor. He struggled to his feet with a frightened oath. As Dan sprang to help him, the diver seized his arms, pinning them to his sides and stared hard into his face, panting and shrieked—

"Where's that knife? I dropped it, I tell you!"

Dan struggled to free himself, but the diver with wild, livid, staring eyeballs, held him fast. The sweat poured from the old man's face. Dan was thoroughly frightened and was about to call loudly for help when McLeod relaxed his hold and sank to the floor, moaning as if in agony.

Dan lifted him up and helped him to a chair. McLeod was as weak as a kitten. He stared helplessly around the room, while the sweat ran down his face in tiny rivulets. Boisterous laughter from the barroom explained why nobody had heard the struggle.

"Come, now," urged Dan. "You had a knife, you tell me, and you lost it. How did the air-hose break?"

"I cut it," McLeod answered, very slowly. "I didn't mean to, but the beast drew me towards him, and kept shooting a black, inky stuff at me, so by and by I couldn't see him for the dark clouds of it in the water. I sawed through three of its ugly hands, and I'll get away all right, only it's got me by the arm, and I've cut into the air-tube over my head, and I've dropped my knife and I can't pick it up.

"Where is that knife, lad?" he whined. "There's no time to lose, for I've got no air, I tell you! They're pulling on the ropes up there, can't you feel 'em? Give me that knife! I've got to cut loose, I tell you! They're trying to pull me up, and the air-tube's cut, and I can't breathe, and I've got to cut away! Don't you hear me?"

He covered his face with his hands, moaning piteously.

"It's no use! It's no use!" he whimpered. "I've lost the knife."

His unkempt, coarse white hair was wet with perspiration. Understanding began to dawn on Dan.

"Come, now," Dan said at last. "Nobody's going to hurt you. You're all right now. Tell me, how did you get to the surface?"

McLeod took his hands from his face and stared at Dan blankly.

"How did they get you up? How did you get to the top?" Dan repeated.

"Get to the top?" the diver moaned. "I didn't."

He covered his face again with his hands.

Dan felt a strange sinking of the stomach as he looked at the moaning creature before him, who was still fighting hopelessly on in his mind, with blank horror always at the end of his tale. For the diver's mind had given way under the strain of the desperate struggle under the waves and recorded no memories beyond that terrific combat, nor gave any glimmer of hope as to the outcome.

Dan had his story. And that same day tender hands took McLeod into their care and ministered to his overwrought nerves and anguished brain.

Fantasy Magazine, April 1935

Self-Portrait
By Farnsworth Wright
Editor, *Weird Tales*

The editor's a gloomy guy, who fusses, fumes and frets;
He puts in all his cheerless life expressing his regrets.
And you should see the things he sees when perched upon his Eyrie;
The shuddering shapes and eldritch forms, and dim things out of Faerie.
Around the eaves the spiders weave their webs, and bat-things flutter,
While vampires drear breathe in his ear of thoughts too wild to utter.
For music he hears werewolves howl all night to serenade him;
This symphony cacophonous a shivering wreck has made him.
Ah, look! what slithering shapes are these that on his desk are crawling?
Their red eyes fix upon his throat with avid lust appalling,
Till (just between ourselves, you know) he scarce can keep from bawling.
With obscene grins and fleshless chins tall skeletons do mock him,
Till he's reduced to a quivering pulp in fear that one might sock him.
Stone wyverns guard the adytum of darkness where he labors;
Ghosts fly about in a grisly rout, and witches beat their tabors.
A murdered lich stands sentinel beside the office portal—
A zombie he, undead, yet dead; immortal, and yet mortal.
So all the day and all the night the editor gives battle
To spooks and warlocks, wizards, snakes, until his jawbones rattle.
So come, ye bards and raconteurs, send him your stories creepy;
Be sure they're weird, for if they're not, they'll merely make him sleepy;
Stories that bite as well as bark, convincing yarns that floor him—
These are, to him, both food and drink; all other kinds just bore him.

The Writer, October 1922

Editorial Prejudice Against the Occult

Said a famous editor not so very long ago in writing to one of his contributors: "... but my dear fellow, if you are aiming to enlist against you the suspicion—nay, the actual *enmity*—of the average editor, send him a Ghost Story, a Fairy Story, or a Dream Story. If you want to be absolutely certain of such an effect, make it a Dream Story!"

These three classes of stories may be said to merge into what is generally understood under the caption, "The Occult." And "the occult" in this general sense of the term is banned by most magazines. Authors who "try one on an editor" are apt to get their tales back in haste; yet there is the well-known fact that readers revel in tales of this general type! Moreover, there is hardly an author of note who has not done good work in this field, or at least tried his hand at "the occult."

It is, for example, to "The Messenger," written in the golden 'nineties, that the partisans of Robert Chambers are apt to turn in his defense when pressed. It appears to be conceded that "The Mark of the Beast" is Rudyard Kipling's high-water mark. Has any comparatively modern tale been reprinted more times than "The Phantom Rickshaw"? Docs not Bram Stoker's finger clasp relentlessly the edge of "The granite brink in Helicon" (Ezra Pound) because of "Dracula"?

Possibly the editorial tradition noted is still laboring under the weight of the Gothic Ghost—the kind of ghost which rattled its chains in "The Castle of Otranto"; but Walpole was not a Mary Wilkins Freeman. The ghosts of the pre-Poe period are quite hopeless unless as material for getting a Ph.D.! They are not the "ghosts" of Arthur Machen, or Rudyard Kipling; of M.R. James, or Algernon Blackwood. They are not even kindred to the "ghosts" of Elliot O'Donnell, Miss Freeman, George Adams Cram, or Ambrose Bierce, to say nothing of William Hope Hodgson and his "Carnacki," or even W.W. Jacobs, who has to sandwich his "ghosts" in between tales of "Ginger Dick" and "Wapping Old Stairs" to get a hearing for them!

What real reader does not know "John Silence"? Who, once having dipped into "The House of Souls" would not set it down as the third of the five books to take into life imprisonment with him—or even the second, if he be a Baconian.

It seems hardly necessary to adduce today's enormous interest in spiritistic phenomena in this connection, although this would be a legitimate argument in favor of "the occult" as showing which way the popular wind is blowing. The word "spiritism" at once conjures up the names of Sir Oliver Lodge and Sir Arthur Conan Doyle, as well as The Proceedings of the Society for Psychical Research. And it is a fact that there is just now—growing up a generation of readers for whom the Doyle of "Sherlock Holmes" is an obsolescent figure, disappearing behind the Doyle who is championing spiritism.

Fairy Stories! Howard Pyle! Andersen! The Gebrüder Grimm! Andrew Lang! Why, the last-named dear old gentleman must have made a comfortable fortune with his kaleidoscopic catena of Fairy Books! It would be interesting to know what proportion of the constant readers of the *Strand Magazine* take it for the monthly fairy tale.

Dreams! "Peter Ibbotson"! "A Dream of Armageddon"! "Gerontius"! "Dream Life" and "Reveries of a Bachelor"! "Dreams"! Du Maurier, H.G. Wells, Cardinal Newman, Donald G. Mitchell, and Olive Schreiner! Could any other common interest conceivably have brought together such a group of diverse intellects? Dreams make queer assortments of literary bedfellows. And it is simply because dreams have invaded the realm of scientific psychology as contrasted with literary, that Sigmund Freud has become one of the great ones of earth. Many of the "intelligentsia" to whom Freud and his satellites Jung and Adler are restaurant-words (there being no longer *households* to have words among the "intelligentsia") have never heard, say, of Jelliffe, or Janet, or Edward Cowles, all of them very much greater psychologists than Freud and his immediate following. Yet there is perhaps nothing today, not even excepting the late excitement about the League of Nations, which has so intrigued the popular mind as Freud's Dream Psychology, and its concomitant, psychoanalysis.

From the day of Joseph, backward and forward, dreams and the occult have been fascinating people's minds with the perennial lure of their mystery. Ghost Stories, Fairy Stories, and Dream Stories—the occult in fiction—have always been unfailingly alluring to the popular mind. The inventor of the ouija board is said upon sound authority to have made more than a million dollars from its sale!

In Erse and Choctaw, in the Hieroglyphics and in the Sumerian; in Kalmuck, and Finnish, and Hebrew, there are and always have been Ghost Stories, and Fairy Stories, and Dream Stories. They have been told and are being told—and read—from the bazaars of Oodeypore to the Steppes; from the lamaseries of Tibet to the Beach of Easter Island. In China, in Afghanistan, in Ireland, and Down in Maine, people are positively clamoring for Ghost Stories and Fairy Stories and Dream Stories.

Why, O why, do not the magazine editors give the people what they want?

Henry S. Whitehead
Frederikstad, Virgin Islands

The Writer, January 1931

Writing the Fantastic Story
By Otis Adelbert Kline

> *William Bolitho said of Mr. Kline, "In this world of scientific fiction, there are chiefs. They must be good. There is Otis Adelbert Kline whom I am sure I would rather read than many fashionable novelists." When asked to tell some of the problems of creating fantastic stories, Mr. Kline wrote us, "The subject you assigned me is a pretty big one. It has so many interesting ramifications that a whole series of articles would scarcely cover it."*

Writing, with me, is a semi-subjective process. I mean by this that I find it necessary, at times, to wait for that temperamental and elusive entity, my Muse, to cooperate with me. Every day I try to write, and I mean TRY. But some days I produce only a few hundred words fit for nothing but filing in the wastebasket. And on the other hand I have, in a single day, produced six or seven thousand words of marketable copy.

So this, the problem of successfully wooing the Muse, is the one which I find most difficult of solution. I have a profound admiration for writers who can sit down at their desks, day after day, and, without fail, bat out two or three thousand words of good, salable material in two or three hours. Most of them will tell you this is the result of practice—of continuous trying. But I've been trying for ten years, and selling stories for eight, and today my Muse is as obstinate and capricious as ever.

Although I had previously written songs, plays, and moving picture scenarios, my first inspiration for writing fiction, strange as it may seem, came from reading books on psychology. And that reading was the result of some previous incidents in my life, so perhaps I had better begin a little farther back.

When I graduated from high school, I decided that I would launch on a musical career, and gave up my plans for going to college. I became a professional songwriter. I also tried my hand at plays and moving picture scenarios, and wrote vaudeville sketches and even plots for burlesque shows. I later became a music publisher. But it was a hard life, with much night work, plugging songs in theatres, dance halls, and cafes, and I tired of it, in spite of the fascination the element of chance gave to the work. Putting out songs was like playing poker; no one could predict a hit with certainty.

I decided on a business career, and went to a business college. Shortly after this, I got a job, and at twenty-two I married. No chance, then, to go to college. But going to college had been a sort of tradition in our family. I had to work every day to keep the well-known and justly unpopular wolf from breaking down the door. But my evenings were my own. I decided to use them for the improvement of what I optimistically called my mind.

I would take one subject at a time, and study. But where should I begin? I recalled that a certain ancient philosopher had once said there are but three things in the universe—mind, force, and matter. Mind controls force, and force moves matter. It was easy to decide which of these things was the more important, so I began by studying psychology—a science which, by the way, is in its infancy—no farther advanced today than were the physical sciences a century ago.

Having read practically everything there was on the subject over a period of years, I began to have some theories about psychic phenomena, myself. I started a ponderous scientific treatise, but didn't carry it far. This medium limited my imagination too much. Then I wrote a novelette, "The Thing of a Thousand Shapes," in which some of my ideas and theories were incorporated. It was turned down by most of the leading magazines in 1922, but early in 1923 a magazine was made to order for the story—*Weird Tales*. It was accepted, and published in the first issue. This was before the word "ectoplasm" was used in connection with psychic phenomena. A German writer, whose translated work I had read, had coined the word "teleplasm," but this did not seem precisely the right term, so I coined the word "psychoplasm." I notice that it is being used today by some writers of occult stories.

I had finished writing the above novelette early in 1921, and decided to try my hand at a novel. I wanted to write an interplanetary story, and I believe the reason for this lay in the following incidents.

As soon as I was able to understand, my father, who was interested in all the sciences, and especially in astronomy, had begun pointing out to me the planets that were visible to the naked eye; had told me what was known of their masses, densities, surfaces, atmospheres, motions, and satellites; and that there was a possibility that some of them were inhabited by living beings. He taught me how to find the Big and Little Dippers, and thus locate the North Star, that I might make the heavens serve as a compass for me, by night as well as by day. He pointed out that beautiful and mysterious constellation, The Pleiades, which inspired the lines in the Book of Job: "Canst thou bind the sweet influences of Pleiades, or loose the bonds of Orion?"

He told me of the vast distances which, according to the computations of scientists, lay between our world and these twinkling celestial bodies—that the stars were suns, some smaller than our own, and others so large that if they were hollow, our entire Solar System could operate inside them without danger of the planet farthest from the sun striking the shell. He told me of the nebulae, which might be giant universes in the making, and that beyond the known limits of our own universe it was possible that there were countless others, stretching on into infinity.

My childish imagination had been fired by these things, and I had read voraciously such books on the subject of astronomy as were available in my father's well-stocked library. He supplemented and encouraged this reading by many interesting discussions, in which a favorite subject for speculation was the possibility that planets, other than our own, were inhabited.

Geology, archaeology, and ethnology were also brought into our discussions. We lived in northern Illinois, which had in some distant geological epoch been the bottom of an ocean, and took pleasure in collecting such fossil remains as were available. Dad and I could become very much excited over bits of coral, and fossil marine animals.

Then there were Darwin, Huxley, Tyndall, and others, with their interesting theories. There was the great mystery of man's advent on this earth, which religion explained in one manner and science in another. We discussed these, and a third possibility, an idea of my father's, that some of our ancient civilizations might have been originated by people who came here from other planets—the science of space-navigation forgotten by their descendants, but the tradition of their celestial advent persisting in their written and oral traditions. That such traditions did persist was beyond dispute. Whence came these traditions that were not confined to related civilizations, but were preserved by widely separated peoples?

It was with this background that I began my first novel in 1921—a tale of adventures on the planet Venus. I called it *Grandon of Terra*, but the name was later changed to *The Planet of Peril*.

The problem of how to get my hero to Venus bothered me not at all, for I had been reading about the marvelous powers of the subjective mind: of telepathy, that mysterious means of communication between minds which needs no physical media for its transmission, and which seems independent of time, space, and matter. I haven't the space to enlarge on this here, but can refer you to the thousands of cases recorded by the British Society for Psychical Research, if you are interested. There was also the many cases of so-called astral projection, recorded by the above society in a volume called *Phantasms of the Living*. My hero, therefore, reached Venus by the simple (try it) expedient of exchanging bodies with a young man on that planet who was his physical twin. He reported his adventures on Venus to an earthly scientist, Dr. Morgan, by telepathy.

Cloud-wrapped Venus is supposed to be in a stage similar to our own carboniferous era. I, therefore, clothed my hypothetical Venus with the flora of such an era—ferns, cycads, and thallophytes of many kinds, including algae, fungi, and lichens of strange and eerie form.

Through the fern jungles and fungoid forests stalked gigantic reptiles, imaginary creatures, but analogous to those ponderous prehistoric Saurians that roved the earth when our coal and petroleum beds were having their inception. There were Herbivora devouring the primitive plants, and fierce Carnivora that devoured the Herbivora and each other, and disputed the supremacy of man. Air and water teemed with active life and sudden dealt—life feeding on death and death snuffing out life.

There were men in various stages of evolutionary development—men without eyes, living in lightless caverns, who had degenerated to a physical and mental condition little better than that of Batrachia. There were monkey-men swinging through the branches and lianas of the fern forests, blood-sucking bat-men living in caves in a volcanic crater—a veritable planetary inferno, and gigantic termites of tremendous mental development that had enslaved a race of primitive human beings.

There were mighty empires, whose armies warred with strange and terrible weapons, and airships which flew at tremendous speed propelled by mechanisms which amplified the power of mind over matter—telekinesis.

After writing and rewriting, polishing and re-polishing, I sent the story out—a bulky script, ninety-thousand words long. At that time there but two possible American markets for that type of story, *Science and Invention* and *Argosy-All Story*, but I had not been watching the Munsey publication and did not know it used this sort of thing. I submitted the story, first, to *Science and Invention*. It was turned down because of the paucity of mechanical science.

When *Weird Tales* came into being, I tried it on this magazine. Edwin Baird, the editor liked it, but finally, after holding it several months, rejected it because of its length. He suggested that I try *Argosy-All Story*, but I didn't do it then. I let it lie around for a long time. Every once in a while I would dig it out of the file and read it over. Each time, I found new places to polish. I was writing and selling a number of other stories in the interval—occult, weird, mystery, detective, adventure, and Western. I also collaborated with my brother, Allen S. Kline, on a novel set in the South American Jungle, called *The Secret Kingdom*. This was later published in *Amazing Stories*.

One day I was talking to Baird, and he asked me what I had done with my fantastic novel. He said I was foolish not to try *Argosy-All Story*. I accordingly recopied my pencil-marked version, and sent it on. Good old Bob Davis, dean of American editors, held it so long I had some hope: that he was going to buy it. But it came back, eventually, with a long, friendly letter asking to see more of my work. I later learned that he had just bought the first of Ralph Milne Farley's famous radio stories, the scene of which was on the planet

Venus, and whose settings, therefore, were somewhat similar to mine.

After that, I spent enough money on express and postage to buy a good overcoat, sending the story around the country, and out of it.

Finally, Mr. Joseph Bray then book-buyer, and now president of A.C. McClurg & Company, told me he would publish it if I would first get it serialized in a magazine. I had turned down a couple of low-priced offers for serialization, but I started over the list again. A.H. Bittner, the new editor of *Argosy*, who has been building circulation for that magazine since he took over the editorial chair, bought the story. A month later, Mr. Bray accepted it for publication as a novel.

The Planet of Peril brought many enthusiastic fan letters to *Argosy*. I received a number of complimentary letters from people all over the country who had read it in magazine or book form. I was overwhelmed with requests for autographs, and all that sort of thing. A baby in Battle Creek, Michigan, was named after me. It was encouraging.

Last September, Grosset & Dunlap reprinted the book in the popular edition. In a bulletin to their salesmen they recently reported that, despite the fact that they had not made any special effort to push it, and that it was a first novel, it was enjoying a continuous and persistent resale—something unusual for a first novel. They suggested that their salesmen remember this item when calling on the trade. This, also, was encouraging.

Since then, *Argosy* has serialized and McClurg has published in book form two more novels—*Maza of the Moon* and *The Prince of Peril*, the latter a companion story to *The Planet of Peril*.

Right now I'm working night and day on a new novel for spring publication, in order to make a deadline date set by my publisher. Also, I've reached the length limit set by THE WRITER'S editor, so that will be all for this time.

BIBLIOGRAPHY

Baird, Edwin (EB).
——. "How to Write a Detective Story," Parts I-XIII, *The Author & Journalist*, December 1929 to December 1930.
——. "What Editors Want," *The Story World and Photodramatist*, October 1923.
Brush, Katharine. *This Is On Me*. New York: Farrar & Rinehart, Inc., 1939.
Burks, Arthur J. (AJB).
——. *Black Medicine*. Sauk City, Wisconsin: Arkham House, 1966.
——. *Land of Checkerboard Families*. New York: Coward-McCann, Inc., 1932.
Cannon, Peter. *Lovecraft Remembered*. Sauk City, Wisconsin: Arkham House, 1998.
Everett, Justin and Jeffrey H. Shanks, eds. *The Unique Legacy of* Weird Tales*: The Evolution of Modern Fantasy and Horror*. Lanham, Maryland: Rowman & Littlefield, 2015.
Finn, Mark. *Blood & Thunder: The Life and Art of Robert E. Howard*. The Robert E. Howard Foundation Press, 2013.
Gordon, Robert J. *The Rise and Fall of American Growth: The U.S. Standard of Living Since the Civil War*. Princeton, New Jersey: Princeton University Press, 2016.
Hanley, Terence E. *Tellers of Weird Tales* blog. tellersofweirdtales.blogspot.com.
Henneberger, Jacob Clark (JCH).
——. Letter to Joel Frieman, October 20, 1968, private collection. A slightly revised version appears in *WT50: A Tribute to Weird Tales*.
——. Letter to Joel Frieman, April 14, 1969, in *WT50: A Tribute to Weird Tales*, Robert Weinberg, ed., 1974.
——. Undated letter to Robert A.W. Lowndes, in *It Is Written* (column), Robert A.W. Lowndes, ed., *Magazine of Horror*, May 1969.
——. Undated letter to Sam Moskowitz, quoted in Sam Moskowitz, "In the Beginning . . .," *Weird Tales*, Winter 1973.
——. Untitled article, in *Deeper Than You Think*, July 1968.
Joshi, S.T.
——. *I Am Providence: The Life and Times of H.P. Lovecraft*: Volumes 1 & 2. New York: Hippocampus Press, 2013.
——. *Lovecraft and a World in Transition: Collected Essays on H.P. Lovecraft*. New York: Hippocampus Press, 2014.
Kantor, MacKinley. "Editors You Want To Know: Edwin Baird," *The Author & Journalist*, November 1929.

Kline, Otis Adelbert (OAK).

——. Letter to Dr. I.M. Howard, April 1, 1941, in "Otis Adelbert Kline's Letters to Robert E. & Dr. I.M. Howard," *OAK Leaves*, Fall 1970.

——. "Writing the Fantastic Story," *The Writer*, January 1931.

Kraft, David Anthony, ed. *The Compleat OAK Leaves*. Clayton, Georgia: Fictioneer Books, Ltd., 1980.

Locke, John. *Ghost Stories: The Magazine and Its Makers*: Volumes 1 & 2. Elkhorn, California: Off-Trail Publications, 2010.

Loftus, Elizabeth F. *Eyewitness Testimony*. Cambridge, Massachusetts: Harvard University Press, 1996.

Long, Frank Belknap (FBL). *Howard Phillips Lovecraft: Dreamer on the Nightside*. Sauk City, Wisconsin: Arkham House, 1975.

Lovecraft, Howard Phillips (HPL).

——. *Collected Essays: Volume 2: Literary Criticism*. Ed. S.T. Joshi. New York: Hippocampus Press, 2004.

——. Letter to J.C. Henneberger, February 2, 1924, Harry Ransom Center, The University of Texas at Austin.

——. *Letters to James F. Morton*. Ed. David E. Schultz and S.T. Joshi. New York: Hippocampus Press, 2011.

——. *Letters to Robert Bloch and Others*. Ed. David E. Schultz and S.T. Joshi. New York: Hippocampus Press, 2015.

——. *Lovecraft Letters Volume 2: Letters from New York*. Ed. S.T. Joshi and David E. Schultz. San Francisco & Portland: Night Shade Books, 2005.

——. *Selected Letters I: 1911-1925*. Ed. August Derleth and Howard Wandrei. Sauk City, Wisconsin: Arkham House, 1965.

——. *Selected Letters II: 1925-1929*. Ed. August Derleth and Howard Wandrei. Sauk City, Wisconsin: Arkham House, 1968.

——. *Selected Letters III: 1929-1931*. Ed. August Derleth and Howard Wandrei. Sauk City, Wisconsin: Arkham House, 1971.

——. *Selected Letters IV: 1932-1934*. Ed. August Derleth and James Turner. Sauk City, Wisconsin: Arkham House, 1976.

——. *Selected Letters V: 1934-1937*. Ed. August Derleth and James Turner. Sauk City, Wisconsin: Arkham House, 1976.

Lovecraft, Howard Phillips and August Derleth. *Essential Solitude: The Letters of H.P. Lovecraft and August Derleth: 1926-1931*. Ed. David E. Schultz and S.T. Joshi. New York: Hippocampus Press, 2013.

Lovecraft, Howard Phillips and Clark Ashton Smith (CAS). *Dawnward Spire, Lonely Hill: The Letters of H.P. Lovecraft and Clark Ashton Smith*. Ed. David E. Schultz and S.T. Joshi. New York: Hippocampus Press, 2017.

Moskowitz, Sam.

———. "The Forgotten Creator of *Weird Tales*: An Introduction . . ." in *Worlds of Weird*. New York: Pyramid Books, 1964.

———. "In the Beginning . . .," *Weird Tales*, Winter 1973.

Pacyga, Dominic A. *Chicago: A Biography*. Chicago, Illinois: The University of Chicago Press, 2011.

Palmer, Frederick. *Modern Authorship: Author's Fiction Manual*. Hollywood, California: Palmer Institute of Authorship, 1924.

Peterson, Theodore. *Magazines in the Twentieth Century*, 2nd ed. Urbana, Illinois: University of Illinois Press, 1964.

Poe, Edgar Allan. *Complete Tales & Poems*. New York: Castle Books, 2002.

Powers, Paul S. *Pulp Writer*. Lincoln, Nebraska: University of Nebraska Press, 2007.

Price, E. Hoffmann (EHP).

———. *Book of the Dead: Friends of Yesteryear: Fictioneers & Others*. Sauk City, Wisconsin: Arkham House, 2001.

———. "Editors You Want to Know: Farnsworth Wright," *The Author & Journalist*, October 1930.

———. "Farnsworth Wright" in *The Weird Tales Story*. Ed. Robert Weinberg. West Linn, Oregon: FAX Collector's Editions, Inc., 1977.

Robillard, Douglas, ed. *American Supernatural Fiction: From Edith Wharton to the* Weird Tales *Writers*. New York: Garland Publishing, Inc., 1996.

Roehm, Rob, ed. *The Collected Letters of Doctor Isaac M. Howard: with Correspondence from Otis Adelbert Kline, E. Hoffmann Price & Others*. The Robert E. Howard Foundation Press, 2011.

Schwartz, Julius. "Titans of Science Fiction: Farnsworth Wright," *Science Fiction Digest*, March 1933.

Swanson, H.N. *Sprinkled with Ruby Dust: A Literary and Hollywood Memoir*. New York: Warner Books, Inc., 1989.

Ward, Harold. *The Complete Exploits of Doctor Death*. Boston: Altus Press, 2017.

Weinberg, Robert. *The Weird Tales Story*. West Linn, Oregon: FAX Collector's Editions, Inc., 1977.

Weisinger, Mort and Julius Schwartz. "Titans of Science Fiction: Arthur J. Burks," *Science Fiction Digest*, May 1933.

Whitehead, Henry S. *Voodoo Tales*. Were, Hertfordshire, UK: Wordsworth Editions Limited, 2012.

Williamson, Jack. *Wonder's Child: My Life in Science Fiction*. Dallas, Texas: Benbella Books, Inc., 2005.

INDEX

OFF-TRAIL PUBLICATIONS
Specializing in the era of American pulp fiction
offtrailpublications.com

For the first half of the 20th century, the pulps ruled America's newsstands. Cheap magazines with eye-catching covers, they were the primary source of popular fiction. Within their pages, genre fiction—adventure, crime, romance, western, science fiction, and hero stories—came of age. OFF-TRAIL PUBLICATIONS is dedicated to reviving these forgotten treasures of entertainment, as well as the forgotten history of the pulps. The typical OFF-TRAIL book combines stories from the pulps with profiles of the relevant authors, editors, magazines, publishers, and genres—fiction and the underlying history that gives it meaning. The *Pulpwood Days* series unearths the history of the pulps buried in the writers' magazines that catered to the field.

History

 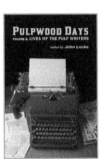

PULPWOOD DAYS: Volume 1: Editors You Want To Know
Edited by John Locke • 180 pages, $16

Numerous articles from the writers' mags by and about pulp editors, with ample biographical profiles. Editors include: Frank E. Blackwell (Detective Story, Western Story), Ray Palmer (Amazing Stories, Fantastic Adventures), Edwin Baird (Weird Tales), and many more.

PULPWOOD DAYS: Volume 2: Lives of the Pulp Writers
Edited by John Locke • 250 pages, $22

This unique collection mines the writers' mags for those rare articles in which pulpsters looked back on their careers—the glories and hardships of the pulp racket. These are hardboiled writing stories from the Pulp Era—when the greatest time in history to sell fiction— the 1920s—was suddenly followed by one of the worst—the '30s. Complementing the twenty pieces are new profiles of the authors: Arthur J. Burks, Tom Curry, Steve Fisher, Hapsburg Liebe, Chuck Martin, Harold Masur, Tom Thursday, Paul Triem, Jean Francis Webb, and many others. Over 100,000 words of pulp history.

Adventure

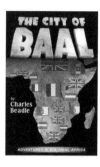 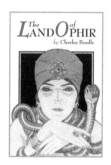  

THE CITY OF BAAL
By Charles Beadle • Introduction by John Locke
7 stories, 240 pages, $20

Authentic stories of African adventure from an author who traveled the lands he wrote about. Lost cities, strange tribes, jungle magic. Six stories from Adventure *(1918-22) and one from* The Frontier *(1925).*

THE LAND OF OPHIR
By Charles Beadle • Introduction by John Locke
Complete 3-part serial, 146 pages, $12

From Adventure *magazine, reprinted for the first time since 1922. A group of globe-trotting adventurers journeys into Africa in a quest for fabled Ophir and its legendary riches. A freewheeling saga full of fascinating characters, action, suspense, mystery, and horror.*

AMAZON STORIES
Volume 1: Pedro & Lourenço
Volume 2: Pedro & Lourenço
By Arthur O. Friel • Introductions by John Locke
Vol 1: 10 stories, 222 pages, $18 • **Vol 2**: 10 stories, 286 pages, $20

Collects Friel's first twenty stories from Adventure *(1919-21), following the strange experiences of two Amazon Basin rubber workers as they explore the jungle. The best of pulp adventure fiction.*

All books available from Amazon.com, other online booksellers, and dealers specializing in the pulps. Complete listing, Amazon links, and latest news at:
offtrailpublications.com

Adventure

THE GOLDEN ANACONDA: And Other Strange Tales of Adventure
By Elmer Brown Mason • Introduction by John Locke
10 stories, 260 pages, $20

Fantastic and horror-laden stories set in the exotic corners of the world known to their globe-trotting entomologist author. From The Popular Magazine *and* All-Story Weekly, *1915-16.*

HOBO STORIES
By Patrick & Terence Casey • Introduction by John Locke
6 stories, 332 pages, $20

The Casey brothers from San Francisco broke into the pulps while still teenagers. Within a few years, they had conned their way into the prestigious pages of Adventure. Hobo Stories *reprints the exploits of a teenage hobo and his dog from* The Saturday Evening Post *(1914) and* Adventure *(1916-21). Included is their story of a teenage pulp writer from* Romance *(1920); and a lengthy introduction which explores the lives of the Caseys and the origins of their hobo stories.*

THE OCEAN: 100th Anniversary Collection
Edited by John Locke
20 stories, 234 pages, $18

Munsey's The Ocean *(1907-08) was one of the first specialized pulps, a sea-story magazine. The best adventure stories are included here, along with 30+ pages of nonfiction material: a history of the pulp, and extensive author profiles.*

THE TEXAS-SIBERIA TRAIL
By Malcolm Wheeler-Nicholson • Intro by Nicky Wheeler-Nicholson
8 stories, 252 pages, $20

Before he founded DC Comics, the Major wrote hardboiled adventure stories for the top pulps. This inaugural collection includes stories set in all four of his real-life arenas: the U.S. southwest border, the southern Philippines, Siberia, and Western Europe. Introduced by the Major's granddaughter, Nicky Wheeler-Nicholson.

J. Allan Dunn

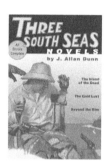

OUTDOOR STORIES

By J. Allan Dunn • Introduction by John Locke

3 stories, 190 pages, $16

> *Presented are all three of Dunn's tales from the ultra-rare* Outdoor Stories *(1927-28). These gripping adventures, set in the exotic places of another day, rank with Dunn's best. The featured story, "New Guinea Gold," is an epic tale of friendship, survival and revenge. Included is a history of* Outdoor Stories, *a biography of editor Edmund C. Richards, and an examination of Dunn's role in the magazine.*

THE PERIL OF THE PACIFIC

By J. Allan Dunn • Introduction by John Locke

Complete 5-part serial, 168 pages, $14

> *Dunn's Japanese invasion epic is future history, published as a five-part serial in* People's *in 1916, but set in 1920.* Peril *pits a force of American irregulars armed with futuristic technology against a relentless naval empire bent on conquest. Dunn uses San Francisco and California's Central Coast as his main settings, drawing upon his well-traveled past more than in any other story he ever published.*

THREE SOUTH SEAS NOVELS

By J. Allan Dunn • Introduction by John Locke

3 stories, 360 pages, $20

> *Dunn began his fiction career as a South Seas specialist. These three early works established him as a fan favorite in* Adventure *magazine. Includes Dunn's first full novel,* The Island of the Dead *(April 1915); also* The Gold Lust *(November 1915) and* Beyond the Rim *(July 1916). Enjoy these colorful epics of modern-day buccaneers who behave a lot like their olden-day counterparts.*

Weird & Weird Detective

THE WEIRD DETECTIVE ADVENTURES OF WADE HAMMOND
By Paul Chadwick
Vol 1: 10 stories, 180 pages, $18 • **Vol 2**: 10 stories, 172 pages, $18
Vol 3: 10 stories, 202 pages, $18 • **Vol 4**: 9 stories, 232 pages, $18

Wade Hammond complete in four volumes. In these chilling adventures, all from the classic 1930's pulps, Detective-Dragnet *and* Ten Detective Aces, *freelance investigator Wade Hammond battles a series of weird enemies. Some of the best of '30s pulp fiction.*

GROTTOS OF CHINATOWN: The Dorus Noel Stories
By Arthur J. Burks • Introduction by John Locke
11 stories, 194 pages, $16

The complete adventures of Dorus Noel from All Detective Magazine *(1933-34). Burks' Manhattan Chinatown is a place of dark mystery, riddled with secret passageways, menaced by hatchetmen. Introduction discusses the history of* All Detective *and the career of the Speed-King of the Pulps, Arthur J. Burks.*

CULT OF THE CORPSES
By Maxwell Hawkins • Introduction by John Locke
2 novelettes, 150 pages, $13.95

Two weird detective stories from Detective-Dragnet *(1931) by a forgotten master. Introduction discusses the weird-detective trend of the early '30s, and the career of Maxwell Hawkins.*

DOCTOR COFFIN: The Living Dead Man
By Perley Poore Sheehan • Introduction by John Wooley
8 novelettes, 178 pages, $16

Weird stories from Thrilling Detective, *1932-33. A former character actor who faked his own death, Doctor Coffin runs a string of mortuaries by night and fights crime at night. One of the strangest detective series.*

Weird & Weird Detective

THE MAGICIAN DETECTIVE: And Other Weird Mysteries
By Fulton Oursler
Introduction by John Locke
7 stories, 210 pages, $18

> *Fulton Oursler was one of the great editors of his time, ruling over the Macfadden publishing empire for two decades. But stage magic was his first love. In this collection of early fiction, Oursler's bewitching imagination takes flight in tales of magic, murder and mystery. Featured is an exploration of the astonishing career of Fulton Oursler.*

GHOST STORIES: The Magazine and Its Makers
Edited by John Locke
Vol 1: 19 stories, 256 pages, $24 • **Vol 2**: 15 stories, 272 pages, $24

> *Macfadden's* Ghost Stories *(1926-31) presented haunted tales in every exciting arena: the Western Front, gangland, aviation, the Klondike, the circus, etc. The personnel behind* Ghost Stories *were a fascinating group: poets and scholars, war heroes and war correspondents, adventurers and Bohemians; a few became prolific pulpsters; a few became bestselling authors. And a few led haunted lives. Vol 1 includes the history of* Ghost Stories, *bios of every editor, and every Vol 1 author. Vol 2 includes bios of every Vol 2 author, every cover artist, and a gallery of all 64* Ghost Stories *covers.*

Weird & Weird Detective

SUPER-DETECTIVE FLIP BOOK: Two Complete Novels

From the pulp *Super-Detective*:

"Legion of Robots" (November 1940) by Victor Rousseau • Introduction by John McMahan •• "Murder's Migrants" (March 1943) by Robert Leslie Bellem and W.T. Ballard • Introduction by John Wooley

2 short novels, 174 pages, $18

> Super-Detective *started as a Doc Savage-like adventure pulp, then changed format to hardboiled detective. The* Flip Book *features a novel from each of the two phases with intros exploring the historical background.*

FROM GHOULS TO GANGSTERS: The Career of Arthur B. Reeve

Edited by John Locke

Vol 1 (fiction): 21 stories, 264 pages, $20 • **Vol 2 (nonfic)**: 260 pages, $20

> *Reeve was the leading American detective-story writer of the early 20th Century, with his scientific detective, Craig Kennedy. The astonishing breadth of his career is explored for the first time here. Vol 1 includes a cross-sction of fiction from all phases of career, including many never-before-reprinted pulp stories. Vol 2 provides a 40-page biography; an extensive Art Gallery of cover repros, interior illos, ads, etc; a 75-page guide to Reeve's work in all media; and more. An "excellent piece of scholarship"—*MYSTERY SCENE, *Spring 2008.*

Gangster

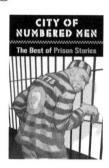

GANG PULP
Edited by John Locke • 19 stories, 294 pages, $24

Hardboiled stories of the criminal underworld from the first year (1929-30) of the gang pulps: Gangster Stories, Racketeer Stories, *etc. These violent tales came under immediate censorship pressure; the history is explored in an in-depth essay. "A remarkable work of popular-culture scholarship"*—MYSTERY SCENE, *Fall 2008.*

IF SHE ONLY HAD A MACHINE GUN
Crime Stories by Richard Credicott
Introductions by Dave Credicott & John Locke
Edited by John Locke & Rob Preston
18 stories, 360 pages, $20

The complete stories of one of the best gang-pulp authors. Includes gang stories from Racketeer Stories, Mobs, *etc., wildly entertaining tales of mob intrigue and mayhem, and the violent whims of molls; and detective stories from* The Dragnet, Dime Detective, *and others. All from 1929-33. A complete biographical profile offers rare insights into the pulps during the early years of the Depression. As a special feature, Dave Credicott provides reminiscences of his father's life.*

CITY OF NUMBERED MEN: The Best of Prison Stories
Introduction by John Locke
12 stories, 278 pages, $20

During Prohibition, famed publisher Harold Hersey turned America's disintegrating prison system into the hardboiled Prison Stories *(1930-31). Included are stories from all issues of this rare pulp, the startling history of* Prison Stories, *cover gallery, and "Tales of an Ink-Stained Wretch," the first comprehensive biography of pulp publishing's most colorful character, Harold Hersey.*

Gangster

THE GANGLAND SAGAS OF BIG NOSE SERRANO
Volume 1: Dames, Dice and the Devil
Volume 2: Horses, Hoboes and Heroes
Volume 3: Hell's Gangster
By Anatole Feldman • Introductions by Will Murray
Each: 4 novels • **Volumes 1-2**: 266 pages, $20 • **Volume 3**: 224 pages, $18

The complete Big Nose Serrano novels from Gangster Stories, Greater
Gangster Stories, *and* The Gang Magazine, *1930-35. Feldman was
the best of the gang pulp authors, and Big Nose was his most inspired
creation, the berserking king of Chicago gangsters.*

QUEEN OF THE GANGSTERS: Volume 1: Broadwalk Empire
Introductions by David Bischoff & John Locke
8 stories, 234 pages, $18

*Tough, rough, remorseless stories from the first woman hardboiled
crime fiction writer; from gang pulps like* Gangland Stories,
Racketeer Stories *and* Mobs. *Margie Harris slammed her typewriter
like a machine gun, mowing down good guys and bad guys alike;
shooting them, knifing them, blowing them up—lacing her prose with
metaphysical commentary on the destinations of their damned souls.
This is the first time her work has been collected. Introduction from
bestselling author David Bischoff.*

All books available from Amazon.com, other online booksellers, and dealers
specializing in the pulps. Complete listing, Amazon links, and latest news at:
offtrailpublications.com

CPSIA information can be obtained
at www.ICGtesting.com
Printed in the USA
LVHW09*0001080918
589549LV00003B/19/P

9 781935 031253